I TOO AM HERE

Selections from the Letters of
JANE WELSH CARLYLE

I still find myself a self-subsisting and alas! self-seeking *me*. Little Felix, in the Wanderjahre, when, in the midst of an animated scene between Wilhelm and Theresa, he pulls Theresa's gown, and calls out, '*Mama Theresa I too am here!*' only speaks out, with the charming trustfulness of a child, what I am perpetually feeling . . .

Jane Carlyle to John Sterling, 15 June 1835

Jenny kiss'd me when we met,
   Jumping from the chair she sat in;
Time, you thief, who love to get
   Sweets into your list, put that in!
Say I'm weary, say I'm sad,
   Say that health and wealth have miss'd me,
Say I'm growing old, but add,
   Jenny kiss'd me.

Leigh Hunt
1784–1859

I TOO AM HERE

Selections from the Letters of
JANE WELSH CARLYLE

With an Introduction and Notes by
ALAN AND MARY McQUEEN SIMPSON

CAMBRIDGE UNIVERSITY PRESS

CAMBRIDGE

LONDON · NEW YORK · MELBOURNE

Published by the Syndics of the Cambridge University Press
The Pitt Building, Trumpington Street, Cambridge CB2 1RP
Bentley House, 200 Euston Road, London NW1 2DB
32 East 57th Street, New York, NY 10022, USA
296 Beaconsfield Parade, Middle Park, Melbourne 3206, Australia

This selection, introduction and notes © Cambridge University Press 1977

First published 1977

Composed in Great Britain at the
University Press, Cambridge

Printed and bound in U.S.A. by
Vail-Ballou Press, Inc., Binghamton, New York

Library of Congress Cataloguing in Publication Data
Carlyle, Jane Baillie Welsh, 1801–1866.
I too am here.
Bibliography: p.
Includes index.
1. Carlyle, Jane Baillie Welsh, 1801–1866
Correspondence. I. Title.
PR 4419.C5A83 1976   824'8 (B)   76–11093
ISBN 0 521 21304 5

Contents

Illustrations

Preface

This book sprang from an appeal which the Carlyles have had for us all our lives – as personalities, as observers of the human scene with extraordinary powers of insight and characterization, as satirical geniuses, and as partners in a marriage in which, it is said, each was both the chief comforter and the chief tormentor of the other.

As the woman in the story, who gave up too much of herself for him, and whom we found both the more enigmatic and the more enjoyable – who could resist her letters? – Jane had the stronger claim.

We decided to make our own selection of these letters and our own assessment of the marriage on the basis of the publications of those two embattled editors: Carlyle's disciple, James Anthony Froude, and Carlyle's nephew, Alexander Carlyle. This was done on a leave of absence in 1974 with very little help from libraries. Since then, we have reviewed all the other publications of her letters, examined many of the manuscript collections, particularly the great collection at the National Library at Edinburgh, and explored the secondary literature on the Carlyles. But what we designed from the first was a book for enjoyment – for bedside, weekend and vacation – with the minimum of scholarly apparatus.

Froude's editing would not pass a severe test for accuracy; and although he printed enough to disturb a Victorian sense of propriety he left many living people unidentified, omitted passages about Jane's health which he thought indelicate and substituted some of his own terms for hers – 'bowels', an omnipresent fact in the Carlyle family, becomes 'interior'. Alexander Carlyle, an unforgiving critic of Froude's editing whenever he thought it injured his Uncle Thomas' reputation, had his own weaknesses. He prints Jane's instruction to her housekeeper in a letter of 1865, 'Be sure to keep all the windows open, that the house may be sweet when Mr. Carlyle returns . . . ' and allows the three dots to replace 'and goes sniffing all thro' it'. So the texts of the letters published in this selection have been derived from the manuscript sources in all but a few instances. Nearly all the letters have been printed before, either in the older collections or in the definitive Duke–Edinburgh edition as far as it goes; but one or two interesting letters are here printed for the first time.

Mary Carlyle once reminded a printer that her Uncle Thomas was 'painfully particular about his punctuation and capital letters'. What were we to do about her Aunt Jane's? We decided to preserve Jane's breathless punctuation as far as it was possible to do so without distracting or annoying her readers. The dashes, the exclamation marks and the italicization (for underlining in the original) convey the nervous energy, the intensity, and the unstudied artistry of their author. We have occasionally supplied a needed comma, expanded a contraction or corrected a mis-spelling. Three full-stops indicate either that the letter has been cut or that the original has been lost.

Many of the letters are undated – her usual custom was just to indicate the day of the week. Successive editors have established these dates and encouraged us to adopt a uniform style instead of cluttering our text with square brackets; in general we have adopted the dates as listed in the catalogue at the National Library of Scotland. We have also adopted a uniform style for the addresses given at the head of the letters. Footnotes have been kept to the minimum; where possible necessary explanations have been inserted in the text; and the Index can be used to identify people and places. Since most of the recipients of the letters are members of the Welsh or Carlyle families we have supplied a table of relationships.

Among the libraries which have helped us we owe a special debt to the National Library of Scotland in Edinburgh, for the generous assistance given to us by Dr Roberts, Mr Ritchie and their staff; we wish also to thank the Librarian of Edinburgh University Library, Mr Fifoot, Mr Finlayson and their staffs for allowing us to consult Jane's manuscript letters to Eliza Stodart; the Keeper of Western Manuscripts at the Bodleian Library, Oxford, for permission to consult Jane's manuscript journals; the New York Public Library for access to copies of Jane's letters which Thomas Carlyle annotated; the Librarian of Trinity College, Cambridge, for permission to consult Carlyle's correspondence; the staff of the Hornel Collection, Broughton House, Kirkcudbright, for their help; and, finally, Joan Murphy and her colleagues at the Vassar College Library for innumerable kindnesses.

Our most fascinating experience with private collections has been the opportunity to consult the Ashburton Papers in the possession of the Marquess of Northampton at Castle Ashby and those from the same collection on loan to Baring Brothers. We are particularly grateful to Lord and the late Lady Northampton for all their kindness and helpfulness; to Dr and Mrs Peter Dalgleish for their hospitality during the visit; and to Mr Tom Ingram, archivist of Baring Brothers, for his generous assistance.

Out of all the scholarship, commentary and criticism which has been devoted to the Carlyles we would like to acknowledge a few special debts: to the Duke–Edinburgh team, General Editor Charles Richard Sanders, Associate Editor K. J. Fielding, Assistant Editors Ian Campbell, John Clubbe and Janetta Taylor, for their magnificent enterprise, *The Collected Letters of Thomas and Jane Welsh Carlyle*, volumes 1–4 (1970) covering the years 1812–28, and volumes 5–7 (1977) the years 1828–34; to Professors Sanders and Fielding and Dr Campbell for their generous hospitality and all their professional wisdom; to Lady Bliss (Trudy Bliss) for the elegance of her selection of Jane's letters which she published in 1949, for much assistance and the pleasures of a visit in 1975; to our old friend, Dorothy Malbon Parker, who urged us to make this selection; to two brilliant essayists, Virginia Woolf (her father, Sir Leslie Stephen, told her that Jane was 'the most wonderful letter-writer in the English language') for her essay 'Geraldine and Jane', and Iris Origo for 'The Carlyles and the Ashburtons: A Victorian Friendship'; and to Thea Holme for her charming and witty study of *The Carlyles at Home*.

Our explorations in 'Carlyle country' were made especially enjoyable by Kathleen and John Macfie, at whose home at 17 Heriot Row, Edinburgh, we finished our selection in the summer of 1975; by artists Tom Fleming and Edith McArthur, and author Henry Donald, whose dramatic recital, 'Carlyle and Jane', was such a delightful feature of the Edinburgh Festival in 1974; by our old friends Wilfred and Dorothy Taylor of *The Scotsman*; by Mr and Mrs D. H. A. Mitchell, Great King Street, Edinburgh, who served us tea from the silver teapot which Jane inherited from her mother; by Mr and Mrs Jack Bullick at Torsonce, Stow, where Carlyle stayed with Henry Inglis; by our guides in Haddington, John McVie, Town Clerk, Graham and Helen Duncan, who live in Jane's old schoolhouse, and the Woods, who live in Jane's old home; by Mr and Mrs Swan, custodians of Carlyle's House at Ecclefechan; by Susan Blacklock at Scotsbrig, where Carlyle's father and mother ended their days, and where we were sped on our way with two dozen eggs of the freshness Jane used to yearn for in Chelsea; by Mr and Mrs George Armour in the lonely beauty of Craigenputtoch; by Mr and Mrs Hugh Mackintosh Robertson at Templand where Carlyle and Jane were married and the views are as marvellous as Carlyle recalled them in his *Reminiscences*; by Alan and Elizabeth Hay of the Carlyle House, Chelsea; and by Jennie and Evelyn Simpson, our companions and comforters in many an adventure.

At Vassar College and Little Compton, Rhode Island, we remember gratefully Elizabeth Runkle Purcell, Chairman of the Board of Trustees, and her fellow trustees who granted us a semester's leave of absence in 1974; Jean and Ralph Connor at whose Bequia home in the West Indies during this leave we made our first selection of Jane's letters; Elizabeth A. Daniels and George Farr of the Department of English and Valenice Castronovo for delightful contributions; Ethel Grauer and Angie Smith for heroic feats with the typewriter; Bill and Virginia Lynch, and Barbara and Frank Flynn for the rigours endured in proof-reading Jane's punctuation.

Our final thanks go to the staff of the Cambridge University Press who have done so much to help us in the preparation of this book.

ALAN AND MARY SIMPSON

President's House
Vassar College
September 1976

Acknowledgements

Thanks are due to the following for permission to publish letters which appear in this book: to the National Library of Scotland and its Trustees for all but nineteen of the letters; to Edinburgh University Library for letters 1 and 61; to the Master and Fellows of Trinity College, Cambridge, for letter 180; to E. A. Hornel's Trustees for letter 172; to the Henry W. and Albert A. Berg Collections, the New York Public Library, Astor, Lennox and Tilden Foundations for letter 8; to the National Trust for material from the Carlyle House, Chelsea (letters 32 and 53); to John Murray, publishers of *Jane Welsh Carlyle: Letters to Her Family 1839–1863* by Leonard Huxley, for letters 63 and 131; finally to the Marquess of Northampton for permission to publish letters 33 and 192.

We were unable to locate texts for letters 48 (to J.T. an anonymous admirer), 58 (Mrs Austin, 18 October 1864), 95 (Charlotte Southam, 26 December 1865), 104 (T.C., 20 August 1842), 111 (Mary Smith, 11 January 1857), 115 (Mrs Austin, 25 December 1857), 118 (Dr Russell, 6 January 1863), 191 (Geraldine Jewsbury to T.C., 26 May 1866). Texts have been taken from Froude, *Letters and Memorials* (1883), from *Strand Magazine* (1915) for letter 95, and from *Autobiography of Mary Smith* (1892) for letter 111.

Chronology

1758   Birth of James Carlyle, Thomas' father
1771   September. Birth of Margaret Aitken, Thomas' mother
1775 or 1776   4 April. Birth of John Welsh, Jane's father, at Craigenputtoch
1776   4 July. *America's Declaration of Independence*
1782   15 December. Birth of Grace Welsh, Jane's mother, at Castlemains, Crawford
1789   14 July. *Fall of the Bastille*
1795   Marriage of James Carlyle (a previous wife, Jannet, had been married in 1791, borne one son John, and died) to Margaret Aitken
       4 December. Birth of Thomas Carlyle at Ecclefechan
1800   Marriage of John Welsh and Grace Welsh
1801   14 July. Birth of Jane Baillie Welsh at Haddington
1809–14   Carlyle studies at Edinburgh University, completing his arts studies in 1813 and returning to begin his preparation for the ministry
1810–12   Edward Irving teaching at Haddington
1815   May. Carlyle family moves from Ecclefechan to the farm at Mainhill
       18 June. *Battle of Waterloo*
1816   Carlyle leaves a teaching position at Annan Academy for another at Kirkcaldy. Friendship with Edward Irving
1817   Carlyle renounces the ministry as a career
1819   19 September. Death of Dr Welsh at Haddington
1820   29 January. *Accession of King George IV*
1821   May. Meeting of Jane Welsh and Thomas Carlyle at Haddington
1822   August. Carlyle has his 'conversion experience' in Leith Walk, Edinburgh
1822–4   Carlyle is tutor in the Buller family
1824   Carlyle publishes translation of Goethe's *Wilhelm Meisters Lehrjahre*. Goethe writes to him

1825 Publication, in book form, of Carlyle's *Life of Schiller*. Carlyle
moves to Hoddam Hill; visited in September by Jane Welsh
1826 May. Carlyle family settle in the farm at Scotsbrig
July. Haddington house sold. Mrs Welsh and Jane Welsh in
Edinburgh. Miniature of Jane by Kenneth McLeay
17 October. Marriage of Jane Welsh and Thomas Carlyle at
Templand, Thornhill. They move to Comely Bank, Edinburgh
1827 Publication of *German Romance*
1828 May. Removal from Comely Bank to Craigenputtoch
1829 'Signs of the Times' published in *Edinburgh Review*
1829–30 Carlyle writing *Sartor Resartus*
1830 26 June. *Accession of King William IV*
1831–2 Carlyle and Jane visit London
1832 22 January. Death of Carlyle's father, James
June. *Passage of the Reform Bill*
1833 August. Emerson visits Craigenputtoch
1834 10 June. Removal to 5 Cheyne Row
7 December. Death of Edward Irving
1835 March. Book I of *The French Revolution* accidentally burnt
1837 May. Lectures on 'German Literature'
June. Publication of *The French Revolution*
20 June. *Accession of Queen Victoria*
August. Jane's visit to Oxford and the Cotswolds with the
Sterlings
December. Helen Mitchell, the maid from Kirkcaldy, hired
1838 May. Lectures on 'The History of Literature or the Successive
Periods of European Culture'. Crayon portraits of Jane and
Carlyle by Samuel Laurence
1839 *Chartism agitation at its height*
May. Lectures on 'Revolutions of Modern Europe'
December. Publication of *Chartism*
1840 Lectures on 'Heroes and Hero-Worship'
1841 Publication of *Heroes and Hero-Worship*
1842 5 February. Death of Jane's mother, Grace Welsh
August. Jane visits the Bullers in Troston
1843 April. Publication of *Past and Present*. Painting of Jane by
Gambardella.
May. Jane's first meeting with Lady Harriet Baring (who
became Lady Ashburton on the death of her husband's
father in 1848)

1844   18 September. Death of John Sterling

1845   Publication of *Oliver Cromwell's Letters and Speeches: with Elucidations*

1848   29 November. Death of Charles Buller

1849   Helen Mitchell, the maid from Kirkcaldy, finally fired

        July. Jane revisits Haddington, writes 'Much Ado About Nothing'

1850   February. Publication of the first of the *Latter Day Pamphlets*

        June. The Bath House ball

        July. *Sir Robert Peel dies*

1851   May–October. *The Great Exhibition*

        October. Publication of the *Life of John Sterling*

1852   July. The sound-proof room begun

        August. Jane's visit to Sherborne House

        14 September. *Duke of Wellington dies*

        25 December. Death of Carlyle's mother, Margaret

1854–6 *Crimean War*

1855   August. Jane in search of lodgings at Rottingdean

1855–6 Jane keeps a journal; appeals to the Tax Commissioners

1857   4 May. Death of Lady Ashburton

        Robert Tait paints 'A Chelsea Interior'

1858   17 November. Lord Ashburton marries his second wife, Louisa Stewart Mackenzie.

1863   October. Jane's accident in Cheapside

1864   April. Jane taken to Dr Blakiston's at St Leonards

        July–September. Jane at Dr Russell's at Holm Hill, Thornhill

        1 October. Jane returns to Cheyne Row

1865   January. Carlyle completes *History of Friedrich II, of Prussia, Called Frederick the Great*

        November. Carlyle elected Rector of Edinburgh University

1866   29 March. Carlyle kisses Jane goodbye as he leaves for Edinburgh

        2 April. Carlyle's Inaugural Address at Edinburgh

        21 April. Death of Jane Carlyle

1881   5 February. Death of Thomas Carlyle

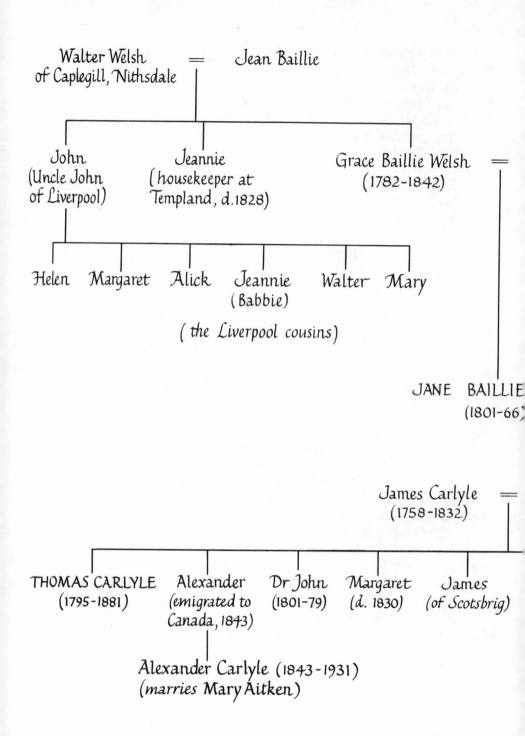

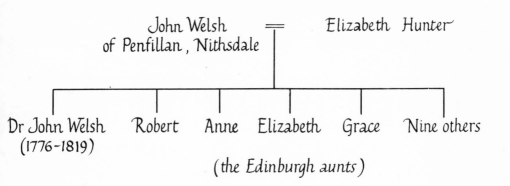

John Welsh
of Penfillan, Nithsdale
=
Elizabeth Hunter

Dr John Welsh (1776-1819) — Robert — Anne — Elizabeth — Grace — Nine others

(the Edinburgh aunts)

WELSH

Margaret Aitken
(1771-1853)

Mary
(marries James
Austin of
The Gill)

Jean
('Craw' Jean,
mother of
Mary Aitken)

Janet
(marries Robert Hanning
and emigrates to Canada)

The Welsh and Carlyle families

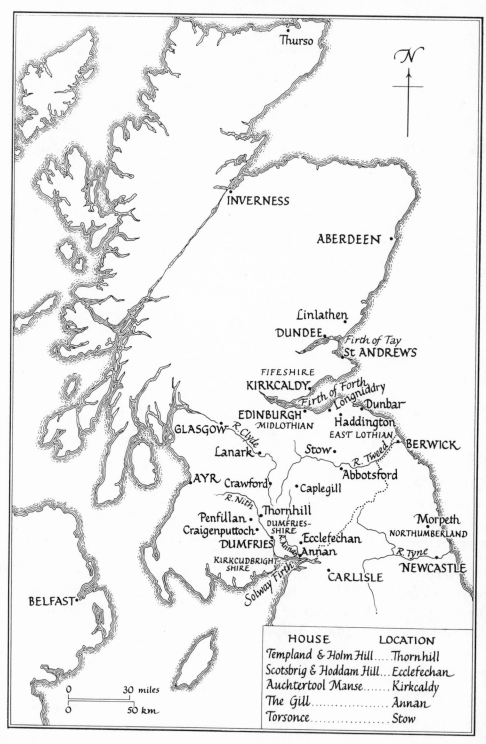

Carlyle country

Introduction

The predictions of her extravagant friend, Geraldine Jewsbury, were often received with laughter by Jane Carlyle, but there is one over which we linger today and wonder whether Jane would have taken it seriously. It appears in a letter of 1849 and is nothing less than Geraldine's estimate of the place which she and Jane might have earned for themselves in the history of women's emancipation.

> I do not feel that either you or I are to be called failures. We are indications of a development of womanhood which as yet is not recognized. It has, so far, no ready-made channels to run in, but still we have looked, and tried, and found that the present rules for women will not hold us – that something better and stronger is needed. . . There are women to come after us, who will approach nearer the fullness of the measure of the stature of a woman's nature. I regard myself as a mere faint indication, a rudiment of the idea, of certain higher qualities and possibilities that lie in women, and all the eccentricities and mistakes and miseries and absurdities I have made are only the consequences of an imperfect formation, an immature growth.[1]

Jane Carlyle was forty-eight at this time, the brilliant wife of Britain's most prophetic voice. Her face looks out at us from the photographs on the walls of 5 Cheyne Row, Chelsea; head on hand, smooth black hair parted in the middle, eyes intent and brooding, mouth composed; both a studied and a studying face. To her intimates she must have seemed a notional woman, full of fascination and problems; affectionate and bitter, radiant and depressed, full of brilliant mockery and plaintive self-pity, beloved and tormented by her husband to whom she was both a ministering angel and a caustic martyr, talking and scribbling with endless vivacity when she was not, in Geraldine's words, 'curled up on the sofa, pale and miserable-looking, as if the damp had struck into your very soul'.

Would she have agreed with Geraldine about their place in history? How did she really feel about her life? When James Anthony Froude became a regular visitor to Cheyne Row, in the 1850s, he

[1] *Selections from the Letters of Geraldine Endsor Jewsbury to Jane Welsh Carlyle*, ed. Mrs Alexander Ireland (1892), pp. 347–8.

wondered what lay behind the strained looks of the great man's bewitching wife, and the answers he eventually gave after both were dead, as their editor and biographer, were to start a controversy which still stirs us.

HADDINGTON

Jane was born on 14 July 1801, the only child of a Scottish country doctor in the county town of Haddington, which is in East Lothian, eighteen miles east of Edinburgh. Haddington was and is a lovely old town. The visitor to the George Hotel, where the London coach to Edinburgh used to stop, and where Carlyle stayed with his friend, Edward Irving, on his first visit to Jane, can look down the High Street lined with its high stone houses to the little alley – the 'pend', it is called – which leads into the Welsh house. John Welsh, Jane's father, came from a long line of John Welshes who had succeeded each other as lairds of Craigenputtoch, a moorland sheep farm of 800 acres in Dumfriesshire, until his father broke with tradition by sending him to Edinburgh University to become a doctor. He quickly made his mark in his Haddington practice; was highly admired; and married a lady of the same name as himself, Grace Baillie Welsh, who was not related to him but came from the same old farming stock. Between them, they had romantic tales of famous ancestors which their daughter, Jane, was to enjoy telling. On her father's side, there was a stiff-necked reformation preacher who married a daughter of John Knox; on her mother's side, a splendid gypsy horse-thief who could steal a horse from under its rider and who 'suffered' at Lanark, that is to say, was hanged, for his accomplishments. When an admirer of Jane heard of this ancestry, he said, 'That explains everything – sprung from John Knox and a gypsy!'

Jane idolized her father, just as the man she was to marry idolized his mother. It was almost more than she could bear at eighteen when Dr Welsh died of typhoid caught from a patient. He had wanted a boy and he educated her, to her impetuous delight, more like a boy than a girl. Her beautiful, wayward mother was of another nature; she was said to be capable of fifteen different humours in an evening. She and Jane were to cherish each other, from that enduring sense of love and duty which bound Victorian mother and daughter, but they were much too intense to be capable of living at peace together.

Jane was an endearing, clever, sharp-witted, sharp-tongued child; applying herself furiously to study and play; often in the little schoolhouse by the Nungate Bridge a whole two hours before the teacher arrived at eight in the morning; mastering Latin and mathe-matics; scribbling verses, a novel, and a five-act tragedy in her teens; adored by her maid, Betty – 'a fleein', dancin', lighthearted thing that naething would hae dauntit'; adored by her tutor, Edward Irving, who later came to love her; and by a whole succession of suitors when in due course she became 'the belle of Haddington'. She seemed born to crave fame and to be deliciously spoilt.

COURTSHIP

When she was twenty, the admiring circle of eligible young men was breached by her man of destiny. He was five years older; a struggling writer in Edinburgh; no gentleman by any reckoning of that time, unless by the standards of nature's nobility; but a true original, with blue eyes as vivid as her black ones, a tongue as sharp as hers, and a huge, enthralling stock of unemployed talents and unrealized dreams.

Thomas Carlyle had been brought up in a stonemason's cottage in Ecclefechan, eldest of eight children born to Calvinist peasants of rock-like character and hand-hewn sense. They had no cultivation beyond the study of the Bible. His mother taught herself to write so that she could keep in touch with him when he left home. They had prayed that he might enter the ministry and they were to bear with him as he worked his way towards a sanctified calling of his own contriving. But their deep, unspoken love and their natural endow-ments, of which he later wrote with such heartfelt eloquence, could not protect him from what he and we would call a gloomy childhood. He felt isolated and repressed; superior in his consciousness of gifts and expectations, but a worrier; full of miseries both real and imagi-nary – some of them springing from his mother's veto on fighting, which left him defenceless against bullies; and already fixed in those habits of sarcasm and self-pity – 'splenetic contempt' was his own description – which stayed with him for the rest of his life. He was introduced to Jane by Edward Irving, who had preceded him as a schoolboy at Annan, a student at Edinburgh, and a teacher at Kirkcaldy, and who was soon to begin his 'shooting-star's' career as a fashionable preacher in London.

Jane became Carlyle's 'fair pupil' as she had once been Irving's. He sent her books, reading lists, literary compositions, rhapsodies on German literature. In February 1822 she wrote:

Mr Carlyle was with us two days, during the greater part of which I read German with him. It is a noble language! – I am getting on famously. He scratched the fender dreadfully – I must have a pair of carpet-shoes and handcuffs prepared for him the next time. His tongue only should be kept at liberty – his other members are most fantastically awkward.[1]

She mimicked him; chided him; flirted with many others as well as him; but got steadily more involved. His hold over her was his power to convince her he was a man of genius. All his contemporaries felt it – his father, his mother, his brothers and sisters, his classmates at Edinburgh, his pace-setter, Irving, or for that matter anyone who was a judge of special talent. But Jane was especially susceptible. He revived the ideal her father had set for her before he died. He re-kindled her own ambition for personal fame. She would help him to be a hero! Perhaps she would join him as a heroine in her own right!

This was a true courtship of intellectuals and it was heady stuff in an age when Rousseau, Byron, Schiller and Goethe set the standards. But life being what it was, it was also provokingly long. Over five years passed before their uncertainties, their worries about what they would live on, and Mrs Welsh's hopes of a much more suitable match, were finally overcome. They were married on 17 October 1826 at Templand in Nithsdale, her mother having just given up the Haddington home to return to her own country. Carlyle was thirty; Jane twenty-five; and perhaps she, at this juncture, was more pressing than he. Genius may have been dragging its feet in obedience to its own imperatives. Or it may only have been that powers of decision were not Carlyle's strong point. Considering the trouble she was going to have, in the next forty years, getting him to decide when he would leave home for an annual holiday, it was no slight feat to get him to the altar.

Was Jeannie Welsh throwing herself away? Only four people came to the wedding, three of her family and one of his. She wrote to a relative,

They would tell you, I should suppose, first and foremost that my intended is *poor* . . . and, in the next place, most likely indulge in some criticisms scarce flattering on his birth (the more likely if their own birth happened to be mean or doubtful) and, if they happened to be vulgar-fine people with disputed preten-sions to good looks, they would, to a certainty, set him down as unpolished and ill-looking. But a hundred chances to one, they would not tell you he is among the cleverest men of his day; and not the cleverest only, but the most enlightened! That he possesses all the qualities I deem essential in *my* husband – a warm true heart to love me, a towering intellect to command me, and a spirit of fire to be the guiding star – light of my life . . .

Such, then, is this future husband of mine; not a *great* man according to the most common sense of the word, but truly great in its natural proper sense; a

[1] Letter to Eliza Stodart, 8 February 1822 (Edinburgh University Library).

scholar, poet, philosopher, a 'wise and noble man', one who 'holds his patent of nobility from Almighty God', and whose high stature of manhood is not to be measured by the inch-rule of Lilliputs! Will you like him? No matter whether you do or not – since *I* like him in the deepest part of my soul.[1]

CRAIGENPUTTOCH

The early years of their married life – the first two at Comely Bank in Edinburgh, the next six at Craigenputtoch in Dumfriesshire – could not have been easy. Jane was everything Carlyle thought a wife should be – devoted, making light of every difficulty, an excellent housekeeper and hostess within their limited means, a good listener, and very proud of him. She always put him first, which was where they both expected him to be. She seems – unless we presume too much from what she chose to say to him and his family – to have subscribed fully to his doctrine, which of course was society's doctrine, that 'the man should bear rule in the house and not the woman'. He, in turn, was devoted to her: their marriage would never quite cease to be a love-match in the very worst of times. But he was solitary, self-absorbed, hag-ridden; often unable to share his innermost life with her; or to give her the attention she craved; or to follow his imperious, erratic course with enough consideration for her. So it seemed to Francis Jeffrey, the celebrated editor of the *Edinburgh Review*, who recognized the quality of this moody, scornful iconoclast and his clever, delicate wife; gave him articles to write; flirted with Jane in his witty, middle-aged way; begged him to relax; and watched, with a mixture of affection and despair, their self-imposed exile in lonely Craigenputtoch for six long years.

How it seemed to Jane is anyone's guess. She could impress Carlyle with a capacity for uncomplaining silence in the face of adversity which stirred him – when he had time to notice it – to the heights of rapturous heroine-worship. But it was also Carlyle who said that his wife had a tongue which could take the skin off at a touch. Probably these were trusting, tender, hopeful years, in the main. She must have seen what they meant to the development of Carlyle's genius – it was at Craigenputtoch that *Sartor Resartus* was written. Also, in its moments of sunswept, wind-scoured beauty, or when guests like Jeffrey or Emerson arrived for hours of talk, the

[1] From a letter to Mrs George Welsh, 1 October [1826], published, inexactly, in J. A. Froude, *Thomas Carlyle, A History of the First Forty Years of His Life 1795–1835* (1882), 1, 356–7 and in corrected form by Alexander Carlyle, *The Love Letters of Thomas Carlyle and Jane Welsh* (hereafter *LL*) (1889).

silent moorland farm had a magic all of its own. But if Craigenputtoch began as an adventure for Jane, it must have ended as a lonely ordeal from which the move to London in 1834 brought a blessed relief. Had they not a nagging feeling that it might have been cowardice, not superior wisdom, that took them there? As for *Sartor Resartus* – 'the candle sometimes burns its way thro' the bushel; but what a waste of light!' When she looked back on Craigenputtoch, in later life, she would recall that her two immediate predecessors, 'at that savage place', had gone mad, while the third had taken to drink.[1]

CHEYNE ROW: THE CREATIVE YEARS

The next decade at 5 Cheyne Row may have been the happiest years of her life, if we pass over the childhood years when she was the centre of such adoring attention at Haddington, and if we feel that it makes much sense to talk about 'a happy year' in an emotional biography as full of black skies as hers. She might have said, 'I had happy moments, happy hours, even happy days, but what sort of statistical absurdity is a happy year in a life like mine? Besides, Carlyle despised happiness.'

Nevertheless, this was the most creative period she would ever enjoy. She made 5 Cheyne Row a home which was to meet their needs for the rest of their lives – thirty-two years in her case and forty-seven in his. 'You are like an Eve and make a little Paradise wherever you are', said Edward Irving wistfully when he saw what she had made of Cheyne Row within a few months of her arrival and of his own death. How she kept it that way, through endless encounters with servants, carpenters, painters, demons outside and 'little beings' inside is one of the richest themes of her letters.

She did her heroic best to advance Carlyle's career – battling with the destroyers of his peace, cheering his gloom, entertaining his friends, reading behind him as he wrote, ministering to every sacred egoism. And she saw her faith justified as he became famous. The first fruits of Cheyne Row were the three volumes of *The French Revolution*, which included the Herculean re-writing of the first volume after John Stuart Mill's maid had accidentally burnt the only manuscript. While waiting for the verdict of the reviewers, Jane persuaded Carlyle to take to the lecture platform in London as he had often talked of doing in America. Thanks to the reputation he was

[1] Letter to Miss Smith, 11 January 1857, in *Jane Welsh Carlyle: A New Selection of Her Letters*, arranged by Trudy Bliss (Victor Gollancz, 1949), p. 157.

making by his writings and his table-talk, his friends had no trouble raising two hundred subscriptions of a guinea each for six lectures on 'German Literature'. Though he had a terrible time getting them prepared and delivered in the spring of 1837, he was pressed to repeat the success in each of the next three years. By the end of 1837 the reviews of *The French Revolution* were out and his reputation made. As honours and invitations poured in, he gave a second series of lectures on the 'History of Literature' in 1838, a third on the 'Revolutions of Modern Europe' in 1839, a fourth on 'Heroes and Hero-Worship' in 1840. 1843 was the year for *Past and Present*; 1845 for *Oliver Cromwell's Letters and Speeches*. By this time he was an international celebrity and Jane had christened herself 'Lion's wife'.

It was also in these years that she won her own measure of independence. She wrote to John Sterling on 15 June 1835,

You did kindly to send the little separate note: the least bit ' *all to myself*', (as the children say) was sure to give me a livelier pleasure, than any number of sheets in which I had but a secondary interest. For in spite of the honestest efforts to annihilate my *I-ity*, or merge it in what the world doubtless considers my better half; I still find myself a self-subsisting and alas! self-seeking *me*. Little Felix, in the Wanderjahre, when, in the midst of an animated scene between Wilhelm and Theresa, he pulls Theresa's gown, and calls out, '*Mama Theresa I too am here!*' only speaks out, with the charming trustfulness of a child, what I am perpetually feeling, tho' too sophisticated to pull peoples skirts, or exclaim in so many words; Mr Sterling '*I* too am here.'

She enjoyed a succession of admiring confidants like Mr Sterling. She polished and perfected her mockery of Carlyle as a way of dealing with his eccentricities. She reigned over the Chelsea circle from her armchair as he did from his. And to the brilliance of a hostess she added the incandescence of an incomparable letter-writer.

But it was also in these years that she discovered what was involved in a marriage where each partner was the chief tormentor as well as the chief comforter of the other. She could laugh about herself. 'They call me "*sweet*" and "*gentle*"; and some of the men go the length of calling me "ENDEARING" and I laugh in my sleeve, and think Oh Lord! if you but knew what a brimstone of a creature I am behind all this beautiful amiability!'[1] But she could also ache and weep. With their history of petted childhoods, thin skins, racked nerves, debauched medication and verbal violence, tranquillity was not to be expected. It was well known that she and Carlyle could not share a bed together; once, when an influx of relatives at Templand forced

[1] Letter to Eliza Stodart, 29 February 1836 (Edinburgh University Library).

them to do so, Carlyle left both the bed and the house in the middle of the night.

It was to be the tragedy of Jane's middle age that Carlyle's success brought so little real satisfaction. She had no children. Her only children were his books and lectures and her own collection of disciples, émigrés, waifs and pets. She had no creative work worthy of her powers. The various efforts of husband, friends and publishers to get her to write a book came to nothing. She was insufficiently armed against any unwelcome shift in Carlyle's own interests or affections. 'I too am here!' with its immature archness had not been enough. She had given him altogether too much of herself and was left defenceless when he seemed to need her less, where she most expected to be, at the centre of his love and admiration.

CHEYNE ROW: THE DIFFICULT YEARS

At the heart of this problem is his relationship with Lady Harriet Baring, later, Lady Ashburton, traces of which can be found in Jane's journal and in her letters to Carlyle. It is also likely that Jane shared her distress with the few confidants, like Mazzini, Geraldine Jewsbury, and her cousin, Jean Welsh, to whom she could trust herself to speak. Lady Harriet was a Jane Carlyle in high society, with every advantage of health, wealth and position as well as wits. She and her husband surrounded themselves with all that was most brilliant in intellectual England. Visits to Bath House, Piccadilly, Bay House at Alverstoke, the Grange at Alresford, the Addiscombe farm, or the Scottish hunting lodges, were like royal commands. Carlyle idolized her, as an Elizabethan poet-courtier idolized his Gloriana. She was 'his glorious Queen', his 'beneficent goddess', his 'daughter of the Sun', 'the lamp of my dark path'. He found a solace in her Junoesque power and serenity which he could not find in Jane. 'Among the many fine things I have loved in you', he wrote to her during her last illness, 'the bright, frank courage of your mind, the healthy promptitude with which you shook away annoyances and walked on as if incompatible with "mud" (in which I may be said to dwell) was always one.' No one was less interested in women as such than Carlyle, and, conscious of no disloyalty himself, as distinct from the inevitable little deceptions, he may have been unable to understand what this homage to another woman was doing to his own marriage. But it was a bitter experience for Jane to have to live with such idolatry – invited to the Baring houses for her husband's sake, competing unequally on Lady Harriet's own ground, half-envious, half-admiring, and at times wholly resentful. There was a celebrity's welcome for Carlyle in the Ashburton world – he was original, exciting, shocking. Any gaucherie he committed was immediately forgotten in a recognized genius. If only she had written a shelf-ful of novels to compete with his histories and sermons! It was not an ordeal that absorbed the whole of her life or came close to breaking all that bound her to Carlyle. Each might have said, in the very depths of their misunderstandings, that if the other was hard to live with, he was even harder to live without. But it gave a rueful hue to all her thoughts about marriage, increased her hunger for affection, and pushed her nearer the brink of nervous collapse.

How different it might have been if she had struck out in earlier years for more independence within the marriage, less dancing attendance on him, a literary career to match his own, a sound-proof study at Cheyne Row for her as well as him! It was not lack of self-will, or incapacity for action, that had kept her in chains. It was partly the bondage of conventional ideas – Haddington notions of decorum, those canons of good taste that the irreverent Geraldine kept bumping into in her relations with Jane. It was partly the weight that Carlyle himself threw against the faddish forms of the feminist movement. Jane was no 'women's libber'. She never said that what Carlyle needed was a liberated wife. What she did say was that he should have had '"a strong-minded woman" for wife, with a perfectly sound liver, plenty of *solid fat*, and mirth and good humour world without end – men do best with their opposites. *I* am too like himself in some things – especially as to the state of our livers, and so we aggravate one another's tendencies to despair.'[1]

Yet it was more than all of this. Dependence – to be appreciated only as Carlyle's wife – galled her to the point of savagery. What stopped her from freeing herself? The truth is she was a divided soul. The real paradox of Jane Carlyle is her uneasy combination of two different natures – one positive, concrete, practical, hard; the other romantic, sentimental, self-pitying, soft. Froude caught something of this split-personality in the way he chose to describe the stillness of her face in death, 'The brilliant mockery, the sad softness with which the mockery alternated, were both gone.' If the fiery half of her nature drove her to the brink of rebellion, the plaintive half kept her enslaved. The result was a victory for what the Victorians called

[1] Letter to Helen Welsh, 19 August 1846 (National Library of Scotland).

'duty', but so often she sounded, to herself and her intimates, like a caged mockingbird. This is the real tragedy behind the headaches, the nervous disorders, the sleepless nights, and the wasted days on the sofa.

And so the years passed away. The death of Lady Ashburton in 1857 removed this source of strain, but there were others as Jane entered her sixties. She saw very little more of Carlyle than she had done when he was forever being swallowed up in 'That eternal Bath House'. There was the sacred half hour in the drawing room each evening when he left his work to be relaxed and brightened by her stories; he called it 'the rainbow of my dripping day'. There were the indispensable daily letters when they were separated. But there was not much more they could call their own. The all-consuming labour in his life at this stage was the interminable struggle with *Frederick the Great*. She had been against this book from the start; how could he make a silk-purse out of a sow's ear? It meant nothing whatever to her. But had she not schooled herself to put his wishes first? When the first volume appeared, she read it aloud to some aging, deaf relatives and told him how magnificent it was. But she read no more. As year followed year in the lengthening torture – it took fourteen years of his life to finish the five volumes – even he came to see what it was doing to her. Knowing how useless he was as a nurse, he redoubled his frenzy to help her in the only way he could, by finishing it.

There were whole winters when she was more or less unwell and weeks when she was never out of doors. Old friends died off, others moved away, and some faithful ones, like the unestrangeable Geraldine, had to endure as many stings as kisses from a Jane who was behaving more and more like a chronic, embittered invalid. Yet it was Geraldine who said, 'If she is cruel sometimes and hard, at others she is more noble and generous than ninety-nine just persons who need no repentance, and as to her *fascination* I appeal to yourself'; and the second Lady Ashburton, whom Jane embraced with all the ardour Carlyle had felt for the first, could testify to her capacity for new friendships. She was worn, but she was not yet beaten.

It was this ability to make light of difficulties, to suffer in silence where his needs were concerned, and to stage astonishing comebacks, which deceived Carlyle. Ever hopeful, beneath his proverbial gloom, he talked of another long trail which they would get through together. What actually happened was a descent into a hell of sickness and depression for nearly two years; a restoration for another eighteen months – she called herself 'a *Living Miracle*' – which a now tender and considerate Carlyle thought was the happiest time since their earliest years together; and then, after a life of so much pain, a painless end as she waited in London to share the newest success of her man of genius. He had gone to the University of Edinburgh to give his Rectorial Address and a telegram had brought the news of 'a perfect triumph'. Too frail to go with him, but in a glow of contentment with the pleasure all their friends were taking in his achievements, Jane was continuing her usual round of calls and letters. During a drive in Hyde Park the little dog, Tiny, which was running beside her carriage, was brushed by another vehicle. Alarmed, she stepped out of the carriage, picked him up and took him in on her lap. Hearing no further instructions, after he had driven around and around the park, the coachman looked back into the carriage over the blinds and caught a glimpse of her lifeless hands. She was driven to St George's Hospital, where Geraldine and Froude were summoned, while Cheyne Row was made ready to receive her.

CARLYLE'S PORTRAIT OF JANE

The first to put his thoughts on paper about this enigmatic being was the man who had lived with her for forty years. Carlyle was devastated by her death and for several years he was to be absorbed in an effort to recapture the spirit of her personality and of all she had been and might have been. From the epitaph which he wrote for her tombstone in the ruined abbey church at Haddington, where she was buried in her father's grave on 26 April 1866;[1] from the memoir of her life which he began a few weeks after the funeral, on receiving some reminiscences from Geraldine, and finished in July of the same year; and from her letters which he collected and annotated for publication in 1868–9 – from these we can study Carlyle's portrait of Jane. Into it he poured not only all his own marvellous powers of evocation, and all the grief of one who had found 'the light of his life as if gone out', but also his sense of insufficiency and guilt.

'Never till her death did I see how much she loved me . . . Nor, I fear, did she ever know (could she have seen across the stormy clouds and eclipsing miseries) what a love I bore *her*.' It is a portrait of the heroine as wife of genius; embodying all the Victorian virtues of nobility, goodness, patience and self-sacrifice; combining them

---

[1] Carlyle's epitaph is reproduced on p. 296 below.

11

with the delicacy of a fairy, 'bright as stars and diamonds'; and all for the sake of a blind, ungrateful, gloomy egotist. 'A noble fight at my side; a valiant strangling of serpents day after day – done gaily by her (for most part) as I had to do it angrily and gloomily.'[1]

It is an ideal picture. Carlyle had always been tenderest when Jane was absent and now she would never return. It is also a picture which reminds us of the childlike quality in their love. Jane had wanted a father to pet and coddle her. Carlyle sorrows over 'my poor Jeannie', 'my poor darling', 'my heroic little woman', more like a father than a husband. His absorption with her memory is a labour of remorse; he is expiating the guilt he felt for being so blind to her sufferings and sacrifices. But it is blindness, not chauvinism, for which he repents. He expresses no remorse for the possibility that his demands may have crippled her talents and that under a different dispensation she might have made as much of her genius as he had of his.

Others were to carry their ideas about 'might have beens' further than Carlyle. Still, he strove tenderly and proudly for a way to make her image survive. Before he had finished the memoir he had plunged into her letters and found them as good or better than the best of their kind. He exclaimed, 'not all the Sands and Eliots . . . or celebrated, scribbling women that have strutted over the world in my time . . . could make one such woman!'[2] He wrote in his Journal in 1867, 'One thing you could do – write some record of her – make some selection of her letters which you think justly among the cleverest ever written, and which none but yourself can quite understand.' He went on to do this, using the method of editorial elucidations which he had developed so brilliantly when he edited Cromwell's letters; but with uncertainties compounded by age, he was not able to decide how or when or with what introduction these 'Letters and Memorials' should eventually be published, or whether they should be published at all. Knowing that this problem, which was also the problem of his own biography, would never be solved by himself, he handed it over, with all the papers involved, to his disciple, Froude. What a responsibility!

[1] Thomas Carlyle, *Reminiscences*, ed. Ian Campbell (Everyman, 1972), p. 122.
[2] *Ibid.* p. 138.

Introduction

Froude's Portrait of Jane

Froude produced a portrait of Jane which was also a study of the wife of genius, but where Carlyle had dramatized her persevering love in the face of his absorption with his mission, Froude found that they had never been in love at all. He thought that Jane may have loved, passionately loved, Edward Irving, but that she felt only affection and admiration for Carlyle. And Carlyle, he thought, felt more deeply about his mother than his wife. The marriage of Jane and Carlyle was a true companionship, but it was not in Froude's opinion a real marriage; Geraldine had told him that Carlyle was the kind of man who should never have married. In his speculation on what might have been, Froude thought Jane would have been far happier if she had married someone of her own class; and that Carlyle's needs could have been served, perhaps not so well but adequately, by a mother, or a sister, or a niece, who kept house for him; or, as George Meredith would have added, by anyone so long as she had 'a nervous system resembling a dumpling'. In this way, if happiness were the most important thing in life, Jane might have been spared the misery which Carlyle's physical constitution, his nervous impatience and irritability, his peasant ideas about women's work, and his preoccupation with his own genius was almost bound to inflict on a wife.

'I married him for ambition', he quotes Jane as saying, and he thinks that without Jane's help Carlyle might not have gone as far as he did. But the price she paid for a success which exceeded her dreams was loneliness, loss of intellectual companionship, loss of his imaginative homage when she most needed it, and the endless drain of his demands on her health and nerves. She was even without the faith of her childhood, because his intellect had destroyed that for her without being able to replace it with his own religion. It had been an extraordinary partnership of genius; but it was also like an abrasion of diamond on diamond until one was half-demolished by the other. Froude thinks there was a bitterness in her soul which Carlyle never saw, and that even the last eighteen months of her life – the Indian summer of their marriage – was not as idyllic as Carlyle thought. The resentment seemed less, but it was still there, for 'she was unforgiving and had more to forgive than anyone knew'.

The painter of this portrait of Jane was Carlyle's devoted disciple. After a literary acquaintance which began in 1849, Froude had been admitted to intimacy with the great man in 1860. He walked and

13

talked with Carlyle two or three times a week, became a kind of son and found Jane one of the most brilliant, haunting women he had ever met. The commission which Carlyle entrusted to Froude – to become, in effect, the editor–biographer of both husband and wife – posed great problems. What sort of description of this celebrated marriage, whose tensions were documented by the papers he had received and by the remorse which Carlyle had poured out, should be given to Victorian England? Froude spurned the idea, both as a historian in his own right and as the disciple of a moralist who put truth-telling above every other value, that his work should read like the conventional lives of the saints. It must be as true to life as he could make it and as Carlyle would want him to make it. What had Carlyle or Jane to fear from the facts of their lives being known? Was not each truly noble? Should they not be painted, for all posterity, as a Rembrandt might have painted them? So Froude worked away at his commission, while Carlyle was still alive, and then, as soon as he was dead, presented the world with three distinct pictures of the Carlyles. The first was Carlyle's image of Jane, as embodied in his penitential memoir, which Froude published within a month of his death in 1881 as part of the *Reminiscences* of Thomas Carlyle. The second was Jane's image of herself and Carlyle, as embodied in *Letters and Memorials of Jane Welsh Carlyle*, which Carlyle had annotated with a view to publication and which Froude published in 1883. The third picture was Froude's own image of both husband and wife, as embodied in one of the great biographies of English literature, the first two volumes appearing in 1882 and the second two in 1884. He held two things back – his belief that Carlyle had once struck Jane and his belief that Carlyle was impotent. In 1887, writing a private journal under what he believed was extreme provocation by his critics, he made each belief a matter of record for his family to use as they thought fit.

THE ANTI-FROUDIANS

If we admit, as many of his enemies did not, the purity of Froude's motives, how much of his picture of Jane and Thomas was fact, and how much fiction? Good judges, relatives and intimates of Carlyle, told him how admirably they thought he had done his duty. But from one segment of the family, which had been very close to Carlyle in his last years, came a bombardment of criticism which was to be sustained by a succession of anti-Froudians for the next half century. Mary Aitken, the daughter of Carlyle's sister, Jean, came to Cheyne Row two years after Jane's death to keep house for Carlyle and to be his secretary. At that time, 1868, she was twenty years old. About a decade later her cousin, Alexander Carlyle, son of Carlyle's brother Alexander, who had emigrated to Canada, came over from Canada and married Mary Aitken. This was in 1879 when Alexander was thirty-seven and Mary thirty-one. Mary's worry about Froude seems to have begun as a worry about whether her own efforts in transcribing Carlyle's papers, and her claims as his niece, would be properly rewarded. She was concerned about whether the masses of correspondence given, or lent, to Froude, would be returned. She may have felt snubbed by Froude; she was 'a modest woman with a lot to be modest about'. She may also have formed her own opinions about Froude's suitability as a biographer of her uncle, though all was cordial up to Carlyle's death. Whatever this background may have been, it was outraged family pride which led Mary to hire her lawyers, write to *The Times*, and denounce Froude for breach of faith and trust, as soon as his publications, beginning with the Memoir of Jane Welsh Carlyle, began to appear. Froude had printed too much; more than the living could bear. Charles Eliot Norton, a Harvard scholar who had met Carlyle after Mary was installed, and who never got on with Froude, took Mary's part. He was editing Carlyle's correspondence with Emerson, so Mary asked him to re-edit the correspondence which Froude had been given as soon as it returned to her hands. When Norton had done his share with vigour and venom, and was too old to continue, the chief sponsorship of the controversy passed to Alexander, who published his *New Letters and Memorials of Jane Welsh Carlyle* in 1903. He was assisted by Sir James Crichton-Browne, a Scottish physician, who undertook to diagnose Jane's sickness and to discharge Carlyle from anything to do with breaking her health. It was the attack on Froude in this book that led his family to publish his last words, *My Relations with Carlyle*. Alexander and Sir James retaliated with *The Nemesis of Froude*, in which Sir James extended his excursions into the diagnosis of the dead by clearing Carlyle of the charge of impotence. Alexander Carlyle lived on until 1931, the indefatigable defender of his uncle's honour against 'Froudacities'.

The anti-Froudians' quarrel with Froude was an altogether larger matter than Froude's portrait of Jane. It embraced the whole question of the commission which Carlyle had given Froude and of the spirit in which Froude had interpreted it. But their determination to vindicate Carlyle's character, which they thought Froude had defamed, inevitably led them into a re-assessment of Jane's. To follow them into every detail of an argument, which was inspired as much by Victorian ideas of reticence and propriety as by differences which we would think important, is unnecessary here. In brief, they believed that Carlyle was neither as selfish, nor as irritable, nor as overbearing as Froude makes out; that life at Craigenputtoch or at Cheyne Row was never as black as Froude painted it; and that Carlyle's remorse had been exaggerated out of all proportion to the facts, perhaps by Carlyle himself, certainly by Froude. David Masson, a close friend of the Carlyles and Professor of English Literature first at London and then at Edinburgh, complained of Froude's insufficient sense of humour; he said he undertook his great biography in the mood of a man driving a hearse. As for Jane, they thought that Froude had let his sympathy, and his sense of theatre, run away with him. There was no such social gulf between Haddington and Ecclefechan as Froude dreams about, no question of Carlyle turning a lady into a drudge; the daughters of Scottish provincial surgeons do not lord it over the educated sons of Scottish peasants. Jane had her disappointments, but why blame Carlyle for them? Her hypochondria was not his doing any more than his dyspepsia (Carlyle's *only* physical complaint, as Alexander carefully insists) was hers. She never achieved literary fame in her own right, but that was because she had no capacity for sustained effort, and not because Carlyle was too selfish to give her a chance. And as to that, they might say, was she not a little self-centred herself? Was not she, rather than he, the really hard one? The thrust of all this anti-Froudian revisionism, in subtle as well as obvious ways, is to elevate the husband, to diminish the wife, to appeal from drama to common sense, and to deprive the marriage of the tragical dimension which Froude had given it.

JANE'S PLACE IN THE HISTORY OF WOMEN

How did Jane really feel about her life? Would she have agreed with Geraldine about their place in history?

Her letters are one witness to her feelings, her friends are another, and each testifies to both sides of her nature. If her mother was capable of fifteen different humours, Jane was always capable of at least *two*. Froude's picture of the middle-aged Jane – disillusioned, disappointed, half-embittered, yet forever rising to do her duty – is perhaps too sombre. Geraldine was a chief source for Froude and many of the most striking passages in her letters are her responses to Jane's discouragements;

My dear child, you ought to know your value better . . . it is a sort of quixotism you have for sacrificing yourself . . . in the nightmare of annoyances under which you are suffering, it is the most wholesome thing you can do to give 'shrewings' right and left . . . better to scold, scold, scold! . . . but do, for God's sake, pitch your virtue in a lower key! An archangel could not go on performing such feats of abnegation as you lay upon yourself.[1]

Yet vivacity and a sense of triumph was as much a part of Jane's history as a sense of failure and frustration. As for the hardness which more than one observer found in her, it can be matched by her displays of tenderness for relations, dependents, favourite friends, her pets, and above all, her husband.

Would she have agreed with Geraldine about their place in history? They were very different people. Geraldine had an enormous, ungratified desire for physical love. Something about her was less than appealing to the objects of her desire, and she blames her frustration on the fact that she was a woman. This was not Jane's problem: a woman who was attractive to most men and who wanted not passion but affection and admiration. Geraldine had a taste for abstractions and thought of herself as a representative of her sex. Jane was intensely individual. Her hopes and woes were all her own. Perhaps only-children are not brought up to consider themselves a part of the human race! Jane was encouraged by her father to think herself unique. She was much less inclined than most of us to attribute her own feelings to other people.

So if Jane was advancing the cause of equality for women, it was not by preaching it. Nor was her practice of self-immolation, for the sake of her genius-husband, a model to be followed, in Geraldine's opinion. It was rather the demonstration she gave of a woman with a mind as good as any man's, who held her own in every male company, pricked their pretensions, poked fun at them, and was perfectly capable, if she had so chosen, of equalling her husband's distinction with achievements of her own, that won Geraldine's praise. So far, said Geraldine, women have been educated to meet the current male idea of a good wife,

a strong taste of housewifery in one generation, a dash of delicate 'feminine' stupidity in another, a gentle flavour of religion, as a sort of ornamental ring-fence

[1] *Letters of Geraldine Jewsbury*, pp. 75–6.

to their virtue . . . not for the saving of their souls, for they must not come it too strong . . . Today they may have a small, graceful tint of learning, and if married, the least-touch in the world of abstract 'George Sandism' but not to come within a mile of the practical.[1]

It was Jane's scornful superiority to the products of this tradition which had been reinforced by the manifold publications of Sarah Stickney Ellis, who considered intellectuality in a woman 'more frequently her bane than her blessing', and indeed everything that set her apart from the 'Mrs Ellis woman' who is developed 'to the extreme of her little possibility', that had earned her, in her friend's opinion, the right to be enrolled among the champions of women's freedom.

Geraldine was one of many who had urged Jane to become a writer. In her letters of 1851 – during Jane's most difficult years – she is begging her to do this not simply as an outlet for frustrations, an 'ark of refuge' from her own troubles, but also because she has so much to teach other women.

If you had had daughters, they would have been educated as few women have the luck to be, and I think you might have enough maternal feeling, sisterly affection, *esprit de corps*, or what you will, to wish to help other women in their very complicated duties and difficulties. Do not go to Mr Carlyle for sympathy, do not let him dash you with cold water. You must respect your own work and your own motives.[2]

Geraldine, with her usual impetuosity, offers to help in any way she can. Should they try writing together?

So begin, begin! half your loneliness comes from having no outlet for your energies, and no engrossing employment . . . You ought to have had a dozen daughters . . . So let your work be dedicated to your 'unknown daughters'. I am one of your children, after a fashion . . . So finally, my dear love, begin to work.[3]

How Jane replied to these entreaties we do not know. Geraldine's editor, Mrs Ireland, tells how Geraldine, as she neared death, kept an old promise to Jane by destroying her letters one by one. We do know that Geraldine, Mrs Paulet and Jane once talked of writing a novel together, made up of letters, and that when the two friends sent her their first efforts she found their manuscript 'too stormy' for her. But Jane's inability to write a book, in the face of all reason, was already an old story by 1851.

[1] *Letters of Geraldine Jewsbury*, pp. 348–9.
[2] *Ibid.* p. 426.
[3] *Ibid.* p. 427.

Nearly thirty years had passed since Carlyle himself had urged her to 'sit down and write . . . begin to write something, if you can, without delay, never minding how shallow and poor it may seem'. That was before they were married, when they were dreaming of the books they might write together and he was saying all the sensible things that could be said to his perfectionist pupil to get her started. She sighed, writhed, joked and entreated. 'Send me an outline of some Tale to work on; else I shall never get on; for no sooner has my brain got up something like a plot, than I perceive it to be the veriest imbecility . . . What a destiny I have chosen! How full of difficulties, disquietudes and dangers! And perhaps, to end in disappointment!... I am a very shuttlecock of a creature. I have no stamina.' He obliged at once with a plan for 'Tales from the German, translated and selected by Jane Baillie Welsh'. He picked the tales, promised an Introduction, talked to publishers, and gaily urged her on, 'Work, work my heroine . . . till we reach the golden, glowing summit.' But he soon had to console her for not having emerged from the foothills.

It is not easy to say when Jane's ambition for literary fame died in either Carlyle's mind or her own. His thought that she might either collaborate with him or do a book of her own was not abandoned easily. After he was famous and she was nearing forty, he could write: 'perhaps we are better as we are'; but he tried again to rouse her interest when her mother's death left her so desolate in 1842: 'My prayer is and has always been that you would rouse up the fine faculties that *are* yours, into some course of real work which you felt to be worthy of them and you.'[1] But three years later we find him saying, 'I know not if you mean to take Egypt's [Geraldine's friend, Lambert Bey] advice and write some book. I have often said you might, with successful effect; but the impulse, the necessity, has mainly to come from within. It is a poor trade otherwise, so we will be content with Goody whether she ever comes to a book or not.'

Jane kept journals and notebooks, most of which she destroyed and none of which she ever showed to Carlyle. Some slight pieces – a fairy-tale, a story from real life, a dialogue between her canary and her mother's watch – may have been shown to close friends. She told Carlyle jokingly in 1852, how Chapman, his publisher, had 'made me again the offer of "very advantageous terms" for a novel of my own'. She might have been brilliantly successful as a reviewer, a short-story writer, a writer of travellers' tales or a diarist. She might have found a way, as Geraldine had hoped, to write about women.

[1] Quoted by Alexander Carlyle in *The Nemesis of Froude* (1903), p. 19.

But whether wilted by the heat of Carlyle's genius, or absorbed by his demands, or worn down by sickness and hypochondria, or simply because it was not in her, the authoress never materialized.

John Forster, life-long friend of the Carlyles and Charles Dickens, tells how shocked Dickens was to hear of her death. He had seen her at Forster's home only a week or two before, radiant with the news of Carlyle's success in Edinburgh, and full of the goings-on she had observed in a house across the street – a perfect beginning for a novel which she would finish for him when they next met. 'How often have I thought of the unfinished novel' said Dickens, 'No one now to finish it. None of the writing women come near her at all.'

HER LETTERS

Instead, she put her genius into her conversation and her letters. There is nothing so evanescent as table-talk – it dies like a facial expression, but from what we know of her conversation it must have been very like her letters. She dined off the experiences which she wrote about the next day. But where we only have scraps of her talk we have hundreds of her letters. The total increases from decade to decade and the end, happily, has not yet been reached. Froude published, in full or in extracts, between three and four hundred of Jane's letters in his biography of Carlyle and in his *Letters and Memorials of Jane Welsh Carlyle* (3 volumes, 1883). Alexander Carlyle published as many more, mostly from the collection originally placed at Froude's disposal but others from his own discoveries. In the first category were *New Letters and Memorials of Jane Welsh Carlyle* (2 volumes, 1903) and *The Love Letters of Thomas Carlyle and Jane Welsh* (2 volumes, 1909); in the second, a score of letters, originally stolen by a clerk of Carlyle's in 1856, which Alexander published in two issues of the *Nineteenth Century* magazine in 1914. About fifty early letters of Jane's, mostly to Eliza Stodart, a childhood friend in Haddington, were published by a great nephew of Eliza's, David G. Ritchie, in 1889. Twenty-seven letters to Joseph Neuberg, a businessman who acted as a literary secretary for Carlyle, made their way through Neuberg's descendants to the National Library of Scotland, to be published by Townsend Scudder in 1931. Over two hundred letters from Jane to a favourite cousin, Jeannie (Babbie) Welsh, and other Welsh relatives – a wonderful goldmine – passed through the hands of Jeannie's daughter to be edited by Leonard Huxley in 1924 as *Jane Welsh Carlyle: Letters to Her Family, 1839–1863*.

This was followed by more from the same quarter in 'A Sheaf of Letters from Jane Welsh Carlyle', *Cornhill Magazine* (October–November 1926).

The editors of the definitive edition of *The Collected Letters of Thomas and Jane Welsh Carlyle* found about 3,000 letters written by Jane, of which 800 had never been published, as compared with about 6,000 by Thomas, of which 3,700 had not been published. More than half of these manuscripts are in the great Carlyle collection started by Carlyle and continued by Alexander in the National Library of Scotland at Edinburgh. The rest are scattered in public and private collections all over the world. In the four volumes of this edition so far published, under the editorship of C. R. Sanders and K. J. Fielding as a cooperative enterprise by Duke University and the University of Edinburgh, the story has been carried as far as the marriage, and the editors estimate that the publication of the whole correspondence will require at least thirty volumes. They point out that in her most active period, 1841–5, judging only by the letters that have survived, Jane was averaging 116 letters a year.

'I never sit down at night, beside a good fire, *alone*, without feeling a need of talking a little, on paper, to somebody that I like well enough, and that likes *me* well enough, to make it of no moment – whether I talk sense or nonsense, and with or without regard to the rules of grammar.' What should a letter be about? Why, about oneself, of course. 'Oh, my dear! I feel so fractious this evening; should like to break something, or box somebody's ears!' This was to an old friend, Mrs Russell, the wife of the doctor in Thornhill who attended her mother in her last illness. Carlyle got the daily letter 'which must be written dead or alive', when they were separated, and she expected the same fidelity from him. He apologized once for the length of a letter and she replied, 'Don't mind length, at least only write longly about yourself. The cocks that awake you; everything of that sort is very interesting. I hasten over the cleverest descriptions of extraneous people and things, to find something "all about yourself" "all to myself".'

But if oneself should become disagreeable to oneself, through sickness or depression, then 'oneself – at least myself – is a sort of Irish bog subject in which one is in danger of sinking overhead; common sense commands therefore to keep out of that'. When she is not talking about herself, Jane is talking about 'everything and everybody' that has caught her eye in the course of the day; at home in Cheyne Row, firing or forgiving a maid, 'earthquaking' (the Carlyle verb for spring-cleaning), annihilating bugs, or shielding a bilious genius from barking dogs and crowing cocks; on her travels, by foot, horseback, coach, omnibus, steamship and train; on her annual migrations into the homes of Scottish relatives or into lodgings by the sea, or into the country houses of the great. There are celebrated people – Carlyle in all his moods, growling, scornful, violent, tyrannical, peaceable, gentle and good; Leigh Hunt, a 'kind of Talking Nightingale'; Tennyson, handsome and noble-hearted, 'with something of the gypsy in his appearance, which, for me, is perfectly charming'; Thackeray, 'very good indeed, beats Dickens out of the world'; Macaulay, 'I used to think my husband the most copious talker, when he liked, that was anywhere to be fallen in with; but Macaulay beats him hollow! in quantity.'[1]

But there are also miraculous ordinary people in this wonderful album of snapshots – a coachful of men, worthy of a French impressionist, a cultivator of scarlet-beans who would have been worth a hundred pounds to Dickens, the caller from Craigenputtoch who looked like a haystack and turned out to be old 'Nancy with the beard', the forlorn lover on a railway platform chanting to his lass in the carriage like a repeating decimal, as he sees her off, '*What for* did ye *no* come to the Ball?'

Two things were forbidden. Outpourings of feelings should be avoided. This was a maxim of that Lady Ashburton who was such a rose in Carlyle's life and such a thorn in Jane's. Jane often referred with approval to her Ladyship's terror and horror of letters which were 'all about feelings' and on one very emotional occasion in her own life – a return to Haddington, her birthplace, after an interval of sixteen years – she poured out her feelings on arrival in a long midnight letter to Carlyle and then destroyed it the next morning. But she was not always so restrained. Feelings inevitably crept into her letters as her nerves or her health deteriorated.

The other prohibition, so far as her own letters were concerned, had to do with scenery. At some early point in her life she must have come to the conclusion that 'the picturesque' and 'the beauties of nature' had been overdone. She once chided Carlyle, who devoured thousands of miles of landscape on foot and horseback in the course of his life and had fantastical powers of describing scenery, by writing: 'If all about feelings in letters is bad, all about scenery is worse.'[2] What he had written, she explained, might charm his future

---

[1] Froude, *Letters and Memorials*, II, 188.
[2] Froude, *Letters and Memorials*, III, 29–30.

biographer or be quoted in a guide-book, but it wasn't what his wife had been waiting to hear.

Jane's powers of description were rarely applied to scenery. Or, for that matter, to many other things which might be meat and drink for another kind of letter-writer. She was intensely interested in the novel and called Carlyle's attention to more than one rising author, but to use a letter as a vehicle for serious criticism would have struck her as dull. Public affairs get only the slightest attention. Politics do not interest her. Science and religion bore her about equally. Art and music are not for her – she gets a conventional thrill out of the Elgin marbles and occasionally remembers her piano. More provokingly, this 'wife of genius', who read every word he wrote until he got bogged down in Frederick the Great, has singularly little to say about his ideas or his message. But this still leaves her a wonderful manager of her own arts.

She has a few things to say about the style, as well as the subject matter, of a good letter. It should be 'offhand, as one speaks'. She opens one letter by saying, 'I will start in promiscuously' and ends another with, 'I am in the habit of letting my pen go its own way and this is the way it has gone.' A marvellous story begins like this, 'I had a visit the other day which turned me upside down with the surprise of it.' Be natural and simple, she seems to be saying, in contrast to the anything-but-natural-and-simple style of her involuted, overheated husband. But of course it was carefully studied simplicity, as we may see from her notebooks, before it became her natural habit.

As a talker and a letter-writer she is essentially a brilliant story-teller. She and Carlyle had shared good stories ever since they first met each other – stories of the Scottish countryside, inherited from their parents and augmented by their own experiences. They repeatedly drew on this household stock of anecdotes to enrich their letters to each other, in ways which would often baffle a third party were it not for Carlyle's elucidations, but, having these, we can see what a good story meant to them. 'I merely pray God to "very particularly damn him"', says Jane of an architect who had broken all his promises. Behind this, Carlyle tells us, sparkles a memory of Old McTurk, paying his rascally reapers in the evening with a half-crown and a 'God damn you!' until he comes to one old woman, the source of all the trouble, who got, 'and God particularly damn *you*, ye bitch!'

Jane was famous for her stories. Carlyle expected some good thing when he joined her at breakfast or dinner and her letters and journals are studded with good things. She had the sharpest eye for the dramatic and the absurd; an excellent ear for conversation, especially in the dialect of Lowland Scots; and a flair for the vivid phrase. 'Today it has blown knives and files; a cold rasping, savage day'; 'went to bed again, and lay till half-past seven, amidst a tearing rumble of carts that seemed to drive over my brain'. 'My head feels as usual to be full of melted lead, swaying this way and that.'

The effects which Carlyle achieved by crashes of thunder Jane managed in little flashes of lightning. Carlyle was one of the noisiest of writers, always shouting, groaning, denouncing, exhorting. Jane rarely raised her voice. Her tone is conversational; collected, playful, affectionate, witty. Her art is like that of a craftsman in jewels or a preserver of butterflies.

In her best vein, unclouded by worry or illness, making fun of herself and the genius she had married, catching a likeness in a line, telling those delicious tales of their lives in 5 Cheyne Row and of her outings in the country, she is endlessly enjoyable.

Did she write for posterity? She would be violating her own precepts if she did. 'My dear', said her friend, the novelist Geraldine Jewsbury, 'how is it that women who don't write books write always so much nicer letters than those who do?' 'Because', retorted Jane, 'they do not write in the "Valley of the shadow" of their future biographer, but write what they have to say frankly and naturally.'[1]

[1] Froude, *Letters and Memorials*, II, 307.

The Letters

I *Courtship*

Jane was nineteen, living with her widowed mother in the family house at Hadding-ton, when Carlyle paid his first call on her. He had been brought over from Edinburgh to stay at the George Hotel by Edward Irving, who meant so much to them in these years as Jane's old tutor and one of Carlyle's few intimates; they were to call him 'the Orator' as he embarked on his dizzy career as a pentecostal preacher in London.

The courtship which began with this visit in May 1821 lasted five years. To an extraordinary degree it was an engagement by correspondence; months would pass without their seeing each other, although the obstacles to a visit hardly seemed insuperable. Between their formal engagement in January 1825 and their marriage in October 1826 there was a period of a whole year when they never saw each other, during which time their plans for setting up house together were the subject of almost comical confusions. Where others might have ridden, or even walked, the intervening miles, they poured out their hearts by mail.

Each was the other's escape from loneliness. Jane's life was the emptier. Although there were suitors and callers and visits to relatives, there was not much in Had-dington for a lively mind to feed on. Carlyle moved around somewhat more, in search of books and employment as a writer, and as a tutor of Charles Buller's sons. He got to London and Paris as well as Edinburgh; but, as Jane told him more than once, he was really intensely isolated.

They clung to each other as young intellectuals, as partners in self-improvement, and as aspirants to a distinction that was moral as well as intellectual. They wanted to make their mark as literary celebrities – Jane called their friendship 'a literary intimacy' – but they also cherished an ideal of 'noble' conduct, which had a girlishly romantic quality in Jane's case and a strongly Puritan flavour in Carlyle's. Their rhetoric can be prosy and stagy, especially when they are trying to be heroic, for neither had yet found his mature style. But 'You and I', wrote Carlyle, 'are two originals for certain "in our own humble way".' Besides their lofty ambitions they shared short tempers, sharp tongues, precarious health, and an irresistible urge to dramatize themselves.

Such love letters! Impetuous Thomas is teacher, preacher, brother and lover by turns. How noble she is! How much talent she has! How proud he is of her! How she must never lose faith in her genius, but work and plan and be guided by him, her guardian spirit. She coquettes; chronicling the importunities of her suitors, submitting to the fates – usually in the person of her mother – who are always preventing her and Thomas from getting together, making and breaking her vows about work, reminding him that all his letters are to be read by her mother, and telling him, for nearly four of the five years, that what he is to expect from her is a profound, sisterly love. What a witch, rogue, gypsy!

Carlyle replies,

The only thing I know is that you are the most delightful, enthusiastic, contemptuous, affectionate, sarcastic, capricious, warm-hearted, lofty-minded,
half-devil, half-angel of a woman that ever ruled over the heart of a man; that
I will love you, must love you, whatever may betide, till the last moment of my
existence; and that if we both act rightly our lot *may* be the happiest of a thousand mortal lots. So let us cling to one another (– if you dare when thus forewarned) – forever and ever![1]

To recapture the flavour of this courtship we can turn over about three hundred
of the original letters in Edinburgh, or read them in the meticulously edited
Duke–Edinburgh edition. Most of them were exchanged between the two lovers;
some of them went to friends and relatives, such as Jane's letters to her girlhood
friend, Eliza Stodart, to her mother, Grace Welsh, or to her future mother-in-law,
Margaret Carlyle. Carlyle's letters are no doubt more impressive than Jane's.
He was five years older, altogether better read, and intent on his mission. While
Jane was bewailing her unfinished projects, he was publishing articles in *Brewster's
Encyclopaedia*, a *Life of Schiller*, a translation of Goethe's *Wilhelm Meister* and a volume of German Romance. This last included a translation of a tale by Musäus
that he had repeatedly urged Jane to do for herself. But if Jane cannot compete
with this sort of range and drive, she is developing her own style.

The letters printed here have been chosen to illustrate her raillery; her eye for a
story; her ill-starred ambition for literary fame; and the special qualities of her
attachment to Carlyle – her faith in him, her deep dependence, and her apparent
lack of romantic or physical passion. They trace the ups and downs of a five-year
courtship and end with an extract from a short story – in every other way a
bumbling story – which Carlyle placed in *Blackwood's Magazine* in 1831.
Behind the thin veil of fiction, in which the hero Jonson woos and marries
Margaret, Carlyle has left us a picture of Jane which deserves a place beside the
magical, irresistible miniature of Jane done in July 1826 by Kenneth McLeay
(see Plate 2*a*).

ON READING ROUSSEAU
AND DYING A MAID

1. TO ELIZA STODART AT EDINBURGH

Haddington/ January 1822

My dear Bess, –

... Do read this book[2] – You will find it tedious in many of its
details, and in some of its scenes culpably indelicate; but for splendour
of eloquence, refinement of sensibility, and ardour of passion it has
no match in the French language. Fear not that by reading Heloise
you will be ruined – or undone – or whatever adjective best suits that

---

[1] Letter of 25 November 1823, in *Collected Letters*, II, 419–20.
[2] Rousseau's *Julie, ou la nouvelle Héloïse* (1761).

fallen state into which women and angels *will* stumble *at a time* – I promise you that you will rise from Heloise with a deeper impression of whatever is most beautiful and most exalted in virtue than is left upon your mind by 'Blairs sermons' 'Paley's Theology' or the voluminous 'Jeremy Taylor' himself – I never felt my mind more prepared to brave temptation of every sort than when I closed the second volume of this strange book – I believe if the Devil himself had waited upon me [in] the shape of Lord Byron I would have desired Betty to show him out – . . . Read the book and ask your heart or rather your judgement if Julia be vicious. *I do not wish to countenance such irregularities among my female acquaintances* but I must confess were any individual of them to meet with *such a man* – to struggle as she struggled – to endure as she endured – to *yield* as she yielded – and to repent as she repented – I would love that woman better than the chastest coldest Prude between Johnnygroats House and Land's end – One serious bad consequence will result to you from reading Heloise – at least if your soul-strings are screwed up to the same key as mine – You will never marry! Alas! I told you that I should die a virgin if I reached twenty[1] *in vain* – Even so will it prove – This Book this fatal Book has given me an idea of a love so *pure* (Yes you may laugh! but I repeat it) so pure, so constant, so disinterested, so exalted – that no love the men of this world can offer me will ever fill up the picture my imagination has drawn with the help of Rousseau – No lover will Jane Welsh ever find like St Preux – no Husband like Wolnar[2] (I dont mean to insinuate that *I should like both* –) and to no man will she ever give her heart and pretty hand who bears to these no resemblance – George Rennie! James Aitken! Robert MacTurk! James Baird!!! Robby Angus! – O Lord, O Lord! where is the St Preux? Where is the Wolnar? – Bess I am in earnest – I shall never marry – and after having laughed so at old maids, it will be so dreadful to be one of the very race at whom I have pointed the finger of scorn – Virtuous Venerable females! how my heart smites me for the illjudged ridicule I have cast on their pure names! What atonement can I make? what punishment shall I undergo? Let me think! – I will – I will write a novel & make my Heroine a Beauty – a Wit – a very *Monster* of *perfection* – an Empress of a thousand *male* hearts – and – she shall live a Maid – and die in an elegant little garret – But I will talk no more on this melancholy subject – So you saw my Aunt! what did you think of her? Poor thing

[1] She was twenty on 14 July 1821.
[2] St Preux and Wolnar are characters in *La nouvelle Héloïse*.

she does not understand love – She never read Heloise – but she has got a husband – such as he is –

Mr Craig Buchanan has put me to the expense of postage[1] twice within the last fortnight – He is improving in his Style and displays some ingenuity in finding out subjects to write upon – He threatens me with a visit in a week or two – It will surely come to a crisis – what do you think of it – He is about the age of Wolnar – but Wolnar had not a bald head – nor a lame leg – neither did Wolnar make puns or pay compliments – I have just had a letter from Thomas Carlyle; he too speaks of coming – He is something liker to St Preux than George Craig is to Wolnar – He has *his* talents – *his* vast and cultivated mind – *his* vivid imagination – *his* independence of soul and *his* high souled principles of honour – But then Ah these *buts*! St Preux never kicked the fire irons –nor made puddings in his teacup – Want of Elegance – Want of Elegance Rousseau says is a defect which no woman can overlook – It is the decree of fate! dear Eliza. it is the decree of fate! so look about for a nice pleasant little garret that has a fine view unclouded by the town smoke and out of reach of the camera obscura and we will take up house together – . . .

A SISTER – BUT NOT A WIFE

2. To Thomas Carlyle at Edinburgh

Haddington/ ca. 17 January 1822

I have read the Tragedies – I thank you for them – They are Byron's. Need *I* praise them. I have also read your eloquent history of Faust – For it too I thank you. It has fewer faults and greater merits than its Author led me to expect – I have moreover read your letter – For *it* I do *not* thank you – It afforded me neither pleasure nor amusement – Indeed, my Friend this letter of yours has, to my mind, more than one fault – I do not allude to its being egotistical – To speak of one's self is, they say, a privilege of Friendship, and I have seen too much of Mr Carlyle to expect that Friendship should have *any* privileges of which he would *not* avail himself. But there is about it an air of levity which I dislike. Which seems to me to form an unnatural union with the other qualities of your head and heart, and to be ill-timed in treating of a subject, to you the most important

[1] The recipient of the letter usually paid for the postage.

of all subjects – your own *destiny*. In a Statesman venturing the hopes of his ambition on one decisive stroke – In a Soldier rushing to the Battle to conquer or to die, I might admire the spirit of gay daring with which you seem to have been animated; But in a man sitting quietly in his chamber contemplating years of labour, unattended with any danger (For I do not see that it is incumbent on you to '*perish*' because you fail in writing a good Novel, good Tragedy, or good any thing else) years of labour the result of which may be neither certain good, nor certain evil, it seems to me, such a *spirit* is unnatural and ridiculous – Besides this there is about your letter a *mystery* which I detest – It is so full of *meaning* words underlined – *meaning* sentences half finished, *meaning blanks* with notes of admiration – and *meaning* quotations from foreign languages that really in this abundance of *meaning* it seems to indicate I am somewhat at a loss to discover what you would be at. I know how you will excuse yourself on this score – you will say that you knew my Mother would see your letter, and that, of course you cared not to what difficulties I, as Interpreter, might be subjected, so that you got your *feelings towards me* expressed. Now Sir, once for all, I beg you to understand that I *dislike* as much as my Mother *disapproves* your somewhat too ardent expressions of Friendship towards me; and that if you cannot write to me as to a Man who feels a deep interest in your welfare – who admires your talents – respects your virtues, and for the sake of these has often – perhaps too often – overlooked your faults – If you cannot write to me as if – as if you were married you need never waste ink on paper on me more.

'*Alles für Ruhm und Ihr*'!![1] – On my word, most gay and gallantly said – One would almost believe the man fancies I have fallen in love with him, and entertain the splendid project of rewarding his literary labours with myself. Really Sir I do not design for you a recompense so worthless. If you render yourself an honoured member of society (and it seems to me that the pursuit of literary fame is, from the talents you possess, an easy – and, from the manner of life you have adopted, an *only* way of raising yourself from obscurity into the estimation of the wise and good) I will be to you a true, a constant, a devoted *friend* – but not a Mistress – a Sister – but not a Wife – *Falling in love* and marrying like other Misses is quite out of the question – I have too *little* romance in my disposition ever to be in love with you or any other man; and too *much* ever to marry without love – Were I a man I would not wait till *others* find your *worth* to say,

[1] 'All for glory and her.'

30

in the face of the whole world, I admire this man and choose him for my friend – But I am a woman Mr Carlyle – and what is worse a young woman – Weakness, timidity and bondage are in the word – But enough of this – why do you force me into such horrid explanations? . . .

You propose coming here – As I do not presume to forbid this house to any one whom my 'excellent Mother' invites, the matter, I grieve to say, rests with yourself. As you neither study *my* inclinations, nor consider *my* comfort, it is in vain to say how much I am averse to your intended visit, and to how many impertinent conjectures it will, at present, subject me, in this tattling, illnatured place – I leave it then to yourself to accomplish it, or not, as you please – with this warning that if you come, you will repent it. I expected that the tasks I assigned you in my last would have stood me instead of Penelope's Web for a while – But I was a fool to expect peace – Patient sufferance I begin to find, is the first lesson to be learned by *one* of the parties in a Romantic Friendship. My Mother knows nothing of your projected visit. She did not see your letter. We were in bad humour with each other when it came, and as, in spite of your *precautions*, and the handsome adjective with which you ushered in your intention of visiting her it seemed to me nowise calculated to improve her temper, I seized the opportunity which a fit of Pet afforded me of laying it aside without showing it – If she *had seen* it I am pretty sure her friendship for *you* would have formed but a brief episode in the history of her affections. If you are so unlucky as to determine on coming, it will be necessary for you to write again and mention your intentions as for the first time – (To what pitiful evasions do you reduce me!) As I do not take the Pet every night no future letter of yours may escape like your last. I beg therefore that you will make no *particular* allusion to any part of this letter; for tho' my Mother knows that I am writing to you she must not see it – I trust however that your *Good Genius* will lead you to make *one* effort of self denial. In that case I shall be glad to hear from you some weeks hence. Earth Air and Sea surely afford subjects enough for a letter to spare you the necessity of confining your ideas to yourself and me. If you think me more *prudent* or rather more *rational* than formerly resolve the difficulty thus. *Now* I am *using* the language of my *own* heart *Then* I was *learning* that of *yours* Here I am Jane Welsh – In Edinburgh I was Mr Carlyle's *Pupil* –

Your sincere Friend –

J. B. Welsh

31

A FINE LADY – OR A LITERARY LADY?

3. To Thomas Carlyle at Edinburgh

Haddington/ 7 May 1822

Dear Sir

I would have returned Delphine[1] long ago had you not sent Henry[2] along with it – She is a most fascinating Being I have liked no body half so well for a great while – I ought not (at least sage people say I ought not) to admire the book, nevertheless I cannot for my life help liking it better than any novel of six volumes I ever read – I declare the idea of having Madame de Stael for an acquaintance in the world of spirits makes me half wish to die – As to Henry He is a downright blockhead and had you not desired me to read it I would have taken an everlasting farewell of his 'probablys' and 'we may supposes' in the first half dozen pages – I have toiled with a vexed spirit through the whole volume, and, after all, the materials I have got would make but a starved Tragedy –

I have neither genius taste nor commonsense – I have no courage no industry no perseverance – and how in the name of wonder can I write a tragedy – I am not at all the sort of person you and I took me for – I begin to think that I was actually meant by nature to be a fine Lady – My friends that is my acquaintances have told me this all along but I would not believe them – For the last month however I have shown lamentable symptoms of a tendency that way – I have spent all my time in riding on horseback, dressing three times a day, singing Italian airs, and playing at shuttlecock! Dear Sir what will cure me? I have just enough of reason left to perceive I am in a bad way – if another such month passes over me – I am a lost woman – even my ambition is expiring very fast. I am as proud of striking the shuttlecock two hundred times as if I had written two hundred admirable verses – the certainty I have felt for some time that I will never excell the hundreds of female Novelists who infest the kingdom is the chief cause of this sudden change in my tastes and pursuits – and what can cure the want of talents? Oh dear me! I shall never hold a respectable place among literary ladies – but I know I can be a first rate fine Lady whenever I please – the temptation is strong; furnish me with an antidote if you can – I am not capable of design-

---

[1] By Madame de Staël (Paris, 1803).
[2] Robert Henry's *History of Great Britain*.

ing a tragedy at present – Indeed I do not see how one can make the story of Boadicea sufficiently interesting. For Mercy's sake sketch it for me and I will if I can fill it up – I am not to be in town during the assembly[1] – possibly my Mother may be there for a day but I will not accompany her – I wish you may be able to read this I am in the most dreadful hurry ever poor wretch was in –

Yours truly
Jane Baillie Welsh

POLE-STARS IN MY LIFE

4. To Thomas Carlyle at Edinburgh

Haddington/ 11 November 1822

My dear friend

If ever I succeed in distinguishing myself above the common herd of little Misses, thine will be the honour of my success. Repeatedly have your salutary counsels, and little well-timed flatteries roused me from inactivity when my own reason was of no avail. Our meeting forms a memorable epoch in my history; for my acquaintance with you has from its very commencement powerfully influenced my character & life. When you saw me for the first time, I was wretched beyond description – grief at the loss of the only being I ever loved with my whole soul [her father] had weakened my body and mind – distraction of various kinds had relaxed my habits of industry – I had no counsellor that could direct me – no friend that understood me – the pole-star of my life was lost, and the world looked a dreary blank – Without plan, hope, or aim I had lived two years when my good angel sent you hither – I had never heard the language of talent and genius but from my Father's lips – I had thought that I should never hear it more – you spoke like him – your eloquence awoke in my soul the slumbering admirations and ambitions that *His* first kindled there – I wept to think, the mind he had cultivated with such anxious, unremitting pains was running to desolation; and I returned with renewed strength and ardour to the life that he had destined me to lead – But in my studies I have neither the same pleasures, or the same motives as formerly – I am *alone*, and no one loves me better for my industry – this solitude together with distrust of my own talents,

---

[1] The General Assembly of Ministers and Elders of the Church of Scotland, which meets annually in Edinburgh in the latter half of May.

despair of ennobling my character, and the discouragement I meet with in devoting myself to a literary life would, I believe, have, oftener than once, thrown me into a state of helpless despondency; had not your friendship restored me to myself, by supplying (in as much as they can ever be supplied) the counsels and incitements I have lost – You see I am not insensible to the value of your friendship, or likely to throw it away; tho' you have sometimes charged me with inconstancy and caprice –

There is no plainer way of testifying my entire approval of the matter contained in your last letter than rigidly adhering to the plan you have sketched for me. This I am endeavouring to do – I immediately commenced an active search through the libraries of my acquaintance for some of the books you named. Hume I have commenced and recommenced so many many times, that I cannot now look with patience on a volume of the same shape and colour. Therefore I preferred acquainting myself with the history of England through the medium of Clarendon. Clarendon however is '*out of fashion*'. My next attempt was on Rollin and that proved more successful. I read his Ancient History in my infancy; but remembered no more of it than the number of volumes. I have already finished the first volume, (writing little foolish reflections as I proceed) – during the last week I have also read the latter half of 'Maria Stuart' – some scenes of Alfieri – and a portion of 'Tacitus' (which by the way is the hardest Latin I ever saw) – when you devoted four hours of my day to the study of history, what did you mean should become of my Italian and my dear dear German? I have no inclination to part with these, and accordingly I mean to devote four hours more, equally '*constantly, faithfully* and *inflexibly*' to the study of languages. What is the reason I cannot read the first part of 'Wallenstein'? I was just beginning to congratulate myself upon my progress in the German Tongue ('Maria Stuart' was so intelligible) and now I find I know nothing at all about it. Have you ever read 'Rosmunda'?[1] If you have not you never saw women in a proper rage. Oh! it is a furious, bloody business – I think Alfieri must have written it with a live coal in his Stomach – . . .

I should like above all things 'to make a hero and heroine such as the world never saw' do let us set about it! the creatures of our joint imaginations will be a most singular mixture of genius and imbecility.

Would to God the alacrity of your execution was equal to the boldness of your projects! – Your last verses are very like Campbell –

[1] A tragedy by Alfieri (1804).

34

pray send me some more. you cannot think what pleasure they afford me. I am ashamed to say I have nothing to send you even '*in my humble way*' . . .

– Write soon

Your very sincere friend

Jane Welsh

WOMAN'S DEPLORABLE FATE

5. To Thomas Carlyle at Edinburgh

Haddington/ 24 March 1823

My dear Friend

I have been longer in writing than usual and this time I cannot plead either excessive occupation or impertinent interruptions – But I have not patience to do anything when my mind is not at rest, and for the last week it has been in a horrible hubbub –

These nonsensical people with their *Heirathsgedanken* and *Heiraths-vorschlagen*[1] will assuredly drive me mad. Like Carlos *ich fürchte die wie die Pest*[2] – to cause unhappiness to others, above all to those I esteem, and would do anything within reach of my duties and abilities to serve, is the cruelest pain I know – but positively I can not fall in love – and to sacrifice myself out of pity is a degree of generosity of which I am not capable – besides matrimony under any circumstances would interfere shockingly with my plans –

The Philosopher that used to thank the gods he was born a man, and not a woman, must have had more sense than the generality of his calling – truly our fate is very deplorable. As soon as a poor girl takes that decisive step called *coming out*, she is exposed to a host of vexations men know nothing of – We are the weakest portion of the human kind, and nevertheless we have to bear two thirds of the burden of sorrows our unwise first Parents left behind them. Really it is very unjust! – What I would give to be a prime Minister or a Commander in chief! An old woman that boiled blankets in this town used to say when I was leaping the mill-dam some dozen years ago, 'that *providence had sticket a fine Callant*'.[3] She understood my character better than anybody I have had to do with since – ' *The*

---

[1] 'Thoughts of marriage' and 'proposals of marriage'.

[2] 'I fear them like the plague'.

[3] I.e. thwarted a fine boy.

35

extreme enviableness of my condition'! Oh dear me – I wish you had a trial of it for one twelvemonth – . . .

Yours Faithfully Jane Welsh

THE IMPORTANCE OF BEING FAMOUS

6. TO THOMAS CARLYLE AT KINNAIRD HOUSE, DUNKELD

Hell [postmarked Thornhill]/ 19 August 1823

My dear Friend

. . . When shall a world know your worth as I do? You laugh at the stir I make about Fame; but I suspect my sentiments on that subject – stript of the 'garb' of my expressions, which is at times fantastic enough – are not very dissimilar to your own – You are not *satisfied* living thus – bowing a haughty genius to the paltry necessity of making provision for your daily wants – stifling the fire of an ambitious soul with hard-learned lessons of humility; or expending it in idle longings and vague, colourless schemes – 'The wheel of your destiny *must* turn' – I have heard you say so – and you have power to turn it – giant power – But when shall all effort be made? when will your genius burst through the obstruction and find its proper place? – it *will* – 'as the bolt bursts on high from the black cloud that bound it' – of *that* I have no fear – but when? Oh that I heard a nation repeat your name! You may call it a mistaken ambition – a weak dependance on the opinion of others – you may call it what you will – but I *will* wish you *famous* as long as there is room for such a wish – . . .

Yours ever Jane Baillie Welsh

YOUR FRIEND – BUT NEVER YOUR WIFE

7. TO THOMAS CARLYLE AT KINNAIRD HOUSE

Haddington/16 September 1823

My dear Friend

. . . You misunderstand me – you regard me no longer as a friend, a sister; but as one who at some future period may be more to you than both – is it not so? is it not true that you believe me, like the bulk of my silly sex, incapable of entertaining a strong affection for a man of my own age without having for it's ultimate object our union for life? 'Useless and dangerous to love you'! 'my happiness wrecked by you'! – I cannot have misinterpreted your meaning! And my God what have I said or done to mislead you into an error so destructive to the confidence that subsists betwixt us, so dangerous to the peace of us both? In my treatment of you I have indeed disregarded all maxims of womanly prudence, have shaken myself free from the shackles of etiquette – I have loved and admired you for your noble qualities, and for the extraordinary affection you have shewn me: and I have told you so without reserve or disguise – but *not* till our repeated quarrels had produced an explanation betwixt us, which I foolishly believed would guarantee my future conduct from all possibility of misconstruction – I have been to blame – I might have foreseen that such implicit confidence might mislead you as to the nature of my sentiments, and should have expressed my friendship for you with a more prudent reserve – but it is of no use talking of what I might or should have done in the time past – I have only to repair the mischief in as far as I can, now that my eyes are opened to it now that I am startled to find our relation actually assuming the aspect of an engagement for life –

My Friend I love you – I repeat it tho' the expression a rash one – all the best feelings of my nature are concerned in loving you – But were you my Brother I would love you the same, were I married to another I would love you the same – and is this sentiment so calm, so delightful – but so unimpassioned enough to recompense the freedom of my heart, enough to reconcile me to the existence of a married woman the hopes and wishes and ambitions of which are all different from mine, the cares and occupations of which are my disgust – Oh no! Your Friend I will be, your truest most devoted friend, while I breathe the breath of life; but your wife! never never! Not though you were as rich as Croesus, as honoured and renowned as you yet shall be –

You may think I am viewing the matter by much too seriously – taking fright where there is nothing to fear – It is well if it be so! But, suffering as I am at this very moment from the horrid pain of seeing a true and affectionate heart near breaking for my sake, it is not to be wondered at tho' I be overanxious for your peace on which my own depends in a still greater degree – Write to me and reassure me – for God's sake reassure me if you can! Your Friendship at this time is almost necessary to my existence. Yet I will resign it cost what it may – will, will resign it if it can only be enjoyed at the risk of your future peace – . . .

Ever Affectionately Yours

Jane B. Welsh

VOCATIONAL GUIDANCE

8. To Thomas Carlyle at 2 Liverpool Terrace, Dover

West Craigs, Corstorphine, Edinburgh/ 10 November 1824

Dearest Friend

. . . So you have been in France, Mr Thomas! in France without me – in the train of that everlasting Princess![1] How fortunate she is to have a carriage with a dickey! – Well, I am flattering myself that your *residence on the Continent* will have made you a bit of a Dandy. At least you will not speak Annandale, surely, after having *travelled* – Apollo and the Nine Muses forbid! It would be so delightful, when I go south, to find you about a hundredth part as 'elegant' as my amiable Cousin [Captain James Baillie]. I am quite sure that I should fall in love with you if you were, and then – 'Oh Heavens what a thing it might be *if it prospered*' – surely you will own no man had ever such inducement to study the Graces – . . .

What do I think of your new project? At first I cordially disapproved it altogether. The translating of all Schiller's works seemed a stupendous and ungrateful task, which would heavily occupy your time and talents for years; and be attended with no advantage to you, except putting some hundreds of pounds in your pocket: the other part of the plan filled me with horror, and on deliberation, I am still decidedly against it. What fellowship is there in Annandale for *you*? Doubtless you might find 'kind Christian souls' there to love you and wonder at you, but without spirits like your own to *understand* you, – without sympathy your life would be without a soul – Oh mercy never think of establishing yourself in Annandale! All your faults are the effects of your isolated way of life: if you seclude yourself altogether from your fellows, as sure as fate, you will sink in a year or two, into the most surly, misanthropic, self-opinionative, dreadfully disagreeable person alive. It was only the other day, you wrote to me that you began to think there were many more worthy

---

[1] The glamorous Kitty Kirkpatrick.

38

people in the world than you counted on; and already are you pro-
jecting to turn your back on them? You will never be so mad!
Certainly the recovery of your health *must* be attended to above all
things else; and if that is not to be brought about in the smoke and
bustle of a City, why then, you must seek it in the quietness and pure
air of the country: But what is to hinder you setting yourself down
within a mile or two of London – in some pleasant place where you
might ride and garden just as in Annandale; and, at the same time,
occasionally enjoy society which would refresh and incite your spirit?
My plan perhaps is foolish: yours is certainly not wise.

As to the translating of Schiller, there is much to be said for and
against. It would employ without fatiguing your mind; it would increase your command of language, and make composition more
easy to you; it would insure you a certain and sufficient income, and
deliver you from anxieties about what you are to do, and how you
are to live. On the other hand, you are likely to be disgusted with the
undertaking before you finish it; there is no exercise for your finest
faculties in turning sentences and choosing words; there is no scope
for your genius in transcribing the thoughts and sentiments of
another; on the contrary I should be afraid that in imitating so long
you might cease to be original, and lastly the task when done, –
however well done will gain you only the praise of a good Translator.
If any of your new Friends would 'help you to the uttermost' and
find you a sinecure which would set you free from care about the
morrow, I would like better that you would follow out your plan of
the 'Lives' (which is certainly the grandest you have yet thought of)
tho' by fits and starts as you felt able for it. But it is only Blockheads
who get sinecures; as it is, this translation perhaps is the very best
thing you could engage in. The only advice I can give you is to do
nothing in haste for fear that you repent at leisure. It is really a high
farce my giving advice to any one and of all people on earth to *you*;
but recollect you bade me. – . . .

God bless you Dear. – Ever ever yours

Jane Baillie Welsh

ON LOVE AND MARRIAGE

9. To Thomas Carlyle at 23 Southampton Street, Pentonville, London

Haddington/ 13 January 1825

My dearest Friend

I little thought that my joke about your farming Craigenputtoch was to be made the basis of such a serious and extraordinary project. If you had foreseen the state of perplexity which your letter has thrown me into you would have practised *any* self-denial (I am sure) rather than have written it. But there is no use in talking of what is *done* – '*cosa fatta ha capo*'.[1] The thing to be considered now is what *to do* . . .

I love you – I have told you so a hundred times; and I should be the most ungrateful, and injudicious of mortals if I did not – but I am not *in love* with you – that is to say – my love for you is not a passion which overclouds my judgement; and absorbs all my regards for myself and others – it is a simple, honest, serene affection, made up of admiration and sympathy, and better perhaps, to found domestic enjoyment on than any other – In short it is a love which *influences*, does not *make* the destiny of a life.

Such temperate sentiments lend no false colouring no 'rosy light' to your project. I see it such as it is, with all the arguments for and against it; I see that my consent under existing circumstances would indeed secure to *me* the only fellowship and support I have found in the world; and perhaps, too, shed some sunshine of joy on *your* existence which has hitherto been sullen and cheerless; but, on the other hand, that it would involve you and myself in numberless cares and difficulties; and expose *me* to petty tribulations, which I want fortitude to despise, and which, not despised, would imbitter the peace of us both.

I do not wish for fortune more than is sufficient for my wants – my natural wants, and the artificial *ones* which habit has rendered nearly as importunate as the other – but I will not marry to live on less; because in that case every inconvenience I was subjected to, would remind me of what I had quitted; and the idea of a sacrifice should have no place in a voluntary union – Neither have I any wish for grandeur – the glittering baits of titles and honours are only for children and fools – But I conceive it a duty which every one owes to

[1] 'A deed is crowned when done.'

society, not to throw up that station in it which Providence has assigned him; and having this conviction, I could not marry into a station inferior to my own with the approval of my judgement, *which* alone could enable me to brave the censures of my acquaintance.

And now let me ask you have you any *certain* livelihood to maintain me in the manner I have been used to live in? any *fixed* place in the rank of society I have [been] born and bred in? No! You have projects for attaining both – capabilities for attaining both – and much more! but as yet you have *not* attained them. Use the noble gifts which God has given you! You have prudence (tho' by the way this last proceeding is no great proof of it) – devise then how you may gain yourself a moderate but *settled* income; think of some more promising plan, than farming the most barren spot in the county of Dumfries-shire – What a thing that would be to be sure! you and I keeping house at Craigenputtoch! I would just as soon think of building myself a nest on the Bass-rock – nothing but your ignorance of the place saves you from the imputation of insanity for admitting such a thought. Depend upon it, you could not *exist* there a twelve-month. For my part I would not spend a month on it with an Angel – Think of something else then – apply your industry to carry it into effect your talents to glide over the inequality of our births and then – we will talk of marrying. If all this were realized I *think* I should have goodsense enough to abate something of my romantic ideal, and to content myself with stopping short on this side idolatry – At all events I will marry no one else – This is all the promise I can or will make. A positive engagement to marry a certain person at a certain time, at all haps and hazards, I have always considered the most ridiculous thing on earth: it is either altogether useless or altogether miserable; if the parties continue faithfully attached to each other it is a mere ceremony – if otherwise it becomes a galling fetter riveting them to wretchedness and only to be broken with disgrace.

Such is the result of my deliberations on this very serious subject. You may approve of it or not; but you cannot either persuade me or convince me out of it – My decisions – when I *do* decide – are unalterable as the laws of the Medes & Persians – Write instantly and tell me that you are content to leave the event to time and destiny – and in the meanwhile to continue my Friend and Guardian which you have so long and so faithfully been – *and nothing more* –

It would be more agreeable to etiquette, and perhaps also to prudence, that I should adopt no middle course in an affair such as this – that I should not for another instant encourage an affection I *may* never reward and a hope I *may* never fulfil; but cast your heart away from me at once since I cannot embrace the resolution which would give me a right to it for ever. This I would assuredly do if *you* were like the generality of lovers, or if it were still in my power to be happy independent of your affection but as it [is] neither etiquette nor prudence can obtain this of me. If there is any change to be made in the terms on which we have so long lived with one another; it must be made by *you* not *me* – I *cannot* make any.

All this I have written with my Mother's sanction; if my decision had been more favourable to you, she might have *disapproved* it but would not have *opposed* it. And this I think is more than you could expect, considering how little she knows you.

I shall not be comfortable till I hear from you again so I beg you will not keep me waiting. God bless you ever affectionately

Yours Jane Welsh

EXPLAINING MY MIND

10. To Thomas Carlyle at Pentonville, London

Haddington/ 29 January 1825

Well! Dearest you have criticised *my* letter – it is now my turn to criticise *yours*. Be patient, then, and good-tempered, I beg; for you shall find me a severer critic than the Opiumeater –

First then, you complain that I have but an imperfect view of your situation and purposes – Now I think, I may complain with equal justice, that you have but an imperfect view of *my* meaning – This, indeed, is, most probably, no fault of yours. I wrote to you after a sleepless night, with an aching head, and an aching anxious heart, and it is no wonder, if, in this condition I failed to express myself as perspicuously as I wished – Thus, in what I said about self-denial, it certainly was *not* my meaning to reproach you with any want of it; but on the contrary to express my confidence in your magnanimity – your willingness, at all times to prefer my happiness to your own. To say that 'had you foreseen how unhappy your letter was to make me, you would not have written it' surely implied that 'in writing it, you had *not* foreseen how unhappy it was to make me'; now, in this case there was no *occasion* for self-denial; and consequently you could not be charged with any want of it – Neither did I imagine, that your proposal was *grounded on my jest* or *taken up in a moment of selfishness*. I have too good an opinion of your sense, to suspect you of making a proposal like this, with no better foundation, and conceived in no better spirit to any one; and too proud a consciousness of your esteem to suspect you of making it to *me*. It was not the idea of our union, but the idea of living at Craigenputtoch, which I took to be grounded on my jest; and this was reasonable enough, seeing that my words were gravely quoted, by way of text to your letter – This much in justice to my understanding!

In the next place, you assure me, that you are not '*hurt* or *angry*'. Thank Heaven you are not! But does not this imply that there is some room for your being hurt or angry – that I have done or said what might have hurt or angered another less generous than you? I think so. Now, room for disappointment there *may* be; but surely there is none for mortification or offence – I have refused my immediate, positive assent to your wishes; because our mutual happiness seemed to require that I should refuse it; but for the rest I have not slighted your wishes, on the contrary, I have expressed my willingness to fulfil them, at the expense of every thing but what I deem to be essential to our happiness: and so far from undervaluing *you*, I have shown you, in declaring I would marry no one else, not only that I esteem you above all the men I have ever seen; but also that I am persuaded I should esteem you above all the men I may ever see – What, then, have you to be hurt or angry at?

The maxims I proceed by (you tell me) are those of common and acknowledged prudence, and you *do not say* it is unwise in me to walk by them exclusively – The maxims I proceed by are the convictions of my own judgement, and being so, it would be unwise in me were I *not* to proceed by them, whether they are *right* or *wrong* – Yet I am *prudent*, I fear, only because I am not strongly tempted to be otherwise – My heart is capable (I feel it is) of a love to which *no* deprivation would be a sacrifice – a love which would overleap that reverence for opinion with which education and weakness have begirt my sex, would bear down all the restraints which *duty* and *expediency* might throw in the way, and carry every thought and feeling of my being impetuously along with it – But the all-perfect Mortal, who could inspire me with a love, so extravagant, is nowhere to be found – exists nowhere but in the Romance of my own imagination! Perhaps it is better for me as it is – A passion, like the torrent in the violence of its course, might perhaps too, like the torrent, leave ruin and desolation behind. In the mean time, I should be very mad, were I to act as if from the influence of such a passion, while my affections are in a state of perfect tranquillity. I have already explained to you the nature of my love for *you*; that it is deep and calm, more like the quiet river, which refreshes and beautifies where it flows, than the torrent which bears down and destroys – Yet it is materially different from what one feels for a statue or a picture –

'Then why not attain wealth and rank' – you say – and it is you who have said it – not *I* – Wealth and rank (to be sure) have different meanings, according to the views of different people; and what is bare sufficiency and respectability in the vocabulary of a young Lady may be called wealth and rank in that of a philosopher: but it certainly was not wealth or rank, according to *my* views which I required you to attain. I merely wish to see you earning a *certain* livelihood, and exercising the profession of a gentleman – for the rest it is a matter of great indifference to me, whether you have hundreds or thousands a year, whether you are a Mr or a Duke – To *me*, it seems, that my wishes in this respect are far from unreasonable, even when *your* peculiar maxims and situation are taken into account: nor was it wholly with the view to an improvement in your external circumstances, that I have made their fulfilment a condition to our union; but also with a view to some improvement in my sentiments towards you, which might be brought about in the meantime. In withholding this motive in my former letter, I was guilty of a false and illtimed reserve. My tenderness for your feelings betrayed me into an insincerity which is not natural to me. I thought that the most decided objection to your circumstances would pain you less than the least objection to yourself; and accordingly let my denial seem to be grounded wholly on the former, while, in truth it is, in some measure grounded on both. But I *must* be sincere, I find, at whatever cost!

As I have said, then, in requiring you to better your Fortune I had some view to an improvement in my sentiments towards you in the meantime: I am not sure that they are proper sentiments for a Husband: they are proper for a Brother, a Father, a Guardianspirit, but a Husband, it seems to me should be dearer still. This, then, independently of prudential considerations, would make me withhold my immediate assent to your proposal. At the same time, from the change which my sentiments towards you have already undergone, during the period of our acquaintance; I have little doubt but, that, in time, I shall be perfectly satisfied with them. One loves you (as Madame de Stael said of Necker) in proportion to the ideas and sentiments which are in oneself; according as my mind enlarges, and my heart improves, I become capable of comprehending the goodness and greatness which are in *you*, and my affection for you increases. Not many months ago, I would have said it was impossible that I should ever be your wife; at present I consider this the most *probable* destiny for me; and in a year or so, perhaps, I shall consider it the only one. 'Die Zeit ist noch nicht da!'[1]

Thus then I have explained my mind to you as clearly and faithfully as I possibly can; and a strange, confused, inconsistent sort of mind it appears to be! However, from what I have said, it is plain (to *me*, at least), what ought to be the line of our future conduct. Do *you* what you can to better your external circumstances; always, however, subordinately to your own principles, which I do not ask you to give up, which I should despise you for giving up, whether I approved them or no – While *I* on the other hand do what *I* can, subordinately to nothing, to better *myself* which I am persuaded is the surest way of bringing my wishes to accord with yours. (And let us leave the rest to Fate, satisfied that we have both of us done what lies with *us* for our mutual happiness) – If nevertheless, you can point out any line of conduct, to *my conviction* better than this, you will find me ready and willing to follow it –

There is one passage in your letter which I cannot conclude without noticing; I mean that in which you talk about *parting*, and *going forth upon our several paths*. I have pondered this passage in various moods; and am at last come to the conclusion that it is to be understood (as we are bound to understand every thing, in the Scriptures, derogatory to the justice and mercy of God) in a metaphorical sense – for I will not believe that you ever seriously thought of parting from me, of throwing off a heart, which you have taught to lean upon you, till it is no longer sufficient for itself! You could never be so ungenerous! *you*, who for years have shown and professed for me the most disinterested, most noble affection! How could I *part* from the only living soul that understands me? I would marry you tomorrow rather! but then, – our parting would need to be brought about by death or some dispensation of uncontrollable Providence – were *you* to will it, *to part* would no longer be bitter, the bitterness would be in thinking you unworthy. If indeed your happiness was to suffer from your intercourse with me in our present relation, I would not blame you for discontinuing it; tho' I should blame you, perhaps, for not examining yourself better before you entered into it – But how can that be? Your present situation is miserable; it *must* be altered; but

---

[1] 'The time is not yet here!'

is it with reference to *me* that it must be altered? Is it *I* who have made it miserable? No! you were as unhappy before we met as ever you have been since: the cause of your unhappiness then must lie in other circumstances of your destiny, which I have no connection with – no real connection, however much I may seem to have, from being frequently associated with them in your mind. It is an alteration in these circumstances which your duty and happiness require from you; and not an alteration in your relation with me – but what need is there of my most weak arguments to dissuade you from a purpose which you can never have entertained, – which, if you had entertained it for one moment, your own heart would have argued you out of, the next. Oh no! we will never part – Never!

Will you be done with this wild scheme of yours? I tell you it will *not* answer; and you must positively play Cincinnatus somewhere else. With all your tolerance of places, you would not find, at Craigenputtoch, the requisites you require; The light of Heaven, to be sure, is not denied it; but for green grass! beside a few cattle fields there is nothing except a waste prospect of heather, and black peat-moss. Prune and delve would you! in the first place there is nothing to prune; and for delving – I set too high a value on your life, to let you engage in so perilous an enterprise – were you to attempt such a thing, there are twenty chances to one, that you should be swallowed up in the moss – spade and all. In short, I presume, whatever may be your *farming* talents, that you are not an accomplished Drover; and nobody but a person of this sort, could make the rent of the place out of it. Were *you* to engage in the concern we should all be ruined together! –

You will write immediately – won't you? and for Heaven's sake say something to make me less unhappy than I am at present – There has been the weight of a mill-stone at my heart for these last two weeks – I would have written sooner, but I have been tormented with headache, as usual, which unfits me for every exertion of thought, while it lasts.

Ever yours Jane B. Welsh

A TEARFUL CONFESSION

11. TO THOMAS CARLYLE AT HODDAM HILL,
ECCLEFECHAN

Templand/ 24 July 1825

My dearest

I thought to write to you from this place with joy; I write with shame and tears. The enclosed letter,[1] which I found lying for me, has distracted my thoughts from the prospect of our meeting – the brightest in my mind for many months, and fixed them on a part of my own conduct which makes me unworthy ever to see you, or be clasped to your true heart again. I cannot come to you cannot be at peace with myself: till I have made the confession which Mrs Montagu so impressively shows me the need of – Let me tell it then out at once; I have deceived you *I* whose truth and frankness you have so often praised have deceived my bosom friend! I told you that I did not care for Edward Irving, took pains to make you believe this – It was false; I loved him – must I say it – *once* passionately loved him – Would to Heaven that this were all! it might not perhaps lower me much in your opinion for he is no unworthy man, and if I showed weakness in loving one whom I knew to be engaged to another, I made amends in persuading him to marry that other and preserve his honour from reproach: but I have concealed and disguised the truth: and for this I have no excuse – none at least that would bear a moment's scrutiny. Woe to me then if your reason be my judge and not your love! I cannot even plead the merit of a *voluntary* disclosure as a claim to your forgiveness. I make it because I *must*, because this extraordinary woman has moved me to honesty whether I would or no – Read her letter and judge if it was possible for me to resist it.

Write I beseech you instantly, and let me know my fate – This suspense is worse to endure than any certainty. Say if you *can* that I may come to you – that you will take me to your heart after all as your own, your trusted Jane and I will arrange it as soon as ever I am able – say no – that you no longer wish to see me that my image is defaced in your soul and I will think you *not unjust*. Oh that I had

---

[1] This letter (printed in *LL*, II, 148–50) was from Mrs Montague, who had heard about Jane's earlier feelings for Edward Irving and urged her to confess them to Carlyle. When Carlyle discovered this letter after Jane's death, he scribbled on it 'some of Mrs Montague's nonsense' – and asked that it *not* be copied.

your answer – never were you so dear as at this moment when I am in danger of losing your affection or what is still more precious to me your respect

Jane B. Welsh

A DESPERATE APPEAL

12. To Thomas Carlyle at Hoddam Hill, Ecclefechan

Templand/ 30 July 1825

Mr Carlyle do you mean to kill me?[1] is it just of you to keep me so long in doubt? Your displeasure I have merited, perhaps your scorn, but surely not this terrible silence. Write then for Heaven's Sake! and kindly if you can, for I am wretched beyond all expression. Had I but strength I would come to you this very day, and when I held you in my arms and you saw my tears you would forget every thing but the love I bear you. Oh I do love you my own Friend. above the whole earth – no human being was ever half so dear to me – none none – and will you break my heart? Alas I thought when we parted that some evil destiny was hanging over us. but the loss of your affection was the very last thing I feared and have I indeed lost it? Speak tell me. It is inhuman to leave me in this suspense. Be your answer what it may I will love and venerate you to the last. You may be no longer mine but I will be yours in life in death through all eternity

Jane B. Welsh

A MOTHER'S EXPLOSION

13. To Thomas Carlyle at Hoddam Hill

Templand/ 25 October 1825

My Dearest,

Your letter was very consolatory to me; and much do I stand in need of consolation: for since you departed this life, I have been the

---

[1] Carlyle had written a reassuring letter protesting his love on 29 July, which had not yet reached her, matching her sincerity with spiritual confessions of his own – 'You know me not; no living mortal knows me, seems to know me. I can no longer love. My heart has been steeped in solitary bitterness till the life of it is gone.'

forlornest, most dispirited of creatures. 'What can be worse than to dwell here, driven out from bliss', amid wind and whist and ill-humour? *Is there any livelier image of hell?* Oh Time bring the roses as fast as you can; for the winter of our discontent is ill to bear!

It was on the day after your departure, that the storm, which has been brewing in my Mother's mind for many weeks, broke forth in copious eloquence. Oh mercy! what cruel, unreasonable things she said; but nothing distressed me so much as her bitter reflections against you, whom she accused of having 'bewitched and poisoned my mind'. She was unjust, I told her; my connection with so wise and honourable a man could be attended with no ill consequence; and, any way, such language, *now*, was out of time, – particularly since it was with her knowledge and consent, that I had come to look upon you as my partner for life. She sulked for four and twenty hours, and then wrote me a long epistle; wherein she demonstrated (*not* by geometrical reasonings) that I was utterly lost to all sense of duty; and took much bootless pains to explain the inconsistency of her conduct towards *you*. 'She *had*, indeed, given her consent to our union' (she said) 'when you should have made yourself *a name and a situation in life*; but only because I asked it, with tears, *upon my bended knees*, at a time, too, *when my life seemed precarious*'!! (to the best of my recollection I was enjoying tolerable health). 'Afterwards, however, when you came to Haddington, when she watched your temper, and perceived its *effect* upon me, it was then her soul was torn &c &c &c' 'A pack of damned nonsense, the whole of it!' 'Temper!' 'effect!' Truly, she has seen her own temper have a hundred times worse effects upon me than ever yours had, without being troubled with such tender solicitude. No! my own Darling! we shall not be parted on this account. Your irritability is the very natural consequence of continual suffering; when you are well, and happy (oh that you were!) you will be the best humoured man alive. And tho' you should never be good-humoured, what then? Do we not love each other? And what is love if it can not make all rough places smooth! Nein! I am not afraid that my happiness will be wrecked upon this rock; nor is my Mother either if the truth were told. I could lay my life this grand objection never entered her head, till she was sitting with the pen in her hand, hunting after an excuse for so much caprice . . .

Nevertheless I am any thing but insensible to her displeasure; and rather than be under it I would make every sacrifice consistent with reason. But it would be folly to make myself the slave of her variable humour – Oh it is heart-breaking, shocking, to live in this manner, with one to whom I am bound by the holiest tie! deprived of her sympathy in the matters which lie next my heart! obliged to be silent on my dearest hopes, except when I am called upon to defend them! How different it would be, if there were that cordial, trustful affection betwixt us which ought to be betwixt parent and child! – but, alas! alas! we understand each other no more! . . .

I was interrupted yesterday by furious rapping at the door – It was my Lancer-Cousin [Captain James Baillie]! arrived in a fine emblazoned chariot with four horses; and all glittering in jewels, from the gold pendant of his rose-coloured cap, to the ruby buckles of his slippers. You never saw such a man! He is, if possible more Adonis-like, witty, and elegant than ever. Such an air! such a voice! such a profusion of little dogs! I wish, in my heart, he were returned, to the place whence he came; for I will confess to you, dear friend, that – you have not the slightest cause to be jealous – jealous! – oh mercy! when I compare this fine gentleman with the *man* I love; what is he after all? A mere painted butterfly, fluttering over the flowery surface of the Earth – the creature of a sunshiny day! while he – my own – is like to the royal Eagle, who soars aloft thro' the regions of ether, and feasts his eye on the glories of the sun . . .

God bless you my dearest – I am yours all

Jane B. Welsh

A MOTHER'S CLAIMS

14. To Thomas Carlyle at Hoddam Hill

Haddington/ 16 March 1826

Oh my Beloved! what a tantalizing letter is this, which was meant to drive away all trouble from my mind! what a Paradise it sets before my eyes, from which I am shut out as with a flaming sword! Would I dare to make myself a beggar within six months – to wed my wild man of the woods and and [*sic*] go and live in his cavern? Yes! Dearest, that I would without fear or misgiving, and deem myself the richest, best lodged Lady in the Land. Indeed I can figure to myself no happier lot on this side Heaven than that which is so touchingly imaged in your own 'Wish';[1] and *that*, it seems to me, might be realized to the letter in a cottage in Annandale as well as in

[1] A poem of Carlyle's published in *LL*, II, 343–4.

any other 'calm home' on the surface of the Earth – and as well moreover in our present circumstances as in more affluent ones . . . Were happiness, then, the thing chiefly to be cared for, in this world; I would even put my hand in yours, *now*, as you say, and so cut the gordian knot of our destiny at once. But, oh my Husband, have you not told me a thousand times and my conscience tells me also that happiness is only a secondary consideration – it must not must not be sought out of the path of duty. And does the happiness that now invites me lie in that path? Should I do well to go into Paradise myself, and leave the Mother who bore me to break her heart? She is looking forward to my marriage with a more tranquil mind, in the hope that our separation is to be in a great measure nominal, – that by living wheresoever my Husband lives she may at least have every moment of my society which he can spare. And how would it be possible not to disappoint her in this hope, if I went to reside with your people in Annandale? *Her* presence *there* would be a perpetual cloud over our little world of love and peace. For the sake of all concerned it would be necessary to keep her quite apart from us – and apart from us – yet so near she would be the most wretched of Mothers, the most desolate woman in the world. Oh is it for *me* to make her so – *me* who am so unspeakably dear to her in spite of all her caprice, who am her only, only child – and her a widow – I love you Mr Carlyle, tenderly, devotedly as ever Woman loved; but I may not put my Mother away from me even for *your* sake – I cannot do it! I have lain awake whole nights since I received your letter, trying to reconcile this act with my conscience; but my conscience will have nothing to say to it – rejects it with indignation –

What is to be done then? Indeed, I see only one way of escape out of all these perplexities. Be patient with me while I tell you what it is. – My Mother, like myself, has ceased to find any contentment in this pitiful Haddington, and is bent on disposing of our house here as soon as may be and hiring one elsewhere. The *where* I perceive rests with me to determine. now, why should it not be the vicinity of Edinburgh after all? and why should not you live with your wife in her Mothers house? Because (you say) my Mother would never have the grace to like you or let you live with her in peace; because you could never have any right enjoyment of my society so long as you had me not all to yourself; and finally, because you, positively, must and will have a door of your own to slam on the face of nauseous intruders. These are objections, it must be allowed, which *sound* almost fatal to my scheme; but – I am greatly mistaken if they are not more sound than substance – My Mother *would* like you – Oh assuredly she would, if you came to live with her as her son. For what is it Dearest that has so prejudiced her against you? Is it not terror lest thro' your means she should be made childless, and a weak imagination that you regard her with disrespect; both which rocks of offence would be removed by this one concession – Besides, as my wedded Husband, you would appear to her in quite a new light; her maternal affection, of which there is abundance at the bottom of her heart, would, of necessity, extend itself to him with whom I was become so inseparably connected; and mere common sense would prescribe a kind motherly behaviour to you as the only expedient to make the best of what could no longer be helped. As to your second objection it seems to me still lighter than the first; for would it not be ridiculous to continue all-together beggars in happiness because the possession of it is encumbered with a trifling tax? to live on joyless and solitary, thus far asunder, rather than give to Duty a few hours each day from our full enjoyment of each other's society? Surely it were better to make the sacrifice required of us without murmuring and verily it would secure its own reward. The hours that remained to us which we might devote exclusively [to] one another would be the dearer for being interrupted –

The intrusions of a mob of idle visitors would *indeed* be a nuisance greater than we could bear – but really I do not see that we should be called upon to bear it – might it not be made a sine qua non in the treaty with my Mother, that we should [be] exempted from having any concern with her company? – and that the door of our study should be made sufficiently strong to keep every living soul of them outside. – Think then Darling, and answer me – Would you live with me in my Mother's house? Say 'No' if you judge that best without fear that I shall take it amiss. Indeed indeed I *would* not sway you tho' I *could* for I know well enough the infinite superiority of your Judgement – Say yes, – and I propose the thing to my Mother – I have no manner of doubt but she will give it a willing, a joyful hearing – Should it however contrary to all human expectation turn out otherwise – why then – let it be as you will! In that case our separation would be *her* doing not mine – I should have [been] mistaken in thinking myself indispensable to her happiness. Oh me! I am much to be pitied – my heart is divided against itself – Would to heaven we saw each others face – for I find it impossible to set these things down on paper as I feel them in my heart – Let me use as many words as I like, my meaning is still but imperfectly expressed –

But I must conclude for the present, or miss another post – I waited
till yesterday that I might answer both your letters at once, in case
you had written as you half promised on Sunday – and Yesterday I
was distracted with headache – Write – the first hour you have leisure.

God forever bless you

I am yours heart and soul

Jane B. Welsh

'HERR IM HAUSE'

15. To Jane Welsh at Haddington
from Thomas Carlyle

Hoddam Hill/ 2 April 1826

Dearest Weibchen –

... in all this royal project, I had taken no distinct account of
your Mother. I merely remembered the text of Scripture: 'Thou
shalt leave father and mother, and cleave unto thy husband, and
thy desire shall be towards him all the days of thy life.' I imagined
perhaps she might go to Dumfries-shire, and gratify her heart by
increasing the accommodations of her father, which she would then
have ample means to do; perhaps that she might even – in short,
that she might arrange her destiny in many ways, to which my
presence must be a hindrance rather than a furtherance. Here I was
selfish and thoughtless: I might have known that the love of a Mother
to her only child is indestructible and irreplaceable; that forcibly to
cut asunder such ties was cruel and unjust.

Perhaps, as I have told you, Love, I may not yet have got to the
bottom of this new plan so completely as I wished: but there is one
thing that strikes me more and more, the longer I think of it. This the
grand objection of all objections, the head and front of offence, the
soul of all my counter-pleading; an objection which is too likely to
overset the whole project. It may be stated in a word: *The Man
should bear rule in the house and not the Woman.* This is an eternal axiom,
the Law of Nature herself which no mortal departs from unpunished.
I have meditated on this ma[ny long] years, and every day it
grows plainer to me; I must not and I cannot live in a house of which
I am not head. I should be miserable myself, and make all about me
miserable. Think not, Darling, that this comes of an imperious
temper; that I shall be a harsh and tyrannical husband to thee.
God forbid! But it is the nature of a man that if he be controlled by
any thing but his own Reason, he feels himself degraded; and incited,

53

be it justly or not, to rebellion and discord. It is the nature of a woman again (for she is essentially *passive* not *active*) to cling to the man for support and direction, to comply with his humours, and feel pleasure in doing so, simply because they are his; to reverence while she loves him, to conquer him not by her force but her weakness, and perhaps (the cunning gypsy!) after all to command him by obeying him. It is inexpressible what an increase of happiness, and of consciousness, wholesome consciousness of inward dignity I have gained since I came within the walls of this poor cottage. My own four walls! For in my state this primeval law of Nature acts on *me* with double and triple force. And how cheaply it is purchased and how smoothly managed! They simply admit that I am *Herr im Hause*, and act on this conviction. Here is no grumbling about my habitudes and whims: if I choose to dine on fire and brimstone, they will cook it for me to their best skill; thinking only that I am an unintelligible mortal; perhaps in their secret souls, a kind of humourist, *facheuse* to deal with, but no bad soul after all, and *not* to be dealt with in *any* other way. My own four walls!

Your mother is of all women the best calculated for being a *Wife*, and the worst for being a *Husband*. I know her perhaps better than she thinks; and it is not without affection and sincere esteem that I have seen the fundamental structure of her character, and the many light capricious half-graces half-follies that sport on the surface of it. I could even fancy that she might love me also, and feel happy beside me, if her own true and kindly character were come into fair and free communion with mine, which she might then find was neither false nor cruel any more than her own. But this could only be (I will speak it out at once and boldly, for it is the quiet and kind conviction of my judgement, not the conceited and selfish conviction of my vanity: this could only be) in a situation where she looked up to *me*, not I to her.

Now, I think, Liebchen, whether your Mother will consent to forget her own riches, and my poverty, and uncertain most probably very scanty income; and consent in the spirit of Christian meekness to make *me* her guardian and director, and be a second *wife* to her daughter's husband! If she can, then I say, she is a noble woman; and in the name of Truth and Affection, *let* us all live together, and be one household and one heart till Death, or her own choice part us! If she cannot, which will do any thing but surprise me, then alas! the other thing cannot be, must not be; and for her sake, no less than for yours and mine, we must think of something else. Explain all this, Jane, in your own dialect; for unless you explain it, it may be dreadfully misunderstood. Then tell me the result without the loss of a moment. Love me always in the centre of your heart, and believe me your own.

T. Carlyle –

A HAPPY ENDING

16. JANE WELSH TO THOMAS CARLYLE AT HODDAM HILL

Haddington/ 10 April 1826

My Dearest

You are thinking, I presume, that I might have done your bidding with less delay; but, the fact is I have not lost one minute that could be saved – Judge if I have – Your letter found me in the saddest domestic *burble* imaginable: our maid-servant lay in one part of the house at death's door with fever and asthma; in another part of it lay my Mother about as ill with an attack of bile; and to crown all, just in this evil nick, a '*fool-creature*' must needs come on a visit – While things were in this way, as you may well conceive, I had no leisure to make the needful disclosures; besides, it was no propitious season for my Mother to hear them in; and a week passed before the household was convalescent and the '*fool-creature*' departed, and my hands thus left free to go about my Master's business. So you see I am no bad Ariel after all.

Eh bien! I have informed my Mother, in a long Letter of all which it concerned her to know (so long a *speech* being, as Jane [Carlyle's sister] says 'beyond the utmost compass of my ability') and the result is – what do you think? that, provided we manage matters aright, you and I are *soon* to be the happiest pair of people in all Annandale!

My Mother does not object to my wedding you in your actual circumstances; on the contrary, she thinks it all things considered the best I can do; and neither does she object to my living with you in your Fatherland which shows a heroism on her part that I did not dare to look for. In short my kind reasonable Mother views our romantic project with all the favour that heart could desire – and not by the cold, bleak light of worldly prudence, but the rosy sun-light of poetry which is in this case *truth*.

And we will not be purchasing our happiness at the cost of hers; for she will live (she says) at Templand and visit us as often as may

55

be: and this arrangement I believe after all, is the very best that the case admits – My Mother is fond of Nithsdale, and we will make her fond of Annandale also. In the one place she will have kind friends about her, whom she dearly likes, and within her the consciousness of doing good to her Father and Sister; in the other she will find you and I, *ourselves a host*, and will not be *fremd* [strange], she declares to me, with your kindred, but esteem them as they deserve. Moreover, the *other* plan, however well it had been proved to answer, could not, I find, have had any permanency – My Grandfather must, in the course of Nature, be taken from us at no distant day; and my Aunt would then be left alone and helpless were not my Mother to become her protector – That must not be – is not to be thought of – In going to live with her now, then, my Mother is only *anticipating* what *must* be, as far as human calculation reaches, her ultimate destination; and in thus anticipating it she will have the comfort of watching over her Fathers declining age, and adding to his scanty accommodations: a comfort which will atone to her Mother's-heart for the *partial* loss of her Daughter's company – On these grounds, she prefers that we should have separate households; and on these grounds I am willing that we should – so what more remains to be *said*? – Are you happy? You must be the most ungrateful of mortals if [you] are not, in the near prospect of having such a Wife! Oh mein Gott *such* a Wife! . . .

For ever Yours
Jane B. Welsh

Mrs Welsh's postcript:

My dear Sir,

Jane has read to me what she has communicated to you respecting our future *destination*, which I trust will meet with your approval. This long perplexing emigration of ours now draws to a close. May God grant that it may draw us *all* together in the bonds of love and happiness with every good wish for your welfare. Believe me in affection what you would wish the Mother of your Jane to be

G. Welsh

THE FINEST LITTLE PAIR IMAGINABLE

17. TO JANE WELSH AT HADDINGTON
FROM THOMAS CARLYLE

Scotsbrig/ 18 June 1826

Liebstes –

... O my little Weibchen! The next Book I write, *another* shall help me to correct and arrange! And my fairest recompense will be the glad look of two kind black eyes, thro' which a soul is looking that belongs to my soul for ever and ever! Let us not despond in the life of honourable toil which lies before us. Do you not think, that when you on one side of our household shall have faithfully gone thro your housewife duties, and I on the other shall have written my allotted pages, we shall meet over our frugal meal with far happier and prouder hearts than thousands that are not blessed with any duties, and whose agony is the bitterest of all, 'the agony of a too easy bed'? In labour lies health, of body and of mind; in suffering and difficulty is the soil of all virtue and all wisdom. By and by, when we have put our house in order, and our hearts in order, and come to understand one another as indivisible portions of the same whole, I predict that we shall be the finest little pair imaginable! A true-hearted dainty lady-wife; a sick and sulky, but diligent, and not false-hearted or fundamentally unkind goodman: and these two fronting the hardships of life in faithful and eternal union, conquering the evils of their lot by wise effort and perseverance, and every conquest not for *self* but for *another self* far dearer! Let us but be true and good, and we have nothing earthly to dread.

As to the *wedding*, I agree with you in heartily recoiling from it. Pity indeed that we could not both fall asleep, and awaken married in each others arms! It would be infinitely finer and far less trouble...

I am always your own

T. Carlyle

18   AN EARLY PORTRAIT OF JANE?

In January 1831 a rather bumbling short story entitled 'Cruthers and Jonson', by Thomas Carlyle, was published in *Blackwood's Magazine*. The best thing about it was the picture of Margaret, whom the hero Jonson woos and marries.

Bright, airy sylph! Kind, generous soul! I could have loved her myself if I had seen her. Think of a slender delicate creature – formed in the very mould of beauty – elegant and airy in her movements as a fawn; black hair and eyes – jet black; her face meanwhile as pure and fair as lilies – and then for its expression – how shall I describe it? Nothing so changeful, nothing so lovely in all its changes: one moment it was sprightly gaiety, quick arch humour, sharp wrath, the most contemptuous indifference – then all at once there would spread over it a celestial gleam of warm affection, deep enthusiasm, – every feature beamed with tenderness and love, her eyes and looks would have melted a heart of stone; but ere you had time to fall down and worship them – poh! she was off into some other hemisphere – laughing at you – teasing you – again seeming to flit round the whole universe of human feeling, and to sport with every part of it. Oh! never was there such another beautiful, cruel, affectionate, wicked, adorable, capricious little gypsy sent into this world for the delight and vexation of mortal man. My own admiration is, how in the name of wonder Jonson ever got her wooed! – I should have thought it the most hopeless task in nature. Perhaps he had a singular skill in such undertakings: at any rate he throve. The cynosure of neighbouring eyes, the apple of discord to all bachelors within many leagues – richer many of them and more showy men than Jonson – preferred Jonson to them all. Perhaps, like Desdemona, she loved him for the dangers he had passed: at all events, she loved him – loved him with her whole soul, the little cozener – though it was many a weary day before he could determine whether she cared one straw for him or not.

II *Self-portrait*

This observer of other people began by studying herself and found the subject fascinating. Jane's descriptions of her excitements, triumphs, trials and depressions make up the conscious half of the self-portrait in her letters. The unconscious revelations are the other half. Both are represented in this selection, which attempts to introduce the whole Jane through sketches of her most characteristic moods.

No one understood many of the paradoxes in her nature better than Jane – how excitement was her rest, how she could rise from death's door to be the life of the party, how dawdling could become a career, how common sense struggled with romance, what toughness lay behind her bright little laugh, what sorrows Carlyle's success concealed, and yet how, if she ever stamped out of his life, she would be back the next day to see how he was taking it!

Of course she also understood her own power to fascinate. All those men she bewitched! All those women who found in her something that every woman finds in herself! All those madmen that sensed in her a fellow-traveller! Deprived of society she chafed at the waste of gifts like hers: 'better be an Owl in a Desert at once and say to-hoo to-hoo than have an articulate speaking tongue in one's head and next to no opportunities to use it'.

Could she see herself as the unsympathetic saw her – the petted child whose ears you wanted to box, the Haddington flirt who never quite outgrew her provincial origins, the story-teller (with that Scots accent!) who never knew when to stop, the actress, the martyr, the neurotic? Not wholly, surely, but more so than most of us, because the power to see ourselves as others see us was one of her gifts. No one with such a precise eye for the chinks in an opponent's armour could have been ignorant of the soft spots in her own.

It is her perception of her emotional life, and the nature of that life itself, that remains ambiguous. She thought of herself, in her later years, as an unrealized woman; but with what conscious or half-conscious or unconscious feelings it is hard to say. She was childless – 'me whose lines have always been cast in Babyless Places!'; often lonely; without the fame she might have won in her own right; a prey to melancholy. She seems to have turned to memories of her father's love, or to a succession of 'everlasting friendships' with other women for the intimacies she missed at home. It seems unlikely that passion was ever part of her life. Unaroused by Carlyle, immune from temptation by other men, shocked by Geraldine's incautious warmth, she was unseduced and unseducing – a brilliant, affectionate, stoical woman, with a haunted look.

59

'EXCITEMENT IS MY REST!'

19. To Jeannie Welsh at Liverpool

5 Cheyne Row, Chelsea/ 23 December 1843

On Tuesday evening I was engaged to assist at Nina Macready's[1] birth-day party – but felt so little up to gaieties on the Monday that I had resolved to send an apology *as usual* when voilà – on the morning of the appointed day arrives a note from Mrs Macready *imploring* me almost with tears in its eyes not to disappoint her and her 'poor little daughter' by sending an apology – that a well aired *bed* was prepared for me &c. &c. This forestalling of my cruel purpose was successful – I felt that I *must* go *for once* – so after spending the day in writing – not to *you* – but to people who, not having the reason you have to believe in my love, needed more than you to have a visible sign from me – I dressed myself and sat down to await *the fly*. 'My dear', says Carlyle, 'I think I never saw you look more bilious; your face is *green* and your eyes all *blood-shot!*' fine comfort when one was about to make a public appearance! 'the first time this season'. In fact I was very ill – had been *off* my sleep for a week and felt as if this night must almost *finish* me. But little does one know in this world what will *finish* them or what will *set them up* again. I question if a long course of mercury would have acted so beneficially on my liver as this party which I had gone to with a sacred shudder! But then it was the *very* most agreeable party that ever I was at in London – everybody there seemed animated with one purpose to make up to Mrs Macready and her children for the absence of 'the Tragic Actor' – and so amiable a purpose produced the most joyous re-sults. Dickens[2] and Forster above all exerted themselves till the perspiration was pouring down and they seemed *drunk* with their efforts! Only think of that excellent Dickens playing the *conjuror* for one whole hour – the *best* conjuror I ever saw – (and I have paid money to see several) – and Forster acting as his servant. This part

---

[1] Daughter of William Charles Macready, a noted Shakespearean actor.

[2] Dickens had just written his *Christmas Carol*. In another letter of this same day Jane sent a copy of it to her uncle, saying, 'It is really a kind-hearted, almost poetical little thing, well worth any Lady or gentleman's perusal – somewhat too much imbued with the Cockney-admiration – of *The Eatable*, but as Dickens writes for "the greatest happiness of the greatest number" (of Cockneys) he could not be expected to gainsay their taste in that particular.'

of the entertainment concluded with a plum pudding made out of raw flour, raw eggs – all the raw usual ingredients – boiled in a gentleman's hat – and tumbled out reeking – all in one minute before the eyes of the astonished children and astonished grown people! that trick – and his other of changing ladies' pocket handkerchiefs into comfits – and a box full of bran into a box full of – a live guinea-pig! would enable him to make a handsome subsistence let the bookseller trade go as it please – ! Then the dancing – old Major Burns with his one eye – old Jerdan of the Literary Gazette (escaped out of the Rules of the Queen's Bench for the great occasion!), the gigantic Thackeray &c. &c. all capering like *Maenades*!! Dickens did all but go down on his knees to make *me* – waltz with him! But I thought I did my part well enough in talking the maddest nonsense with *him*, Forster, Thackeray and Maclise – without attempting the Impossible – however *after supper* when we were all madder than ever with the pulling of crackers, the drinking of champagne, and the making of speeches; a universal country Dance was proposed – and Forster *seizing me round the waist*, whirled me into the thick of it, and *made* me dance!! like a person in the tread-mill who must move forward or be crushed to death! Once I cried out 'oh for the love of Heaven let me go! you are going to dash my brains out against the folding doors!' to which he answered – (you can fancy the tone) – 'your brains! who cares about their brains *here*? *let them go*!'

In fact the thing was rising into something not unlike the *rape of the Sabines*! (*Mrs Reid* was happily gone some time) when somebody looked [at] her watch and exclaimed 'twelve o'clock!' Whereupon we all rushed to the cloak-room – and *there* and in the lobby and up to the last moment the mirth raged on – Dickens took home Thackeray and Forster with him and his wife '*to finish the night there*' and a *royal* night they would have of it I fancy! – ending perhaps with a visit to the watch-house.

After all – the pleasantest company, as Burns thought, *are* the *blackguards*! – that is; those who have just a sufficient dash of blackguardism in them to make them snap their fingers at *ceremony* and 'all that sort of thing'. I question if there was as much witty speech uttered, in all the aristocratic, conventional drawing rooms thro'out London that night as among us little knot of blackguardist literary people who felt ourselves above all rules, and independent of the universe! Well, and the result? Why the result my dear was, that I went to bed on my return and – slept like a top!!!! plainly proving that *excitement* is *my rest*! To be sure my head ached a little next morning but the coffee cleared it – and I went about the dinner for Mrs Cunningham without much physical inconvenience.

See what a letter I have written! – and such writing! – but I must stop now for the post hour is at hand . . .

Your own

J.C.

HERO-WORSHIPPING

20. To Thomas Carlyle at Scotsbrig

Pier Hotel, Ryde/ 9 August 1843

Dearest

. . . And now let me tell you something which you will perhaps think more *questionable* than the placing of the Mudie girls[1] – a little piece of Hero-worship that I have been after. My 'youthful enthusiasm', as John Sterling calls it is not extinct then, as I had supposed; but must certainly be *immortal*! Only think of its blazing up for – *Father Mathew*! – You know I have always had the greatest reverence for that Priest – and when I heard he was in London, attainable to me, I felt that I *must* see him, shake him by the hand, and tell him I loved him considerably! I was expressing my wish to see him to Robertson the night he brought the Ballad-collector – and he told me it could be gratified quite easily. Mrs Hall had offered *him* a note of introduction to Father Mathew, and she would be pleased to include my name in it. 'Fix my time then.' He was administering the pledge all day long in the Commercial Road. I fixed next evening.

He (Robertson) called for me at five, and we rumbled off in omnibus all the way to *Mile End* – that hitherto for me unimaginable goal! Then there was still a good way to walk – the place, the new lodging, was a large piece of waste ground, boarded off from the Commercial Road, for a Catholic cemetery. I found 'my youthful enthusiasm' rising higher and higher as I got on the ground and saw the thousands of people all hushed into awful silence, with *not a single exception* that I saw – the only *religious* meeting I ever saw in Cockneyland which had not plenty of scoffers hanging on its out-skirts.

The crowd was all in front of a narrow scaffolding from which an

---

[1] The finding of suitable 'situations' for two Mudie sisters, left fatherless, with a feckless mother, was one of Jane's good works. She enlisted her friend Geraldine Jewsbury's aid in the matter.

American Captain was then haranguing it – and Father Mathew stood beside him, so good and simple-looking! Of course we could not push our way to the front of the scaffold, where steps led up to it – so we went to one end, where there were no steps or other visible means of access, and handed up our letter of introduction to a Policeman. He took it and returned presently, saying that Father Mathew was coming. And he came – and reached down his hand to me – and I grasped it – but the boards were higher than my head, and it seemed that our communication must stop there. But I have told you – I was in a moment of enthusiasm – I felt the need of getting closer to that good man. I saw a bit of rope hanging, in the form of a festoon, from the end of the boards. I put my foot on it – held still by Father Mathew's hand – seized the end of the boards with the other – and, in some, to myself, up to this moment, incomprehensible way – flung myself *horizontally* onto the scaffolding at Father Mathew's feet!! He uttered a scream! for he thought (I suppose) I must fall back – but not at all – I jumped to my feet, shook hands with him and said – what? 'God only knows.' He made me sit down on the only chair a moment, then took me *by the hand* as if I had been a little girl and led me to the front of the scaffold to see him administer the pledge. From a hundred to two hundred took it – and all the Trage-dies and theatrical representations I ever saw, melted into one, could not have given me such emotion as that scene did. There were faces both of men and of women that will haunt me while I live – faces exhibiting such concentrated wretchedness, making, you would have said, its last deadly struggle with the powers of darkness. There was one man, in particular, with a baby in his arms – and a young girl that seemed of the 'unfortunate' sort, that gave me an insight into the lot of humanity that I still wanted. And in the face of Father Mathew, when one looked from them to him, the mercy of heaven seemed to be laid bare. Of course I cried – but I longed to have laid my head down on the good man's shoulder and taken a hearty cry *there* before the whole assembled multitude!!

He said to me one such nice thing. 'I dare not be absent for an hour', he said. 'I think always if some dreadful drunkard were to come, and me away; he might never muster determination perhaps to come again in all his life, and *there* would be a man *lost*!'

I was turning sick and needed to get out of the thing, but in the act of leaving him – never to see him again thro all time most prob-ably – feeling him to be the very best man of modern times (*you* excepted), I had another movement of youthful enthusiasm which you will hold up your hands and eyes at. Did I take the pledge then? No – I *would* tho, if I had not feared it would have been put in the newspapers! No, not *that*; but I drew him aside, having considered if I had any *ring* on, any, any *handkerchief*, anything that I could leave with him in remembrance of me, and having bethought me of a pretty memorandum-book in my reticule, I drew him aside and put it in his hand, and bade him keep it for my sake and asked him to give me one of his medals to keep for his! – and all this in tears and the utmost agitation!! Had you any idea that your wife was still such a fool! I am sure *I* had not. The Father got thro' the thing admirably. He seemed to understand what it all meant quite well, inarticulate tho I was. He would not give me a common medal but took a little silver one from the neck of a young man who had just taken the pledge for example's sake, telling him he would get him another presently, and then laid the medal into my hand – with a solemn blessing. I could not speak for excitement all the way home. When I went to bed I could not sleep; the pale faces I had seen haunted me, and Father's Mathew's smile; and even next morning I could not anyhow subside into my normal state until I had sat down and – written Father Mathew a long letter – accompanying it with your *Past and Present*! Now my dear, if you are ready to beat me for a distracted Gomeril [good-natured fool] I cannot help it. All *that* it was *put into my heart to do, Ich könnte nicht anders . . .*

Bless you always, love to them all.

Your

J.C.

LION'S WIFE

21. TO MRS STIRLING (SUSAN HUNTER) AT DUNDEE

5 Cheyne Row, Chelsea/ 8 January 1841

My dear Susan,

I always thought you a woman of admirable good sense; and I rejoice to see that marriage has not spoiled you. This speaks well for your Husband too; for I defy any woman, unless she be no better than a stone, to hinder herself from taking something of the colour of the man she lives beside all days of the year. We women are naturally so impressible, so imitative! the more shame to men if we have all the failings they charge us with! Our very self-will, I believe which they make such a fuss about, is, after all, only a reflex of their own! . . .

In fact, in my character of *Lion*'s Wife here I have writing enough to *do*, by constraint, for disgusting even a Duchess of Orleans. Applications from young Ladies for autographs, *passionate* invitations to dine, announcements of inexpressible longings to drink tea with me – all that sort of thing which as a provincial girl I should have regarded perhaps as high promotion, but which at this time of day I regard as very silly and tiresome work, fritters away my time in fractionary writing, against the grain, and leaves me neither sense nor spirit for writing the letters which would suggest themselves in course of nature. Dear Susan I am sorry to say this world looks always the more absurd to me the longer I live in it! Human beings always the more like sheep! But thank heaven I am not the shepherd set over them, so let them go their way while we who are a little higher than the sheep go ours! Now dont be fancying that I am growing into a '*proud Pharisee*', which were even a degree worse than a sheep! Not at all! I have a bad nervous system, keeping me in a state of greater or less physical suffering all days of my life, and *that* is the most infallible specific against the sin of spiritual pride that I happen to know of . . .

What a likeable man, by the way, your Brother in Edinburgh is, so intelligent and so unpretentious, a combination not often to be found in Edinburgh, so *quietly* clever and *quietly* kind. I love quiet things, and *quiet good* things still carry me to enthusiasm.

Your affectionate

J. Carlyle

22. To Thomas Carlyle at Scotsbrig, Ecclefechan

30 July 1865

. . . ' *The Good, the Beautiful, and the True*' came last evening – 'to inquire how I was after my journey, and to tell *me* who knew nothing about it and cared less, how he had written letters of introduction for Dr Carlyle and sent them to the Captain of some steamer, &c. &c. and how his wife had set her heart on having a lock of *your* hair and *mine* set in a brooch, and he had promised her to try and *complete* her wishes! And it ended – for happily everything *does* end – in his begging and receiving the last *pen* you used – to be kept under a glass case! I have seldom seen a foolisher Hero-worshipper! But the greatest testimony to your fame seems to me to be the fact of *my* photograph – the whole three, two of them very ugly (Watkins's) – stuck up in Macmichael's shop-window!! Did you ever hear anything so preposterous in your life! And what impertinence on the part of Watkins! He must have sent *my three* along with your *nine* to the whole-sale man in Soho Square, without leave asked! But it proves the interest or curiosity *you* excite – for being neither a 'distinguished authoress', nor 'a celebrated murderess', nor an actress, nor a '*Skittles*'[1] (the four classes of women promoted to the shop-windows) it can only be as *Mrs* Carlyle that they offer me for sale!...

EARTHQUAKING

23. TO MRS AITKEN AT DUMFRIES

October 1843

... Carlyle returned from his travels 'very bilious', and continues very bilious up to this hour. The amount of bile that he does bring home to me, in these cases, is something 'awfully grand'! Even thro that deteriorating medium however he could not but be struck with a 'certain admiration' at the immensity of needlework I had accom-plished in his absence, in the shape of chair-covers, sofa-covers, window curtains, &c. &c., and all the other manifest improvements into which I had put my whole genius and industry and so little money as was hardly to be conceived! For three days I think his satisfaction over the rehabilitated house lasted – on the fourth, the young lady next door took a fit of *practising* on her accursed piano-forte, which he had quite forgotten seemingly, and he started up *disenchanted* in his new library, and informed Heaven and Earth in a peremptory manner that '*there* he could neither think nor live', that the Carpenter must be brought back and 'steps taken to make him a *quiet* place somewhere – perhaps best of all *on the roof* of the house'. Then followed interminable consultations with the said Carpenter, yielding, for some days, only plans (wild ones) and *estimates*. The room on the roof could be made all that a living author of irritable nerves could desire – silent as a tomb, lighted from above – but – it would

---

[1] A famous beauty, kept by Lord Hartington among others, who produced a traffic jam whenever she rode in Rotten Row. Earned her nickname by telling some guardsmen who were blowing insults at her 'if they didn't hold their bloody row, she'd knock them down like a row of bloody skittles'. James Laver, *Manners and Morals in the Age of Optimism 1848–1914* (New York, 1966).

cost £120! Impossible, seeing that we may be turned out of the house any year! So one had to reduce one's schemes to the altering of rooms that already were. By taking down a partition and instituting a fire-place where no fire-place could have been fancied capable of existing, it is expected that some bearable approximation to that ideal room in the clouds will be realised.

But my astonishment and despair, on finding myself after three months of what they call here 'regular mess', just when I had got every trace of the work-people cleared away, and had said to myself, 'Soul, take thine ease, or at all events thy *Swing,* for thou hast carpets nailed down and furniture rubbed for many days!' just when I was beginning to lead the dreaming, reading, dawdling existence which best suits me, and alone suits me in cold weather, to find myself in the thick of a new '*mess*' – the carpets, which I had nailed down so *well* with my own hands, tumbled up again – dirt, lime, whitewash, oil-paint, hard at work as before – and a prospect of new cleanings, new sewings, new arrangings stretching away into *eternity* for anything I see – Well, as my Helen says (the strangest mixture of Philosopher and perfect idiot that I have met with in life), 'when one's doing *this,* one's doing nothing else anyhow!' And as one ought to be always doing something, this suggestion of hers has some consolation in it . . .

IN HER GYPSY TENT

24. To John Welsh at The Baths, Helensburgh

5 Cheyne Row, Chelsea/ 18 July 1843

Dearest, dear, only Uncle of me!

I would give a crown that you could see me at this moment through a powerful telescope! You would laugh for the next twelve hours. I am *doing the rural* after a fashion so entirely my own! To escape from the abominable paint-smell and the infernal noise within doors, I have erected *with my own hands* a gipsy-tent in the garden, constructed with clothes lines, long poles, and an old brown floor cloth! under which remarkable shade I sit in an arm-chair at a small round table, with a hearth rug for carpet under my feet, writing materials, sewing materials, and a mind superior to Fate!

The only drawback to this retreat is its being exposed to 'the envy of surrounding nations' – so many heads peer out on me from all the windows of *the Row*, eager to penetrate my meaning! If I had a speaking-trumpet I would address them once for all – 'Ladies & Gentlemen, I am not here to enter my individual protest against the progress of civilisation! nor yet to mock you with an Arcadian felicity which you have neither the taste nor the ingenuity to make your own! but simply to *enjoy Nature* according to ability, and to get out of the smell of new paint! So, pray you, leave me to pursue my innocent avocations in the modest seclusion which I covet!'

Not to represent my contrivance as too perfect, I must also tell you that a strong puff of wind is apt to blow down the poles, and then the whole tent falls down on my head! This has happened once already since I began to write, but an instant puts it all to rights again. Indeed without counteracting the indoors-influences by all lawful means, I could not stay here at present without injury to my health, which is at no time of the strongest. Our house has for a fortnight back been a house possessed with seven devils! – a painter, two carpenters, a paper-hanger, two nondescript apprentice-lads, and '*a spy*' – all playing the devil to the utmost of their powers – hurrying and scurrying 'upstairs, downstairs, and in my Lady's chamber'! affording the liveliest image of a Sacked City!

When they rush in at six of the morning and spread themselves over the premises, I instantly jump out of bed, and 'in wera desperation' take a shower-bath. Then such a long day to be virtuous in! I make chair and sofa covers – write letters to my friends – scold the work-people, and suggest improved methods of doing things. And when I go to bed at night I have to leave both windows of my room wide open (and plenty of ladders lying quite handy underneath), that I may not, as old Sterling predicted, 'awake dead' of the paint.

The first night that I lay down in this open state of things, I recollected Jeannie's house-breaker adventure last year, and not wishing that all the thieves who *might* walk in at my open windows should take me quite unprepared, I laid my policeman's rattle and my dagger on the spare pillow, and then I went to sleep quite secure. But it is to be confidently expected that in a week more things will begin to subside into their normal state – and meanwhile it were absurd to expect that any sort of *Revolution* can be accomplished with *rose water*.

There! – the tent has been down on the top of me again, but it has only upset the ink.

Jeannie appears to be earthquaking with like energy in Maryland Street but finds time to write me nice long letters nevertheless, and even to make the loveliest pincushion for my birthday – and my birthday was celebrated also with the arrival of a hamper, into which I have not yet penetrated. Accept kisses *ad infinitum* for your kind thought of me, dearest Uncle. I hope to drink your health many times in the Madeira when I have Carlyle with me again to give an air of *respectability* to the act. Nay, on that evening when it came to hand, I was feeling so sad and dreary over the contrast between this 14th of July – alone, in a house like a sacked city – and other 14ths that I can never forget, that I hesitated whether or no to get myself out a bottle of the Madeira there and then, and try for once in my life the hitherto unknown comfort of being dead-drunk. But my sense of the respectable overcame the temptation . . .

My husband has now left his Welshman and is gone for a little while to visit the Bishop of St David's. Then he purposes crossing over somehow to Liverpool, and after a brief benediction to Jeannie, passing into Annandale. He has suffered unutterable things in Wales from the want of any adequate supply – of tea! The *Spooney*! For the rest, his visit appears to have been pretty successful – plenty of sea-bathing – plenty of riding on horse-back – and of *lying under trees*! I wonder it never enters his head to lie under the walnut-tree here at home – *it is a tree*! – leaves as green as any leaves can be even in South Wales! – but it were too *easy* to repose under that; if one had to travel a long journey by railway to it, then indeed it might be worth while!

But I have no more time for scribbling just now; besides, my pen is positively declining to act. So, God bless you Dear and all of them.

Ever your affectionate

Jane Carlyle

DEFYING THE MESMERIST

25. To John Welsh at Liverpool

5 Cheyne Row, Chelsea/ 13 December 1847

My dearest Uncle

I write to you *de profundis* – that is to say, from the *depths* of my tub-chair, into which I have migrated within the last two hours out of the still lower depths of my gigantic red bed, which has held me all this week, a victim to the 'inclemency of the season'! Oh, Uncle of my affections, such a season! Did you ever feel the like of it? *Already* solid ice in one's water jug! – 'poor Gardiners all *froz* out', and

Captain Sterling going at large in *a dress of skins* the same that he wore in Canada! I tried to make head against it by *force of volition* – kept off the fire as if I had been still at 'Miss Hall's', where it was a fine of sixpence to touch the hearthrug, and *walked*, walked, on Carlyle's pernicious counsel (always so for *me* at least) to '*take the Bull by the horns*' instead of following Darwin's more sensible maxim: 'in matters of health always *consult your sensations*'. And so, 'by working late and early, I'm come to what ye see'! in a tub-chair – a little live bundle of flannel shawls and dressing-gowns, with little or no strength to speak of, having coughed myself all to fiddle-strings in the course of the week! and 'in a dibble of a temper', if I had only anybody to vent it on!

Nevertheless I am sure 'I have now got the turn', for I feel what Carlyle would call '*a wholesome desire*' – to smoke! which cannot be gratified, as C. is dining with Darwin; but the tendency indicates a return to my normal state of health.

The next best thing I can think of is to write to *thee*; – beside one's bedroom fire, in a tub-chair, the family affections bloom up so strong in one! Moreover I have just been reading for the first time Harriet Martineau's outpourings in the 'Athenaeum', and '*that* minds me', as my Helen says, that you wished to know if I too had gone into this devilish thing. Catch me! What I think about it were not easy to say, but one thing I am very sure of, that the less one has to do with it the better. And that is it all of one family with witchcraft, demoniacal possession – is in fact the selfsame principle presenting itself under new scientific forms and under a polite name. To deny that there is such a thing as Animal Magnetism, and that it actually *does* produce many of the phenomena here recorded is idle – nor do I find much of this, which seems wonderful because we think of it for the first time, a whit more wonderful than those common instances of it which have never struck us with surprise, merely because we have been used to see them all our lives. Everybody, for instance, has seen children thrown almost into convulsions by someone *going through the motions* of tickling them! Nay, one has known a sensitive Uncle shrink his head between his shoulders at the first *pointing of a finger towards his neck*!

Does not a man *physically tremble* under the mere *look* of a wild beast or fellow-man that is stronger than himself? Does not a woman *redden all over* when she feels her lover's eyes on her? How then should one doubt the mysterious power of one individual over another? – or what is there more surprising in being made *rigid* than in being made *red*? in falling into sleep, than in falling into convulsions? in following somebody across a room, than in *trembling* before him from head to foot? I perfectly believe then in the power of magnetism to throw people into all sorts of unnatural states of *body*; could have believed so far *without* the evidence of my senses, and *have* the evidence of my senses for it also.

I saw Miss Bölte magnetised one evening at Mrs Buller's by a distinguished magnetiser who could not sound his *h*'s, and who maintained nevertheless that mesmerism 'consisted in moral and intellectual superiority'. In a quarter of an hour by gazing with his dark animal-eyes into hers, and simply holding one of her hands, while his other rested on her head, he had made her into the image of death – no marble was ever colder, paler, or more motionless, and her face had that peculiarly beautiful expression which Miss Martineau speaks of – never seen but in a dead face or a mesmerized one. Then he played cantrups with her arm and leg, and left them stretched out for an hour in an attitude which no awake person could have preserved for three minutes. I touched them and they felt horrid – stiff as iron. I could not bend them down with all my force. They pricked her hand with the point of a penknife; she felt nothing. And now comes the strangest part of my story. – The man, who regarded Carlyle and me as Philistines, said, '*Now* are you convinced?' 'Yes,' said Carlyle, 'there is no possibility of doubting but that you have stiffened all poor little Miss Bölte there into something very awful.' 'Yes,' said I pertly, 'but then she wished to be magnetised; what I doubt is whether anyone could be reduced to that state without *the consent of their own volition*. I should like for instance to see anyone *magnetise me*!' 'You think I could not?' said the man with a look of ineffable disdain. 'Yes,' said I, 'I defy you!' 'Will you give me your hand, *Miss*?' 'Oh by all means'; and I gave him my hand with the most perfect confidence in my force of volition and a smile of contempt. He held it in one of his and with the other made what H. Martineau calls some 'passes' over it – as if he were darting something from his finger ends. I looked him defiantly in the face as much as to say, 'You must learn to sound your *h*'s, Sir, before you can produce any effect on a woman like *me*!' And whilst this or some similar thought was passing thro my head – flash – there went over me from head to foot something precisely like what I once experienced from taking hold of a galvanic ball, only *not nearly* so violent. I had presence of mind to keep looking him in the face as if I had felt nothing and presently he flung away my hand with a provoked look, saying, 'I believe you would be a very difficult subject, but nevertheless if I had *time* given me, I am sure I could mesmerize you; at least I never failed with anyone yet.'

Now if this destroyed for me my theory of *the need of a consenting will*, it as signally destroyed *his* of *moral and intellectual superiority*; for *that* man was superior to *me* in nothing but animal strength, as I am a living woman! I could even hinder him from *perceiving* that he had mesmerised me by *my* moral and intellectual superiority! Of the *clairvoyance* I have *witnessed* nothing – but one knows that people with a diseased or violently excited state of nerves *can* see more than their neighbours. When my insane friend[1] was in this house he said many things *on the strength of his insanity* – which in a mesmerised person would have been quoted as miracles of clairvoyance . . .

Your devoted niece

Jane Carlyle

A SPECTACLE OF WOE

26. To Jeannie Welsh at Auchertool

5 Cheyne Row, Chelsea/ 19 May 1846

Dearest Babbie,

Few deaths could have surprised me more than Mr Liddle's; he had so little the look of one born to die young! I can well believe that all who were in habits of intimacy with him will long mourn the loss of such a cheerful kindly soul. For me, I am got to that with it now, that I can no longer feel sorry for the one who *dies* but only for the friends he leaves behind to miss him – one escapes so much suffering by dying young! – all the good one *could possibly* have enjoyed in longer life is not it seems to me to be put in the balance against the evil which one *must necessarily* have suffered, surviving one after another of all one loved – one after another of all one's beautiful illusions and even most reasonable hopes, surviving in short one's original self! You cannot understand *yet* how life may grow to look no such blessing – even for those who have no claim to be considered exceptionally unfortunate – long may it be before you feel this as I do! it is a weary, dreary feeling, almost making one regret the feelings of acute sorrow out of which it grows. And yet it is well to be prepared for it – that one may have it in as gentle a degree as possible by beginning early to pitch one's hopes from the world rather low – and by laying

---

[1] Plattnauer.

in as many good thoughts and good actions as one possibly can to look back upon for comfort, when one ceases to feel any comfort in looking forward. I have not got into a Socinian zeal for the '*pleasures of a good conscience*' tho' the foregoing sentence might lead you to that idea. I do not pretend to know by experience what the 'pleasures of a good conscience' may really be – but I fancy them like all other *pleasures* that I *have* experience of, a feeble refuge against the pressure of existence as it hardens gradually into old age – stript of all its early poetical illusions – but without any Socinian self-conceit. I *may* say to you of my own knowledge that the natural sadness of the latter part of one's life may be cruelly *embittered* by the reflection that one's best years, which might perhaps have produced something good have been suffered to run to waste, fertile only of tares and nettles! – But enough of moralizing.

I have not been well – as Mrs Paulet said – but not more ill than when Mrs Paulet spread such fine news of my improved looks! – People must talk – about other people's looks and much else that comes readiest – but what they say *for talking's sake* is not worth a minute's recollection. Ach Gott! how little even those who like one, *divine* of one's actual state – unless one *put oneself into words* and hardly even then can the generality of one's friends tell whether one is glad or sorrowful – feeling pain or pleasure! – I called at the Macreadys' the other day – in a humour that a person under sentence of death need hardly have envied. For days and weeks a cheerful feeling had not been in my mind – but of course one does not make calls to show oneself as *a spectacle of woe*. I talked talked – about the feats of Carlyle's horse &c. – and they laughed till their tears ran down. I could not *laugh* – but no matter – perhaps my own gravity made the things I was saying only more amusing by contrast. By and by Mrs Macready who is in the family-way began to talk of the dreadful 'depression of spirits' she occasionally laboured under. 'Ah, said I, everyone I suppose has their own fits of depression to bear up against if the truth were told.' – 'Do you say so?' said Miss Macready. 'Oh no surely! some people are never out of spirits – *yourself* for example, I really believe you do not know what it is to be ever sad for a minute!!! one never sees you that you do not keep one in fits of laughter!' I made no answer – but congratulated myself on having played my part so well. I wish I could find some hard work I *could* do – and saw any sense in doing. If I do not soon it will be the worse for me.

Meanwhile all *around* me goes on as usual – C. is just *getting done* with *his* work – speculating about 'where to go'. The usual people come about; but seldomer I think – seeing that I am less disposed to amuse them – new people come – but I have lost my talent for 'swearing everlasting friendships'. All my talents seem to be going one after another . . .

God bless thee Babbie, love me while you can.

Ever your affectionate,

Jane Carlyle

MUSING ON MARRIAGE

27. To Jeannie Welsh

Fragment, on a torn sheet.

10 January 1843

just because, in virtue of his being *the least unlikable* man in the place, I let him dance attendance on my young person, till I came to *need* him – all the same as my slippers to go to a ball in, or my bonnet to go out to walk. When I finally agreed to marry him, I *cried* excessively and felt excessively shocked – but if I had then said *no* he would have left me – and how could I dispense with what was equivalent to my slippers or bonnet? Oh if I might write my own biography from beginning to end – without reservation or false colouring – it would be an invaluable document for my countrywomen in more than one particular – but '*decency forbids*'!

28. To Jeannie Welsh at Liverpool

Croydon/ 4 April 1849

. . . Little Lewes came the other night with his little wife – speaking gratefully of you all – but it is Julia Paulet who has taken his soul captive!! he raves about her 'dark luxurious eyes' and 'smooth firm flesh' – ! his wife asked 'how did he know? had he been feeling it?' In fact his wife seems rather *contemptuous* of his raptures about all the women he has fallen in love with on this journey, which is the best way of taking the thing – when one *can*.

I used to think these Lewes a perfect pair of love-birds always cuddling together on the same perch – to speak figuratively – but the female love-bird appears to have hopped off to some distance and to be now taking a somewhat critical view of her little shaggy mate!

In the most honey-marriages one has only to *wait* – it is all a question of time – sooner or later 'reason resumes its empire', as the phrase is . . .

THE GODMOTHER

29. TO HELEN WELSH AT LIVERPOOL

5 Cheyne Row, Chelsea/ 20 January 1849
Dearest Helen,

. . . I have been interrupted dreadfully these two weeks, but the wonderfulest 'go' of all has been *a child*! Yes indeed! I have had a child – to keep, – to sit at meat with, and *sleep* with (good God!) and dress dolls for, and wash and comb and all that sort of thing – and also (– most fatiguing of all –) to *protect* it from Mr C. who gave manifest indications of a tendency to wring its neck! Where did I pick the creature up? – Ah my Dear! the creature picked up *me* – 'quite promiscuously'. I went some six weeks ago to call at the Macreadys' – and dined at the children's dinner and was reminded that I had a godchild, *by seeing it*. Not one godmotherly thing had I ever done towards that child! and really it was a godchild to be proud of, so now I took it on my knee and kissed it and, like a fool, asked 'will you go with *me*?' 'I should like it very much' said the child. '*That she would*' said the mother, 'and you need not be afraid of her misconducting herself for she is a good child.' I saw the thing had been taken *on the serious* so I backed out of it as well as I could, 'some time we shall see! – when I come again *with a carriage*'. Well! ten days ago I went there again with Anthony Sterling – and was asked gravely by the eldest daughter if I 'meant to take Jane Lydia back with me?' 'She had never ceased talking about *her visit* since I had been there.' I was in for it! so I said 'not to-day'; (it was necessary to prepare C.'s mind as well as my own) 'but if her Mother would bring her any day she liked to name I should do my best with her.' So Saturday was named – and the little creature delivered over to me in a transport of joy, (hardly mutual) to stay 'as long as I could be troubled to keep her.' I modestly suggested that three days and three nights – just the time that Jonah was in the whale's belly – would probably be enough of it for *her* as well as for me – and the Mother went and I remained alone – with a child of six years – very

75

stirring and very small and delicate! during the first day I 'ran horses' at her bidding, and performed my new functions with a determined energy – but the night came; I durst not put her to sleep in the spare room – for fear of her crying in the night – and awaking Mr C., and being herself very miserable, so after infinite perplexity in getting off her clothes (all *sewed* together) I laid her in my own bed, where she soon commenced – singing! – after an hour's waiting upon her I left her still awake – when I went up again she was asleep but lying right *across* the bed – at twelve I placed her properly, and went into bed myself, but of course not to sleep: all night long she pitched into my breast with her active little heels – and when she awoke at seven and threw her arms about my neck calling out 'Oh I am so glad to be here!' I had not once closed my eyes, and in this state to have to wash and dress her and play at horses again! it was a strange and severe penalty for being a God-mother. Next night I put her in the spare bed at all risks – with a good fire and trusted in Providence – and she did very well there – but I had got some cold by the job and the idea of being *laid up* in such a cause after having got so far thro' the winter on foot – was very vexatious. So I kept the house a few days and when the child's time came Anthony Sterling took her home for me!! I have a great quantity more to tell you about this '*go*' and other things – but Mr C. has been bothering ever since I began to write about helping him to pack a boxful of old clothes and things for Scotsbrig – and in an hour I have to be off to Mrs Buller so I will finish this letter to Babbie. God bless you all

Your affectionate
Jane Welsh

AN AFFINITY WITH MADMEN

30. TO JEANNIE WELSH AT LIVERPOOL

5 Cheyne Row, Chelsea/ After 22 August 1844

Dearest,

You may well say *in this instance at least* that while others talk I act. Certainly I have been *acting* – with a vengeance! You will wonder if I have not become insane myself when I tell you *the sequel* – would to Heaven I could call it *the solution*! Last Sunday evening Carlyle and I had just finished an early dinner preparatory to setting off on a Cockney-Sunday-excursion to the Regent's Park to be helped out with tea at Mrs Macready's – when I heard a gentleman's voice at the door inquiring for *me*. I had heard that voice only once before in my life but I recognized it instantly as Sir Alexander Morison's. What on earth had brought so busy a man to my own house? – Was he come to tell me that *He* had committed *suicide* or *escaped*? I rushed upstairs to him as white as milk – tearing my muslin gown by the way to an extent that would have tried even the temper of Ann Jane. – With an impassive air, that operated like a shower-bath on me at the moment, the good old Doctor delivered me a letter from my friend[1] – stating that he had appeared before the Committee on the previous day, been pronounced *cured* and now only waited till some friend should 'take him out' – a formality it seemed which could not be dispensed with. Would I *send someone*? I told Sir Alexander of course that I would come myself next morning if C. could not leave his work. But what then? – suffer him so soon as I had emancipated him to rush out into space under the first excitement natural to recovered liberty – and without either money or plan from all I could learn? – The thing was not be to thought of, so when Sir Alexander asked: 'But where will he go?' I looked imploringly at Carlyle who, good as he always is on *great* occasions, said directly 'Oh he must come *here* for a while till he sees what is to be done next.' And so it was settled and I had no difficulty in bringing *himself* to consent to the arrangement!!

Thro' unavoidable hindrances I was obliged to spend nearly *the whole day* in the Lunatic Asylum and a *happier* day I hardly ever passed [in] my life. At seven at night I landed him here in *a fly* and here he has been ever since and will be for some time yet. Whether it be the consciousness of having done a good action – or that he discovers a faculty and nobleness of Character in him, which he had before not allowed himself opportunity to discover; I cannot say – but the fact is that Carlyle seems to take to him most *lovingly* and shows him the uttermost kindness!! Still I have much to keep me anxious for not only does his future lie most perplexedly before us but – whatever the Drs and Committee have judged, I do not consider him by any means *sane*. He is horribly excitable – and has many wild whims in his head which might at any moment, by injudicious treatment, be exploded into madness – and his whole bearing and manner of speech is quite changed – *for the better* – so far as that goes – never did he seem half so clever or noble or highbred – but this very superiority alarms one. I know that *I* can keep him from any new crisis so

---

[1] Plattnauer, a German whom the Carlyles had befriended and who had gone mad and been confined in an asylum.

long as he is beside *me* – my influence over him is without limit – but then he cannot be *always* with *me* – and I tremble at the thought of what will become of him when left to himself. God knows – perhaps I frighten myself needlessly and his present state is but the *natural* consequence of the past five weeks.

Mrs Buller is worrying herself to death with the fear of his killing me – in these days of *insane* murders. Just as Jeffrey used to warn me against William Glen but no madman will ever hurt a hair of *my* head. I have too much *affinity* with them . . .

Love and kisses to all
Ever your affectionate
Jane Carlyle

EVERLASTING FRIENDSHIPS

31. TO JEANNIE WELSH AT LIVERPOOL

5 Cheyne Row, Chelsea/ 6 August 1843

My own Babbie

Have you *comprehended* me the least in the world? I fear not – I fear that your faith in me, steadfast as it is, must have received a *shock* more or less, from this prolonged silence. If so, now hear '*the solution*' and be sorry for having doubted a moment. Babbie I *could* not write to you while my husband was there, because I could and would and needed to write to *thee* more confidentially than to *him* even, and I felt that it were placing you in an embarrassing predicament to send you letters which he naturally would wish to see and which you would not feel at liberty to show him – better – easier and more prudent to write always straight to himself than to be writing as it were *for* him *thro'* you, or else *for* you to the exclusion of him. Not that I have had any mysteries of iniquity to communicate – but all my bits of household troubles – all my sympathy with *you* in *your* troubles, which with *two* such men[1] must have been considerable – all my amusement at their *planlessness* – their *lionizing* &c. &c. – all my apprehensions of having John landed with *me* – all in short of the *intimate little* things which it came naturally to say to Babbie and to no person else, all *that* it would have puzzled you to repeat to *them* –

---

[1] Carlyle and his brother John had just left Babbie's house when Jane wrote this letter. Jane was out of humour with Carlyle; he had been suggesting that she might want to take a house on the Lancashire coast where his mother might join her and enjoy the seabathing, but Jane had other ideas.

and when I tried to *compose* a letter to you - a letter for the public – Ach Gott I found it not possible – I have got so into the way of *splashing* off whatever is on my mind when I write to you, without forethought or back-thought that I must go on so, if at all, to the end of the chapter. Well! now the coast is clear again – and now my Babbie how do you do? For *me* I have been but indifferently all last week – Carlyle would perhaps tell you that I had been to Tunbridge Wells, and that feeling out of sorts next day I took an immense dose of shower bath to enable me to *do* the Kay Shuttleworths. The step I believe was *too* energetic – all that cold water drove my cold not *away* but *in* – and so I have been in a *curious* and rather wretched state ever since.

I seriously think of going for three or four days to the Isle of Wight on Tuesday – for the good of my body – through my body of my soul – going actually with Old Sterling. The poor old fellow is utterly broken down of late weeks and one may go with him any-where now, into the deserts of Siberia even without apprehension of being ravished! In fact he ought not to be from home alone – is too feeble to be without some one to take care of him – . . .

Your own
Cousin and Sister and Friend

32. To Miss Barnes at King's Road, Chelsea

Auchtertool House, Kirkcaldy/ 24 August 1859

My dear Miss Barnes

How nice of you to have written me a letter, '*all out of your own head*' (as the children say)! and how very nice of you to have remarked the *Forget-me-not*, and read a meaning in it! – It was certainly *with inten-tion* I tied up some *Forget-me-nots* along with my farewell roses; but I was far from sure of your recognising the intention, and at the same time not *young* enough to make it plainer. *Sentiment*, you see, is not well looked on by the present generation of women; there is a grow-ing taste for *fastness* or, still worse, for strongmindedness! – so, a discreet woman (like me!!) will beware always of putting her *senti-ment* (when she has any) in evidence – will rather leave it, as in the Forget-me-not case, to be *divined* thro' *sympathy*; and, *failing the sympathy*, to escape notice.

And you are actually going to get married! *you*! *Already*! And you expect me to *congratulate* you! – or 'perhaps not'. I admire the judiciousness of that '*perhaps not*'. Frankly, my Dear, I *wish* you all happiness in the new life that is opening to you; and you are marrying under good auspices since your father approves of the marriage. But, congratulation on such occasions seems to me a tempting of Providence! The Triumphal-Procession air which, in our Manners and Customs, is given to Marriage at the outset – that singing of *Te Deum before* the battle has *begun* – has, since ever I could reflect, struck me as somewhat senseless and somewhat impious! If ever one is to pray, if ever one is to feel grave and anxious, if ever one is to shrink from vain show and vain babble – surely it is just on the occasion of two human beings binding themselves to one another for better and for worse till death part them; just on that occasion which it is customary to celebrate only with rejoicings, and congratulations, and *trousseaux*, and – white ribbon! good god!

Will you think me mad if I tell you that when I read your words 'I am going to be married', I all but *screamed*? Positively, it took away my breath, as if I *saw* you in the act of taking a flying leap – into Infinite Space. You had looked to me such a happy happy little girl! Your Father's only daughter, and he so fond of you, so proud of you as he evidently was! After you and he had walked out of our house together that night, and I had gone up to my own room, I sat down there in the dark, and took 'a good cry'! – You had reminded me so vividly of my own youth, when I, also an only daughter – an only child – had a Father as fond of me, as proud of me! I wondered if you knew your own happiness! Well! knowing it or not, it has not been enough for you, it would seem! Naturally – youth is so insatiable of happiness, and has such sublimely insane faith in its own power to make happy and be happy!

But of your Father? Who is to cheer *his* toilsome life and make home bright for *him*? His companion thro' half a life time gone! his dear '*bit of rubbish*' gone too – tho' in a different sense! Oh little girl! little girl! *do* you *know* the blank you will make to him?

Now, upon my honour, I seem to be writing just such a letter as a raven might write if it had been taught! Perhaps the henbane I took in despair last night has something to do with my mood today – Anyhow, when one can only ray out darkness, one had best clap an extinguisher on oneself – And so God bless you –

Sincerely yours
Jane W. Carlyle

33. To Louisa, the second Lady Ashburton
at Addiscombe, Surrey

5 Cheyne Row, Chelsea/ 18 October 1864

Come at last! Oh dearest of created *Ladies*, 'past present and to
come'! I wonder if you have any adequate conception how your
coming has been watched and waited for, by the person now addressing you, and that persons better half? From day to day, since this
day week, expectation and disappointment alternating! Every day
the one or the other of us has ridden or driven up to Bath House, to
examine the windows and the gate; sometimes even to cross-question
Hannah, who had never more positive information to give, than
that you 'might arrive any day' – 'Every day' – till yesterday; just
the day when ones perquisition would have had happy results! for
yesterday I had to stay at Home to nurse 'a chill' – and Mr C. was
made too late out, by an *inburst* of Mrs Cameron [the photographer]
and Mr Watts (the Artist), the former hardly to be restrained from
forcing her way into Mr C.'s bedroom while he was changing his
trousers!! – I told *her* as Baillie told *me*, when I was pursuing Mr
Heath 'to the Back' with your message; 'It is a dangerous affair,
rather, that you are there entering on, Mam!' So when your note
arrived this morning it was *news* that it told! – Oh my Darling! my
Darling! how I love you! how glad I am – nay it is but just towards
him to say how glad *we* are – at the prospect of having you here
tomorrow night! *Will* you really come? Bless you for even *intending*
it! But at all events you will arrange for my seeing you, one way or
another, with the least possible delay? And Mr C. is *really impatient*
to see you, also. If you heard how eloquently he was talking of your
'exquisite kindness and *loveableness*, and *beautiful transparency of soul*',
on the way home that evening, and on several occasions since, you
would know whether he has the 'eyes to see, and heart to understand' which a certain young Lady would have persuaded you he had
not!

Oh my Darling! my Darling! who that comes near to you, and is
cared for by you can help loving you with a whole heartful of love!
I am almost frightened at myself when I feel how dear, how indispensable you are become to me! I had fancied myself too calmed
down with years and other things, ever to have bother with my *heart*
any more! Yes! I was henceforth to take just such tepid pleasures of

friendship as the Gods provided me; leaving aside all strong feelings that can tend to pain and anxiety. If you were to tire of me now –! if you were to die, before me –! if you were anyhow taken away out of my Life –! why, I should fall into as great trouble as I ever was in when young and excitable about a 'lost love' –

Meanwhile I shall see you tomorrow evening?

Yours devotedly
Jane Carlyle

III *Portrait of Carlyle*

Most married couples who have lived and worked at the same address for as many years as Jane and Thomas Carlyle, have managed to see much more of each other than they did. They spent most of the day and all of the night in separate rooms. He took his long walks and rides alone or with others. More of their holidays were spent apart than together. Their marriage was an intimacy of breakfasts (though when she was very sick, they might go for months without even breakfasting together), teas, evenings, and letters, in the midst of long separations. But whatever the physical distance, he was always close to her mind and her nerves.

Her letters are dotted with scores of those little sketches of her husband that amused both him and their friends and impressed as good a judge as Dickens with her powers of characterization. The physical description is missing. A wide-awake hat might be mentioned, but we don't learn from Jane that he was tall, erect, over five feet eleven, lean and spare. This was less, perhaps, because she was writing to people who knew what he looked like than because she was more interested in character than appearance. If she alludes to the beard he grew in middle age, it is to tell the Thackeray children that the time he saved by no longer shaving was spent wandering about the house bewailing the state of the world! It is worth remembering (for she does not tell us) that the Carlyle she lived with for all but the last eight years of her life was clean-shaven – with those intense eyes and the stubborn underlip; – and that all the famous, brooding, bearded Carlyles, which artists like Millais, Watts, Whistler, and Boehm, and the genius-photographer Julia Margaret Cameron, have made immortal, were done after her death.

Some other things are missing from these sketches which a different observer might have chosen to illuminate. She seizes on facts; she rarely speculates. Carlyle's melancholy, for example, is a fact to be described, not something she tries to explain. She also takes Carlyle's genius for granted and makes very little attempt to explain that. She called herself 'Lion's Wife', but rarely wrote as if she were a prophet's disciple. Carlyle was a hero, a sage, a saviour of society to hundreds of thousands of his countrymen. Was he a hero to his wife? She once quoted Erasmus Darwin as lightly asking, 'What the deuce is Carlyle's religion? Or has he any?' But nowhere in her correspondence does she attempt a serious answer. He was her 'Man of Genius'; to be celebrated, sheltered and lovingly satirized; but not to be analysed as an intellectual or a moralist; or not, at least, in her letters. We can see how she adopted his favourite expressions – 'Pray come to Tea with me to-morrow evening at seven, if my husband's particular friends "the Destinies", *alias* "the Upper Powers", *alias* "The Immortal Gods" . . . don't interfere to keep you away"; but there is no evidence on which to judge whether she shared his faith.

Finally, though we see Carlyle in many different veins – great in big things, tender at bottom, infusing his hope into her despair – it is the gloomy, growling,

83

inconsiderate, inconsistent, unpractical Carlyle that predominates. 'Wae, wae! Ay di mi, Ay di mi!' Apostle of Silence? 'As if that man *could* enjoy or yet *endure* perfect silence for one week!' This was the Carlyle she served up for entertainment and we should not forget that, generally speaking, no one got more fun out of it than he did.

She never pointed out, as David Masson did after Carlyle's death, that his denunciations and jeremiads would often end with a huge peal of laughter at something that had tickled his sense of absurdity; or that he must have enjoyed his misery when he complained of a particular listener, 'a man might as well pour his sorrows into the long hairy ear of a jackass'. But in their own way, if only by all that inside talk, the 'coterie-speech' that preserved the memory of so many good stories, her letters remind us of all the tremendous delight they got out of the human spectacle when they were not sorrowing over it.

Of course they snapped at each other. 'You know we never travel together – he does not like the *fash* of a woman with band-boxes.' 'At night I sit in the same room with Mr C. and must not fidget him with 'the scratching of my pen' while he is reading or correcting proofs.' And there were always kind friends to feed a sense of injury; 'You will see the mighty man of genius is not so easily managed as a pet-bird', wrote the sculptor Thomas Woolner to Mrs Tennyson, 'I think if he could see his wife's weak state so keenly as he can spiritual truths, he would not let his plans interfere with her little projects for health-seeking.' Perhaps the bitterest letter she ever wrote is the tearful complaint in this selection about Carlyle's insensitivity. What a brute to think that scornful bullying would bring the best out of her! How much better her father understood her!

Poor Jeannie! He could be 'gey ill to deal wi'', as his mother always said.

FOR HIS MOTHER

34. To Mrs Carlyle at Scotsbrig

1 September 1834

... I must tell you what Carlyle will not tell of himself – that he is rapidly mending of his Craigenputtoch gloom and acerbity. He is really at times a tolerably social character, and seems to be regarded with a feeling of mingled terror and love in all companies, which I should expect the diffusion of Teufelsdröckh [i.e. *Sartor Resartus*] will tend to increase ...

For his mother

35. TO MRS CARLYLE AT SCOTSBRIG

2 May 1835

... I have just had a call from an old rejected lover who has been in India these ten years – tho he has come home with more thousands of pounds than we are ever likely to have hundreds or even scores, the sight of [him] did not make me doubt the wisdom of my preference. Indeed, I continue quite content with my bargain – I could wish him a little *less yellow*, and a little more *peaceable*; but that is all!...

36. TO MRS CARLYLE AT SCOTSBRIG

23 December 1835

... You are to look upon it as the most positive proof of my regard that I write to you in my present circumstances; that is to say with the blood all frozen in my veins and my brains turned to a solid mass of ice. For such has for several days been the too cruel lot of your poor little daughter-in-law at Lunnon; the general lot indeed of all Lunnon, so far [as] I can observe. When the frost *comes* here, '*it comes*', as the woman said with the four eggs, and it seems to be somehow more difficult to guard against it than elsewhere; for all the world immediately takes to coughing and blowing its nose with a fury quite appalling. The noise thus created destroys the suffering remnant of senses spared by the cold and makes the writing of a letter or any other employment in which thought is concerned seem almost a tempting of Providence. Nevertheless I am here to tell you that we are still in the land of the living, and thinking of you all, from yourself the head of the nation, down to that very least and fattest child, who I hope will continue to grow fatter and fatter till I come to see it with my own eyes. I count this fatness a good omen for the whole family; it betokens good-nature, which is a quality too rare among us. Those '*long, sprawling, ill-put-together*'[1] children give early promise of being 'gey ill to deal wi''.

That one of them who is fallen to my share conducts himself pretty peaceably at present, writing only in the forenoons. He has finished a chapter much to my satisfaction, and the poor book begins

[1] 'A lank, sprawling, ill-put-together thing.' Such had been my mother's definition to her of me as a nurseling – T.C.

85

to hold up its head again. Our situation is further improved by the introduction of Ann Cook into the establishment, instead of the distracted Roman Catholics and distracted protestants who preceded her. She seems an assiduous kindly honest and thrifty creature; and will learn to do all I want with her quite easily. For the rest, she amuses me every hour of the day, with her perfect incomprehension of everything like ceremony. I was helping her to wring a sheet one day, while she had the cut finger, and she told me very flatly it was *'clean aboon my fit'* [ability]. 'I should get at it by practice', said I; 'for weaker people than I have wrung sheets.'–*'May be sae,'* returned she very coolly, *'but I ken-na where ye'll find ony weaker; for a weaklier-like cretur I never saw in a' my life.'* Another time when Carlyle had been off his sleep for a night or two, she came to me at bedtime to ask, 'if Mr Carlyle bees ony uneasy thro the nicht, and's ga'an *staiveren* [stumbling] about the hoose wull ye bid him gee us a cry [awaken us] at five in the morning'! . . .

I am much better off this winter for society than I was last. Mrs Sterling makes the greatest possible change for me. She is so good, so sincerely and unvaryingly kind, that I feel to her as to a third Mother. Whenever I have blue devils, I need but put on my bonnet and run off to her, and the smile in her eyes restores me to instant good humour. Her Husband would go thro fire and water for me and if there were a third worse element would go through that also. The Son is devoted to Carlyle and makes him a real friend which among all his various intimate acquaintances and well-wishers he cannot be said ever to have had before – this family then is a great blessing to us. And so has been my study of Italian which has helped me thro many dullish hours. I never feel anything like youth about except when I am learning something, and when I am turning over my Italian dictionary I could fancy myself thirteen: whether there be any good in fancying oneself thirteen after one is turned of thirty I leave your charity to determine.

We sit in hourly nay in momentarily expectation of the meal &c. which has not yet arrived, but will soon I am sure for I dreamt two nights since that I saw them fetching it out of the waggon. Meanwhile we sup on arrowroot and milk – the little bag being done . . .

For his mother

37. TO MRS CARLYLE AT SCOTSBRIG

22 September 1837

. . . You know the saying 'it is not lost which a friend gets' and in the present case it must comfort you for losing him. Moreover, you have others behind – and I have only him – only him in the whole wide world to love me and take care of me – poor little wretch that I am. Not but what numbers of people love me after their fashion far better than I deserve – but then *his* fashion is so different from all these and seems alone to suit the crotchety creature that I am. Thank you then for having in the first place been kind enough to produce him into this world and for having in the second place made him scholar enough to recognise my various excellencies and for having in the last place sent him back to me again to stand by me in this cruel east wind. God bless you all. . . I will write you a letter all to yourself before long God willing . . .

CARLYLE AT WORK

38. TO JOHN WELSH AT LIVERPOOL

5 Cheyne Row, Chelsea/ 4 March 1837

Dearest Uncle of me,

'Fellow-feeling makes us wondrous kind'! You and my aunt have had the influenza: I also have had the influenza; a stronger bond of sympathy need not be desired: and so the spirit moves me to write you a letter; and if you think there is no very 'wondrous kindness' in *that*, I can only say you are mistaken, seeing that I have had so much indispensable writing to *do* of late days, that like a certain Duchess of Orleans I was reading about the other week, 'when night comes, I am often so tired with writing, that I can hardly put one *foot* before the other'!

But with respect to this influenza Uncle, what think you of it? above all *how* is it, and *why* is it? For my part with all my cleverness, I cannot make it out. Sometimes I am half persuaded that there is (in Cockney dialect) '*a Do at the bottom on it*'; medical men all over the world having merely entered into a tacit agreement to call all sorts of maladies people are liable to, in cold weather, by one name, so that one sort of treatment may serve for all, and their practice be thereby greatly simplified. In more candid moments, however, I cannot help thinking that it has something to do with the '*diffusion of useful knowledge*': – if not a part of that knowledge, at least that it is meant as a counterpoise; so that our minds may be preserved in some equilibrium; between the consciousness of our enormous acquirements on the one hand, and on the other the *generally diffused* experience, that all the acquirements in the world are not worth a rush to one, compared with the blessedness of having a head clear of snifters! However it be, I am thankful to Heaven that I was the chosen victim in this house, instead of my Husband. For had he been laid up at present, there would have been the very devil to pay. He has *two* printers on his book [*The French Revolution*] that it may if possible be got published in April; and it will hardly be well off his hands when he is to deliver a course of lectures on German Literature to 'Lords and Gentlemen', and 'honourable women not a few'. You wonder how he is to get thro such a thing; So do I, very sincerely, the more as he proposes to speak these lectures extempore, Heaven bless the mark! having indeed no leisure to prepare them before the time at which they will be wanted.

One of his lady-admirers (by the way he is getting a vast number of lady-admirers) was saying the other day that the grand danger to be feared for him was that he should commence with '*Gentlemen and Ladies*', instead of '*Ladies and Gentlemen*', a transmutation which would ruin him at the very outset. He vows however that he will say neither the one thing nor the other, and I believe him very secure on that side. Indeed I should as soon look to see gold pieces or penny loaves drop out of his mouth, as to hear from it any such hum-drum unrepublican-like commonplace. If he finds it necessary to address his audience by any particular designation, it will be thus – '*Men and Women*'! or perhaps in my Penfillan grandfather's style, '*Fool-creatures come here for diversion*'. On the whole if his hearers be reasonable, and are content that there be good sense in the things he says, without requiring that he should furnish them with *brains* to find it out; I have no doubt but his success will be eminent. The exhibition is to take place in *Willis's Rooms*; 'to begin at three and end at four *precisely*', and to be continued every Monday and Friday thro the first three weeks of May. '*Begin precisely*' it may, with proper precautions on my part, to put all the clocks and watches in the house half an hour before the time; but as to '*ending precisely*'! *that* is all to be tried for! There are several things in this world which once set agoing, it is not easy to stop; and *the Book* is one of them. I have been thinking that perhaps the readiest way of bringing him to a *cetera desunt* (*conclusion* is out of the question) would be, just as the clock strikes four, to have a lighted cigar laid on the table before him – we shall see!

The *French Revolution* done and the Lectures done; he is going somewhere (to Scotland most probably) to rest himself awhile – to lie about the roots of hedges and speak to no man, woman, or child, except in monosyllables! a reasonable project enough, considering the worry He has been kept in for almost three years back. For my part having neither published nor lectured, I feel no call to refresh myself by such temporary descent from my orbit under the waves; and in Shakespearean dialect, I had such a '*belly full*' of travelling last year as is likely to quell my appetite in that way for some time to come. If I had been consulted in the getting up of *The Litany*, there would have been particular mention made of steamboats, mail-coaches and heavy coaches among those things from which we pray to be delivered; and more emphatic mention made of 'such as travel by land or sea' . . .

Yours
Jane Welsh Carlyle

39. To Mrs Carlyle at Scotsbrig

5 Cheyne Row, Chelsea/ 6 May 1839

Our second lecture '*transpired*' yesterday, and with surprising success – literally surprising – for he was imputing the profound attention with which the audience listened, to an awful, sympathising expectation on their part of his momentary, complete break-down, when all at once they broke into loud plaudits, and he thought they must all have gone clean out of their wits! But, as does not happen always, the majority were in this instance in the right, and it was *he* that was out of *his* wits to fancy himself making a stupid lecture, when the fact is, he really *cannot* be stupid if it were to save his life. The short and the long of it was, he had neglected to take a pill the day before, had neglected to get himself a ride, and was out of spirits at the beginning; even I who consider myself a perfectly un-prejudiced judge, did not think he was talking his best or anything like his best, but the '*splendids*', '*devilish-fines*', '*most trues*', and all that which I heard heartily ejaculated on all sides, showed that it was a sort of mercy in him to come with bowels in a state of derangement, since if his faculties had had full play, the people must have been all sent home in a state of excitement bordering on frenzy. The most practical good feature in the business, was a considerable increase of hearers – even since last day – the audience seems to me much larger than last year, and even more distinguished. The whole street was blocked up with 'fine yellow' (and all other imaginable coloured) 'deliveries'[1] – and this is more than merely a dangerous flattery to one's vanity – the fashionable people here being (unlike our Scotch *gigmen* and *gig-women*) the most open to light (above all to *his* light) of any sorts of people one has to do with. Even John Knox, tho' they must have been very angry at him for demolishing so much beautiful architecture, which is quite a passion with the English, they were quite willing to let good be said of, so that it was indisputably true. Nay, it was in reference to Knox that they first applauded yesterday. Perhaps his being a countryman of their favourite Lecturer's might have something to do with it! But we will hope better things, tho we thus speak.[2]

You will find nothing about *us* in the *Examiner* of this week. Leigh Hunt who writes the notices there did not arrive at the first lecture in time to make any report of it – having come in an omnibus which took it in its head to run a race with another omnibus after a rather novel fashion, that is to say, each trying which should be *hindmost*. *We* go to lecture this year very commodiously in what is called *a Fly* (a little chaise with one horse) furnished us from a livery stable hard by at a very moderate rate. Yesterday the woman who keeps these stables sent us a *flunkey* more than bargain, in consideration that I was 'such a very nice lady' – showing therein a spirit above slavery and even above *Livery*. Indeed as a foolish old woman at Dumfries used to say, 'everybody is kind to *me*' and I take their kindness and am grateful for it without inquiring too closely into their motives. Perhaps I am a genius too as well as my husband – Indeed I really begin to think so – especially since yesterday that I *wrote down* a parrot! which was driving us quite desperate with its screeching. Some new neighbours that came a month or two ago brought with them an accumulation of all the things to be guarded against in a London neighbourhood, viz., a pianoforte, a lap dog, and a Parrot. The two first can be borne with as they carry on the glory within doors, but the Parrot since the fine weather has been holding forth in the

---

[1] 'Fine yellow *deliveries* and a' !' exclaimed a goosey maidservant at Mainhill, seeing a carriage pass in the distance once (in little Craw Jean's hearing) – T.C.
[2] Common preachers' phrase in Scotland – T.C.

Garden under our open windows. Yesterday it was more than usually obstreperous – so that Carlyle at last fairly sprang to his feet declaring he could 'neither think nor live'. Now it was absolutely necessary that he should do both. So, forthwith, on the inspiration of conjugal sympathy, I wrote a note to the Parrot's mistress (name unknown) and in five minutes after Pretty Polly was carried within and is now screeching from some subterranean depth whence she is hardly audible. Now if you will please recollect that at Comely Bank I also *wrote down* an Old Maid's house-dog, and an only son's pet bantam-cock, you will admit, I think, that my writings have not been in vain.

My Mother is still in Liverpool having been detained there by an operation which had to be performed on one of my Uncle's eyes – but as he is doing very well I suppose she will now be thinking of Templand. She was very happy here last time – and very sensible to Carlyle's kind treatment of her. He had been 'everything' she said 'that heart could desire'. When I wonder will *you* be justified in saying as much of *me*? . . .

40. TO MRS CARLYLE AT SCOTSBRIG

20 May 1839

. . . The last lecture was indeed the most splendid he ever delivered – and the people were all in a heart-fever over it. On all sides of me people who did not know me, and might therefore be believed, were expressing their raptures audibly. One man (a person of originally large fortune which he got thro in an uncommon way, namely, in *acts of benevolence*) was saying, 'He's a glorious fellow. I love the fellow's very faults', &c., &c. – while another answered, 'Aye faith is he – a fine, wild, chaotic, noble chap', and so on over the whole room. In short we left the concern in a sort of whirlwind of '*glory*' not without '*bread*' – one of the dashing facts of the day being a Queen's carriage at the door – which had come with some of the household. Another thing I noticed of a counter tendency to one's vanity was poor Mrs Edward Irving sitting opposite me in her weeds, and looking as ugly as sin – with sorrowful heart enough, I dare say. And when I thought of her lot and all the things that must be passing thro her heart, to see her husband's old friend there, carrying on the glory in his turn; while *hers*! – What was it all come to – She seemed to me set there expressly to keep me in mind 'that I was but a woman'; like the skeleton which the Egyptians place at table in their feasts to be a memorial of their latter end . . .

41. TO MRS STIRLING AT DUNDEE

8 January 1841

. . . For my Husband he is as usual – never healthy, never absolutely ill – protesting against 'things in general' with the old emphasis – with an increased vehemence just at present, being in the agonies of getting under way with another book. He has had it in his head for a good while to write a life of Cromwell and has been sitting for months back in a mess of great dingy folios, the very look of which is like to give me lock-jaw . . .

42. TO JEANNIE WELSH AT LIVERPOOL

10 January 1843

. . . Dear I will tell you a secret but see that you keep it to yourself – Carlyle is no more writing about *Oliver Cromwell* than you and I are! I have known this for a good while – you will wonder that I should not have known it all along – the fact is his papers were a good time more resembling hierogliphics than finished manuscript. I could not be at the trouble of making them out – then when I came to find, on days when I chanced to look, pages about *the present fashion of men's coats* – about the rage for novelties – puffing every thing or anything except '*Cromwell Oliver*' – I had no misgivings – I know he has such a way of tacking on extraneous discussions to his subject – but when I found at last a long biography of that *Abbot Samson*! then indeed – I asked what on earth *has* all this to do with Cromwell – and learned that Cromwell was not begun – that probably half a dozen other volumes will be published before that. Nevertheless for I know not what reason he lets everybody go on questioning him of his Cromwell and answers so as to leave them in the persuasion he is very busy with that and nothing else. Absolutely I will not begin another sheet . . .

1a *Jane's birthplace:*
   a doctor's house
   in Haddington

1b *Carlyle's birthplace:*
   a stonemason's
   cottage at
   Ecclefechan

2a *Jane in the year of
her marriage:
a miniature by
Kenneth McLeay*

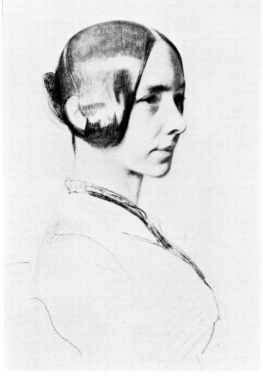

2b *Jane in her late
thirties: a
drawing by
Samuel Laurence*

3 *Carlyle at 37: a drawing by Daniel Maclise*

4a No. 5 (now 24)
Cheyne Row, Chelsea

4b The garden at Cheyne Row

43. To Mrs Russell at Thornhill

5 November 1844

. . . I suspect that my Man-of-Genius-Husband has forgotten old Mary as completely as if she had never been born, Oliver Cromwell having, as the servants at Craigenputtoch used to say 'taken the whole *gang* to himsel'. The wife of Sir Fowell Buxton has been many times heard to wish that the *Blacks* (*her* Husband's fixed idea) were all at the bottom of the red Sea; and I am afraid I have often been undutiful enough of late months to wish the Memory of Cromwell 'at the bottom of *something*', where I might hear less about it. It *is* at the bottom of rubbish enough, I am sure; to judge from the tremendous ransacking of old folios and illegible manuscripts which Carlyle is always going on with, but still he manages to bring it up, in season and out of season till I begin to be weary of him (the Protector) great man tho he was. But as everything comes to an end with patience; he will probably get himself written at last, and printed and published, and then my husband will return to a consciousness of his daily life and I shall have peace from the turmoils of the *Commonwealth*. For if Carlyle thinks of nothing else but his *book* whilst he is *writing* it; one has always this consolation that he is the first to forget it when it is *written* . . .

44. To Thomas Carlyle at Galway, Wales

Benrydden/ 20 July 1849

. . . I suppose Forster has sent you a Bradford paper containing the report of our meeting for 'Roman Liberty' . . . In fact, the Bradford *gentlemen* on the platform were like Bess Stodart's legs, 'no great things'. – but the Bradford *men*, filling the Hall to suffocation, were a sight to see! to cry over, 'if one liked'! – such ardent, earnest, half-intelligent, half-bewildered countenances! as made me, for the time being, almost into a friend of the species and advocate for *fusion de biens* [St Simonian Socialism]. And I must tell you – I 'aye thocht meikle o' you', but that night I 'thocht mair o' you than ever'. A man of the people mounted the platform, and spoke – a youngish, intelligent looking man, who alone of all the speakers seemed to *understand* the question, and to have *feelings* as well as

notions about it – he spoke with a heart-eloquence that '*left me warm*'.
I never was more affected by public speaking. When he ceased I did
not throw myself on his neck and swear everlasting friendship, but I
assure you, it was in *putting constraint on myself* that I merely started
to my feet and shook hands with him – all the *gentlemen* imitated my
example and shook hands with him – Then 'a sudden thought'
struck me: *this* man would like to know *you* – I would give him my
address in London. I borrowed a pencil and piece of paper, and
handed him my address. When he looked at it he started as if I had
sent a bullet into him – caught my hand again, almost squeezed it to
'immortal smash', and said, 'Oh! *it is* your husband! – Mr Carlyle
has been my teacher and Master! I have owed everything to him for
years and years!' I felt it a credit to you really to have had a hand
in *turning out* this man – was prouder of that heart-tribute to your
genius than any amount of Reviewer-praises, or of aristocratic
invitations to dinner . . .

45. TO THOMAS CARLYLE AT CHELSEA

Craigenvilla, Edinburgh/ 24 August 1857

. . . Oh my Dear! What a magnificent book[1] *this* is going to be!
The best of all your Books! I say so who *never flatter*, as you are too
well aware; and who am 'the only person I know that is always in
the right'! So far as it is here before me; I find it forcible, and vivid,
and sparkling as *The French Revolution*, with the geniality, and composure, and finish of *Cromwell* – a wonderful combination of merits!
And how you *have* contrived to fit together all those different sorts
of pictures, belonging to different Times, as compactly and smoothly
as a bit of the finest mosaic! Really one may say of these two first
Books at least, what Helen said of the letters of her sister who died –
you remember? 'So *splendidly* put together; one would have thought
that hand couldn't have written them!' . . .

[1] *Frederick the Great.*

46. To Thomas Carlyle at Chelsea

Sunny Bank, Haddington/ 30 August 1857

... I am reading *the sheets* to them – *they* most likely will not live to see the finished Book. You never saw more *ardent* listeners! My godmother with her head bent forward, hearkening with her blind eyes as well as her ears, might sit for a picture of *Attention*! And every now and then one or other asks some question or makes some remark that shows how *intelligently* they listen. Miss Jess said one good thing: 'To look merely to the *wording*, it is so *brief*, so *concise*, that one would expect some obscurity in the narrative, or at least that it would need a great effort of attention to understand it; instead of which the meaning is as clear as glass!' And Miss Donaldson said, 'I see more than ever in this, my Dear, what I have always seen in Mr Carlyle's Books; and what I think distinguishes him from all the writers of the present day; a great love of Truth – and, *what is more* (observe the fine discrimination!) *a perfect detestation of lies*!'

I was afraid having to read in a voice so high pitched, my reading would not do justice to the thing; but Miss Donaldson asked me last night, 'My Dear, does Mr Carlyle read what he writes to you bit by bit?' 'Oh, dear no! – he does not like reading aloud.' 'Then I suppose you read it often over to yourself? For I was noticing that in reading those sheets, you did it so *natural-like*: just as if it was coming out of your *own* head!' ...

I was dreaming last night about going to some strange house – among strange people – to make representations about *cocks*! I went *on my knees* at last, *weeping*, to an old man with a cast metal face and grey hair, and while I was explaining all about how you were an author and couldn't get sleep for these new *cocks*, my auditor flounced off, and I became aware he was the man who had three serpent-daughters and kept people in glass bottles in Hoffman's Tale! I forget his name – but knew it well enough in my dream.

A kiss to Nero.[1]

Yours ever

J.W.C.

---

[1] Her dog.

47. TO THOMAS CARLYLE AT SCOTSBRIG

5 Cheyne Row, Chelsea/ 11 July 1858

Botkin (what a name!) your Russian translator, has called. Luckily Charlotte had been forewarned to admit him if he came again. He is quite a different type from Tourgueneff, tho' a tall man, this one too. I should say he must be a Cossack – not that I ever saw a Cossack or heard one described! – *instinct* is all I have for it! He has flattened high-boned cheeks – a nose flattened towards the point – small, very black, deep-set eyes, with thin semi-circular eyebrows – a wide thin mouth – complexion whitey-grey, and the skin of his face looked thick enough to make a saddle of! He does not possess himself like Tourgueneff, but bends and gesticulates like a Frenchman.

He burst into the room with wild expressions of his 'admiration for Mr Carlyle'. I begged him to be seated and he declared 'Mr Carlyle was the man for Russia'. I tried again and again to 'enchain' a rational conversation, but nothing could I get out of him but rhapsodies about you in the frightfullest *English* that I ever heard out of a human head! It is to be hoped that (as he told me) he *reads* English much better than he *speaks* it – else he must have produced an inconceivable translation of *Hero Worship*. Such as it is, anyhow, 'a large deputation of the Students of St Petersburg' waited on him (Botkin), to thank him in the strongest terms for having translated for them Hero Worship and made known to them Carlyle – And even the young Russian ladies now read *Hero Worship* and 'unnerstants it thor – lie'. He was all in a perspiration when he went away – and so was I!

I should like to have asked him some questions; for example how *he* came to know of your works (he had told me he had had to send to England for them 'at extreem cost') but it would have been like asking a cascade! The best that I could do for him I did – I gave him a photograph of you, and put him up to carrying it in the top of his hat . . .

48. To J.T. (an anonymous admirer)

5 Cheyne Row, Chelsea/ 11 February 1863

I wish, dear sir, you could have seen how your letter brightened up the breakfast-time for my husband and me yesterday morning, scattering the misanthropy we are both given to at the beginning of the day, like other nervous people who have 'bad nights'. I wish you could have heard our lyrical recognition of your letter – its 'beautiful modesty', its 'gentleness', and 'genuineness'; above all I wish you could have heard the tone of real feeling in which my husband said, at last, 'I do think, my dear, that is the very nicest little bit of good cheer that has come our way for seven years!' It might have been thought Mr C. was quite unused to expressions of appreciation from strangers, instead of (as is the fact) receiving such almost every day in the year – except Sundays, when there is no post. But, oh, the difference between that gracious, graceful little act of faith of yours, and the intrusive, impertinent, presumptuous letters my husband is continually receiving, demanding, in return for so much 'admiration', an autograph perhaps! or to read and give an opinion on some long, cramped MS of the writer's; or to – find a publisher for it even! or to read some idiotic new book of the writer's (that is a very common form of letter from lady admirers) – say a translation from the German (!) and 'write a review of it in one of the quarterlies'! 'It would be a favour never to be forgotten'! I should think so indeed.

Were I to show you the 'tributes of admiration' to Mr C.'s genius, received through the post during one month, you, who have consideration for the time of a man struggling, as for life, with a gigantic task – you, who, as my husband says, are 'beautifully modest', would feel your hair rise on end at such assaults on a man under pretence of admiring him; and would be enabled perhaps, better than I can express it in words, to imagine the pleasure it must have been to us when an approving reader of my husband's books came softly in, and wrapped his wife in a warm, beautiful shawl, saying simply – 'There! I don't want to interrupt you, but I want to show you my good-will; and that is how I show it.'

We are both equally gratified, and thank you heartily. When the shawl came, as it did at night, Mr C. himself wrapped it about me, and walked round me admiring it. And what think you he said?

He said, 'I am very glad of that for you, my dear, I think it is the only bit of real good my celebrity ever brought you!'

Yours truly,

Jane W. Carlyle

The letter which called out so many praises was this:

Mrs Thomas Carlyle. Madam, – Unwilling to interrupt your husband in his stern task, I take the liberty of addressing you, and hope you will accept from me a woollen long shawl, which I have sent by the Parcel Delivery Co., carriage paid, to your address. If it does not reach you, please let me know, and I shall make inquiries here, so that it be traced and delivered. I hope the pattern will please you, and also that it may be of use to you in a cold day.

I will also name to you my reason for sending you such a thing. My obligations to your husband are many and unnameably great, and I just wish to acknowledge them. All men will come to acknowledge this, when your husband's power and purpose shall become visible to them.

If high respect, love, and good wishes could comfort him and you, none living command more or deserve more.

You can take a fit moment to communicate to your husband my humble admiration of his goodness, attainments, and great gifts to the world; which I wish much he may be spared to see the world begin to appreciate.

I remain, &c.,

J.T.

SERVING-UP CARLYLE

49. To John Sterling at Floriac, Bordeaux

5 Cheyne Row, Chelsea/ 1 February 1837

My ever dear John Sterling

. . . One great comfort, however, under all afflictions, is that *The French Revolution* is happily concluded; at least it will be [a] comfort when one is delivered from the tag-raggery of printers' devils that at present drive one from post to pillar. Quelle vie! Let no woman who values peace of soul ever dream of marrying an author! that is to say if he be an honest one, who makes a conscience of *doing* the thing he pretends to do. But this I observe to you in confidence: should I state such a sentiment openly, I might happen to get myself torn in pieces, by the host of my Husband's lady-admirers, who already I suspect, think me too happy in not knowing my happiness. You cannot fancy what way he is making with the fair Intellectuals here! There is Harriet Martineau presents him her ear-trumpet with a pretty blushing air of coquetry which would almost convince one out of belief in her identity! And Mrs Pierce Butler, bolts in upon his studies, out of the atmosphere as it were, in riding-habit, cap and whip (but no shadow of a horse, only a carriage – the whip, I suppose, being to whip the cushions with, for the purpose of keeping her hand in practice) – My inexperienced Scotch Domestic remaining entirely in a nonplus whether she had let in '*a leddy or a gentleman*'! And then there is a young American Beauty – such a Beauty! 'snow-and-rose-bloom' thro'out – not as to clothes merely but complexion also – large and soft, and without one idea, you would say, to rub upon another! And this charming creature *publicly* declares herself his '*ardent admirer*'; and I heard her with my own ears call out quite passionately at parting with him 'Oh Mr Carlyle I want to see you – to talk a long long time about – *Sartor*'!! Sartor of all things in this world! What *could* such a young lady have got to say about Sartor can you imagine? And Mrs Marsh the moving Authoress of the Old Man's Tales reads Sartor when she is ill in bed; from which one thing at least may be clearly inferred that her illness is not of the head.

In short my dear friend; the singular author of Sartor appears to me at this moment to be rather in a perilous position, in as much as (with the innocence of a sucking dove, to outward appearance) he is leading honourable women not a few entirely off their feet. And who can say that he will keep his own! After all, in sober earnest, is it not curious that my Husband's writings should be only completely understood and adequately appreciated by women and mad people? I do not know very well *what* to infer from the fact . . .

I am ever affectionately

Yours

Jane W. Carlyle

50. To Mrs Aitken at Dumfries

5 Cheyne Row, Chelsea/ March–April 1844?

. . . I found Carlyle in a bad way, complaining of sore throat and universal misery, and in this state nothing I could say hindered him from walking out in the rain – and his throat became so much worse during the night that I was afraid he was going to be as ill as when poor Becker attended him at Comely Bank. He had asked a gentleman to dinner on Sunday and two more to tea – Dodds and John Hunter of Edinburgh, and *two more* came 'on the voluntary principle', and all these men *I* had to receive and entertain, on my own basis, and to show me, I suppose, that they were not too much mortified in finding only me, the unfortunate creatures all staid till eleven at night – then I put a mustard blister to the Man's throat, and put him to bed with apprehensions enough, – but to my astonishment he went almost immediately to sleep, and slept quite peaceably all night and next morning the throat was miraculously mended. We kept him in bed to breakfast almost by main force however, and John ordered him to live on slops to complete his cure but he told John in very decided *Annandale* that 'he had a great notion he would follow the direction of *Nature* in the matter of eating and getting up, and if Nature told him to dine on a chop it would be a clever fellow that should persuade him not to do it' . . .

51. POSTSCRIPT OF A LETTER TO JOHN FORSTER, AT 58 LINCOLN'S INN FIELDS

Chelsea/ 11 December 1849

Oh Lord! I forgot to tell you – I have got a little dog [Nero]. and Mr C. has *accepted* it with an amiability! To be sure when he comes down gloomy in the morning, or comes in wearied from his walk the infatuated little beast dances round him on its hind legs as *I* ought to do and can't, and he feels flattered and surprised by such unwonted capers to his honour and glory.

52. TO MRS RUSSELL AT THORNHILL

5 Cheyne Row, Chelsea/ 3 July 1856

Dearest Mrs Russell –

Your letter quite warmed my heart and gave me a pull towards Scotland, stronger than I had yet felt. I think it in the highest degree unlikely, and certainly it will not be my own fault if I am there without seeing you. But we have no programme positively laid out yet for the summer, or rather the autumn. Mr C. always hithers and thithers in a weary interminable way before he can make up his mind what he would like most to do. And so, as I don't like wandering in uncertainties, with a net of '*ifs*' and '*buts*' and '*perhapses*' and '*possibly*' and '*probably*' about my feet; I have got into the way of standing aside, and postponing my own plans, till *he* has finally got to some conclusion. His present '*most probably*' is that he will go to his sister's at a farm within a few miles of Annan, and 'enjoy perfect solitude for a time'. I mean, in that case, to stream off after 'my own sweet will'; as he would not need me with him at *The Gill,* and indeed there would be no room for me there, and I should only complicate his case. When he has settled to go there, or anywhere else where I am not needed, I shall proceed to scheme out a pro-gramme for myself and I *want* to go to Scotland too, and I want to see you, and to see my cousins in Fife, and my old people at Had-dington. But I do not take up all that practically at the present stage of the business, in case he take some new thought, with which my wishes could not so easily combine.

I don't see any hope of his quitting London anyhow till the begin-ning of August, at soonest, which is a pity; the present month would be passed so much more pleasantly in the green country than here, where everything seems working up to *spontaneous combustion.* I was thinking the other night, at the 'most magnificent ball of the season', how much better I should like to see people *making hay,* than all these Ladies in laces and diamonds, waltzing! One grows so sick of diamonds and bare shoulders, and all that sort of thing, after a while! It is the old story of the Irishman put into a Sedan chair *without a bottom,* 'If it weren't for the honour of the thing, I might as well have walked!'

I shall write dear Mrs Russell whenever I know for certain what we are going to do. And, as I have great faith in the magnetic power of wishes, I pray you to wish in the meantime that I may come – as I, on my side, shall not fail to wish it *strongly.*

I am just going off this burning day to – sit for my picture!! rather late! But I have a friend who has constituted herself a portrait-painter, and she has a real genius for the business; and Ruskin told her she must paint a portrait with no end of pains, must give it '*twenty sittings at the least*'. And I suppose she thinks I am the most *patient* woman she knows, and may give her these *twenty sittings,* out of desire for her improvement. As she is a clever charming creature I don't feel all the horror that might be expected of my prospect.

My kind regards to your husband and father.

Yours affectionately,

Jane W. Carlyle

53. To Miss Barnes at King's Road, Chelsea

22 September 1861

... For the rest; I should have enjoyed this beautiful place excessively, if Eve hadn't eaten that unfortunate apple, a great many years ago! in result of which there has, ever since, been *always a something* to prevent one's feeling oneself in Paradise! The '*something*', of the present occasion, came in the form of *Lumbago*! not into my own back, but into Mr C.'s; which made the difference, so far as the whole comfort of my life was concerned! For it was the very first day of being here that Mr C. saw fit to spread his pocket handkerchief on the grass – just after a heavy shower – and sit down on it! – for an hour and more – in spite of all my remonstrances!! The Lumbago following in the course of nature; there hasn't been a day that I felt sure of staying over the next, and of not being snatched away – like Proserpine – as I was from *the Grange* last winter! For what avail the '*beauties of nature*', the '*Ease with dignity*' of a great House, even the Hero Worship accorded one, against Lumbago? Nothing, it would seem! – less than nothing! – Lumbago, my Dear, it is good that you should know in time, admits of but one consolation – of but one happiness! – viz: '*perfect liberty to be as ugly and stupid and disagreeable as ever one likes*'! – and that consolation, that happiness, that liberty reserves itself for the domestic hearth! As you will find when you are married, I daresay.

And so, all the ten days we have been here, it has been a straining on Mr C.'s part to tear his way through the social amenities back to Chelsea! – while I have spent all the time I might have been enjoying myself in expecting to be snatched away! ...

54. To Mrs Russell at Holm Hill

23 February 1862

... The longer I live, the more I am certified that *men*, in all that relates to their own health, have not common sense! whether it be their Pride, or their Impatience, or their Obstinacy, or their ingrained Spirit of Contradiction that stultifies and misleads them, the result is always a certain amount of idiocy or distraction, in their dealings with their own bodies! I am not generalising from my own

Husband. I *know* that *he* is a quite extravagant example of that want of common sense in bodily matters, which I complain of. Few *men* (even) are so lost to themselves as to dry their soaked trousers on their legs! (as he does) or swallow five grains of mercury *in the middle of the day*, and then walk or ride three hours under a plunge of rain! (as he does) &c. &c. But *men* generally – all of them I have ever had to do with – even *your* sensible Husband included you see! – drive the poor women, who care for them to despair, either by their wild impatience of bodily suffering, and the exaggerated moan they make over it, or else by their reckless defiance of it, and neglect of every dictate of Prudence . . .

55. To Thomas Carlyle at Scotsbrig

10 April 1866

. . . Alas, I missed Tyndall's call! and was 'vaixed'! He left word with Jessie that you were 'looking well and every body worshipping you'! and I thought to myself: a pity if he have taken the habit of being *worshipped*, for he may find some difficulty in keeping it up, *here*!

. . . Frederick Elliot, and – Hayward! – were at Lady Williams. Hayward was raging against the Jamaica business – would have had Eyre cut into small pieces and eaten him raw. He told me *women* might patronize Eyre – that women were naturally cruel, and rather *liked* to look on while horrors were perpetrated. But no *man* living could stand up for Eyre *now*! 'I hope Mr Carlyle does, I said. I haven't had an opportunity of asking him, but I should be surprised and grieved if I found *him* sentimentalising over a pack of black brutes'! After staring at me a moment, 'Mr *Carlyle*! said Hayward – 'Oh yes! *Mr Carlyle*! one cannot indeed swear what *he* will *not* say! *His* great aim and philosophy of life being '*the smallest happiness of the fewest number*'! . . .

CHIEF TORMENTOR, CHIEF COMFORTER

56. To Helen Welsh at Liverpool

5 Cheyne Row, Chelsea/ 6 December 1850

Dearest Helen,

'The Immortal Gods' are not favourable to writing this day. Firstly we have 'a London Fog' coming on, and if it advance at the same rate in half an hour more I should need candles to write by; secondly my morning hours have been unavoidably taken up in rehabilitating my chief winter-gown, and now I am in momently expectation of Mrs William Wynn who is in town for two days and has written that she will come today betwixt 2 and 4 – and then, today I *must* write to John Carlyle who asked last night in a letter to his brother that 'Jane would write to him *herself* about that accident' – with all this bearing me away from you, however I feel as if it would be a sort of sin not to tell you at once how grateful I feel for your and Jeannies letters containing such kind and also – oh how rare in this world!, such *judicious* sympathy – and to relieve you also from any painful speculating about my accident *more than the occasion requires*. The day before yesterday I was sensible, for the first time, of a considerable diminution of the pain, it has been growing less and less ever since; I really *think* it is going away altogether; I hope there will be no return of it; and from the first minute I could assure myself it was *beginning* to feel better I began to cheer up my heart – O God forbid that I should die a *lingering* death, trying the patience of those about me; beside a Husband who could not avoid letting me see how little patience his own ailments have left him for anybody else's – should *such a thing* come upon me in reality, I should go away from here, I think, and ask *one of you* to tend me and care for me in some little place of my own – even my low spirits about the thing which in the first days I *could* not conceal from him – nor in fact did I think there was any obligation on me to *keep up appearances* with *him* brought down on me *such* a tempest of *scornful* and wrathful words, such charges of 'impatience', 'cowardliness', 'impiety', 'contemptibility' that I shut myself up altogether and nothing should ever wring from me another expression of suffering to him – the more thankful did I feel for your and Jeannies kind toleration of my anxiety – so well both of you just hit the right tone of treating such a state of mind, speaking hopefully to me and at the same time not making *light* of my accident, nor *mocking* at my fears. I wonder after all [how] I come to be grown such a coward, for I was certainly one of the bravest little children alive – used to bear pain like an Indian – take hissing Ganders by the neck – and show myself up to every emergency. I suppose my bravery active and passive must have been like most of my other good qualities, 'for the occasion got up' – *assumed* to gain my Father's approbation, to be *praised* by him and kissed, and 'loved very much indeed'. Oh! that was the right handle to take me up by – not 'shoring [scolding] me out of creation' for my faults and weaknesses, not trying to make me heroic by *abusing* as 'contemptible and impious'! . . .

> God bless you all – this letter is half for Babbie
> > Yours affectionately
> > Jane Welsh

57. To Margaret Welsh at Liverpool

> 5 Cheyne Row, Chelsea/15 July 1842

My dear Maggie

It was a good thought in you to send me the little purse, and I feel very grateful to you for it. This last birthday was very sad for me as you may easily suppose, very unlike what it was last year and all former years – and I needed all the heartening kind souls could give me. But by your kindness and that of others the day was got over with less of a forsaken feeling than could have been anticipated. Only think of my husband too having given me a little present! he who never attends to such *nonsenses* as birthdays, and who dislikes nothing in the world so much as going into a shop to buy anything, even his own trowsers and coats; so that to the consternation of Cockney-tailors *I* am obliged to go about them. Well he actually risked himself in a jeweller's shop and bought me a very nice smelling-bottle! I cannot tell you how *wae* his little gift made me as well as glad – it was the first thing of the kind he ever gave me in his life – in *great* matters he is always kind and considerate, but these little attentions which we women attach so much importance to he was never in the habit of rendering to any one – his up-bringing and the severe turn of mind he has from nature had alike indisposed him towards them. And now the desire to replace to me the irreplaceable makes him as good in *little* things as he used to be in great . . .

> Ever your affectionate Cousin
> > Jane Carlyle

58. To Mrs Austin at The Gill, Annan

5 Cheyne Row, Chelsea/ 18 October 1864

Oh, little woman! you will come to our aid, if possible; but if impossible, what on earth are we to do for eggs? At this present Mr C. is breakfasting on shop-eggs, and doesn't know it; and I am every morning expecting to hear in my bed an explosion over some one too far gone for his making himself an illusion about it. All the people who kept fowls round about have, the maids say, during my absence ceased to keep them, and the two eggs from Addiscombe three times a week are not enough for us both; I, 'as one solitary individual' needing three in the day – one for breakfast, one in hot milk for luncheon, and one in my small pudding at dinner. When I left Holm Hill, Mrs Russell was in despair over her hens; thirty of them yielded but three eggs a day. Yours, too, may have struck work; and in that case never mind. Only if you could send us some, it would be a mercy.

Only think of my getting here every morning a tumbler of milk warm from the cow, and all frothed up, just as at the Gill and at Holm Hill, to my infinite benefit. The stable-fed cow does not give such delicious milk as those living on grass in the open air; but still it is milk without a drop of water or anything in it, and milked out five minutes before I drink it. Mr C. says it is a daily recurring miracle. The miracle is worked by our Rector's wife, who keeps two cows for her children, and she has kindly included me as 'the biggest and best child'; and with a key into their garden my cook can run to their stable with a tumbler and be back at my bedside in ten minutes. Indeed, it is impossible to tell who is kindest to me; my fear is always that I shall be stifled with roses. They make so much of me, and I am so weak. The Countess of Airlie was kneeling beside my sofa yesterday embracing my feet, and kissing my hands! A German girl said the other day, 'I think, Mrs Carlyle, a many many peoples love you very dear!' It is true, and what I have done to deserve all that love I haven't the remotest conception.

All this time I have been keeping better – getting some sleep, not much nor good; but some, better or worse, every night, and the irritation has been much subsided. Yesterday afternoon and this afternoon it is troubling me more than usual. Perhaps the damp in the air has brought it on, or perhaps I have been overdone with people and things; I must be more careful. I have always a terrible consciousness at the bottom of my mind that at any moment, if God will, I may be thrown back into the old agonies. I can never feel confident of life and of ease in life again, and it is best so.

I cannot tell you how gentle and good Mr Carlyle is! He is busy as ever, but he studies my comfort and peace as he never did before. I have engaged a new housmaid, and given warning [*i.e. notice*] to the big beautiful blockhead who has filled that function here for the last nine months; this has been a worry too. God bless you all.

Your affectionate
Jane W. Carlyle

Ever so few eggs will be worth carriage.

IV *Victorian housewife*

Jane Carlyle's letters are so vivid and so filled with the minutiae of everyday living that her readers can know intimately – even feel – what it was like to be a woman living in a middle-class household in Victorian England. They become familiar with every room in Number 5 Cheyne Row, sense her pride and share her frustrations in keeping it watertight, warm, clean, free from bugs and smoothly running. When to the normal cares of managing a 'massive old concern' (the Cheyne Row house was over a hundred years old when the Carlyles leased it) were added the demands of a genius-husband that the business be conducted silently and peaceably, it became a herculean labour.

Carlyle did the house-hunting in the spring of 1834 and sent back descriptions of his finds. Jane's preference was for the Cheyne Row house with 'the broad staircase and abundant accommodation for *crokery*'! She did the packing at Craigenputtoch and stayed with her mother at Templand until Carlyle sent for her. They moved in on 10 June of that year and were to live the rest of their lives in that 'excellent old house'. They leased it for an annual rent of £35, improved it, and finally obtained a thirty-one year lease in 1852 at the same rent. Although Carlyle, in his restlessness, threatened to leave it in favour of any number of other abodes – a house in Scotland, a return to Craigenputtoch, some 'crib of a house on the Isle of Wight', a cottage on the Ashburton estate – all 'mythical' places – Jane went on tidying it, polishing it, painting old furniture, buying bargains in couches, making decorative screens, curtains, sofa covers, and ignoring all schemes for its abandonment.

She was obviously 'house-proud', and appears to have relished the terrific upheavals which the annual 'earthquaking' produced. At least her health improves when Carlyle is on his summer travels, and she is in her gypsy tent in the garden, with the house like a sacked city and full of seven devils in the shape of painters, carpenters, paper-hangers, apprentice lads and a 'spy'. 'When I am *single*', she writes to Jeannie Welsh (30 June 1843), 'and when a domestic earth-quake is going on there is no leisure for *feeling* lonely.'

The exertions of 1843, so eloquently described in the letter to Jeannie Welsh reproduced in this chapter, were all in vain so far as Carlyle was concerned, for after three days in his new library, he found he could neither think nor live because of the piano next door, so up went all the carpets and in rushed the legions of 'incarnate demons' to take out a partition in one room and install a new fireplace. Such a finale to her cleaning struck the maid Helen with a 'temporary idiocy' and nearly reduced her mistress to tears. And when the new uproar subsided, he found he couldn't write in there any more than beside the piano; 'it was all so strange to him'. The sound-proof room under the roof, which he dreamed of for years, was not achieved until 1853, and even then, the 'silent apartment' turned out the noisiest in the house, and 'the cocks still crowed and the *macaw* still *shrieked*, and Mr C. still stormed'. Lighted by a skylight, the attic room proved ferociously hot in summer and freezing in winter. Carlyle finished *Frederick the Great* there in 1865, a year before his wife's death, and quit the room; thereafter it became the servant's quarters.

During the Carlyle tenancy, the Cheyne Row house saw many famous visitors: John Stuart Mill, Leigh Hunt, Erasmus Darwin, John Sterling, author and clergyman; his brother, Captain Anthony Sterling; and his father Edward Sterling, chief leader-writer for *The Times* (variously referred to by the Carlyles as 'the Thunderer', 'the Whirlwind', and '*Stimabile*'); Harriet Martineau, Edward Irving, Richard Monckton Milnes (afterwards Lord Houghton), Charles Buller, Robert Owen, Count d'Orsay, Mazzini, Lord Jeffrey, Cavaignac, Louis Blanc, Kingsley, Dickens, Browning, Thackeray, Arthur Hugh Clough, Emerson, Tennyson, Ruskin, G. H. Lewes, Froude, T. H. Huxley – in short, literary London.

Moncure Conway, an American preacher, pastor at South Place Chapel, Finsbury from 1864 to 1881, was a regular visitor to Cheyne Row in the 1860s. He left this description of his visits which Reginald Blunt quotes in *The Carlyles' Chelsea Home* (1895):

I used to go once or sometimes twice in the week, towards nine in the evening. By that time Carlyle was stretched on the floor [in the drawing-room upstairs] his back cushioned against the wall, the bowl of his long clay pipe in the fireplace, so that the smoke might not disturb his invalid wife. She reclined on the sofa beside him. After greetings their conversation was resumed, and Carlyle went on pouring out such good stories as those treasured in his wife's letters. Mrs. C. took a lively share in the talk with that easy freedom not usual in oppressed wives, and with so much point and sparkle that I sometimes wondered that there were not more clashings between these swords that had got into one sheath. One could not look upon Mrs. Carlyle's face then without reading in it love and reverence for her husband.

Number 5 was re-numbered Number 24 during Carlyle's lifetime. The house fell into disrepair after his death in 1883; it had strange occupants – a lady who took in stray cats and dogs and a servant who, after that lady's death, 'took in worse'. In 1895 a committee headed by Mr (afterwards Sir) Leslie Stephen purchased it with monies raised by public subscription, formed a Memorial Trust to restore and administer the property, and began the search for the original furnishings. Today it is owned by the National Trust, furnished as Jane left it, her ornamental screen, her sofa, her piano – all in place, as if the Carlyles had just departed for a weekend in the country.

THE CHOICE OF CHEYNE ROW

59. To Thomas Carlyle at 4 Ampton Street,
London

Templand/ 27 May 1834

. . . Now you wish the furniture and Goody off immediately.
Dearest, 'it shall be done'! There is no earthly objection to my sailing
on Friday first (but on the contrary every motive to hasten to you
at the soonest possible), except *one*, and that one is not of consequence enough to stand in the way of your wishes and my own. It
was only in case of there being no *outrake* for me if I joined you so
soon, that I spoke in my last of waiting till the Friday following.

. . . And now, my Darling, with respect to those two houses, I
declare to thee they look both so attractive on paper that I cannot
tell which I ought to prefer, and *should* like to see with my bodily
eyes before you decide. I have a great liking to that massive old
concern with the broad staircase and abundant accommodation for
crokery! And dressingrooms to one's bedrooms is charming! I should
not quarrel with the quantity of room even tho' (like my china
assiettes) it might be asked 'what we had to put in it'. But is it not
too near the river? I should fear it would be a very foggy situation in
winter and always dampish and unwholesome. And then the wains-
coating up to the ceilings, is it painted? If in the original state,
hardly any number of candles (never to speak of 'only two') will
suffice to light it. And another idea presents itself along with that
wainscoat – if bugs have ever been in the house! Must they not have
found there, as well as the inmates, 'room without end'? The other
again does not attract me so much, but to make up for that, suggests
no objections; so keep them *both* open, if you can, till I come. And if
you are constrained to decide, that you may not let both or either
slip thro your hands, do it with perfect assurance that Goody will
approve your choice. The neighbourhood to our friends I would not
let be a material point in your deliberations. *You* have a pair of
effectual legs to take you wherever you please; and for me, my chief
enjoyment, I imagine, will always be in the society of my own heart's
Darling and within my own four walls, as heretofore.

My Mother sends her kindest regards. She is in the most gracious,
bountiful mood – giving me gowns, etc., has even bought a superior
silk handkerchief for Alick! and a gown for little Sister Jenny whom

she never saw! What a mercy for you, Dearest that I have not *her* turn for managing the finance department! We should soon sit rent free in the King's bench. And now I must conclude – a mean return for your long precious letter – but I have a headache today and must not drive it beyond bounds. God Almighty bless you my love – before many days I shall see your face again.

Your own Jane

THE ARRIVAL THERE

60. THOMAS CARLYLE'S NOTE

'Tuesday, June 10, 1834', it appears, was the date of our alighting amid heaped furniture, in this house, where we were to continue for life. I well remember bits of the drive from Ampton Street; what damp-clouded kind of sky it was; how, in crossing Belgrave Square, *Chico,* her little canary-bird, whom she had brought from Craigen-puttoch in her lap, burst out into singing, which we all ('Bessy Barnet', our romantic maid, sat with us in the old hackney-coach) strove to accept as a promising omen. The business of sorting and settling, with two or three good carpenters, &c., already on the ground, was at once gone into, with boundless alacrity, and (under such management as hers) went on at a mighty rate; even the three or four days of quasi-camp life, or gypsy life, had a kind of gay charm to us; and hour by hour we saw the confusion abating, growing into victorious order. Leigh Hunt was continually sending us notes; most probably would in person step across before bedtime, and give us an hour of the prettiest melodious discourse. In about a week (it seems to me) all was swept and garnished, fairly habitable; and continued incessantly to get itself polished, civilised, and beautified to a degree that surprised one. I have elsewhere alluded to all that, and to my little Jeannie's conduct of it: heroic, lovely, pathetic, mournfully beautiful, as in the light of eternity, that little scene of time now looks to me. From birth upwards she had lived in opulence; and now, for my sake, had become poor – so nobly poor. Truly, her pretty little brag (in this letter) was well founded. No such house, for beautiful thrift, quiet, spontaneous, nay, as it were, unconscious – minimum of money reconciled to human comfort and human dignity – have I anywhere looked upon where I have been . . .

JANE'S DESCRIPTION OF THE HOUSE

61. To Eliza Stodart at 22 George Square, Edinburgh

5 Cheyne Row, Chelsea/ 1834

Our well-beloved Friend and Cousin –

. . . Well! is it not very strange that I am here? sitting in my own hired house by the side of the Thames as if nothing had happened; with fragments of Haddington, of Comely Bank, of Craigenputtoch interweaved with *cockneycalities* into a very habitable whole? Is it not strange that I should have an everlasting sound in my ears, of men, women, children, omnibuses, carriages glass coaches, streetcoaches, waggons, carts, dog-carts, steeple bells, door bells, Gentlemen-raps, twopenny-post-raps, footmen-showers-of-raps, of the whole devil to pay, as if plague, pestilence, famine, battle, murder sudden death and wee Eppie Daidle were broken loose to make me diversion. – And where is the stillness, the eternal sameness, of the last six years? Echo answers at Craigenputtoch! There let them 'dwell with Melancholy' and old Nancy Macqueen; for this stirring life is more to my mind, and has besides a beneficial effect on my bowels. Seriously I have almost entirely discontinued drugs, and look twenty percent better, every one says, and 'what every one says must be true'. This being the case you may infer that I am tolerably content in my new position; indeed I am more and more persuaded that there is no complete misery in the world that does not emanate from the bowels.

We have got an excellent lodgment; of most antique physiognomy, quite to our humour; all wainscoated, carved and queer-looking, roomy substantial, commodious; with closets to satisfy any Bluebeard, a china-closet in particular that would hold our whole worldly substance converted into china! Two weeks ago there was a row of ancient trees in front, but some crazy-headed Cockneys have uprooted them – behind we have a garden (so called in the language of flattery) in the worst order; but boasting of two vines which produced two bunches of grapes, in the season, which 'might be eaten'; and a walnut-tree from which I have gathered almost sixpence worth of walnuts. 'This large and comfortable tenement' we have, *without bugs*, for some two or three pounds more rent than we paid for the pepper box at Comely Bank. This comes of our noble contempt for fashion – Chelsea being highly unfashionable. The only practical disadvantage in this circumstance is that we are far from most of our acquaintance; a disadvantage which I endeavour to obviate by learning to walk. My success is already considerable. I have several times walked ten miles without being laid up. Besides, we are not wholly isolated. Leigh Hunt lives a few doors off. The celebrated Mrs Somerville is at Chelsea Hospital within five minutes walk, and Mrs Austin is coming to introduce me to her to-morrow – and within a mile I have a *circle* of acquaintances ...

Your truly attached Friend
Jane W. Carlyle

A DAY WITH HER MOTHER

62. To Thomas Carlyle at Scotsbrig

12 October 1835

... I have not been a day in bed since you went – have indeed been almost quite free of headache and all other aches, and every body says Mrs Carlyle begins to look better – and what every body says must be true. With this improved health every thing becomes tolerable, even to the peesweep Sereetha (for we are still without other help). Now that I do not see *you* driven desperate with the chaos, I can take a quiet view of it, and even reduce it to some degree of order. Mother and I have fallen naturally into a fair division of labour, and we keep a very tidy house. Sereetha has attained the unhoped-for perfection of getting up at half after six *of her own accord*, lighting the parlour fire, and actually placing the breakfast things (nil desperandum me duce!). I get up at half after seven and prepare the coffee and bacon-ham (which is the life of me, making me always the hungrier the more I eat of it). Mother in the interim makes her bed and sorts her room. After breakfast, Mother descends to the inferno, where she jingles and scours and from time to time scolds Sereetha; till all is right and tight there. I, above stairs, sweep the parlour, blacken the grate – make the room look cleaner than it has been since the days of Grace Macdonald – then mount aloft to make my own bed (for I was resolved to enjoy the privilege of having a bed of my own) then clean myself (as the servants say) and sit down to my Italian lesson. A bit of meat roasted at the oven suffices two days cold and does not plague us with cookery. Sereetha can fetch up tea things, and the porridge is easily made on the parlour fire – the kitchen one being allowed to go out (for economy) when the pee-sweep retires to bed at eight o'clock . . .

A 'LITERARY' DAY

63. To Jeannie Welsh at Liverpool

August 1844?

. . . With my improved health the standard of my occupations has proportionately elevated itself. I sat down the other day to a deter-mined critical reading of Voss's *Homer* – the only translation which gives a person ignorant of the Greek any adequate idea of the real Homer. I am horribly rusted in my German I find, so that I get on with it very slowly, but the task is very well worth the pains. *That* employs two or three hours in the morning. Then I am translating – or to speak accurately – I have *bought foolscap for translating* something which I did one half of, years ago, and which I should like to see in print before I die. Then I am making extensive and enlightened repairs of the household linen! I *mean* to have a piano! – and *I think* a great deal! Perhaps like the old woman at Haddington, I also '*repent* a great deal'. But I do not *cultivate* that branch of morality. I have always indeed considered *remorse* the most wasteful of all the virtues, devouring a great deal of good faculty which might be turned to practical account . . .

EARTHQUAKING

64. To Jeannie Welsh at Liverpool

5 Cheyne Row, Chelsea/ 12 July 1843

Dearest Babbie,

The sympathy between us continues to be perfect in all respects – both materially and morally – to a degree unprecedented I really believe except in the case of the *Siamese twins*! Unfortunately it is not oftenest sympathy in bliss! at this moment? – Oh good Heavens, after all! – The unspeakable is going on in this house! – Every morning at six of the clock a legion of devils rush in under the forms of Carpen-ters, Painters, whitewashers, and non-descript apprentice-lads who grind, grind, grind, with pumice-stones, and saunter up and down the stairs whistling and singing as if I had hired them to keep me in *music*! – At the first sound of this *Legion* spreading itself over the premises, I spring out of bed – dash down stairs, and 'in wera desperation' take a shower-bath! – After which I feel more up to standing the noise – and smell, and hideous discomfort! I am oil-painting the staircase and passages and the wood of the Library – so you may conceive the smell in this warm weather! Sterling predicts my *death* in consequence – various persons remonstrate against my staying – above all sleeping – in it – but what can I do? If I were not here to look after what is a-doing I can see that there would be fifty blunders made – and to leave Helen alone during the night – or to bring any stranger in to keep her company while the house is in such disorder would be equally inexpedient – 'death' indeed were to be avoided on any terms and if I saw *that* likely to ensue I would accept a sleeping room in Sterling's house – but by keeping my bed room door always closed and sleeping with the two windows wide open I do not feel the smell very bad thro' the night – 'And *the thieves* Cousin? two wide-open windows and plenty of ladders lying quite handy in the court underneath them?' – My dear, when one is painting and papering one's house, one has no time to think of thieves! – It did occur to me last night in lying down, that 'heavy bodies' [A phrase of Helen's] might drop in thro' the night and be at my pillow before I heard them – but my nerves are pretty strong at present – I took the precaution to lay the Policeman's rattle on the spare pillow – and went to sleep without thinking more about them – a curious contrast to Mr Lambert next door – father of the young pianists – who sleeps in the back room of the ground floor – 'for protection to his house' – he told me – and besides his quick-eared dog has ever in readiness a loaded gun – pistols he says are 'worth nothing in such cases'. I told him that rather than pass my life in such a state of armed defence, I would adopt Darwin's plan of leaving all the plate &c. every night on the lobby table – I told him also of your screams of delight in seeing 'a small cannon' carried into his house last year – and thinking what an unexpected reception the next thieving party was likely to encounter. He laughed himself till the tears ran down but told me 'the small cannon' was a small steam engine – he seems to be some sort of military engineer. All this passed between us yesterday morning when in return for an amiable note of regrets about the noise &c. which I had felt it polite to write to him, he came himself to assure me 'he had never heard the noise' – and to *offer me 'his protection'* – (in the virtuous sense of the word of course) – from all he said, he left me with the idea that *he* stood much more in need of *my* protection than I did of *his* . . .

Your own

J.C.

BUGS IN HELEN'S BED

65. TO THOMAS CARLYLE AT SCOTSBRIG

5 Cheyne Row, Chelsea/ 18 August 1843

Dearest

. . . You ask the state of the house. Pearson and Co. *are* out of it. *Both the public rooms* are in a state of perfect habitableness again – a little still to be done in the needlework department, but nothing (like Dodger's Boy's nose) 'to speak of'. Your bedroom, of which the ceiling had to be whitened and the paint washed, &c. &c., will be habitable by tomorrow. The front bedrooms into which all the confusion had been piled are still to clean – but that will soon be done. My own bedroom also needs to have the carpet beaten and the bed-curtains taken down and brushed; all this would have been completed by this time but for a most unexpected and soul-sickening mess which I discovered in the kitchen – which has caused work for several days. Only fancy, while I was brightening up the outside of the platter to find in Helen's bed a new colony of bugs!! I tell you of it fearlessly *this time*, as past victory gives me a sense of superiority over the creatures. She said to me one morning in putting down my breakfast, '*My*! I was just standing this morning, looking up at the corner of my bed, ye ken, and there what should I see but two *bogues* – I hope there's nae more.' 'You *hope*? said I immediately kindling into a fine phrenzy; 'how could you live an instant without making sure? A pretty thing it will be if you have let your bed get full of bugs again!' The shadow of an accusation of remissness was enough of course to make her quite *positive*. 'How was *she* ever to have thought of *bogues*, formerly? *What a thing to think about*! But *since*, she had been just *most particular*! To be sure these two must have come off these Mudies' shawls!'[1] I left her protesting and appealing to posterity, and ran off myself to see into the business. She had not so much as taken off the curtains – I tore them off distractedly – pulled in pieces all of the bed that was pullable, and saw and

---

[1] The Mudies were two sisters, left in straitened circumstances, whom Jane befriended and tried to find employment for.

killed *two*, and in one place which I could not get at without a bed-key, *beings* (as Mazzini would say) were clearly *moving*!! Ah, mercy mercy, my dismay was considerable! Still it was not the acme of horror this time, as last time, for now I knew they *could* be annihilated root and branch. When I told her there were plenty; she went off to look herself, and came back and told me with a peremptory note that '*she* had looked and there was not a single *bogue* there!' It was needless arguing with a wild animal. I had Pearson to take the bed down, and he soon gave me the pleasant assurance that 'they were pretty strong!' Neither did he consider them a *recent importation*.

Helen went out of the way at the taking down of the bed, not to be proved in the wrong to her own conviction – which was 'probably just as well', as she might have saved a remnant in her petticoats, being so utterly careless about the article. Pearson, who shared all my own *nervous sensibility*, was a much better assistant for me. I flung some twenty pailfulls of water on the kitchen floor, in the first place, to drown any that might attempt to save themselves – then we killed all that were discoverable, and flung the pieces of the bed, one after another, into a great tub full of water, carried them up into the garden, and let them steep there two days – and then I *painted* all the joints – had the curtains washed and laid by for the present, and hope and trust there is not one escaped alive to tell. *Ach Gott*, what disgusting work to have to do! – but the destroying of bugs is a thing that cannot be delegated. In the course of the bug investigation I made another precious discovery. That her woollen mattress was getting itself absolutely eaten from under her with moths. *That* had to be torn up next, all the wool washed and boiled and teazed – and I have a woman here this day making it up into a mattress again. I have small apprehension of bugs anywhere else. In *your* bed I had *ocular conviction* that there were none, when it was in pieces; in my *own* I have inferential conviction, for they would have been sure to bite *me* the very *first* Adam and Eve of them; in the front room nothing is discoverable either – but I shall take that bed all down for security's sake before I have done with it – either *that*, or go up and *sleep in it a night* – but then imagination might deceive me, and even cause spots! 'The troubles that afflict the just', &c.

We have warm weather these two days – not oppressive for *me*, but more summer-like than any that has been this season.

Oh, I always forgot to tell you that in the railway carriage going to Ryde my next neighbour was Robert Owen (the Socialist); he did not know anything of me, so that I had the advantage of him. I found something of old Laing in him, particularly the voice. I like him on the whole, and in proof thereof gave him two carnations.

Your affectionate
Goody

NEW EARTHQUAKES COMMANDED

66. To Jeannie Welsh at Liverpool

5 Cheyne Row, Chelsea/ 2 October 1843

... My husband has been returned this fortnight back, and since then I have not written to you – have not written to anyone – have not *done* anything except occasionally mend my stockings and read in the dreamy novels by the Gräfin Hahn Hahn (Countess Cock cock! What a name!) She is a sort of German George Sand *without the genius* – and *en revanche* a good deal more of what we call in Scotland *gumption* – a clever woman, really – separated from her husband of course, and on the whole very good to read when one is in a state of moral and physical collapse. For the rest nothing can exceed this great city in these weeks, for absence of all earthly objects of interest! Even Darwin has been gone for a month! – the last to go. But I had the pleasure of meeting him yesterday in Cadogan Place, having returned the night before. To give you the most striking illustration that occurs to me of the desert state of things; I saw the other day a little girl of six years old playing her hoop in the centre of Piccadilly!! A cab *did* come at last and as nearly as possible ran over her – but skipping from under the horse's belly, literally, she recommenced her hoop-playing, with the same assiduity as before.

And within doors is not a whit more gay I can assure you than without. Carlyle returned, as usual from his journeyings in quest of health, as bilious and out of sorts as he went away. Blue pill with castor-oil 'and the usual trimmings' had to be taken at the very out-set, then by the time the distress of *that* was over it was time to be feeling the intolerable influences of – London!

The house was approved of as much as I had flattered myself it would be – and between ourselves he would have been a monster if he had not exhibited some admiration more or less at my magnificent improvements effected at such small cost – *to him*. The upstairs room is now a really beautiful little drawing room with a sofa – easy chair – ottoman – cushions – stools – every conceivable luxury! – all covered

– and all the chairs covered also – with a buff and red chintz made by my own hands ! ! ! Mrs Carlyle's picture is over the mantelpiece – but then yours and my uncle's are on the mid wall with Jean Paul between – and you cannot think how beautiful you both look on the pretty new paper.

All this and his own bedroom new carpeted and smartened up amazingly – to say nothing of the old big press in the china closet transformed by the female genius into a glorious resplendent Chinese-cabinet! could not fail to yield him 'a certain' satisfaction and obtain me some meed of praise – but – alas alas – never can one get out of the shadow of that *but*! – but after two or three days he began to find 'there was no getting on in that upstairs room for want of the closet or some equivalent to fling one's confusion in'!! – 'best to accumulate no confusion' said I – 'Oh there must be a place for keeping all sorts of papers for a *year* or so, till one has made up one's mind what to burn and what not'! This was a first ground for quarrel with the room – and then – oh then – one day when he had been home about [a] week Miss Lambert took a fit of playing – the *first* – but that only made it the more intolerable – for he had fallen into a false security through her prolonged silence. The next day again she played half an hour in the morning which was sufficient to set all his nerves up for the rest of the day – and it was solemnly declared that 'no life of Cromwell or any other book could ever be written alongside of that damnable noise'. Then Mr Chancellor's cock had awoke him, he said, at six for two mornings (he had not however come down to breakfast till ten) and 'that bedroom was uninhabitable' – 'Could one get a piece of ground to build some *crib of a* house upon at the Isle of Wight, did I think?' – In fact just all the old eternal story commenced again! – I must fetch back Pearson to *consult* about the possibility of excluding noise – etc., etc., in the meanwhile.

Accordingly Pearson was here yesterday – kept in consultation for *three* hours! the whole result being plenty of *possibilities* – and a positive order for a pair of window boards to be all stuffed with cotton! to fasten on the back windows or the front (viz. in *your* room) at pleasure – and as these will prevent the sleeping with windows *open*, zinc pipes are to be introduced thro' the walls to let in a sufficiency of fresh air! You are to observe by the way that it is only when the windows are wide open that this distant cock ever makes itself heard and – that the simple expedient which Pearson suggested – of *shutting the window* and *opening the door* would have solved the problem effectively and much more cheaply than all this apparatus of stuffed shutters and zinc pipes! But then if the shutters make even the front room quiet enough for *him* to sleep in – and the zinc pipe brings in air enough for *him* to breathe; the piano-problem is also solved! for his present bedroom where alone the piano-noise is not clearly audible, is to be converted into his study – the partition taken down between the two front rooms, that the *two* four-posted beds may have room to stand up *there*! Until we can get a lease of the house (which is not procurable) and then a *silent* room, *twenty feet long, lighted from above*, is to be built on the roof!!!

So here is a quite other prospect than that of quiet order which I was looking forward to for the next twelve months at least! And I assure you it is with a heart-rending sigh that I resign myself to the thought of lifting and altering all the carpets again, before they have been well down, and having carpenters plasterers and white-washers as before, besides the inconvenience of having one's spare room as it were annihilated – for could *you* for instance sleep in a double-bedded room with Carlyle? However there may be many plans before a definitive one gets *carried into effect* – and anyhow I cannot help it – and at least as Darwin says I 'have always the consolation of knowing that he will need some *new* arrangements in six months or so'. – But indeed Babbie if you saw how pretty the upstairs floor is in its actual state and knew all the toil and scheming I had in bringing it into such order you would not wonder that I am fretted. Your room too with the blue carpet from his bedroom (his had got the drawing-room one) and the position of the bed altered looked so like the Templand bedroom – all the little things in it arranged as they were *there* – that one could almost deceive oneself into its being the same – and all this to be overturned. Well well, I cannot help it and what *is* the use of talking – *such* woes are but very petty ones after all! . . .

Your own

J.C.

NEW EARTHQUAKES EXECUTED

67. To Jeannie Welsh at Liverpool

5 Cheyne Row, Chelsea/ 25 October 1843

. . . When that letter arrived hoping that my troubles would pass over with the blue pill – I was already up to the ears in them – Pearson with his troop of incarnate fiends carpenters bricklayers

whitewashers plasterers had already spread themselves *per ogni dove* –
and Helen, at sight of such unexpected finale to her cleaning labours,
had been struck with a temporary idiocy – so that I had to follow her
about and supply her with wits as well as with active help at every
turn, and with such heart as you can imagine – besides having to
ward off the deluge of confusion from the man himself – who conducted himself on the occasion much like a half-conjuror – finding
that he had not the counter-spell to allay the storm which himself had
raised, he raged and lamented and all but rent his garments and
tore his hair. The front bedrooms were to have been thrown into one
in *two* days according to Pearson – in *ten* days the workmen had
finished there! – then the room had to be instantly fitted up for
Carlyle's sleeping room – at least so long as the people should be
breaking out a chimney and instituting a small fireplace in his dressing
room, which last plan had dawned on his mind as the probablest
escape from the pianoforte – another *week* they were messing *there* –
Carlyle unable to sleep in the new room – not for noise – his *stuffed*
window shutters fastened on with as many screws and bolts as if they
were for the windows of a mad house almost wholly exclude all noise
from the street – but merely from the nervousness always incident
with him on 'finding himself in a new position'. There were wander-
ings about during the night – fires kindled with his own hands, bread
and butter eaten in the china-closet! all sorts of what shall I say –
strange things upon my honour done – and I all the while lying awake
listening with a bouncing heart but *afraid* to meddle with him – even
to offer any assistance. Then the sort of days sure to follow that sort
of nights! I will not try to *describe* – to have overlived them was
botheration enough – no sooner were the workmen out of the dressing
room than back he must be moved bag and baggage into his old
bedroom – and at this point of the business I caught a fine rheumatism in the back of my head and shoulders – in consequence of spending a whole forenoon in papering the broken parts of the plaster and
all the afternoon of the same day in nailing carpets – *that* is a thing
that Helen *can not* do – and the hands of me are absolutely blackened
and coarsified with the quantity of it I have had to transact this
season. To make the mess still thicker, the dining-room grate which
you may remember was a perpetual source of execration, was
finally voted insupportable for another twenty-four hours – another
must be got – and then – as all our things are never to be made like
other people's but on some *superior* plan of our own – the new grate –
with cover of Dutch tiles – needed ever so much of the chimney to be

pulled down and a man building and plastering at it for two days and a half – of course all the carpets and furniture of that beautifully clean room had to be removed also. Ten days ago I nailed down the carpets of *it* – and readjusted the things and today I have nailed down all the stair and passage carpets – at last. There is still a good piece of work for me in the front bedroom which will be all the fitter for your and our visitors' reception in consequence of what it has undergone – but if he had only allowed me to do these things when I was about it in the summer it would have spared a world of fash [bother] – and such a sickening feeling towards 'household good' as I do not remember ever in my life before to have experienced. I am physically ill of the long continued discomfort and the cinderella labours in which I have had to put forth the activity of a maid of all-work – along with improvisation and inventive faculty of a woman of genius.

The fact is I have spoiled Mr C. – I have accustomed him to have all wants supplied 'without visible means' until he has forgotten how much head and hands it takes to supply the common resource of a good round outlay of money. When one had not any money – it was all well – I never grudged my work – but now that we have enough to live on, it would be good sense in him to say 'get in a carpenter to nail your carpets' and a few other such considerate suggestions. No matter, I shall get my hands kept clean and put into mitts for a time so soon as I have patched together a carpet for the new bedroom – and will lie on the sofa, by heaven, for two weeks and read French novels!

It was not that I was so *eternally* in motion from morning till night that I could not write to you – one can always find a half hour during which it is possible to sit still if one looks for it, but my temper was so bad that I could not compose it to write even to you – and as I have said my health has been bad as well as my temper – indeed these two things with me pretty invariably go with one another.

I will tell you of all the rest – that is about people &c. &c. next time. Write you little false hearted gipsy. Love to them all.

Ever your affectionate

Jane Carlyle

THE RENOVATION OF NUMBER 5

68. CARLYLE'S HEADNOTE TO THE LETTERS DESCRIBING THE UPROAR

This was the year [1852] (only first year, alas!) of repairing our house; 'architect' (Helps's) was 'Mr Morgan', a very honest man, and with workmen honest though inexpert; he himself had no talent for managing the chaos he created here, and indeed he at length fell sick, and left it to end by collapse. My own little heroine was manager, eye, inventress, commandress, guiding head and soul of everything; and made (witness this drawing-room, and compare it with the original, *i.e.* with every other in the street) a real triumph of what without her would have been a puddle of wasteful failure. She feared no toil howsoever unfit for her, had a marked 'talent in architecture' too – in fact, the universal talent of applying intellect, veracity, and courage to things gone awry for want of those qualities. My noble darling! few women have had such an outfit of talent, far fewer such a loving nobleness and truth of heart to urge it into action and guide it there. Meanwhile, to escape those horrors of heat and dust, I fled (or indeed was dismissed) to Linlathen, to my excellent T. Erskine's, where I morbidly and painfully stayed three weeks, gentlest and best of hospitality able to do little for me. I remember trying to bathe in the summer mornings – bad bathing coast. Most of my leisure went in translating what is now the Appendix to *Friedrich*, vol. vii of 2nd edition.

69. TO MRS RUSSELL AT THORNHILL

5 Cheyne Row, Chelsea/ 13 July 1852

Dearest Mrs Russell

I might be excused for forgetting my own birthday this time, and even my own *name* and address, and everything about me, except the one terrific fact that I am in a house under what is called 'thorough repair'! – Having never had to do with London workmen, you cannot form any adequate idea of the thing. Workmen who spend three-fourths of their time in *consulting how the work should be done* and in going out and in after 'beer', were not, at least, in my day, *known* in Scotland; and then a thorough *repair*, complicated by the altering of chimneys and partitions and by heat at eighty two degrees in the shade, were a wild piece of work with any sort of workmen! The Builder promised to have all done in six weeks, painting included – if he get done in six *months* it is as much as I hope! – Meanwhile I run about in the great heat, carrying all my furniture in my arms from one room to another – and sleep or rather *lie about* like a dog, just where I see a cleared space. I am needed here to keep the workmen from falling into continual mistakes; but why Mr Carlyle who is anything rather than *needed* stays on, I can't imagine. Nor do I know when I shall get away nor where I shall go. We were to have gone both of us to Germany but that is all knocked on the head now – at least for the present. If you saw me sitting in the midst of falling bricks and clouds of lime dust, and a noise as of battering-rams, you wouldn't wonder that I should make my letter brief . . .

And now to the business: will you lay out five shillings on old Mary in some judicious way for me, and will you give my little packet to Margaret,[1] and tell them I still think of them both kindly . . .

Ever affectionately yours,

Jane Welsh Carlyle

70. To Thomas Carlyle at Linlathen, Dundee

27 July 1852

. . . Now *you* are not here to point out the horrors of every thing so eloquently, I don't care the least in the world about the noise, or the dust, or the tumble heels over head of the whole house. All I am concerned about is to get it rapidly on – which as Builders and Builders men are at present constituted, seems pretty much of an impossibility.

Yesterday I wrote to Mr Morgan to take back the third carpenter and bestow him on somebody with more patience and a less correct eye than myself. But it's worse than useless plaguing you, in your cool clean retirement there with the worries from which you have just fled away. Best you should forget the sound of our hammering altogether – so I will henceforth fight my own battle with the house, without saying a word about it . . .

[1] Old Mary Mills and Margaret Hiddlestone were her mother's two maids, whom Jane regularly remembered with gifts of money and tea.

71. To Thomas Carlyle at Scotsbrig

10 August 1852

. . . Oh, my Dear! what a comfortless letter! In your last from Linlathen you said you were 'decidedly better', and now you seem to be again 'all nohow'! I hope it has only been the fag of the journey. Don't fret about the house; it is getting on pretty fast now, and will be satisfactory when finished. For my part I am got quite used to the disturbance, and begin to like the, what shall I say? – *excitement* of it – to see something *going on* and to help its going on – fulfils a great want of my nature. I have prevented so many mistakes being made, and afforded so many capital suggestions, that I begin to feel rather proud of myself, and to suspect I must have been a *Builder* in some previous state of existence. The Painter is my chief delight; he does his work so thoroughly; he is only in your bedroom as yet, but he has rubbed it all down with pumice stone, till it looks as smooth as paper. And I have never been at all inconvenienced by any smell! Perhaps the house may be *habitable* a week or two sooner than I guessed, tho' I hardly think the workmen will be fairly out of it sooner. I shall 'see my way' better next week. The weather is capital for drying both paint and plaster – that is *one* blessing! My *half* of the low room is kept always tidy – the bedding, and tables with their legs in the air, as if in convulsions, which show themselves *above* the screen, often make me laugh. When the noise is *very* great I *practise* on the piano! I do quite well, in short; and don't see how I can be spared till things are done to my mind, and the chaotic heaps of furniture restored to their proper places. Decidedly nobody but myself can do *that* . . .

R. TAIT'S 'A CHELSEA INTERIOR'

72. To Mrs Russell at Thornhill

20 November 1857

My dearest Mary
. . . My chief impediment has been that weary Artist who took the bright idea last Spring that he would make a picture of our sitting room[1] – to be 'amazingly interesting to Posterity a hundred

---

[1] *A Chelsea Interior* by R. Tait, reproduced on the jacket.

years hence.' I little knew what I was committing myself to when I let him begin. – For the three months before I went to Scotland, he came and painted twice a week; while I was in Scotland he came four times a week; and for the last six weeks has has been overstanding me like a night-mare *every day*!! except when, please God, the fog is so black that he can't *see*! These lower rooms are where I have been always used to live *at this season*; and to keep up fire there, and in the drawingroom as well – besides in Mr C.'s study at the top of the house, is a great expence, when coals are seven and twenty shillings a cart load; and is also a great *trouble* to one servant. So I have kept my ground hitherto; always hoping he would get done – but my Heavens! he will make this great 'Work of Art' last him into 1860, I begin to think! A whole day painting at my portfolio! Another whole day over my workbox and so on. Not the minutest object in these three rooms, opening into one another, but what is getting itself represented with Vandyke fidelity! And all the while the floor *won't* be *flat* for the life of him. I suspect he aims at more than post-humous fame from this picture: hopes, perhaps, some admirer of Mr C.'s, with more money than wit to guide it, may give him a thousand pounds for Mr C.'s 'Interior' – the portraits of Mr C. himself, and Mr C.'s wife, and Mr C.'s dog inclusive! The dog is the only member of the family who has reason to be pleased with his likeness as yet! – This will be the second time my dog has appeared in the Exhibition! . . .

V Upstairs and downstairs

'I think, talk and write about my own servants as much as Geraldine does about her lovers', Jane is reported to have said. And so she does! Her letters are as full of her searches for the 'perfect treasure', the 'jewel', of a housemaid, as they are of her frustrations when she has tried them all and found them wanting.

An endless parade winds its way through Comely Bank, Craigenputtoch and Cheyne Row as one adventure follows another. During her thirty-two years at Cheyne Row she had successively thirty-nine servants – a single maid-of-all-work for twenty-six of these years and then both a cook and a housemaid for the last six. They slept in the dark, chilly, stone-flagged basement at Number 5 until the very end of her life, when Carlyle's evacuation of his study under the roof, after the completion of *Frederick the Great*, offered the alternative of being frozen in winter or roasted in summer at a higher elevation. There were farm girls from Fife and East Lothian, mutinous, savage Irishwomen, teen-age waifs from the hovels of Victorian London – all of them acutely observed by a too demanding employer who wanted to improve their minds and take them to her bosom. How bewildering many of them must have found her!

Carlyle thought that the first servant they ever had was the best of the lot. This was Grace Macdonald, at Comely Bank, whose definition of a 'thorough Lady' was one 'who had not entered her own kitchen for seven years' – a prescription which Jane often ruefully recalled but could never have observed herself. When the neat little terrace house in Edinburgh was exchanged for the isolated farm at Craigenputtoch, troubles began. She tells Mrs Carlyle how Betty disappeared in 'an explosion', how the next one was 'as deaf as a door-nail' and the third 'as ignorant as a sucking child'. There would be many a similar tale of woe.

Bessy Barnet, who, with Chico, the canary, Jane and Thomas, made up the party of four that drove up to Number 5, Cheyne Row in 1834, was an engaging exception. A burst of song from Chico, as the hackney-coach crossed Belgrave Square, proved a good omen for downstairs as well as upstairs, but before the year was out, Bessy had to go back to Scotland to take care of her family. She later married a Doctor Blakiston, the second son of a baronet, and returned in 1863 to offer her husband's services at St Leonards, the south coast resort, to a desperately-ill Jane. Carlyle called her 'our romantic maid'. Her successors would have their affairs, but none would be so blessed as Bessy!

Between Bessy's departure in 1834 and Helen Mitchell's arrival in 1837 nothing succeeded. Jane Ireland, who was found reading *Wilhelm Meister* by an unscoured grate, was sent home as incompetent. Impartial justice was meted out to an Irish Protestant and an Irish Catholic, each of whom was dismissed in a matter of weeks, though only the latter got Carlyle's personal attention: 'To your room at once; wages tomorrow morning; disappear!' Sarah Heather, contracted to 'Sereetha', reminded them of the lapwing on their Scottish moors with its ineffectual flight and its mournful cry of 'Peesweep!' 'Peesweep' she became, until she, too, flew away. Anne Cook came from Annandale, had 'a misfortune' in the big city, and was sent back to Scotland, with a 'God alone can help her!'

Ellen, her successor, seemed a 'sweet girl' and lasted six months.

It was Helen Mitchell, from Kirkcaldy, who made history. Carlyle notes: She stayed with us about eleven years and was, in a sense, the only servant we ever got to belong to us, and be one of our household, in this place . . . A very curious little being; mixture of shrewdness, accurate observancy, flashes of an insight almost genial, with utter simplicity and even folly. A singular humble loyalty and genuine attachment to her mistress never failed in poor Helen as the chief redeeming virtues. Endless was her mistress's amusement (among other feelings) with the talk and ways of this poor Helen . . . [her sayings] were to me also among the most amusing things I ever heard.

From her arrival in 1837 to her final departure in 1849, Jane's letters are full of 'Helenisms'. 'How expensive!' was Helen's comment on a picture of the Virgin, when Jane took her to the National Gallery, 'How dilatory!' was her favourite word for the English weather. Helen read a lot; had opinions; was the strangest mixture of philosopher and perfect idiot; the very faithfullest of mortals. Once when Jane was writhing in the agonies of a migraine, and Helen could do nothing for her mistress, she rubbed her cheek against Jane's, as if she were a little child, and Jane found it wet with tears. But she drank; and drink undid her in the end.

There is an interval of two years, 1846–8, when it looked as if life might be kind to Helen. She left Cheyne Row to look after her brother, who sounded as if he might be doing well for himself as a manufacturer of coach-fringe in Dublin; but she quarrelled with him and returned to the Carlyles. A few months later she was dismissed, after a final bout with the bottle. Jane got her other positions in London, but she could not keep them and went back to Kirkcaldy. Without the love of her mistress to keep her sober, she tried to drown herself, was dragged from the river, but died a few months later.

Helen was followed, as she had been preceded, by another succession of disasters. While she was in Ireland there was Isabella, nicknamed *Pessima* by Carlyle – 'the Worst!' then a nameless 'Old Half-Dead Slowcoach'; after her, Chelsea Anne, who stayed until Helen's return and left to marry a butcher. After Helen's final departure came a 'loveable' but soon to be 'dreadful' Elizabeth; Emma, who roasted fowls with their crops in; and finally Irish Fanny, a dashing creature, who eloped with a labourer after being 'exploded' by Carlyle – probably the labourer who, 'ignorant that lath and plaster was not a floor', came plunging down into Carlyle's bedroom until he caught himself by the arm-pits, fast swinging, 'astonished in the vortex of old laths, lime, and dust'.

Next after Helen Mitchell for permanence was Anne III – 'a thoroughly good respectable woman – the best character I ever had in the house'. Appearing first in 1851 she returned in the summer of 1853 to replace Irish Fanny and stayed five years before Jane dismissed her. 'Little Charlotte', a fifteen-year-old whom Jane treated as a daughter, lasted three years, 1858–61, but was cherished as friend and protégé as long as Jane lived.

Not for nothing did Jane say to Louisa, Lady Ashburton, 'So much of one's comfort depends on one's servants (the more's the pity) that if I followed the dictates of *Nature*, my next question to anyone dear to me, after asking, "how are you?"

would be "what sort of servants have you got?" The 'cares of bread' grew no lighter with two servants than they had been with one. Old Jane, who was one of them for a month in 1860, was 'an arrant old humbug' who could not speak a word of truth, could not cook, and decamped with eight bottles of ale. Tall Charlotte lasted three months. Matilda was rushed to the hospital with a strangulated hernia after one month. Margaret managed a year. There was a prodigious downstairs row in 1863, with its inevitable dismissals, and an even more monstrous betrayal of trust in 1864, when a treacherous Mary gave birth to an illegitimate child in the famous crockery pantry, now a small room at the end of the dining room, while an innocent Carlyle was sharing a cup of tea with Geraldine Jewsbury in the adjoining room. And all this in the depths of Jane's illness, when she was under Dr Blakiston's care at St Leonards-on-Sea.

The knaves were sacked. A respectable widow of fifty, Mrs Warren, was installed in November, 1864, to outlast her mistress, while Jessie Hiddlestone, the daughter of her mother's old servant, was brought from Thornhill to be the second servant. Jessie was less appreciative of Jane's kindness than Jane expected her to be, but the whole household, including Silvester, Carlyle's coachman, was ecstatic at the news of Carlyle's Rectorial triumph in 1866 and plunged into desolation by Jane's death.

Why had Jane so much trouble? It is not enough to talk about temperament. Her mother was notorious for her vagaries, but she kept a servant like Betty Braid until she became a member of the family and Jane's own life-long friend. Jane thought enviously of other Haddington servants like Mrs Davidson's Mary Jeffreys, who had 'served her mistress with the same relish for fifty years'. It was certainly not lack of feeling; she sent gifts to her mother's old servants with religious regularity as long as they lived and longed to feel the same concern for her own. It was not impracticality; she demonstrated her efficiency as a manager every time she undertook an 'earthquaking'. Nor was it just Carlyle, though she often said, 'with no Husband to *study*, housekeeping is mere play'. A cynic might suggest that being an avid collector of people, as others might collect coins or butterflies, she was constantly driven to enlarge the collection. But there was more to it than that.

Being as clever as she was, and as impatient at having to spend so much of her time and thought on 'these mean perplexities', she sometimes put her finger on her own problems: 'If I could give over watching her!' she says of Maria, her housemaid in 1862, 'But when one has so little communication with the outerworld – above all with the outer *air* it is difficult to avoid occupying oneself morbidly with the affairs within doors.' Or again, in speaking of Jessie Hiddlestone: 'As a Servant, she is better than the average, as a woman, I do not think *ill* of her; but I mistook her entirely at the first, and see less good in her than perhaps there is, because I began by seeing far *more* good in her than she had the least pretension to. At my age, and with my experience, it would have well beseemed me to be less romantic!'

Once more it was the romantic, sentimental, self-pitying side of Jane that got in the way of her common sense. She notes in a letter to Mrs Russell of 16 October 1865 that Carlyle gets on famously with Jessie Hiddlestone. She 'is ready to *fly* at his word. Perhaps one reason why she is better for *him* than for the rest of us, is that *he* never pays the slightest regard to a servants *humours*; remains sublimely unconscious of them, so long as he gets his bidding done!'

But if Jane's problems were complicated by her enthusiasms, they were also part of the universal experience. The lot of a 'maid-of-all-work', living in the basement or the attic of a Victorian house, rising at five, drawing water from a well in her flag-stoned cellar, carrying coals up as many as four flights of stairs and slops down them, washing clothes, cooking, cleaning, answering door-bells, and responding to every other beck and call until long after nightfall, seems grim enough to be an occasion for drink. It was a lonely post. 'Followers' were thought to lead to 'misfortunes' and sternly discouraged in most households; maids 'scrambled for their living' out of what was provided for those above stairs; wages were meagre. Anne III, 'a higher grade servant' than the Carlyles had hitherto employed, was paid sixteen pounds a year; Fanny had been paid thirteen; most of the others had twelve – this at a time when the Bullers were paying more than a pound a week for Jane's board and lodging at a good hotel. The threat of a 'warning' (a month's notice) without a 'character' (a reference) might keep rebellion down, but it could not extinguish it. Harriet, Lady Ashburton, with her thirty household servants at the Grange, might be spared rows and explosions; but high and low below-stairs expected to make their 'betters' suffer in little ways. It was perhaps the chief pleasure in their obscure and often tragic lives.

HELEN: DISMISSING, THEN FORGIVING HER

73. To Mrs Carlyle at Scotsbrig

5 Cheyne Row, Chelsea/ Autumn 1840

Dear Mother,

. . . At present I have got a rather heavy burden on my shoulders, the guarding of a human being from the perdition of strong liquors. My poor little Helen has been gradually getting more and more into the habit of tippling – until, some fortnight ago, she rushed down into a fit of the most decided drunkenness that I ever happened to witness. Figure the head of the Mystic School and a delicate female like myself up till after three in the morning, trying to get the maddened creature to bed; not daring to leave her at large for fear she should set fire to the house or cut her own throat. Finally, we got her *bolted* into the back kitchen, in a corner of which she had established herself all coiled up and *fuffing* like a young tiger about to make a spring, or like *the Bride of Lammermoor* (if you ever read that profane book).

Next day she looked black with shame and despair; and the day following, overcome by her tears and promises and self-upbraidings, I forgave her again, very much to my own surprise. About *half an hour* after this forgiveness had been accorded I called to her to make me some batter – it was long of coming – and I rang the bell – no answer. I went down to the kitchen to see the meaning of all this delay – and the meaning was very clear; my penitent was lying on the floor, dead-drunk, spread out like the three legs of Man [The Isle of Man], with a chair upset beside her, and in the midst of a perfect chaos of dirty dishes and fragments of broken crockery; the whole scene was a lively epitome of a place that shall be nameless. And this happened at ten in the morning! All that day she remained lying on the floor insensible, or occasionally sitting up like a little bundle of dirt, executing a sort of *whinner*; We could not imagine how she came to be so long of sobering, but it turned out she had a whole bottle of whiskey hidden within reach, to which she crawled till it was finished throughout the day.

After this, of course, I was determined that she should leave. My friends here set to work with all zeal to find me a servant – and a very promising young woman came to stay with me until a permanent character should turn up. This last scene '*transpired*' on the Wednesday; on the Monday she was to sail for Kirkcaldy. All the intervening days, I held out against her pale face, her tears, her despair – but I suffered terribly for I am really much attached to the poor wretch who has no fault under heaven but this one. On the Sunday night I called her up to pay her her wages and to inquire into her future prospects. Her future prospects! it was enough to break any body's heart to hear how she talked of them. It was all over for her on this earth, plainly, if I drove her away from me who alone have any influence with her. Beside me she would struggle – away from me she saw no possibility of resisting what she had come to regard as her Fate. You may guess the sequel – I forgave her a third time, and a last time.

I *could* not deny her this *one* more chance – the creature is so good otherwise. Since then she has abstained from drink, I believe, in *every* shape – finding abstinence, like old Samuel Johnson, easier than temperance – but how long she may be strong enough to persevere in this rigid course, in which lies her only hope, God knows. I am not very sanguine. Meanwhile I feel as if I had adopted a child, I find it necessary to take such an incessant charge of her – bodily and mentally – and my own body and soul generally keep me in work enough, without any such additional responsibility . . .

Affectionately yours,
Jane W. Carlyle

HELEN'S FIDELITY

74. To Mrs Russell at Thornhill

April 1843

. . . Only think! I have still the same little maid. Indeed I need never speak of her *going* again till she be actually *gone*. Nothing could be more determined than I was to part with her that time when I wrote for Margaret. But she absolutely *would not go; would not seek herself a place*! She seems really to have much the same notion of the indissolubility of our relation, that the old Scotch Butler had of his and his Master's, in whose service he had been forty years. When his Master told him his temper was become absolutely insufferable, and they two must positively part, he answered with a look of disdainful astonishment, 'And where the deevil wud ye gang to?' Helen did not exactly ask *me* where I *wud gang to*, but she asked in a tone of the most authoritative remonstrance, 'what would become of me, I should just like to know; fancying *you* ill and *me* not there to take proper care of you? I think *that would* be a *farce*!' To tell her what would become of her under such astonishing circumstances, quite exceeding my gift of prophecy; what could I do but just to bid her 'stay where she was, then; only trying whether she could not behave herself more like a reasonable creature'? And to do her justice, she *has* been a *little* more reasonable latterly . . .

HELEN 'ON LOVE'

75. To Jeannie Welsh at Liverpool

28 May 1843

. . . Poor John! he has recovered his spirits with a rapidity! 'You will see', says Helen, while clearing away the breakfast things the other morning, 'that Mr John Sterling will very soon be married again! – but indeed I don't, for *my* part, think there is any *love* in the world nowadays like what used to long ago! If one hears of it at all it is just *momentary and away*! *There* was No. 4 how soon *she* got over the death of *her* lover! – and Mr Brimlicombe the milkman was married seven months after *his* wife's death! – But I *do* think', she resumed after some interruption of dusting, 'that Mr Carlyle *will be* (admire the tense) a very *desultory widow*! He is so *easily put about* – and seems to take no pleasure *in new females*'! . . .

HELEN'S DEPARTURE FOR IRELAND

76. To Mrs Russell at Thornhill

24 September 1846

. . . My chief object in writing today however is to ask once more about Margaret Hiddlestone. Is there any earthly chance of my getting her *now*? Helen *is* going – this time – for certain – and she could never have gone at a time when I should have been sorrier to lose her. For her conduct during the last year has been quite exemplary. And so, for once, virtue is getting its reward. A Brother in Ireland has been rising into great prosperity as a manufacturer of coach-fringe – thanks to the immense consumption of it on the railways – he has now two hundred girls in his pay, and in point of money (if he tells the truth) quite a *gentleman*. He has never done anything for Helen hitherto beyond coming to see her for *a quarter of an hour* when his business called him to London – never given her to the value of a farthing – but suddenly he is seized with a fit of brotherly love – comes here last evening, and invites her to go to Dublin and be his housekeeper – engaging that should he hereafter *marry* he will settle an ample provision on her. Of course nothing could be done with such an offer but accept it. Helen cries about leaving me – but to be made a Lady of all on a sudden does not fall in one's way every day! For myself, I am far from feeling the confidence *she* does in this Brother's promises and prospects; still I can do no other under the circumstances than encourage her to try this opportunity of providing herself an independent home. And so all that remains is to look out for another in her place . . .

HELEN'S 'UNSPEAKABLE' SUCCESSORS

77. To Mrs Russell at Thornhill

5 Cheyne Row, Chelsea/ End of December 1846

Dearest Mrs Russell

I am recovering out of one of my serious *colds* just in time to write you my New year's good wishes. Nothing could be more inconvenient than my falling ill the very week after my poor little Helen went away – she understood so well how to do with her Master when I was not there, and kept my mind so easy about *material* things that an illness in her time was of comparatively little moment. But with *her* departure every thing went to sixes and sevens. The new maid whom an old servant in Edinburgh had selected for me,[1] proved to have been selected more on account of her pretentions to '*freegrace*' than of any '*works*' she was capable of – in fact, my Aunt Ann, it turned out, had had a hand in her education. If I had only known *that* sooner, she should never have sailed to London at *my* expense! But I relied on the practical understanding which old Betty used to manifest before she became an enthusiast for the free church – and made myself sure of being able to *do* better or worse with any servant of her recommending. Alas – the girl had come out of a family where eight servants were kept – fancied it would be nice to get to London where she had 'seven cousins', and was willing to undertake anything till she got there. And then she satisfied herself within the first twelve hours that it was 'too lonely' to be a single servant – that all-work 'spoiled her hands', and having with all her 'free-grace' no more sense of *duty* than a cat, she threw up her engagement for six months at the end of six days! – and declared that if she were not allowed to depart (to the Cousins) she 'would take fits' as she had 'once done before in a place that did not suit her, and lie in bed for a year' ! ! ! – I being already laid in bed thro' the fatigue and unusual exposure to cold which I had had in trying to set her a-going, the chance of *her* taking to bed was not to be risked. So Carlyle bade her go then in the Devil's name, rather glad to be rid of such a 'lump of selfish dishonest fatuity' on any terms. She 'could not' repay her expenses; so she walked off with her two guineas, as happy as a pig – on a Sunday morning! leaving me very ill in bed, my Cousin Helen here on a visit, and no servant in the house! So much for the whim of bringing a servant from Scotland!

A lady in the neighbourhood who was meaning to discharge her cook at any rate, on account of her constant *rows* with the other servants, goodnaturedly dispatched her to *us* at a moment's warning; and this woman – an old half-dead grumbling soul,[2] but a degree better than nothing, has been acting as a provisional Help, till I should get well enough to look out for a permanent and more effective one . . .

Now I have engaged a girl whose face and history so far as I know

---

[1] This was 'Pessima', selected by Betty Braid.
[2] This was 'Slowcoach'.

it promise well. She is to come the last day in the year, and I am brutally sending my cousin home the same day, that I may have a fair chance at *settling* the newcomer into her *place* myself – full time, for Carlyle has been giving signs of having reached the limits of his human patience – and if he do not soon have a pair of shoes cleaned for him, and his Library swept, he also will 'take fits'. Oh how I wish that Margaret had come to me! All this would have been spared us, even my illness, for I was *quite well* of cold when that horrid free-church woman arrived, and might have continued so with proper care of myself. I wonder if Margaret would have taken the place if I had given out all the heavy clothes to wash. I cannot fancy our *work* hard, for Helen who did it all, washing included, for eleven years was far from healthy – in fact asthmatical. I have one blessing here, however, in the way of service which I ought to be thankful for – our postman's wife, who has baked the best possible bread for us a long time, and who, living at hand, is always going and coming, since I have been in a puddle, to help me in the quietest and nicest way . . .

> Ever your affectionate
> Jane Carlyle

CHELSEA ANNE

78. To Mrs Russell at Thornhill

6 March 1847

. . . The new maid who came at New Year's Day continues here, and promises to become a fixture. She is a remarkable cleanly, orderly, quiet, little woman, with a superior faculty for *cooking*. I have been extremely lucky, I think, in realizing so useful and res-pectable a servant out of the great sink of London, by means of a newspaper advertisement. She has a lover, a butcher, who is extreme-ly attentive – but they are a *rational* pair and not likely to marry till he gets a business of his own – and meanwhile it rather pleases me to know of a little *decent* love-making going on in the house. By and by I shall have her trained into all my *ways* – which are many – and some of them curious for the Cockney intellect – and then I hope to be even better off than I was before; for this one has no tendency to drink, and has more *solidity* than Helen had . . .

79. To Helen Welsh at Liverpool

25 May 1847

... Anne is today and will be tomorrow the same as she was yesterday – good so far as she goes – but not 'going the whole hog' with the *emphasis* one could wish. However, the being a little slow, a little *ineffectual*, is perhaps the least offensive fault she could have; and *some* fault, being human, she *must* have. She is perfectly orderly and *respectable*, and likes me as much as it is in [her] languid nature to like any mistress. I miss the *enthusiasm*, the *birr*, that was in Helen; the-ready-to-fly-at-every-thing-ness; but on the other hand things go on equably, without *flare-ups*, and having to help her a little with her work is perhaps good for me in the main.

I wish *you* had only one servant instead of three – you would find your problem, I am sure, much less complicated. They spoil one another ...

80. To Mrs Carlyle at Scotsbrig

December 1847

... The little servant I got last New Year's Day has turned out a real godsend – so quiet and orderly and honest. The house was never so peaceably managed since I was Mistress. I have not had to transact *one* scold since this girl came to me. She is an excellent cook, and the only objection I had to her in the beginning – a sort of want of *enthusiasm* for things in general and *my* work in particular, has gradually disappeared. She seems now quite as much interested in us as Helen was, tho' she does not make such a prodigious *fuss* about it. I have heard nothing from the said Helen for a long while; her last letter was so full of nonsense about *her* 'servants', and 'Country House', and 'housefuls of visitors', that I had not patience to answer it ...

HELEN'S FINAL DISMISSAL

81. TO JEANNIE WELSH AT LIVERPOOL

5 Cheyne Row, Chelsea/ 27 February 1849

Dearest Babbie

. . . Monday came however – and we must return– the Ashburtons were to come to town that day, and we were to dine at Bath House Tuesday. We drove to our own door where Mr C. and the luggage were to be deposited, I going on to Knightsbridge with Anthony to settle about a governess for him. But Mr C. knocked in vain for a good while and we were speculating about breaking in at a window and storming at Helen[1] for having gone out when she knew we were coming – when the door opened to a twentieth blow and an apparition presented itself which I shall remember as long as I live. There stood Helen – her mouth all over blood, her brow and cheeks white with chalk from the kitchen floor – like an excessively *ill got up* stage-ghost! her dark gown ditto – her hair hanging in two wild streams down her neck – her crushed cap all awry – and on her face a hideous smile of idiotic self-complacency!

Nothing *could* be more drunk! We ordered her downstairs but she refused to be '*used in that way*' so Mr C. had to drag her down! – and leave her on the kitchen floor. I walked off, with the *sublime calm* which always comes to me in purely *material* trouble, followed by Anthony to Mrs White to tell her to come to the rescue – when we came in Mr C. was on his knees lighting the parlour fire. Anthony then drove off coolly remarking that 'as I seemed to have affairs of my own to attend to he could not expect me to come and settle his'. Mr C. retired to his study – there was no fire in the kitchen either. Mrs White lighted one and proceeded to get dinner cooked while the little beast stormed at her for 'daring to do *her* work'. I tidied things upstairs – the whole house was beastly – she has been drunk every day of our absence and having *drinking parties* in the house. That it escaped being either burnt or robbed is a miracle.

About five in the afternoon – (we came at one) – she got her legs and rushed out into space for more drink – staggered home at ten

---

[1] In the autumn of 1848 Chelsea Anne married her butcher and went to live in Jersey. Helen, having quarrelled with her brother, returned to replace Anne. The episode above took place when the Carlyles returned from a visit to the Anthony Sterlings.

and fell insensible on the kitchen floor – she had had *half a pint of rum*, and a quart of ale – in addition to the *half pint of gin* she had taken in the morning. Mrs White got her into bed with difficulty, took away by my desire all combustibles and bolted her in (as she believed). I was to open the outer door to Mrs White at seven in the morning, and barred and chained it for the night as usual. When I came down at seven the bars and chain were all undone and there was a sound as of an animal rolling on the kitchen stairs. The little beast had been out! with a bonnet and shawl on the top of her night clothes and had more drink – at night she got her senses again – and was told by Mrs White that she must get ready to leave the house next day. – *I* would not see her at all. Providence under the form of Miss Bölte had sent a most promising looking servant here the very day we came home. Miss Bölte knew nothing of the exigency, but this servant 'had come in her way and she could not resist sending her to me, to see if the sight of her would not tempt me to put away that dirty little Helen'. Did you ever know such luck? I liked the girl – found her character satisfactory and engaged her to come as soon as I could get the little beast out of the house. She tried her old despair and tears upon me – but in vain this time – I had found her a shocking dirty stupid servant ever since she came and now I knew why – she had been all the time partially drunk. When I was not to be moved by tears she took to bed, and swore she would not go. I told her thro' Mrs White – that I would take her at two on Friday in Capt. S.'s carriage to the house of her dearest friend – who lives at Camden Town and has a room to let, or I would put her on board a Kirkcaldy steamer and pay her expenses – whichever she liked – if she insisted on lying in bed I would send for a Policeman and have her taken to the Station. She saw there was no irresolution more, rose and dressed herself – and agreed to go to Camden Town. I spoke hardly ten words to her all the way – explained the circumstances to the woman of the house – put two sovereigns into *her* hands, that she might pay herself the present shelter afforded her – and came away desiring never to see her (Helen) again in this world. She may go to the Devil her own way – I have bothered myself enough in trying to hold her back.

The new servant [Elizabeth Sprague] came on Saturday – and bodes well to be an immense blessing to us. And now tho' I have not told you half what I had to tell I must make an end for the present – and try to walk off the headache I got at a dinner at Thackeray's last night where you were not – love to them all. Your affectionate

J. Carlyle

THE DEAF ONE

82. To Jeannie Welsh at Liverpool

5 Cheyne Row, Chelsea/ 5 March 1851

Dearest Babbie

. . . Yesterday I got up about four in the afternoon, and came down to – engage a new servant! a thing very repugnent to me even in the perpendicular position – and horrible to think of on the flat of my back. I told you I think that the *last new one* had gone deaf on New Year's Day. She has never recovered yet and has been a very heavy handful latterly; as I have had to do all the door-answering in the first instance, (having to go to seek *her* to *open* it.) How it gets opened when I am out of the house, I have no conception! Then instead of exerting her other faculties to make up for the defect of hearing, she grows more and more nervous and helpless – not to be wondered at poor thing! having a most delicate fine-lady organisation to begin with. Still I thought if *I* who was used to her and so hated new faces and new ways could not make shift to *go on* with her, *who* would be likely to *begin* with her? And nobody knows how long it would have been before I should have mustered inhumanity enough to give her warning on account of her deafness – to say nothing of courage enough to front another change. But a week ago she *took the initiative* and told me with the most *placid* indifference that she 'meant to leave in a month' as she should certainly 'die of grief' if she went on '*listening to bells and never hearing them*'! 'But what will you do?' I asked. – 'Oh! (she had it all cut and dry) I will go into a *kitchen* where I shall have fellow servants to speak loud to me and have nothing to do with the bells, or *the up-stairs*.' I could not but approve her purpose – provided she get it 'carried out'. So yesterday I was engaging another – equally refined – *less sensitive* looking but *more sentimental* – with I should say a great tendency to '*George Sandism* and all that sort of thing'. I remarked that she did not look very strong – the answer was 'perhaps I look more delicate for being in mourning – mourning (for her mother) is *such a denial* to a young person, everyone, I think, looks best in colours'. But she has a three year's character and can cook – especially *fish* her mistress said – 'all sorts of fish in all sorts of ways' – pity we never *eat* fish hardly – I suppose I shall get hardened to changes like other people – certainly I am taking this one *easily*. To be sure there has been no *row* – the general accompaniment of change – and which puts one all bilious at the outset. I really *am* very sick Babbie dear! and must not begin another sheetkin.

Kindest love to Uncle and all the rest,

Your ever affectionate

Jane Carlyle

IRISH FANNY

83. To Thomas Carlyle at Poste Restante, Dresden

5 Cheyne Row, Chelsea/ 13 September 1852

Oh, my Dear!

... Fanny is really a nice servant; a dash of Irish 'rough and ready' in her, but a good cleaner and a good cook, and a perfect incarnation of *The Willing Mind!* Very tidy too in her own person, under all circumstances. An awful complication revealed itself two or three days after she came, which she stood by me under with a jolliness that was quite admirable. When the new painted kitchen was capable of being slept in, she fell to taking the bed in pieces to give it 'a good washing'. Anne who would never be at the trouble to look to her bed, pretended, when she did finally take it down by my express order before she went away, to have found 'nothing worth mentioning'! – 'just *four* bugs', and these '*very small ones*', like the girl's illegitimate child. Well I was sitting writing here when Fanny came and said, 'Do step down, mam, and see what I have kept to show you' – and when I had gone down, not knowing what she had been at, there lay her bed all in pieces, and beside it a large basin of water containing the drowned bodies of something like two hundred bugs!! The bed perfectly swarmed with these 'small beings' – was in fact impregnated with them beyond even *my* cleansing powers! We gathered it all up and carried it out into the garden to be sold to a Broker, who is coming for certain rubbish of things; and I went the same day and bought a little iron bedstead for the kitchen, for £1-2s.-6d. The horror of these bugs quite maddened me for many days; and I would not tell you of them at the time, that you might not feel them prospectively biting you; but now I think we are 'quite shut of them'. The Painter's consolation, that he knew 'fine houses in Belgrave Square where they were crawling about the drawing room floors', did not help me at all.

The poor white cat no longer gives offence to Nero – I suppose she 'couldn't stand the muddle', like that girl who went away for she also went away, into infinite space two weeks ago![1] Darwin says, if I can put up with 'a cat with a bad heart', I may have his. 'That minds me' (as Helen used to say) of an Italian, living with Mazzini at present, who is beating Saffi hollow in 'the pursuit of *English* under difficulties' – sitting down by some Englishman the other day, he said 'fluently' 'Now let *we* have a nice *cat* together!' . . .

Affectionately yours,
J.W.C.

ANNE III AND THE BUGS

84. TO MRS RUSSELL AT THORNHILL

5 Cheyne Row, Chelsea/ 10 October 1856

. . . from the day I left Scotland quite other things than happiness and tranquillity have been 'thrown into my system'! I arrived here with a furious faceache; Mr C. having insisted on my sitting in a violent draught all the journey; *that* kept me perfectly sleepless all night in spite of my extreme fatigue – and so I began to be ill *at once* and have gone on *crescendo* in the same ratio that my worries have increased. Figure this! (*Scene* – a room where everything is enveloped in dark yellow London *fog*! for air to breathe, a sort of *liquid* soot! – breakfast on the table – 'adulterated coffee', 'adulterated bread', 'adulterated cream', and 'adulterated *water*'!) Mr C. at one end of the table, looking remarkably bilious – Mrs C. at the other looking half dead! Mr C.: 'My dear, I have to inform you that my bed is full of *bugs* or fleas or some sort of animals that crawl over me all night'!!

Now, I must tell you; Mr C. had written to me at Auchtertool, to 'write *emphatically* to Anne about keeping all the windows open; for, with her horror of fresh air, she was quite capable of having the house full of bugs when we returned' – and so I imputed this announcement to one of these fixed ideas men, and especially husbands, are apt to take up, just out of sheer love of worrying! Living in a universe of bugs *outside*, I had entirely ceased to fear them in my own house – having kept it so many years perfectly clean from all such abominations. So I answered with merely a sarcastic shrug, that was

---

[1] This was 'our Beauty' who, according to Carlyle, 'was as perfect a fool as the sun ever shone on, and at the end of a week *left*, finding it "quite impossible to live in any such muddle".'

no doubt very ill-timed *under the circumstances*, and which drew on me no end of what the Germans call *Kraftsprüche*! But clearly the practical thing to be done was to go and examine his bed – and I am practical – *moi*! So instead of getting into a controversy that had no basis, I proceeded to toss over his blankets and pillows – with a certain sense of injury! But, on a sudden, I paused in my operations. I stooped to look at something the size of a pinpoint. A cold shudder ran over me. As sure as I lived it was an *infant bug*! And Oh, heaven, that bug, little as it was, must have parents – grandfathers and grandmothers, perhaps! I went on looking *then* with frenzied minuteness – and saw – enough to make me put on my bonnet and rush out wildly, in the black rain, to hunt up a certain trustworthy carpenter to come and take down the bed. The next three days I seemed to be in the thick of a domestic Balaklava – which is now even, only subsiding – not subsided. Anne, tho I have never reproached her with carelessness (decidedly there was not the vestige of a bug in the whole house when we went away) is so indignant that the house should be turned up after *she* had 'settled it', and that 'such a fuss should be made about bugs, which are 'inevitable in London' that she flared up on me, while I was doing her work, and declared 'it was to be hoped I would get a person to keep my house cleaner than she had done; as she meant to leave that day month!' To which I answered, 'very good' – and nothing more.

And now you see; instead of coming back to anything like a home, I have come back to a house full of bugs and *evil passions*! I shall have to be training a new servant into the ways of the house (when I have got her) at a season of the year when it will be the most uphill work for both her and me. As to this woman, I kept her these three years because she was a clever *servant*, and carried on the house without any bother to me – but I never liked her *as a woman*; from the first week I perceived her to be what she has since on all occasions proved herself, cunning, untrue, and intensely selfish. The atmosphere of such a character was not good – and nothing but moral cowardice could have made me go on with her. But I did so dread always the bothers and risks of '*a change*'! Now however that it is *forced* on me, I console myself by thinking, with that 'hope which springs eternal in the human mind', that I may find a servant, after all, whom it may be possible to not only train into my ways – but *attach to me*!

What a fool I am! Oh I should so like a Scotchwoman! if I could get any feasible Scotchwoman. These Londoners are all of the cut of this woman. I have written to Haddington where the servants used to be very good – to know if they can do anything for me. I suppose it is needless asking *you*; of course, if there had been any 'treasure' procurable you would have engaged her yourself. But do you really know nobody I could get from Nithsdale? How stupid it was of Margaret not to come when I wanted her. I am sure it is harder work she must have at the Castle.

Oh, my Darling – I wish you were here to give me a kiss and cheer me up a bit with your soft voice – In cases of this sort, Geraldine with the best intentions is no help. She is *unpractical*, like all women of genius!

She was so pleased with your letter. 'My Dear,' she said to me, 'how is it that women who don't write *books* write always so much nicer *letters* than those who do?' I told her – it was, I supposed, because they did not write in the valley of the shadow of their possible future biographer – but wrote what they had to say frankly and naturally . . .

Your affectionate
Jane W. Carlyle

ANNE'S GENTILITY

85. To Mrs Russell at Holm Hill

March 1857

. . . The last two or three days I have been more anxious about my maid than about myself – she has excellent health – has not been an hour unable for her work since she came to us three and a half years ago! But the other day she cut her finger severely – did not come to tell me, but fussed on with it herself; and it bled half a pint, and was badly wrapped up; and kept her awake all the night after, with the pain of it. To which I impute the bilious attack she had next day. She is going about again now quite well, only a little weak – but for three days I had *two* strangers – that is to say, *new hands* – in the house (I have one of them still), to fill her *one* place – and so inadequately! And had to wait on *her* myself, instead of being waited on. I must tell you an instance of Anne's taste for *gentility* – It was in shaving a *bath-brick* that she cut her finger. Today when she opened the door to the Lady Alice Hill (a lovely girl whom Anne *respects* very much as the daughter of real live Marchioness) – Lady Alice, who is the most bewitching little monkey in the world, said, 'Oh Anne, what ails your hand?' (the finger was wrapt in a

bit of *scarlet* cloth!!) 'I have cut it, my Lady.' – 'How did you cut
it?' 'Well, I did it in cutting up a –*fowl*!!' She told me this substitu-
tion herself. 'You know Ma'm,' said she, in telling of Lady Alice's
kind enquiries, 'I couldn't go and say to a *real* young Lady that I did
it, cutting a *bath-brick*! *that* sounded so *common*! I thought a *fowl*
was more the thing!! 'Did Lady Alice say she hoped you *flung away
that fowl*?' I asked her . . .

ANNE'S DISMISSAL

86. To Mrs Russell at Holm Hill

February 1858

. . . And besides my affairs with Anne have become critical; and
I waited to be delivered from the worry of *that*. We are at a clear
understanding at last, Anne and I; and never was a relation of
five-and-a-half years duration broken off more – what shall I say? –
politely! The married woman who for many years has come in to help
in any ceremony, or press of work, had 'thought it but fair' I should
know Anne was meaning to leave at the end of March, when her
Niece was to go into business as a Milliner. Anne was going to stay
three months with her to teach her housekeeping! and would then
find 'a situation with a single gentleman who kept an under servant
to do all the rough work'. Don't she wish she may get it? – 'That is
the reason', said Mrs Newnham, 'that she doesn't care a bit now
whether she pleases you or not.' – As this woman never said a word
to me of any servant of mine before, I took her information as authen-
tic, and thanked her for it. Anne was at her Mother's that Sunday
night and came home quite *gracious* and continued gracious for a
week! Had the Niece's scheme been visited by the 'pigs' which
'run thro''? I took no more notice of her good temper than I had
done of her bad. One day Geraldine was here (she came back the
very day I last wrote to you); she fell a-talking about Anne; how her
face 'looked less diabolic'. 'It may look as it likes,' I said; 'if she
does not give me warning on the 29th of February, I shall give her
warning and be done with it.' Geraldine has a way, when amused, of
raising her voice to a scream; and she screamed out 'you cannot give
her warning on the 29th, my Dear, for it isn't Leap-year!' I had just
heard Anne sweeping in my bedroom and any loud speaking may
be heard thro' the door between the two rooms. I said 'speak low',

but the shot had clearly told, I fancy. Anne came up so soon as Geraldine was gone, and while arranging the fireplace said carelessly, 'The coals will not last out another week, Ma'am; I should say they will be done by Saturday.' 'Very well, more must be had in on Saturday'; and I went on reading. 'And,' continued Anne, 'if you could by any means *suit yourself*, I should like to leave on – ' 'The 29th of March', I interrupted her. 'Yes, you will leave then whether I am suited or not; if I had not been so helpless these two months back, I should not have troubled you to stay even till then.' Neither of us said another word and both had spoken in the most natural tone! I went on with my reading and she swept up the hearth, and I call that quite a dramatic ending, for all so quiet it was! . . .

MISS CAMERON: THE LIEUTENANT'S DAUGHTER

87. To Mrs Russell at Thornhill

5 Cheyne Row, Chelsea/ 29 March 1858

Dearest Mary

Considering how often one makes experience that evils are worse in the expectation than in the reality, it is wonderful perverseness, that one lets the expectation always do its worst, without drawing comfort from that well known law of things. Here have I looked forward for weeks back to the 29th of March as a day of horrors! and now it is come, and I find myself preparing to pass my evening very composedly in writing a letter to *you*! the most of the forenoon having gone in – '*sitting*' to Mr Tait for the finishing touches to my portrait in that immortal picture of his!! And yet Anne left at midday, and I heard the new servant come in about half an hour ago! Had I 'trusted in Providence' (as your dear Father would have advised) ever so much; I could not indeed have forseen *how* Anne's *Exodus* would be smoothed for me; but I *might* have foreseen that some way or other it would be smoothed, so as to try my sick nerves less than it threatened to do, in prospect.

But first, I must tell you the *adventure* of my new servant; for it *is* of the nature of an adventure, my last choice of a servant! – how it will turn out, Heaven only knows! Either it will be a grand success, or an absurd mistake. It cannot turn out in a medium way. Oh, my Dear!

only fancy! I have hired a '*Miss* Cameron' (from Inverness), 'Daughter of a half-pay Lieutenant'! (swamped in numerous progeny – as in the case of the 'wee wifie that lived in a *shoe*, so many Bairnies he didn't know what to do'!). Miss Cameron is 31 years old, has an intelligent, *affectionate* face, a low, pleasant voice, a manner at once modest and self-possessed; and 'has known enough of life' she says, 'to desire above all things *a quiet home*'. Imagine! a servant coming to one in *London* for a *quiet* home! and knowing anything of life beyond 'beer', 'wages' and 'holidays'! So far, excellent! wonderful! but now for the drawbacks! Miss Cameron, having never filled but *one* 'situation', that of *Lady's maid* and Companion at General Osborne's for eight years, does not know – naturally – whether she can clean a house, and cook a dinner, *till she have tried*!! hopes that she will soon *learn*, if I will '*have patience*' and tell her or get her told *how*!!! And I hope so, too, most sincerely.[1]

THE EMOTIONAL MARIA

88. To Mrs Russell at Liverpool

15 September 1862

... Mr C. was very glad of course to see me back. As for Maria; she went into a sort of hysterics over me! seizing me in her arms, and kissing me all over, and laughing in a distracted manner. A charming reception from one's Housemaid, certainly, if it weren't that such *emotional* natures have always *two* sides; this loving and loveable one; and another, as quick to anger and jealousy and all unreasonableness! – all this impetuous affection for me wouldn't prevail with her to make any *sacrifices* for my sake; or to exert herself for my sake in any manner which was not agreeable to her inclinations. It is just the emotionalness of the Wesleyan Methodist, having its source in the senses rather than in the Soul! ...

[1] In a later letter Mrs Carlyle says that 'Miss Cameron' turned out to be an 'Irish Imposter; was convicted of lying and theft'; and after 'lasting just a fortnight and three days', ran away between 10 and 11 at night. *New Letters and Memorials of Jane Welsh Carlyle*, ed. Alexander Carlyle (1903), II, 179.

TRIALS OF CHANGING HOUSEMAIDS

89. TO MRS RUSSELL AT HOLM HILL

20 October 1862

Now Mary, Dear! pray don't let the echoes of your voice die out of my ears, if you can help it!... Yes! I am changing my housemaid! I have foreseen for long, even when she was capering about me, and kissing my hands and shawl; that this emotional young lady would not *wear well*; and that some fine day her self-conceit and arrogance would find the limits of my patience. Indeed, I should have lost patience with her long ago if it hadn't been for her cleverness about Mr C.'s books, which I fancied would make *him* extremely averse to parting with her; as cleverness of that sort is not a common gift with housemaids. But not at all – at least not in prospect – He says she is 'such an affected fool' and so heedless in other respects that it is quite agreeable to *him* 'that she should carry her fantasticalities and incompetences elsewhere'! She had calculated on being indispensable, on the score of the Books, and was taking, since soon after my return from Scotland, a position in the House which was quite preposterous; domineering towards the cook, and impertinent towards me! picking and choosing at her *work* – in fact not behaving like a *servant* at all, but like a *lady*, who, for a caprice, or a wager, or anything except wages and board, – was condescending to exercise light functions in the house, *provided* you kept her in good humour with gifts and praises. When Mr C.'s attention was directed to her procedure, he saw the intolerableness as clearly as I did; so I was quite free to try conclusions with the girl – either she should apologise for her impertinence and engage (like Magdalen Smith) 'to turn over a new leaf',[1] or she should (as Mr C. said) 'carry her fantasticalities and incompetencies elsewhere'! She chose, of course, the worser part; and I made all the haste possible to engage a girl in her place, and make the fact known; that so I might protect myself against *scenes* of reconciliation, which to a woman as old and nervous as I am, are just about as tiresome as scenes of altercation! All sorts of *scenes* cost me my sleep, to begin with! and are a sheer *waste* of vital power, which one's *servant* at least ought really not to cost one!

[1] The poisoner, who was reported to have made this resolve on the eve of her execution.

I am going to try a new arrangement; *that* of keeping two women, experienced, or considering themselves so – to do an amount of work between them which any one good experienced servant could do singly, having hitherto proved unmanageable with me. I have engaged a little girl of the neighbourhood (age about fifteen) to be *under* the Scotchwoman. She is *known* to me as an honest, truthful, industrious little girl. Her parents are rather superior people in their station. The Father is a Collector on the boats. She is used to work, but not at all to what Mr C.'s Father would have called 'the curiosities and niceties' of a house like this. So I shall have trouble enough in licking her into shape. But *trouble* is always a bearable thing for me in comparison with *irritation*. The chief drawback is, that the mother is sickly, and this child has been her mainstay at home; and tho both Parents have willingly sacrificed their own convenience to get their child into so *respectable* a place, my fear is, that after I have *had* the trouble of licking her into shape, the Mother, under the pressure of home difficulties, may be irresistibly tempted to take her home again. Well! there is an excellent Italian proverb, 'The person who *considers* everything will never decide on anything!' Meanwhile, Elizabeth looks much more *alive* and cheerful since she had this change in view – and I shall be delivered from the botheration of two rival Queens in the kitchen at all events! That I shall have to fetch the Books, and do the sewing myself, will perhaps – 'keep the Devil from my elbow'! . . .

THE EXPENSE OF IT

90. To Mrs Russell at Holm Hill

15 December 1862

. . . You say get a thorough good cook at any wages! Yes – if the *wages* were all the difference! But when you have agreed to give sixteen guineas a year and ten pounds more for extras (the cost of a 'good plain Cook') you find that she requires a 'Servants Hall' and 'a bedroom upstairs' and accommodations which your house, not having been built on purpose for so dignified an individual, does not possess. And still worse, you find that she objects to making bread, and that with the power of cooking some hundreds of dishes which you don't want she has to be taught to [do] Mr C.'s little plain things just as an ignorant servant would, and that she disdains to *be* taught, and that she thinks her gifts quite wasted on a household unworthy of them – as, indeed they would be.

I saw one woman of this sort whose appearance pleased me much – and I agreed to the sixteen guineas and the ten for extras (!!!) but she was 'engaged to Lord Clarendon's Coachman and would like to have leave to receive his visits occasionally', and there was no dress kitchen for such a visitor! – and no bedroom upstairs for her 'great number of trunks'! And this was only 'a good plain Cook' – 'a professed woman Cook' gets 60 or 70 guineas a year of mere wages – No what would suit me best, if good, is what is called 'a General Servant who is a plain cook' the wages of these is from twelve to fourteen pounds and 'everything found' – that is the sort of girl I have engaged with[1] – calculating on having to teach her to make bread and most of the things Mr C. requires but also calculating that she knows enough of roasting and boiling to learn these modifications without giving me too much trouble. We shall see! . . .

91. To Mrs Austin at The Gill, Annan

5 Cheyne Row, Chelsea/ 1 January 1863

Dear little Woman –

A letter was to have preceded that box – a letter of apology for its rubbishy contents – only to be excused indeed by my knowledge from of old how *you* could make somethings out of nothings! a capital talent which, I daresay, is inherited by these remarkably 'world-like' girls of yours. But I had been kept in such a constant bother with teaching the new cook how to make bread, and to make everything that was wanted of her, that I never could find time for writing; and now your kind acknowledgement of the said rubbish shows that my apology was not needed . . . But why not have taken a cook ready trained out of a Gentleman's family? Simply, my dear, because cooks ready trained out of Gentlemen's families have wages entirely disproportionate to any work they would have here, – £20 at the least; – and that is not the worst; all their accommodations are expected to be in keeping with their wages; and they would look down on people living so economically and quietly as we do! Now, I think it is more pleasant, or rather less unpleasant, to look down on one's promoted 'maid-of-all-work', than to be looked down upon by one's 'professed cook' . . .

Your affectionate
Jane W. Carlyle

[1] This is Mary, later to be called 'the worst of girls'.

ROWS BELOW STAIRS

92. To Mrs Russell at Holm Hill

5 Cheyne Row, Chelsea/January 1863

Dearest Mary

You thought I must be *ill* that I did not write; and now that three days have brought no answer to your inquiry, I shouldn't wonder if you are thinking I must be *dead!*

... The illness I have had, and am still having, has been caused palpably enough by a mental shock which struck me deadly sick at stomach, and struck the pain into my back, in the first moment of it. And tho' my mind has recovered its balance, these consequences still remain. One expects to hear of something sentimental, romantic, at least exciting, when anybody speaks of having had a great mental shock. My Dear! lower your expectations; bring them down to the level of the meanest prose! For what I have to tell you is again about – my servants!!! But take up the servant as a human being – a fellow-creature – and read my paltry tale as a psychological illustration; and it *is* enough to throw one into a fit of misanthropy, besides making one sick at stomach and breaking one's spine in two!

When I wrote last I was looking forward to better times below stairs. The new cook seemed a decent young woman; not bright or quick, but one who would, with a little teaching and a good deal of patience, be made to *do*. 'Flo' was clever and assiduous, and thoughtful and helpful; the only thing to be guarded against with *her* was the tendency to praise and pet her overmuch, and so – spoil her; as I had spoilt Charlotte! But I was helped in *that* by the want of personal *attraction* for me in the child. There was something dry and hard, something *unyouthful* in her manner, and voice, which coupled with her extraordinary cleverness and assiduity, sometimes reminded me of the 'Changelings' in Fairy Legends.

Well! as the days went on, a change seemed to come over the spirit of the new Cook's 'dream'. She grew more and more gloomy, and sullen, and indifferent; till she grew exactly into her Scotch predecessor *translated into English* – minus the utter blockheadism!!! I was careful to make no remarks on her before Flo; but Flo was constantly *blurting out* aggravating instances of negligence and disagreeableness on the part of the newcomer. At last one day my dissatisfaction reached a climax; and I told this Mary that I perceived she would not suit, and that I thought it better to tell her so in the first month. And again my weary spirit was wandering thro' space in search of a Cook, beset by far greater difficulties than '*Cœlebs in search of a Wife*'! The only person that looked delighted was Flo, – as delighted as she looked when I gave Elizabeth warning.

Next day I was just putting on my bonnet to go out on this miserable search, when the Cook said to me; she thought it very strange to be *going* in this way! that she had 'never gone out of any place before in less than a year at the least'. 'Whose fault is it?' I said – 'Do you consider it *possible* for me to keep a woman who shows no sort of interest in doing or learning the work she has undertaken to do here?' 'Well,' said the woman with a half sob, 'I am aware I have made myself very disagreeable; but it wasn't easy, to be good tempered and to try to please, with Flo, every time she came down stairs, telling me the dreadfullest things that you said of me and of everything I did!!!' that I was 'nothing but a stupid dirty maid-of-all-work, fit for nothing but a Tradesman's house, where I could get tumbling about among a lot of rough workmen.' And 'Oh far worse things than that!' Astonishment took away my speech for a moment. I had not said *one word* of the woman to the child, knowing that she carried everything to her Mother.

I rung the bell for Flo. – 'What is all this,' I asked, 'that you have been telling Mary – as said of her *by me*?' 'Well, Ma'm,' said Flo, very red, '*I couldn't help it!* Mary was always asking me what you said about her – You *know* you *were* Mary! (*like a viper*); and I was *obliged* to tell her *something*!' 'You were *obliged* to invent horrible lies, were you?' – 'If I didn't tell her something, Ma'm, she wouldn't leave me alone!' – 'Oh you wicked girl!' burst in Mary, 'What was *I* asking you when you tried to set me against the Place and the Mistress from the first night I entered the house!' '*I?*' said Flo – 'I only repeated what Elizabeth said!' 'And the Mistress would be a little surprised,' said Mary, 'if I were to tell her what you told *me*!' 'Oh, I will tell her myself,' said Flo; '*if you please*, Ma'm, Elizabeth said, a woman that was her fellow-servant in Scotland, told her before she came here that you were a she-devil! Elizabeth said *that* tall chair (pointing to a *prie Dieu*) was *for strapping you to when you were mad*!!!' It was at this point that the sickness came into my stomach and the pain into my back! 'Good God' I said, when I could speak, 'is it possible that you who have lived beside me these two months, who have never got a cross look or harsh word from me, who have *seen* my behaviour to that very Elizabeth, could say the like of this?' 'If you please, Ma'm, it wasn't me that said it, it was Elizabeth!' 'Oh, you lying bad girl,' broke in Mary, 'I see it all now! that you were set on driving me out of the place; and I shouldn't wonder if you did the same by Elizabeth.' – The same thought had just flashed on myself. It was from the day that Maria left and *this child* came, that Elizabeth began to grow, from a mere obedient blockhead, into a sullen, disobliging blockhead, seeming to rather take pleasure in poisoning Mr C. than not!

In her case there wasn't even *invention* needed. The imp had only to do what I was constantly warning her against, viz: to *repeat* the strong things Mr C. said of her (Elizabeth's) cookery and self generally, to drive the woman to fury, and make her the unbearable creature she became. Flo seeing herself unmasked, began to cry very hard, repeating again and again, 'You will never to able to bear me again, I know! I have been so *treacherous*! You were so kind to me; and I was so fond of you! and I have been so very treacherous, ooh-ooh-oo-oh.' I didn't know what on earth to do. I didn't feel justified in turning her off on the spot, and to keep her was like keeping a poisonous viper at large in the house. The only thing I was clear about was to withdraw my warning to Mary, whose behaviour had been sufficiently excused by the influences acting on her. Flo's Mother, hearing of the row, came over to try and shift the blame on Mary. I rung the bell and said to Mary, 'Mrs Morrison has accusations to make against you, Mary; you had better hear them yourself, and answer her – as *I* know nothing about it.' And then ensued an altercation, between the two women (while I sat with my feet on the fender and my back to them) in which Mrs Morrison came by the worse; having only drawn out a *fuller* statement of Flo's horrid conduct. She went away imploring me to 'try her' (Flo) a little longer; it would be a lesson she would never forget, etc., etc. And I said, 'She can stay for the present till I see what comes of her.' But three days after, the child herself said, 'I can never be happy here after having been *so* treacherous, and I had better go away.' 'I am glad you think so', I said; 'so the sooner you go the better – today, if you like' – and in one hour she was gone! My paragon little Housemaid! Three days after, she came over, tears all dried, looking hard and bold, to ask me to 'see a Lady' for her. 'What sort of a character do you think I can give you?' I asked. 'Well!' said the child, 'I have *told a few lies* and I *have been treacherous*; but that is all you can say against me'! The dreadful child!

I saw a girl that I thought would suit me, the same day Flo left;

but she couldn't come for a month, and her Aunt who wished me to wait for her, offered to come and help Mary, till the girl was free. So I have a great, jolly, clever, elderly woman in the kitchen, except for the two last days of the week, when she is engaged elsewhere – and Mary does nicely upstairs. This woman is a capital Cook; and I almost wish the present arrangement, tho' an expensive one, could last – now that I have got used to the big woman, who 'thoroughly understands her business'. But she has a Husband and couldn't stay with me in permanence.

Now! do you wonder I fell ill? (Think of Mr C's impatience as a running accompaniment to all this disgusting worry!) . . .

God bless you both.

Your ever-affectionate,

Jane Carlyle

RETURN OF BESSY BARNET

93. To Mrs Russell at Holm Hill

5 Cheyne Row, Chelsea/ 3 June 1863

. . . Well! some weeks ago, Mr C. was just come in from his ride, very tired, and, to do him justice, very ill-humoured, when Mary put her head in at the Drawingroom door and said, 'Mrs Blackett wished to know if she could see me for a few minutes'. I went out hurriedly, knowing Mr C.'s temper wouldn't be improved by hearing of people, he *didn't want*, coming after me! I told Mary to take the Lady into the Diningroom (where there was no fire), and before going down myself, put a shawl about me, chiefly to show her she mustn't *stay*. On entering the room, the Lady's back was to me; and she was standing looking out into the (so called) *garden*: but I saw at once it wasn't the Mrs Blackett I had seen. This one was very tall, dressed in deep black, and when she turned round, she showed me a pale, beautiful face, that was perfectly strange to me! But *I* was no stranger to *her* seemingly; for she glided swiftly up to me like a Dream, and took my head softly between her hands and kissed my brow again and again, saying in a low dreamlike voice, 'Oh, you Dear! you Dear! you Dear! Don't you know me?' I looked into her eyes in supreme bewilderment! At last light dawned on me, and I said one word – '*Bessy*?' 'Yes, it is Bessy!' – and then the kissing wasn't all on one side, you may fancy. It was at last, Bessy – *not*

Mrs Blackett, but Mrs Blackiston, who stood there, having left her husband in a cab at the door, till she had seen me first. They were just arrived from Cheshire, where they had gone to see one of his sons, who had been dangerously ill, and were to start by the next train for St Leonards where he is the chief Physician – They had only a quarter of an hour to stay. He is a good, intelligent-looking man; and while he was talking all the time with Mr C., Bessy said beautiful things about him to me, enough to show that if he wasn't her first love, he was at least a very superior being in *her* estimation. They pressed me to come to them at St Leonards, and I promised indefinitely that I would.

About a fortnight ago, Bessy walked in one morning after breakfast. She 'had had no peace for thinking about me; I looked so ill, she was sure I had some disease! Had I?' I told her, 'none that I could specify, except the disease of *old age*! general weakness and discomfort'. Reassured on that head, she confided to me that 'I looked just as Mrs Blackiston had looked when she was dying of cancer'!! And she had come up, certain that I had a cancer, to try and get me away to be nursed by *her*, and attended by her husband. Besides she had heard there was so much small-pox in London; 'and if I took it, and *died* before she had seen me again, she thought she would never have an hour's happiness in the world again'! Oh, Bessy, Bessy, just the [same] old woman – an imagination morbid almost to insanity! 'Would I go back with her that night anyhow?' 'Impossible!' 'Then when would I come and she would come up again to fetch me?' That I would not hear of, but I engaged to go so soon as it was a little warmer. And today I have written that I will come for two or three days on Monday next.

She is not *still* wearing mourning for Mr Badams, but for the Mother and Eldest Brother of her Husband, who have both died since her marriage, and who received the announcement of that event 'very coolly' (not to be wondered at – being an old Baronet family). Dr Blackiston is the second son of a Baronet.

And now I mustn't begin another sheet. I shall be anxious to hear how your new Cook shapes.

Your ever affectionate
J. W. Carlyle

KNAVERY BELOW STAIRS

94. TO MRS RUSSELL AT HOLM HILL

5 Cheyne Row, Chelsea/ 12 November 1864

Dearest Mary

... At the beginning of this cold, during the time I was constantly retching; and could swallow *nothing*; I got a *moral shock* which would, I think, have *killed* me at St Leonards; and all it *did* to me, I think was to astonish and disgust me! I told you I was parting with my big beautiful Housemaid because she was an incorrigible goose, and destructive and wasteful beyond all human endurance. As a specimen of the waste, figure three pounds of fresh butter at 20 pence a pound regularly consumed in the *kitchen*, and half a pound of tea at 4/- made away with in *four days*! Then, as a specimen of the destruction – figure *all, every one* of my beautiful, fine – and some of them quite *new* – table napkins actually 'worn out' of existence! Not a rag of them to be found and good sheets all in rags; besides a boiler *burst*, a pump well gone irrecoverably *dry*, a clock made to strike *fourteen* every hour – and all the china or crockery in the house either disappeared or cracked! To be sure, the Housemaid was not *alone* to bear the blame of all the mischief – and the Cook was to be held responsible for the waste of the victuals at least. But Mary – the one who attended me at St Leonards – tho the slowest and stupidest of servants – had so impressed me with the idea of her trustworthiness, and her devotion to *me*, that I could accuse *her* of nothing but stupidity and culpable weakness in allowing the other girl, seven years her junior, to *rule* even in the *larder*! Accordingly I engaged an elderly woman to be Cook and Housekeeper, and Mary was to be Housemaid, and wait on *me* as usual. Helen (the Housemaid) meanwhile took no steps about seeking a place, and when I urged her to do so, declared she couldn't conceive *why* I wanted to part with her! When I told her she was too destructive for my means, she answered excitedly: 'Well! when *I* am gone out of the house, and can't bear the blame of *everything* any longer; you will *then* find out who it is that makes away with the tea and the butter and all the things!' As there was nobody *else* to bear the blame but Mary, and as I *trusted her* implicitly; I thought no better of the girl for this attempt to clear herself at the expense of nobody knew who! especially as she would not explain when questioned. When I told slow, innocent Mary, she looked quite amazed, and said, 'I don't think Helen knows what she is saying sometimes; she is very strange!'

Well, Mary asked leave to go and see her family in Cambridgeshire before the new servant came home, and got it, tho very inconvenient to me. When she took leave of me the night before starting, she said in her half-articulate way, 'I shall be always wondering how you are, till I get back.' She was to be away near a week. Mrs Southam, who sat up at night with me last winter, my Charlotte's Mother, came part of the day to help Helen. She is a silent woman, never meddling; so I was surprised when she said to me, while lighting my bedroom fire the day my cold was so bad: 'Helen tells me, ma'm, you are parting with her?' 'Full time,' said I, 'she is a perfect goose.' 'You know best, ma'm,' returned the woman; 'but I always like ill to see the innocent suffering for the guilty!' 'What do you mean?' I asked; 'who is the innocent and who is the guilty?' 'Well, ma'm,' said the woman, 'it is known to all the neighbours round here – you will be told some day, and if I don't tell you now, you will blame me for having let you be so deceived. Mary is the worst of girls! She had an illegitimate child in your house on the 29th of last July. It was her *second* child – and all the things you have been missing have been spent on her man and her friends. There has been constant company kept in your kitchen since there was no fear of your seeing it; and whenever Helen threatened to tell you, she frightened her into silence by threats of poisoning *her* and cutting her own throat!!'

Now, my Dear, if you had seen the creature Mary you would just as soon have suspected the Virgin Mary of such things! But I have investigated, and find it all true. For two years I have been cheated and made a fool of, and laughed at for my softness, by this half-idiotic-looking woman; and while she was *crying* up in my room, moaning out: 'What would become of her if I died?' and witnessing in me as sad a spectacle of human agony as could have been anywhere seen; she was giving suppers to men and women downstairs; laughing and swearing – oh I can't go on. It is too disgusting!

I shall only say that while she was in labour in the small room at the end of the dining room, Mr Carlyle was taking tea in the dining room with Miss Jewsbury talking to him!!! Just a thin small door between them! The child was not born till two in the morning when Mr C. was still reading in the Drawingroom.

By that time Helen had fetched two women – one of whom took the child home to be nursed – Need one ask where all my fine napkins

5 *Jane at 41:*
a painting by Spiridione Gambardella

6a *Harriet,*
Lady Ashburton

6b *Carlyle in his*
early fifties

7a *Jane in her early fifties: a photograph dated 28 July 1854*

Thomas Carlyle (Chelsea, 1865)

7b *Carlyle in the last year of Jane's life: an engraving after a photograph by Elliott & Fry*

"born of respectable parents, and
having enjoyed the advantages
of a liberal education" (like
Judge Somebody's malefactor
who "instead of which", had
gone about the country stealing
turkies!!!) should be withheld
from doing a thing, by just
the feeling that she ought to!
altho' if she had ought to
not to she would have
done it at the first opportunity!
No! — You have no belief
in such a make of woman, —
you! — You are too good
for believing in her! And —
one can't do better than believe
all women born to a sense
of duty "as the sparks fly
upwards" — as long as one
can!

For the rest: I should have
enjoyed this beautiful place
receptively; if Eve had'nt
eaten that unfortunate apple
a great many years ago!
in result of which there has
ever since, been always a
something to prevent one's feeling
oneself in Paradise! The
"something", of the present
occasion, came in the form
of Lumbago — not into
my own back but into
Mr C's; which made no
difference, so far as the
whole comfort of my life
was concerned! For it was
the very first day of being
here that Mr C saw fit
to spread his pocket handkerchief

8 *Letter from Jane to Miss Barnes (22 September 1861),*
concerning Carlyle's lumbago

went, when it is known that the Creature had not prepared a rag of clothing for the child?

Imagine coming to the knowledge of all this when I was *retching* at any rate!

Of course the wretch on her return *in a cab* last Tuesday, bringing the wretched Boy–Father along with her, in broad daylight, to have his dinner, was met by a small packet containing her wages and the news 'it was all found out'. She hurried the Papa into the cab again and they drove off together!...

God bless you, dearest.

Jane Carlyle

LITTLE CHARLOTTE

95. To Charlotte Southam at The Wilderness, near Sevenoaks

5 Cheyne Row, Chelsea/ 26 December 1865

Dear little Woman!

I have been literally *drowned* in letters, for some weeks back; and *off* my sleep at the same time, which makes my head not worth two-pence for writing with.

This – and not neglectfulness of you, has been the reason I did not thank you sooner for that other and better photograph of yourself. Even this one does you no justice – at least does you no justice *when you are good*. But I *have seen* you sufficiently like it when the Devil has got into you, and spread a sort of *cloud* of sullenness over your naturally kind and intelligent look! Oh yes! when I first knew you, and for long after, you were the nicest, brightest looking creature one could wish to see! – Pity one can't keep always young!

I am not *well*, ever, but I have not been positively *ill* this long time.

Except one day that I was in bed with sick headache, I have been out in my Brougham from three to four hours *every day* of my life since I returned from Scotland!! and I go out to dinner occasionally even in this winter weather!...

All the other people who came about in your time still come about – little changed except in the colour of their hair.

Mr C. is much in his usual health – taking his fill of idleness – if *reading* all day long can be called idleness! He will have to go to Edinburgh to make a Speech the last week of March, if the weather keeps favourable and my health *ditto*, I shall perhaps accompany him.

157

Mrs Warren continues to be a great comfort to me; and I brought with me from Dumfriesshire, a capital housemaid – whose Mother and Grandfather were servants to my mother and grandfather, so the House goes on without any bother to me, and at no greater expense than when I did half the work myself, and had to teach the other half! But with all her cleverness, and nice looks, I have none of the *love* for Jessy I had for *you*! No servant has ever been for me the sort of *adopted* child that *you* were! . . .

Affectionately yours,

Jane Carlyle

SERVANTS AT THE GRANGE

96. To Helen Welsh at Liverpool

The Grange, Alresford, Hants/ 6 December 1851

Dearest Helen,

Your note followed me here without delay and now here is the direct address for you. Recollect moreover that when one is on a visit, the time seems always much longer than when in the monotonous routine of home – so by next week it will be seeming a month since I had news of my Uncle. Also to touch your heart as much as possible; let me add; that the very day after I arrived, I took cold which has been keeping me indoors till I am grown quite *low*, and *imaginative*, after my bad fashion, to an even unusual degree. Happily there are no visitors here except the old Countess of Sandwich, Lady Ashburton's Mother, and the days pass quite calmly in – dressing dolls! If I had to sit thro' long dinners and take part in '*wits*', I could not hold out on my legs 24 hours. But that doll-dressing suits me entirely. There is to be a fine Christmas tree for Lady A.'s school children and *seven* dolls form part of the gifts. They were bought *naked*, except for a wrappage of silkpaper and a piece of cotton wool on each of their noses to prevent damage to that interesting feature and Lady A., tho' not much given to a credulous faith in her fellow creatures, *actually* hoped that her Lady's Maid and the Housekeeper, and *their* numerous subordinates would *take an interest* in these dolls and dress or assist *her* dress them. But not a bit – not only did they show themselves *impassive* in the *dressing* question but not a rag of ribbon or any sort of scrap would they produce so that Lady A. had to *insist* on the Housekeeper giving some pieces of *furniture chintz* to make frocks for the dolls and to write to London, to her *ci devant*

Lady's maid for some scraps!! – The very footman won't *carry the dolls* backwards and forwards! When told to bring one or to desire Josephine (the Lady's Maid) to bring one they simply disappear and no doll comes! – I remarked on this with some impatience yesterday, and Lady A. answered, 'Perfectly true, Mrs Carlyle – they *won't bring the doll*! – I know it as well as you do – but what would you have me do? – turn all the servants men and women out of the house on account of these dolls? for *it would* come to *that* – if I made a point of their *doing anything in the doll line*! Perhaps it would be the right thing to do – but then what should we do next week without servants when all the company come?' Such is the slavery the grandest people live under *to what they call* their *'inferiors'* . . .

Your affectionate
J.C.

97. To Helen Welsh at Liverpool

The Grange, Alresford, Hants/ 27 December 1851

Dearest Helen

Our Christmas Tree came off with great success on Wednesday evening – It stood in the middle of the Servant's Hall which was profusely decorated with evergreens, and inscriptions written in red berries '*God* Save the Queen' – 'Long live Lord and Lady Ashburton', etc., etc. The tree was a fir tree six feet high – stuck quite full of apples and walnuts gilded with dutch leaf – lighted coloured wax tapers, and little bundles of comfits; the presents, of which the seven dolls were much the finest, lay on a table erected all round the tree and covered with white cloths; the forty-eight children with their school mistress and Mothers and most of the servants, were ranged round while Lady A., attended by his Lordship, the Clergyman and his wife and two daughters, Mr C. and myself, distributed the presents, calling up each child by name and saying something graceful and witty along with the doll, top, or whatever it might be. Mr C. had begged to have a map of the world in pieces given to *him*, which was done very cleverly. 'Thomas Carlyle – the *Scholar*', shouted her Ladyship and the *Scholar* himself advanced. '*There* is a map of the world for *you* – see that you put it all together and make the pieces fit.' The *scholar* made his bow, and looked as enchanted as any little boy or girl among them. There was afterwards some *mumming* executed before us by country lads in paper dresses – and then we came away leaving the children and their Mothers to enjoy

159

the mugs of tea with large junks of currant loaf spread for them on a long table. The whole thing had a very *fine effect* – and might have given occasion for a laudatory newspaper paragraph, but one reflection that I could not help making rather spoiled it for *me* – viz., that the whole forty-eight presents had cost just two pounds twelve and sixpence; having been bought in the Lowther Arcade, the most rubbishy place in London – with a *regard* of *expense* that would have been meritorious in the like of us, but which seemed to me – what shall I say? – *incomprehensible* – in a person with an income of £40,000 a year – and who gives balls at the cost of £700 each, or will spend £100 on a china jar! I should have liked each child to have got at least *a frock* given it – when one was going to look munificent. But everyone has his own notions on spending money.

For the rest, it has been what Miss Farrar would call 'a dreadful *slow* Christmas', except for the servants who had a ball last night which lasted till six in the morning – we upstairs were in the reactionary state of our company spirits of last week. But Thackeray and Miss Farrar come today – and the steam must be got up again.

And now I must end, having several other letters to write – to the young Countess amongst others (Blanche Airlie) who continues to send me letters *so* confidential, that I feel as if I were being constituted *dry nurse* to her soul! – without having been 'trained to the business'. Love to you all, kisses to my Uncle.

Your affectionate

J.W.C.

VI *Outings*

Descriptions of her travels brought out the very best in Jane's talents as a story-teller. She called these expeditions 'outings', which was the term Londoners used for trips into the country. 'Outings' followed a seasonal pattern. There was a regular annual migration to escape the summer heat of London. The Carlyles fussed in June, took wing in July and were rarely back before September. Christmas and springtime were occasions for 'outings' which might last as long as a month. There were other rhythms which might or might not coincide with this pattern – the labours which brought Thomas to bed with a book and then discharged him, after the delivery, into a country convalescence, and the ups and downs of Jane's mental and physical health.

They sometimes took their 'outings' together, but more often separately, with perhaps a coming together in the middle before parting again. Whether they did or did not was more of Carlyle's determination than Jane's. Sometimes he needed solitude, or the stimulation of other company, and sometimes he needed her. It was his will or whim that prevailed, and she took it for granted that this should be so. But she also needed to get away from him or to have him get away from her. The annual 'earthquaking' at Cheyne Row could only be done in his absence, and it was obviously a relief to be spared, from time to time, the commotions which his presence involved, whether she had spring cleaning to do or not.

Planning an outing was often an ordeal. Carlyle's difficulty in deciding when and where he wanted to go and when he was coming back was the subject of some of Jane's funniest and angriest letters. But 'outings' were a necessity in their lives. As much as Jane might complain about disliking 'locomotion', or about 'country dullness' when she found herself bored, anyone with her interest in 'everybody and everything' got lots of enjoyment out of travel. It was a life-saver from some of her worst depressions. She also found, as ordinary mortals do, that if it was nice to get away, it was nice to get back again.

With roots as deep as theirs, the scenes of their childhood were often visited: Templand, where her mother lived until her death; Scotsbrig, the home of Mrs Carlyle; Haddington, where she was born; Edinburgh and other towns in Lowland Scotland where relatives, friends, or old servants were living. Other ties, made after they became famous, took them through English country houses, especially those of Lord and Lady Ashburton in Hampshire where they spent long periods. Jane had one or two intimates whose homes provided 'houses of refuge', such as Geraldine Jewsbury's in Manchester and Seaforth House, near Liverpool, where Geraldine's friend, Mrs Paulet, lived in comfort and quiet. The attractions of sea air and bathing also took them to the towns and villages overlooking the English Channel.

Methods of travel made some revolutionary leaps in their lifetime, with the railway and the steamship. In 1842 Carlyle got from London to Templand by first taking a morning train from Euston to Liverpool, then the mail-coach through Carlisle, Annan and Dumfries, to arrive finally at Templand at ten o'clock the next day. In 1858 a night train from London took him to Scotland before breakfast. Jane wrote:

> It was wonderful to reflect, while breakfasting at nine, that *you* had probably already breakfasted at *The Gill* in Scotland! After all, Railways are a great thing! only inferior to the Princess of China's *flying bed*, Prince Houssain's *flying carpet* and Fortunatus's *wishing cap*! Transported over night from here to there! from Chancellor's dungheap, the retired cheesemonger's dogs, and twopence worth of nominal *cream* away to 'quiet', 'fresh air', and 'milk without limit'! in *one night*! If it weren't for the four fat men in the carriage with you, wouldn't it be like something in a Fairy Tale?

Ships were going through the same revolution. Jane describes a tour of the 350-foot *Great Britain* in one of her Liverpool letters; but the sea was not her element. Unlike Thomas, whose work on Frederick the Great took him for 'a wild huntsman's rush' through Germany, she never went abroad and never went to Scotland by boat if she could possibly avoid it.

There was nothing in their lifetimes to suggest that the Industrial Revolution would bring the millennial reign of the horse to an end. Jane loved to be driven; would take a London omnibus to the end of the line if there was no better opportunity; and wept with joy when Carlyle surprised her with a present of a brougham. The stage-coach and the faster mail-coach were the standard conveyances, and a good deal of walking was expected of the traveller between leaving the coach and reaching his destination – two miles was only a step.

The first of the following letters describes her journey back from Scotland by the mail-coach in September 1836. She had run away from the London heat, and the higher temperatures of her husband's nervous system, to spend two months with her mother at Templand. The letter is a thank-you to her aunt and uncle who had entertained her en route at Liverpool. It tells of her frenzy when she thought that the mail-coach had gone off without her, after a stop for lunch, and how a distraught Carlyle met her omnibus in the Strand when she reached London. The second is a description of a visit to Oxford, Blenheim Palace at Woodstock, a few miles north-west of Oxford and the Cotswolds in the summer of 1837, with Edward Sterling, the 'Thunderer' of *The Times*, and his wife Hester, the parents of Carlyle's friend, John Sterling.

Next comes a series of letters during a three-week visit in August 1842 to the Bullers at Troston Rectory, which is a few miles from Bury St Edmunds, Suffolk. Thomas had a high regard for Mr and Mrs Charles Buller, Sr. Charles Buller had served with distinction in India, and his sons, Charles and Arthur, had been tutored by Thomas in Edinburgh. The Bullers had been quick to see the merits of both Thomas and Jane, in those days, and it was Mrs Buller who urged Jane to stay with them when she was struggling to recover from the shock of her mother's death. Her son Charles, Carlyle's pupil, seemed destined for a brilliant future in English public life as a reforming M.P. The younger son, Reginald, an airy, clever young man when Carlyle had known him in Edinburgh, was now settled in a rich country living, Troston Rectory, where, according to Carlyle, he would placidly vegetate for the rest of his days as an 'utterly stupid, somnolent Reverend Incumbent'. We get wonderful glimpses of Reginald's care of souls, and of the efforts his parents made to restore Jane's health through country drives, calls on the county families, and the nightly games of chess.

The final letter describes a weekend visit to Sherborne, Dorset, in August 1852, to see Mrs Macready, wife of the famous actor, William Macready, and an old friend, who was dying. This is a tale of adventures on the road there and back – of coaches, flys, gigs, barouchettes, parasols, gallant gentlemen and 'unfortunate females'.

A RETURN FROM LIVERPOOL ON THE MAIL

98. To Mrs Welsh at 3 Maryland Street, Liverpool

5 Cheyne Row, Chelsea/ 5 September 1836

My dear Aunt,

Now that I am fairly settled at home again, and can look back over my late travels with the coolness of a spectator; it seems to me that I must have tired out all men, women, and children that have had to do with me by the road. The proverb says '*there is much ado when cadgers ride*'. I do not know precisely what '*cadger*' means; but I imagine it to be a character like *me*, liable to headaches, to sea-sickness, to *all* the infirmities 'that flesh is heir to', and a few *others* besides; the friends and relations of *cadgers* should therefore use all soft persuasions to induce them to remain at home.

I got into that Mail the other night, with as much repugnance and trepidation as if it had been a Phalaris's brazen bull, instead of a Christian vehicle, invented for purposes of mercy not of cruelty. There were three besides myself when we started, but two dropt off at the end of the first stage, and the rest of the way I had, as usual, half the coach to myself. My fellow-passenger had that highest of all terrestrial qualities which, for me, a fellow-passenger can possess, *he was silent*. I think his name was Roscoe, and he read sundry long papers to himself, with the pondering air of a lawyer.

We breakfasted at Litchfield, at five in the morning, on muddy coffee and scorched toast, which made me once more lyrically recog-nise in my heart (not without a sigh of regret) the very different coffee and toast with which you helped me out of my headache. At *two*, there was another stop of ten minutes, that might be employed in lunching or otherwise – feeling myself more fevered than hungry, I determined on spending the time in combing my hair and washing my face and hands *with vinegar*. In the midst of this solacing operation I heard what seemed to be the Mail resuming its rapid course, and quick as lightning it flashed on me, 'There it goes! – and my luggage is on the top of it! – and *my purse* is in the pocket of it! – and here am I stranded on an unknown beach, without so much as a sixpence in my pocket to pay for the vinegar I have already consumed!' Without my bonnet, my hair hanging down my back, my face half dried, and the towel with which I was drying it firm grasped in my hand, I dashed out – along – down, opening wrong doors, stumbling over steps, cursing the day I was born, still more the day on which I took a notion to travel, and arrived finally, at the bar of the Inn in a state of excitement bordering on lunacy. The bar-maids looked at me 'with weender and amazement'. 'Is the coach gone?' I gasped out. 'The coach? Yes!' 'O! and you have let it away without *me*! O! stop it – cannot you stop it?' and out I rushed into the street, with streaming hair and streaming towel, and almost brained myself against – the *Mail*! which was standing there in all stillness, without so much as horses in it! What I had heard was a heavy coach! And now, having descended like a maniac, I ascended again like a fool, and dried the other half of my face, and put on my bonnet, and came back 'a sadder and a wiser' woman.

I did not find my Husband at the *Swan with Two Necks*; for we were *in*, a quarter of an hour before the appointed time. So I had my luggage put on the backs of two porters, and walked on to Cheapside, where I presently found a Chelsea omnibus. By and by, however, the omnibus stopt, and amid cries of '*No room, Sir*', '*Can't get in*', Carlyle's face, beautifully set off by a broad-brimmed white hat, gazed in at the door, like the Peri, who '*at the Gate of Heaven, stood disconsolate*'. In hurrying along the Strand, pretty sure of being too late, amidst all the imaginable and unimaginable Phenomena which that immense thorough-fare of a street presents, his *eye* (Heaven bless the mark) had lighted on *my trunk* perched on the top of the omnibus, and had recognised it. This seems to me one of the most indubitable proofs of *genius* which he ever manifested. Happily, a passenger went out a little further on, and then he got in.

My Brother-in-law had gone two days before, so my arrival was most well-timed. I found all at home right and tight; my maid seems to have conducted herself quite handsomely in my absence; my *best room* looked really *inviting*. A bust of Shelley (a present from Leigh Hunt), and a fine print of Albert Dürer, handsomely framed (also a present) had *still further ornamented it* during my absence. I also found (for I wish to tell you all my satisfaction) every grate in the house furnished with a supply of coloured clippings! – and the holes in the stair-carpet all darned, so that it looks like new. They gave me tea and fried bacon and staved off my headache as well as might be. They were very kind to me, but on my life, every body is kind to me! and to a degree that fills me with admiration. I feel so strong a wish to make you all convinced how very deeply I feel your kindness! and just the more I would say, the less I am able to say anything . . .

God bless you all. Love to all, from the head of the house down to Johnny.

Yours affectionate

Jane W. Carlyle

A JAUNT TO OXFORD WITH THE STERLINGS

99. To Thomas Carlyle at Scotsbrig

Folley Arms, Great Malvern, Worcestershire/ 11 August 1837

Husband of me

. . . Allons donc! my run-away husband – On Monday (being the 7th of August 1837) I arose and put on clean raiment, and having for the hundredth time recommended to Ellen my roses and silver spoons, and myself to the Great disposer of all, I seated myself beside Mr and Mrs Sterling in their new carriage, with much the same sensations as I might have felt beside Mr and Mrs Graham in their new balloon; to drive wheresoever the wind listed, and be landed where it should please the pigs: so great was the horror of doubt and fluctuation which involved our whole expedition to my thinking! The same day however, about eight in the evening, we actually gained Oxford as proposed; and descended '*da carrozza*' less fatigued and more pleased with our day's-work than '*I as one solitary individual*' had anticipated. – On my life, there is '*a fund of vitality*' in that man, which covereth a multitude of sins. What a taste he still has for '*innocent pleasures*'! what a power of *getting up a sentiment* about anything or nothing! I, who at half his age have already exhausted all that, can do nothing but stare at his preternatural effervescences and raptures. – *The Angel Inn*, where we staid at Oxford, gave me a rather unpleasant impression of the *tone* of that place (for travellers always get very decided and of course infallible impressions of places from the Inns where they eat or sleep) – not that the bread butter et cetera was not first rate, and the silver forks in 'good' style: what disgusted me was to observe in every bed room, *laid before the looking glass, a bible* and *book of prayers* with a small hassock underneath (and this preparation I was told was universal thro' all the Inns at Oxford) *my* particular hassock (of green cloth) had a drawing printed on it, which I was at the pains to examine – it represented a sportsman (for consistency's sake let us hope a *parson*) in the midst of a stubble field taking aim at three birds which he could not fail to hit, the tips of their wings being touching the muzzle of his gun! Moreover the Waiters, all large elderly men, had a sort of 'mazed abstractedness and sad gravity of look which gave one a notion they must have some time or other been unsuccessful graduates: while the Maids *my-ladied* us at such a rate, and made their reverences so profoundly that the free Breton-blood rushed to my face in very shame for them – From all which I inferred that Oxford was a place much under the domination of Cant – Cant in its two most killing shapes, of *Religion* that *keeps its hassock* and *Respectability* that *keeps its gig.*

The Colleges however, which we saw the best part of during Tuesday forenoon under the guidance of Jacobson, interested me beyond measure – not only as being a splendid memorial of past ages but as shaping for me into actual stone and mortar, and painted glass, and illuminated manuscripts and square-capp'd black-gowned figures et cetera, the vague notions I had gathered in my girlhood, out of novels and histories, of a Great English University – But nothing of all that I saw gave me so lively an emotion of pleasure as – a very small thing indeed – neither more nor less than *Guy Fawkes's Lantern* preserved under a glass case! and what gave Mrs Sterling the liveliest emotion of *dis*pleasure, was a question I addressed, with no ill intention but in pure unsophisticated curiosity, to the Gentleman who showed us the Bodleian Picture Gallery, viz: 'how came it that I saw no picture of Oliver Cromwell there, seeing that they had raked together so many insignificant persons of his time?' A broad stare was all the answer I received to this natural enquiry, from which the gentleman's features did not relax so long as I remained in his company. I hope he is now more at ease. There were also many gloriously illuminated manuscripts shown me, which I could have spent much more time in looking at than Mr Sterling would allow – especially a Plato and Tacitus – and a greek testament bound in solid silver having a carved ivory Monk in relief on one side and on the other a Greek inscription purporting that 'the Maker thereof particularly wished God would bless himself and his family' –

And there was Queen Elizabeth's Latin exercise-book (putting me very much in mind of my own) along side of Tippo Saib's gold-lettered *Koran*! But I should need more sheets than one to enumerate all the curiosities and niceties I saw.

With all its magnificence it seems to me that the Bodleian Library must be a most perverse place to study in; for this reason above all, that the numerous private libraries left to it in donation, of which it is chiefly composed, are and *must be* kept *apart* and *entire*; so that instead of *one* great Library arranged under general heads, you have as it were a great many little libraries arranged under one general roof. They told me the inconvenience of this was obviated by the perfection of the catalogues, to which I can only say the perfection of the *catalogues* must be much beyond the perfection of the *Librarians*. One of whom, grown grey in the service, I made as red as a lobster with asking him simple questions which he could nowise answer.

On the Afternoon of the same day we visited Blenheim where amidst much that was note-worthy I remarked most note-worthy of all, and a sort of epitome of the whole, two pictures hung on the same wall, – the one, Old Sarah in her loneliness and her pride, – the other Miss Glover in – her blue satin! (Miss Glover, for to be sure you do not know it, being a trashy actress's daughter, at present officiating as Mistress to his grace of Marlborough, a man of seventy with a wife living in London). I could not but wish that a picture might have spoken for once, and the beautiful termagant might have there and then opened her tinkler-jaw on that trumpery damsel, and asked her in the Devil's name what *she* was doing in *her* Blenheim as '*one of the family*' (to use our Cicerone's delicate phraseology) ? – but so is it ever, pride before destruction – the haughty spirit before a fall! –

We slept that night at a country Inn near Burford, some sixteen miles on the other side of Blenheim, and proceeded hither, next day, by Cheltenham and Tewksbury (not without poking into every crevice of the old church at the latter place) – across the Severn (a marvellously clear flowing river for England) and so thro' a country as full as it could cram of apple-orchards growing on the greenest sward, – patches of the yellowest corn, – thatched homesteads up to the knees in hollyhocks, – and all soft, sweet, picturesque objects, which Nature in her profusion could be suffered to have flung together. For Malvern itself, it only half pleases me – the situation is magnificent, it stands a little way up on a hill or hills, from the top of which you see over *ten* counties, and the window of our sitting-room commands the richest, most extensive prospect I ever saw with my eyes – but as a village it is preposterous – at a little distance it looks as if it had been built with a pack of cards – all so white and twostoried and formal! at hand you find it consists of a great many smart, roman-cemented cockney-built *villas* with a sprinkling of '*gin pallace*'-looking Hotels, grouped stupidly, or in strait lines at regular distances – all which seems so out of character on the slope of a romantic hill and alongside of a fine old Monastery and some two or three *old* houses in the gothic style! – But it will do well enough for all I am likely to *want* with it – Pray heaven you may not find me fallen into that arch-sin – a taste for description of natural scenery.

For the present then you are to figure your *povera piccola* settled in one of these gin-pallace Hotels (*of course* the most aristocratic – when my Lord this and My Lady that breathe the same atmosphere that we breathe –) tolerably well off as to things temporal, but for the spiritual part looking forward to better times; we have private rooms like the rest of the *great* people, and are served with excellent food, and Mrs S. sews at her worsted work, and I work at your purse and the Inevitable exclaims '*By Jove, Hester this tranquillity is – delicious!*' but from the fierce tone he begins in, tho' sinking into dieaway softness at the close, I am always expecting the '*delicious*' will come out a '*damnable*' – and when there is no more to be done 'we go about worship' and so to bed where I for one, tho' quiet enough, sleep no better than at Chelsea – that is to say badly as can be. For all this we pay some guinea a-day *each*! – the more's the pity for him that pays it all. By the way there is certainly a good deal of practical kindness in supporting *me* here at any such rate – However they both seem to think themselves obliged by having my company – and show me all the attention possible – so that I go by the name of '*the young Lady*' in the house – and in short tout va bien – so far. How long it will go so well is another question – He talks of being absent a month. But I guess that either he will return sooner, or I will separate myself from the Great Balloon and alight in a parachute, before that time. I have stood the travelling better than I expected hitherto – going at ones own time in ones own carriage, with an officious Stephen to look after ones odds and ends, and officious Landlords to serve up tender roast chickens and 'exquisite sherry' is a very different sort of thing from dashing over the country in dismay, in doubt and destitution at the blast of a mail coach horn – But I *must* stop. God bless you my beloved. Write instantly on receipt of this – to my present Address –

and tell me if you think of coming back – I do not want to hurry you – but – it is so long that we have not seen each other – at least to me it seems long – Love to all – Again God bless my – Genius –

Jane Carlyle

Pray say something pretty to the Sterlings – they send *you* their kindest regards.

You had better enclose this letter to my Mother – It will give me more time to swallow the *fresh air* on the hills if I make it stand for two –

A VISIT TO THE BULLERS

100. To Thomas Carlyle at Chelsea

Troston, near St Edmundsbury, Suffolk/ 11 August 1842

Here I am then, Dearest, established at Troston Rectory, my clothes all in the drawers; one night over, and for the rest, the body and soul of me 'as well as can be expected'. The journey was less fatiguing than we had supposed; the coach got into Bury at three o'clock instead of five – and Mr Buller and the carriage revealed themselves immediately to my searching eyes – except my parasol, left in the Fly, I committed no further stupidity. At 11 o'clock I ate a small biscuit and a bit of Fannie's barley sugar – and at 2 I ate the Ghent loaf,[1] or the greater part of it, and a very good little loaf it proved to be – grey rye with currants in it – I had also thro' the politeness of the gentleman in the grey jacket, a glass of water, slightly flavoured with *onions*. We did not sit in the *coach* on the railway; they put us into a railway carriage, only leaving the luggage in the coach. The country, most part of the way, reminded me of East Lothian; hereabouts it is richer, and better wooded. The harvest was going on briskly – this to show you that I did *not* sit 'with my eyes on the apron of the gig'.

My reception here was most cordial: Mrs Buller met me with *open arms* (literally), and called me 'dear, *dear* Mrs Carlyle', which from a woman so little expansive, was highly flattering. She looks dreadfully ill – as if she were only kept alive by the force of her own volition, and is more out of spirits than I ever saw her. No wonder! for little Theresa is gone away, and they feel her loss as much as if she had been their real child. Theresa's Mother has fallen ill – of con-

[1] A loaf Carlyle had brought back for her from Ghent.

sumption, the doctors say – and is ordered to the south of France, as the only means of prolonging her life for a year or so. She wished to have her child go with her, and Mrs Buller could not resist her wishes, under such circumstances. So the little thing was sent off to her, *attended by a governess*, three days ago. The Mother is a most amiable and unfortunate woman, Mrs Buller says, and she seems to have been on the most intimate terms with her. But Mrs Buller reads George Sand, like me.

This Rectory is a delightful place to be in, in warm weather; but in winter it must be the reverse of comfortable – all the room-windows opening as doors into the garden, vines hanging over them, &c., &c. It is a sort of compromise between a country *parsonage*, and an aristocratic *cottage*; and compromises never are found to answer, I think, in the long run. It stands in the midst of green fields and fine tall trees – with the church (if such an old delapidated building can be called a church) within a bowshot of it. Around the church is a little quiet-looking church-yard, which, with the sun shining on it, does not look at all sad. A foot-path about half-a-yard wide, and overgrown with green, and strewn with fallen apples, cuts across the bit of green field between the church and the Rectory, and being the *only road* to *the church*, one may infer from it several things!

I went into the church last night with Reginald while Mrs Buller was having her drive; and when I looked at *him* and *it*, and thought of the four hundred and fifty living souls who were to be saved thro *such* means, I could almost have burst into tears. Anything so like the burial-place of revealed religion you have never seen, nor a *Rector* more fit to read its Burial-Service! The churchbell rings, night and morning, with a plaintive clang. I asked, 'Was it for prayers?' 'No, it was to warn the gleaners that it was their time to go out and to come in.' '*Monsieur, cela vous fera un*', &c.[1]

Let no mortal hope to escape night-noises so long as he is above ground! *Here*, one might have thought that all things, except perhaps 'the small birds rejoicing', would let one alone, and the fact is that, with one devilry after another, I have had hardly any sleep, for all so dead-weary as I lay down. Just as I was dropping asleep between eleven and twelve, the most infernal serenade commenced, in comparison of which the shrieking of Mazeppa[2] is soothing melody. It was an ass, or several asses, braying as if the devil were in them, just under my open window! It ceased after a few minutes,

[1] *Grand plaisir*, perhaps – T.C.
[2] A wild horse.

and I actually got to sleep, when it commenced again, and I sprang up with a confused notion that all the Edinburgh Watchmen were yelling round the house, and so on all night! An explosion of ass-brays every quarter of an hour! Then, about four, commenced ever so many cocks – challenging each other all over the parish – with a prodigious accompaniment of *rooks* cawing – ever and anon enlivened by the *hooing* and *squealing* of a child – which my reminiscences of East Lothian instructed me was some varmint of a creature hired to keep off the crows from the grain. Of course, today I have a headache, and if succeeding nights are not quieter, or if I do not *use* to the noise, my stay will not be very long. I am now writing in my own room (which is very pleasant to sit in), taking time by the forelock, in case my head should get worse instead of better, and then, if you were cut out of your letter, '*you would be vaixed*'.

The post leaves Ixworth in the evening, but it is two miles to Ixworth, and the letters get there as they can – Mrs Buller generally takes her afternoon drive in that direction. Letters come in the morning, and this morning I found the French newspaper on the table for me.

I breakfast with Mr Buller and Reginald at nine, preferring that to having it brought to my own room as Mrs Buller recommended.

I will not write any more today, but take care of my head, which needs it. So you must give my love to Jeannie,[1] and a kiss – and bid her do the best she can on that short commons till I am rested. God bless you, my dear husband. I hope you are rested, and going to Lady Harriet; and I hope you will think of me a great deal, and be as good to me when I return as you were when I came away – I do not desire any more of you.

Your own

J.C.

101. To Thomas Carlyle at Chelsea

Troston/ 14 August 1842

My Dearest

There were *two* notes from you this morning – one on each side of my plate – the *first*, having the address of Bury, only, came along with the *third*; so be sure you keep by Ixworth in future. As for '*Keeting*',

---

[1] Jeannie Welsh (Babbie, Jane's cousin) was at Cheyne Row with the maid Helen to look after Carlyle during Jane's visit to the Bullers.

it turned out on investigation to be neither more nor less than Mrs Buller's way of writing *Rectory*.

It is much better with me now, and I find myself quite *hefted* to my new position. But I shall not soon forget the horrors of the first day; feeling myself growing every moment worse – away from you all – and *desperated* by the notion of confessing myself ill, and going to bed and causing a fuss among strangers!

After having written to you, I tried sauntering among the trees – tried lying on the sofa in my own room – tried eating dinner (which is rationally served up here at three o'clock), and finally tried a drive in the carriage with Mrs Buller, all the while saying nothing. But instead of admiring the beauties of Livermere Park, which they took me to see, I was wondering whether I should be able to 'stave off' fainting till I got back. On 'descending from the carriage', I had finally to tell Mrs Buller I was ill and would go to bed. She came upstairs after me, and offered me *sal volatile*, &c.; but seeing that I would have *nothing*, and wanted only to be let alone, she, with her usual good-breeding, *pinned the bell-rope to my pillow*, and went away. A while after, feeling myself turning all cold and strange, I con-sidered would I ring the bell; I did not, and what came of me I cannot tell – whether I fainted, or suddenly fell dead-asleep – but when I opened my eyes, as it seemed, a minute or two after, it was quite dark, and a maid was lighting a night lamp at the table! I asked what o'clock it was? 'Half past eleven! Would I have tea?' No. 'Did I want anything?' No. She was no sooner gone than I fell *naturally* asleep; and when cocks awoke me after daylight, I was quite free of pain, only desperately wearied.

The *asses* did not return the second night, nor last night, and I manage better or worse to weave the *dogs*, *cocks*, and *rooks* into my dreams. My condition has undergone a further amelioration from having the mattress laid above the down-bed – it was like to choke me – besides that I lately read somewhere horrible things about the '*miasma*' contracted by down-beds from all their various occupants through successive generations! – and my imagination got disagree-ably excited in consequence. For the rest; nothing can be better suited to my wants than the life one has here – so that I feel already quite at home, and almost wishing that *you* were Rector of Troston! What a blessed exchange would it be for those poor people, whom I hear at this moment singing feckless psalms! I could almost find in my heart to run over to the old tower and give them a word of admonition myself. Reginald does not *preach* in the morning – he reads service merely, and preaches in the afternoon. I shall go *then* to see 'how the cretur gets thro with it'. I have not made out yet whether there is a downright *want* in him, or whether his faculties are sunk in the shamefulest indolence. He is grown very much into the figure of Mr Ogilvie in miniature. When he speaks I dare not look at his Mother, and feel it a mercy for his father that he is so deaf. The old people do not mean to remain here – the *climate* does not suit Mrs Buller in winter – but they have not made up their minds whether to remove altogether or to hire some place during the cold weather. Oh dear me! 'They have trouble that have the worl'[1] and trouble that want it.' I do not know whether it be worst to be *without* the power of indulging one's reasonable wishes or to *have* the power of indulging one's whims. So many people we know seem to have no comfort with their money, just because it enables them to execute all their foolish schemes.

Jeannie writes to me that when you discovered my parasol you 'crossed your hands in despair' as if you had seen 'the sun's perpendicular heat' already striking down on me. I thought you would be vexing yourself about it – but I have not missed it in the least – the drive here the first day was *cold*; and since then I have had a parasol of Mrs. Buller's, who rejoices in two. And now goodbye dearest – I have two nice long letters from Jeannie to return some acknowledgment for.

Your own
Jane C.

102. To Thomas Carlyle at Chelsea

Troston/ 15 August 1842

Dearest

It was the stupidest-looking breakfast this morning without any letters! – the absence of the loaf or the coffee-pot would have been less sensibly felt! However there is no redress against these London Sundays.

I went to church yesterday afternoon, according to programme – and saw and heard 'strange things upon *my* honour'!

The congregation consisted of some thirty or forty poor people – chiefly adults – who all looked at me with a degree of curiosity rather '*strong*' for the place. Reginald ascended the pulpit in his white *vestment*, and, in a loud, sonorous, perfectly Church-of-England-like tone, gave out the Psalm – whereupon there arose at the far

---

[1] Scots word meaning riches.

end of the mouldering church, a shrill, clear sound, something between a squeal of agony and the highest tone of a bagpipe! I looked in astonishment, but could discover nothing – the congregation joined in with the invisible thing, which continued to assert its predominance – and it was not till the end of the service that Hesketh informed me the strange instrument was 'a clarionet'!! Necessity is the mother of invention!

The service went off quite respectably; it is wonderful how little faculty is needed for saying prayers *perfectly well*! But when we came to the sermon! – greater nonsense I have often enough listened to - for, in fact, the sermon (Mrs Buller with her usual sincerity informed me before I went) 'was none of *his*; he had scraped together as many written by other people as would serve him for years – *which was much better for the congregation*', but he delivered it exactly as daft Mr Hamilton used to read the newspaper – with a noble disdain of everything in the nature of a *stop* – pausing just when he needed breath at the end of a sentence, or in the middle of a word, as it happened! In the midst of this extraordinary exhortation an infant screamed out, 'Away, mammy! Let's away!' and another bigger child went off in whooping cough! For my part, I was all the while in a state between laughing and crying – nay, doing both alternately. There were two white marble tablets before me, containing, one, the virtues of a wife and the sorrow of her husband (Capel Loft), the other a beautiful character of a young girl dead of consumption – and both concluded with 'hopes of an immortality through Jesus Christ'. And there was an old sword and sword-belt hung on the tomb of another Loft – killed in Spain at the age of 28; he also was to be raised up thro Jesus Christ. And this was the Gospel of Christ I was hearing – made into something worse than the cawing of rooks. I was glad to get out, for my thoughts rose into my throat at last, as if they would choke me; and I privately vowed never to go there, when worship was going on again!

We drove as usual in the evening, and also as usual played the game at chess – 'decidedly improper', but I could not well refuse. I sat in my own room reading for two hours after I went upstairs – slept indifferently – the heat being extreme and the cocks indefatigable; and now Mrs Buller has sent me her revised *Play*, begging I will read it, and speak again my candid opinion as to its being fit to be acted. So goodbye, dearest, I shall have a letter tomorrow. Love to Babbie. I wish she had seen the Queen.

Affectionately yours,
Jane Carlyle

A visit to the Bullers

103. TO THOMAS CARLYLE AT CHELSEA

17 August 1842

...Yesterday after breakfast, Mr Buller said we should go to Ampton in the evening – a beautiful deserted place belonging to Lord Calthorpe – 'unless', he added, raising his eyebrows, '*you* have letters to take to Ixworth'. Of course I said my writing was not so urgent that it could not be let alone for a day. And to Ampton we went, where Reginald and I clambered over a high gate with spikes on the top of it, and enjoyed a stolen march through gardens unsurpassed since the original Eden, and sat in a pavilion with the most Arabian-tale-looking prospect – 'the Kingdom of the Prince of the Black Islands' it might have been! – and peeped in at the open windows of the old empty house – empty of people, that is – for there seemed in it everything mortal could desire for ease with dignity: such qualities of fine-bound books in glass bookcases, and easy-chairs, &c., &c.! And this lovely place Lord Calthorpe has taken some disgust to – and has not set foot in for years and never, he says, means to set foot in it again! Suppose you write and ask him to give it to us! He is nearly mad with evangelical religion, they say. Strange that he does not see the sense of letting somebody have the good of what he cannot enjoy of God's providence himself! Look at this delicious and deserted place, on the one side, and the two thousand people standing all night before the Provost's door, on the other! 'And yet you believe', says Mrs Buller, 'That it is a *good* spirit who rules this world.'

You never heard such strange discourse as we go on with during the hour or so we are alone together before dinner! How she contrives, with such opinions or no-opinions, to keep herself so serene and cheerful, I am perplexed to conceive; is it the old story of the 'cork going safe over the falls of Niagara, where everything weightier would sink'? I do not think her so *light* as she gives herself out for – at all events, she is very *clever*, and very good to *me*...

I wish I heard that Helen's leg was whole. If I had had the smallest notion it was to continue so long bad, I would not have come away. I like very ill the notion of Babbie cinderellaing while I am playing the fine lady here – poor little Babbie in her 'flowered dressing gown'! Since you absolutely have not the pluck to kiss her for me, give her at least my warmest regards and say I will write to her next time...

104. TO THOMAS CARLYLE AT CHELSEA

20 August 1842

... They are very anxious you would come, 'and bring Miss Jeannie along with you. Regy would be delighted to have a young lady' – more delighted, I imagine, than the young Lady would be to have Regy! although he does improve on acquaintance. Laziness, and what his mother calls 'muddling habits', are the worst things one can charge him with – one of the people who, with the best intentions, are always unfortunate; but he is very sweet-tempered and kindly; deserves really the only epithet that remained to him – seeing that there was already 'the clever Buller' and 'the handsome Buller' – viz.: 'the good Buller'. If he were not so completely the victim of snuff, I should think an attractive Babbie might be beneficial to him; but I would as soon undertake the reformation of a drunkard as of anybody that snuffs as he does ...

105. TO THOMAS CARLYLE AT CHELSEA

23 August 1842

... To begin where I left off. On Sunday, after writing to you, I attended the afternoon service! Regy looked so *wae* when I answered his question 'whether I was going?' in the negative, that a weak pity induced me to revise my determination. 'It is a nice pew, that of ours,' said old Mr Buller; 'it suits *me* remarkably well, for being so *deep*, I am not *overlooked*; and in virtue of *that*, I read most part of the *femme de qualité* this morning'!! 'But don't', he added, 'tell Mr Regy this! Had Theresa been there, I would not have done it, for I like to set a good example'! I also turned the depth of the pew to good account; when the sermon began, I made myself, at the bottom of it, a sort of Persian couch out of the praying-cushions; laid off my bonnet, and stretched myself out very much at my ease. I seemed to have been thus just one drowsy minute when a slight rustling and the words 'Now to father, son, and holy ghost', warned me to put on my bonnet, and made me for the first time aware that I had been asleep! For the rest, the music that day ought to have satisfied me; for it seemed to have remodelled itself expressly to suit my taste – *Scotch* tunes, produced with the nasal discordant emphasis of a Scotch country-congregation, and *no* clarionet. I noticed in a little square gallery-seat, the only one in the church, a portly character, who acts as blacksmith, sitting with a wand, some five feet long, in his hand, which he swayed about majestically as if it had been a sceptre! On inquiring of our man-servant what this could possibly mean or symbolise, he informed me it was 'to beat the bad children'. 'And are the children here so *bad* that they need such a functionary?' 'O, they will always, them little '*uns*, be doing mischief in *the church*! it's *a-wearisome* for the poor things! – and the rod keeps them in fear'!!

In the evening, the drive, as always, with this only difference, that on Sunday evenings Mr Buller only *walks* the horse – from principle! After this conscientious exercising, the game at chess! My head had ached more or less all day, and I was glad to get to bed, where I was once more fortunate enough to get slept without any violent disturbance. The next day, however, my head was rather worse than better; so that I would fain have '*declined from*' calling on Lady Agnes; but Mrs Buller was bent on going to Livermere, and so as I did not feel up to walking, it was my only chance of getting any fresh air and exercise that day. To Livermere we went, then, before dinner, the dinner being deferred till five o'clock to suit the more fashionable hours of our visitees. 'The Pagets' seem to be extremely like other mortals, neither better nor bonnier nor wiser. To do them justice, however, they might, as we found them, have been sitting for a picture of high-life *doing* the amiable and the rural in the country. They had placed a table under the shadow of a beech-tree; and at this sat Mr Byng studying the 'Examiner', Lady Agnes reading – 'O, nothing at all, only some nonsense that Lord Londonderry has been printing; I cannot think what has tempted him', and a boy and girl *marking* for a cricket-party, consisting of all the men-servants, and two older little sons, who were playing for the entertainment of their master and mistress and their own; the younger branches ever and anon clapping their hands and calling out 'What fun!' I may mention for *your* consolation that Mr Byng (a tall, gentlemanly, *blasé*-looking young man) was dressed from head to foot in unbleached linen – while Babbie may take a slight satisfaction to her curiosity *de femme*, from knowing how a Paget attires herself of a morning, to sit under a beech-tree – a white-flowered muslin pelisse over pale blue satin – a black lace scarf fastened against her heart with a little gold horse-shoe, her white neck tolerably revealed, and set off with a brooch of diamonds – immense gold bracelets – an immense gold chain, a little white silk bonnet with a profusion of blond and flowers – thus had she prepared herself for being rural! But, with all this finery, she looked a good-hearted, rattling, *clever haveral* [i.e. foolish] sort of a woman. Her account of Lord Londonderry's sentimental *dedication* to his wife was perfect – 'from a goose *to* a goose'! – and she defended herself with her pocket handkerchief against the wasps, with *an energy*!

When we had sat sufficiently long under the tree, Mrs Buller asked her to take me thro the gardens, which she did very politely, and gave me some carnations and verbinium; and then thro *the stables*, which were, indeed, the finer sight of the two . . .

106. To Thomas Carlyle at Chelsea

25 August 1842

. . . I hope you have the same refreshing rain in London which is reviving our drooping spirits here; for it is easy to see, altho you try to put the best face on *everything* for me at a distance, that you are suffering horribly from the heat. My only consolation in thinking of your being in the town and I in the country in such weather is that, if you *might* have felt a less degree of suffocation, sitting out of doors here during the day, certainly the improvement would have been counterbalanced by the superior suffocation of *our* nights. Even with both door and window wide open, it is hardly possible to realise a breath of air; the cottage roof collects and retains the heat so very much more than any other sort of roof I ever lived under. After the first few days, I was obliged to give up remaining during the mornings in my own room; my head got into a swimming condition, as when I poisoned myself with the charcoal.[1] Mrs Buller, I find, retires out of *her* room into some back apartment; but even there I am sure the closeness is very hurtful to her. The drawing-room is the coolest place, and that is left to myself till Mrs Buller comes down; except for occasional inroads of *Mr* Buller and Regy to seek some volume of a French novel – repeated cargoes of which are sent for from Rolandi's. 'A very bad stock, this last', I observed last night. 'Yes,' says Mr Buller, raising his eyebrows – 'when French novels are decorous, they are monstrous stupid!' . . .

You may tell Babbie that my ardour for nightcap muslin, that morning, was the most superfluous in nature! for except twice, to mend a hole in my black silk stockings, I have not had a needle in

[1] An accident at Craigenputtoch.

my hand since I left London – nor wished to – neither have I so much as wound the skein for my purse. I do a little in the way of reading – and of writing as you know – and a great deal of nothing at all. I never *weary*, and yet there is no company comes, and, except the evening drive and the chess, we have no *amusements*. The chess, however, is getting into the sphere of a *passion*. Mr Buller 'does not remember *when* he had such good playing as this'; and so, to make hay while the sun shines, he must have a game before dinner as well as the one after tea – sometimes a game will last two hours – and then there is generally three hours consumed in the drive – so that there remains no more time on my hands that I can find ways and means to get rid of without calling in the aid of needlework. Last night we drove to a place called *New* House; which is in fact a very *old* house, bearing the date 1612. The wainscoat [and] floors were polished to such a pitch with wax and turpentine, that I am certain I could have skated on them! The Lady, a married sister of Mr Loft's, showed me an original portrait of 'Fergusson, the self-taught Philosopher, who had been her Mother's preceptor': I was ashamed to ask, 'What does't doe?'[1] I never heard of him in my life. There were various pictures besides – Queen Elizabeth, Charles II, and honourable women not a few. To-night we are to go, if it fairs, to take tea at a show place called The Priory, belonging to 'Squire Cartwright', Mrs Buller is infinitely kind in her exertions to find me amusement . . .

A JOURNEY TO SHERBORNE HOUSE

107. To Thomas Carlyle at Scotsbrig

Chelsea/ 5 August 1852

You recollect, Dear, that Macready told me of *two* routes; recommending that by Frome as the quickest and least fatiguing: so I rendered myself at the Paddington station on Friday morning, with my night-things in a bag on one arm and my 'Blessed'[2] in a basket on the other. *He* gave me no trouble, kept himself hidden and motionless till the train started, and then looked out cautiously, as much as

---

[1] Typical coterie speech. Carlyle explains that Anne Cook, the maid, announced Lord Jeffrey as 'Lurcherfield', and on being corrected asked, 'But what is a "Looard", then? What diz't duih?'

[2] Her dog, Nero.

to say, 'Are we safe?' The journey to Frome was quite a *rest* after that morning's work (carrying down all the books from the top landing-place into the back parlour!) and I descended from the train quite fresh for the thirty miles by coach.

But when I inquired about the coach to Sherborne, I was told there was *none*!! 'A coach passing through Sherborne passed through Frome, without coming to the Station at *eleven* in the morning three hours *before* the time we were at! no other since many months back!' My first thought was; What a mercy *you* were not with me! my next, that the Macreadys could not blame *me* for keeping them waiting – and then I '*considered*,' like the piper's cow and *resolved* – *not* to stay all day and night at Frome, but to take a Yeovil coach which started at five, and which could take me, I was told, to a wayside Inn within eight miles of Sherborne, and there I hoped to find a fly '*or something*'! Meanwhile I would proceed to the town of Frome, a mile from the Station, and get something to eat and even to drink, 'feeling it my duty' to keep my heart up by all needful appliances. I left my little bag at the Station, where the coach came, and set my dog quite free, and we pursued our way as calmly and naturally as if we had known where we were going.

Frome is a dull dirty-looking place, full of Plumbers; one could fancy the Bennett controversy[1] must have been a godsend to it. I saw several Inns and chose *The George* for its name's sake.[2] I walked in and asked to have some cold meat and a pint bottle of Guinness's porter! They showed me to an ill-aired parlour and brought me some cold Lamb that the flies had been buzzing round for a week – even Nero disdained to touch it! I ate bread however, and drank *all* the porter! and 'the cha-arge' for that feeble refection was – 2s. 6d.! Already I had paid one pound eight and sixpence for the train. It was going to be a most unexpectedly costly journey to me! But for that reflection I could almost have laughed at my forlorn position there.

The Inn and Town were 'so disagreeable' that I went presently back to the Station, preferring to wait there. One of the men who had informed me about the coach came to me as I was sitting on a bench and remarked on the beauty of the scene, especially of some scarlet beans that were growing in *his own* piece of garden. 'Ah,' he said, 'I have lived in London and I have lived abroad – I have been

[1] Carlyle, in a note to this letter, says this was 'something in the newspaper', but remembered nothing further.
[2] 'The George' was – and is – the name of the inn at Haddington.

here and there, backwards and forwards, while I was in service, *with them as never could rest*, but I am satisfied now, that the only contentment for Man is in growing his own *VEGETABLE*! Look at them beans,' he said again. 'Well! tomorrow they'll be ready, and I'll be pulling them, and boiling them, and – eating them – ! – and *such* a taste! No agriculture like *that* in Piccadilly!' Then he looked sympathisingly at me and said, 'I'm going to get you something you'll like, and that's a glass of cool, fresh, clear water – and he went away with a jug to his garden and fetched some water from a little spring well – and a great handful of mignionette. 'There! there's something sweet for you, and here's *splendid* water! – that you won't find the like of in Piccadilly.' I asked him how it was going with Mr Bennett? 'Huh! I hear no complaints, but *I* goes to neither one nor other of them, and follows my own notions! *I* finds agriculture the thing!' He would have been worth a hundred pounds to Dickens, that man!

I had the *coach* all to myself for a while, then a young gentleman got in who did exactly the right thing by me, neither spoke to me nor looked at me till we stopt at Castle Carey (*Yeovil* pronounced Youghal? – *Castle Carry*? I grew quite frightened that I had been somehow transported into Ireland)! There the young gentleman went into the Inn, and said to me first, '*Excuse the liberty I take in asking*; but *would* you take anything – a little wine and water?' I thought *that* very *polite* – but I was to meet with 'something more exquisite still' before I got to Sherborne. At the Sparkford Inn – eight miles from Sherborne – I got out and asked had they a *fly*? '*Yes*! but one of its wheels was broken and it was gone to be mended'! 'Had they any other conveyance that was *whole* – a gig or cart?' 'Yes, they had a nice little gig and I should have the loan of a cloak to keep me warm' (the evening was rather chill). So I went in, and sat down in a parlour where an old gentleman was finishing off with cheese and bread. He soon made himself master of my case, and regretted he was not going back to Sherborne that night, as then he would have taken me in *his* carriage; and presently he offered something else more practical, viz., to try to recover my parasol (my Mother's, the one she bought with the sovereign you gave her,[1] and which I had got new covered), left stupidly in the roof of the coach, and never recollected till the coach with its four horses had thundered past the window! If the landlady would tell the coachman about it next day, and get it there, he, the old gentleman, would bring it to Sherborne House. I

[1] A sovereign to each of them, on returning home with a pocketful from my 'first lecture'. Ah, me! – T.C.

went into the Lobby to tell the Landlady, some five or eight minutes after the coach had started, and told her in presence of a gentleman who was preparing to start in a *barouchette* with two horses. He looked hard at me, but said nothing – and a minute or two after I saw *him* also drive past the window. Some twenty minutes after, I started myself, in a little gig, with a brisk little horse, and silent driver. Nothing could be more pleasant than so *pirring* thro quiet roads in the dusk – with the moon coming out. I felt as I were *reading about myself in a Miss Austen novel*! But it got beyond *Miss Austen* when, at the end of some three miles, before a sort of Carrier's Inn, the gentleman of the barouchette stept into the middle of the road, making a sort of military signal to my driver, which he repeated with impatience when the man did not at once draw up! I sat confounded expecting what he *would* do next. We had halted; the gentleman came to my side, and said, exactly as in a book: 'Madam! I have the happiness of informing you that I have reclaimed your parasol and it is here in my carriage ready to be restored!' 'But how on earth?' I asked. 'Madam, I judged that it would be more pleasing for you to take the parasol along with yourself, than to trust to its being brought by the other gentleman – so I just galloped my horses, overtook the coach as it was leaving this court, reclaimed the parasol, and have waited here knowing you could take no other road to Sherborne for the happiness of presenting it to you!' (to an ostler) 'Bring the parasol!' It was brought and handed to me. And then I found myself making a speech in the same style, caught by the infection of the thing. I said: '*Sir*! this day has been full of mischances for me, but I regard this recovery of my parasol so unexpectedly as a good omen, and have a confidence that I shall now reach my destination in safety – accept my thanks, tho it is impossible to give any adequate expression to my sense of your courtesy!' I never certainly made so long and formal a speech in my life. And how I came to make anything like it I can't imagine unless it were under mesmerism! We bowed to each other like first cousins of Sir Charles Grandison and I *pirred* on. 'Do you know that gentleman?' I asked my driver. 'Never saw him before.'

I found Sherborne House without difficulty – and a stately beautiful house it was and a kind welcome it had for me. The mistake had been discovered in the morning, and great anxiety felt all day as to my fate. I was wonderfully little tired, and able to make them all (*her* too) laugh with my adventures. But I must positively interrupt this penny-a-lining and go to bed. It is true *to the letter*, all I have told.

A journey to Sherborne House

My two days at Sherborne House were as happy as could possibly be with that fearfully emaciated, dying woman before my eyes. They were all doing their best to be cheerful – herself as cheerful as the others. She never spoke of her death except in taking leave of me; when she took my head in her hands and kissed it and gave me her solemn blessing and asked me to come again, with *you*, to see William and the children when *she* should be gone. *That* was a dreadful trial of my composure. I am so glad I went; it pleased her and all of them so much!

The journey back by Dorchester went all right, and was less expensive, for I came by the second class, and so saved the nine shillings my *gig* had cost me. It was a weary long way, however, from a quarter before nine till half after seven flying along in one shape or other, with only ten minutes' delay (at Southampton). My only *adventure* on the road back was *falling* in with a young *Unfortunate Female* in the Chelsea boat, the strangest compound of Angel and Devil that I ever set eyes on, and whom, had I been a great, rich Lady, I should decidedly have – brought home to tea with me, and tried 'to *Save*'! The helpless thought that *I* had nothing to offer her *instead* alone prevented me. I could not leave her however, without – speaking to her! – and my words were so moving – through my own emotion that she rushed from me *in tears* to the other side of the vessel. You may feel *a certain* curiosity to know what I said. I only recollect – something about 'her Mother, alive or dead! and her evident superiority to the life she was leading'. She said '*Do you think so, ma'm?*' with a look of bitter wretchedness and forced gaiety that I shall never forget. She was trying to *smile defiantly*, when she burst into tears and ran away . . .

I made a frantic appeal to the workmen the other day, since when we have been getting on a little more briskly. The *Spokesman* of them, a *dashing* young man, whom you have not seen, answered me – 'My *dear* (!) Madam! you must have *patience*! indeed you must! it will be all done – someday!'

. . . My health continues wonderfully good . . . Today I dine at the Brookfields', for what poor Helen used to call 'a fine change'. . .

Ever yours affectionately,

Jane W. C.

VII *In search of her lost youth*

In July 1849, after Carlyle had set off on a trip to Ireland, Jane began an 'outing' of her own, with several stops in England and plans for a round of visits in Scotland. It seems to have been at Rawdon, near Bradford in Yorkshire, where she was staying with William Edward Forster, that the notion seized her to make Haddington her first stop in Scotland and to do so incognito. She had only twice been to Haddington since the days before her marriage in 1826; once in 1829, when she and Carlyle were returning to Craigenputtoch from a visit with Jeffrey, and once in 1833, when she went there alone from Edinburgh and visited her father's grave. She had talked about going back, since that date, but had never been able to face it. She wrote a letter on Monday, 23 July to Dr John Carlyle at Scotsbrig, explaining her plans; set off with Forster as her escort on Tuesday morning for an overnight halt at Morpeth in Northumberland; said goodbye to him after dinner on Wednesday – he was joining Carlyle in Ireland – and reached Haddington the same evening. All worked up by her adventures after her arrival that night, she wrote Carlyle a long midnight letter which she destroyed the next morning, sending instead the businesslike note we print here. Dr John Carlyle got a part of the story in a letter which she wrote from her cousin's manse at Auchtertool, near Kirkcaldy, on 28 July; but the fascinating 'Much ado about nothing', dated Auchtertool Manse, 2 August, seems to have been written as a journal; it was only discovered by Carlyle after her death. The charming letter to Mr Lea, 'grown old like a golden pippin', who had seen her flight over the churchyard wall, was written several weeks later – prompted, perhaps, by the opportunity to give him a copy of the new edition of *Cromwell* as a memento of the visit.

The special quality of Jane's sentiment – the intense self-absorption, the attachment to family and dependents, the feeling of rue – is beautifully revealed by these records.

A BLESSING FROM HERE

108. To Thomas Carlyle at Galway, Sligo

George Inn, Haddington/ 26 July 1849

My dear Dear –

I wrote you a long – very long letter last night, at midnight, from this same place – But this morning instead of putting it in the post office I have torn it up. You may fancy what sort of a letter, 'all about *feelings*' (as Lady A. would say) an excitable character like me would write in such circumstance after a long railway journey,

and a three hours pilgrimage – all up and down and across and round
about Haddington – And you can also understand how after some
hours of sleep, I should have reacted against my last night's self,
and thought all that *steam* best gathered back into the vale of *silence*.

I have now only time to write the briefest of notes – but a *blessing
from here* I *must* send you – to no other mortal would I or indeed
could I write from this place at this moment – but it comes natural
to me to direct a letter to *you* here, and that is still *something*, is it
not? –

I will give you all my news so soon as I have slept a night at
Auchtertool. I expect Walter and Jeannie will meet me at the station
in Edinburgh where I shall be at a quarter after twelve.

I am not too much tired – my journey has been made as easy for
me as possible. From Rawdon to Morpeth, on Tuesday; William
Edward most kindly accompanying me there, and seeing me off next
day – 'I looked so *horribly helpless*', he said, 'that he could not reconcile it to his conscience to leave me a *chance* at losing myself.'

I was wandering about till after dark last night and out again this
morning at six – but I must leave all particulars till a more leisure
moment – and till my heart is a little calmer than just at present. I am
so glad I came here on this incognito principle. It is the only way in
which I could have got any good of the dear old place – God bless it!
how changed it is and how changed am I! – but enough just now.

Ever your affectionate,

Jeannie Welsh

'MUCH ADO ABOUT NOTHING'

109. A JOURNAL

This was probably written as a journal, and only found by Carlyle after Jane's
death.

Auchtertool Manse/ 2 August 1849

On Tuesday, 24th July 1849, I left Rawdon, after breakfast, and
at five of the afternoon reached Morpeth; where I had decided to
pass the night. William Forster escorted me thus far, and stayed to
start me by the 2 o'clock train next day; – out of pure *charity*, having
adopted Donovan's[1] theory of me, that I am wholly without *observ-
ing Faculty*, with large *Reflectiveness* turned inward; – a sort of woman,
that, illadapted for travelling by railway, alone, with two boxes, a

---

[1] A quack physiognomist, &c., of the time – T.C.

writing-case, and carpet-bag. Anyhow, I was much the better of such a cheerful companion; to stave off the nervousness about Haddington; not to speak of the *material* comforts, – a rousing fire, brandy-negus, &c. – which he ordered for me at the Inn, and which I should not have had the audacity to order, on my own basis.

After a modest dinner of chops and cherrytart; we walked by the River-side in a drizzling rain (*that* was at *my* suggestion); then back to the Phoenix for tea, chess, and speculative talk till midnight; when I went to bed expecting no sleep to speak of, and of course slept unusually well; for the surest way to get a thing in this life is to be prepared for doing without it, – to the exclusion even of hope.

Next morning was bright as diamonds, and we walked all about the Town and neighbouring Heights; where, rendered unusually communicative by our isolated position, I informed William Edward that my maternal grandmother was 'descended from *a Gang* of Gipsies'; was in fact grandniece to Matthew Baillie who '*suffered* at Lanark', – that is to say, was *hanged* there, – a genealogical fact Forster said which made *me* at last intelligible for him, – 'a cross betwixt John Knox and a Gipsy how that explained all'. – By the way, my uncle has told me since I came here, that the wife of that Matthew Baillie, Margaret Euston by name, was the original of Sir W. Scott's *Meg Merrilies*. Matthew himself was *the last of the Gipsies*, – could steal a horse *from under* the owner, if he liked, but left always the saddle and bridle; a thorough *gentleman* in his way, and sixfeet four in stature!

But to go back to Morpeth, we again dined at the Phoenix; then Forster put me into my carriage, and my luggage in the van and I was shot off towards Scotland; – while himself took train for – *Ireland*!

From Morpeth to Haddington is a journey of only four hours; again 'the wished for come too late'! rapidest travelling to Scotland now, and no *home* there any more!

The first locality I recognised was *the Peer Bridge*: I had been there *once* before, a little child, in a postchaise with my Father; he had held his arm round me while I looked down the ravine; it was my first sight of the Picturesque, *that*. I recognised the place even in passing it at railway speed, after all these long long years.

At the Dunbar station an old lady in widow's dress, and a young one, her daughter, got into the carriage which I had had so far all to myself; a man in yeomanry uniform waiting to see them off. 'Ye'll maybe come and see us the *morn'snicht*?' said the younger lady from the carriage. '*What for* did ye *no* come to the Ball?' answered the yeoman, with a look 'to split a pitcher'? The young lady *tchick-tchicked* and looked deprecatingly, and tried again and again to *enchain* conversation; but, to everything she said, came the same answer; '*What for* did ye *no* come to the Ball?' – The poor young lady then tried holding her tongue; her lover (only her *lover* would have used her so *brutally*) did the same; but rested his chin on the carriage-window to scowl at her with more convenience. The interest was rising; but one could see who of them would speak first. 'Oh!' broke out the young lady, 'I'm just mourning!' '*What for*?' – 'Oh, just *that* ball!' – '*What for* then did [ye] *no* come?' growled the *repeating decimal*; 'I waited an *oor* for ye!' and he got his upper lip over the strap of his cap and champed it – like a horse! – Squeal went the engine; we were off; the young lady '*just mourned*' for a minute or two, then fell to talking with her Mother; for me, I reflected how 'the feelings were just the same there as here',[1] and the Devil everywhere busy!

Before these ladies got out at Drem I had identified the pale, old, shrivelled widow with a buxom bright-eyed rosy Mrs Frank Sheriff of *my* time. The Daughter had not only grown up but got herself born in the interval. What chiefly struck me, however, indeed confounded me, was to be stared at by Mrs Sheriff as a stranger, or even *foreigner*! (for, when I asked her some question about the road, she answered with that compassionate distinctness which one puts on with only *foreigners* – or *idiots*.) I began to think my precautions for keeping *Incognita* in my native place might turn out to have been superfluous.

One of these *precautions* had the foolishest little consequence. In leaving London, I had written the addresses for my luggage on the backs of other peoples visiting-cards, 'without respect of persons'; a stupid practice when one thinks of it! – but at Morpeth I removed three of the cards, leaving one to the carpet-bag, carpet-bags being so confoundable; I was at the pains however to rub off *my own* name from *that* card, which, for the rest, happened to be Mrs Humphrey St John Mildmay's. Well! at Longniddry, where I had to wait some fifteen minutes for the cross-train to Haddington, '*there came to pass*' a *Porter*! who helped me with my things, and would not leave off helping me – quite teased me in fact with *delicate attentions*. At last he made me a low bow and said he was 'not aware that any of the family were in this quarter'. I believe I answered; '*quite well I thank*

[1] As Carlyle's mother had said when she read *Wilhelm Meister*.

you'; for I was getting every instant more *excited* with my circumstances. He shut the carriage-door on me, then opened it again and
said with another low bow; 'Excuse me, Ma'm but I was in the
service of the Brother of Mr Humphrey St John Mildmay.' I am
positive as to my answer this time, that it was; '*Oh thank you No! I am
quite another person!*'

A few minutes more and I was at the Haddington Station; where
I looked out timidly, then more boldly, as my senses took in the utter
strangeness of the scene; and luckily I had '*the cares of luggage*' to keep
down *sentiment* for the moment. No vehicle was in waiting but a
dusty little Omnibus licensed to carry – *any number*, it seemed! for on
remarking there was no seat for me I was told by all the *Insides* in a
breath; 'never heed! come in! *that* makes *no* difference!' And so I was
trundled to *The George Inn*, where a Landlord and Waiter, both
strangers to me, and looking half-asleep showed me to the best room
on the first floor, – a large old-fashioned, three-windowed room,
looking out on *The Fore Street*, – and, without having spoken one
word, shut the door on me, and there I was at the end of it! –
Actually in the George Inn, Haddington, alone, amidst the silence
of death!

I sat down quite composedly at a window, and looked up
the street, – towards our old House; it was the same street, the
same houses; but so silent, – dead, *petrified*! it looked, the old place,
just as I had seen it at Chelsea in my dreams – only *more* dreamlike! –
Having exhausted that outlook, I rung my bell, and told the silent
Landlord to bring tea, and took order about my bedroom. The
tea swallowed down; I notified my wish to view 'the old Church
there', and the keeper of the keys was immediately fetched me. In
my part of stranger-in-search-of-the-Picturesque, I let myself be
shown the way which I knew every inch of, – shown the 'the
school-houses' where myself had been *Dux*, – 'the play-ground',
'the *Boo*lin green', and so on to the church-gate, which so soon as
my guide had unlocked for me, I told him he might wait – that I
needed him no further.

The Church-yard had become very full of graves. Within *the
Ruin* were two new *smartly got up* tombs; *His* [her father's] looked old,
old; was surrounded by nettles; the inscription all over moss; except
two lines which had been quite recently cleared. – *by whom*? Who had
been there, before *me*, still caring for *his* tomb after 29 years? The old
Ruin knew, and could not tell me! that place *felt* the very centre of
eternal silence – silence and sadness world without end! When I

returned to the sexton, or whatever he was, he asked would I not walk thro the church; I said yes, and he led the way, but without playing the Cicerone any more; he had become pretty sure there was no need. *Our* pew looked to have never been new-lined since *we* occupied it; the *green* cloth was become all but *white* from age! I looked at it in the dim twilight till I almost fancied I saw my beautiful Mother in her old corner, and myself a bright-looking girl in the other! It was time to 'come out of *that*'! Meaning to return to the Churchyard next morning, to clear the moss from the inscription; I asked my conductor where he lived – with the key. 'Next door to the house that was Dr Welsh's', he answered, with a sharp glance at my face; then added *gently*; 'excuse me mem for mentioning *that*, but the minute I set eyes on ye at the *George*, I *jaloosed* it was *her* we all looked after whenever she went up or down.' 'You won't tell of me?' I said, crying, like a child caught stealing apples; and gave him half a crown to keep my secret, and open the gate for me at eight next morning. Then turning, up the waterside by myself, I made the circuit of *The Haugh, Dodd's Gardens* and *Babbies Butts*, – the customary evening walk in my teens; and except that it was perfectly *solitary* (in the whole round I met just two little children walking hand in hand, like *the Babes of the Wood*) the whole thing looked exactly as I left it 22 years back! the very puddles made by the last rain I *felt* to have stepped over before. – But where were all the living beings one used to meet? What could have come to the place to strike it so dead? I have been since answered; the railway had come to it, and ruined it. At all rates 'it must have taken a great deal to make a *place* so dull as that'! – Leaving the lanes I now went boldly thro' the streets, the thick black veil, put on for the occasion, thrown back; I was getting confident that I might have ridden like *the Lady Godiva* thro Haddington, with impunity, – so far as recognition went. – I looked thro' the sparred door of our old coachhouse, which seemed to be vacant; the House itself I left over till morning, when its occupants should be asleep. Passing a Cooper's shop which I had once had *the run of*, I stept in and bought two little *quaighs*; then in the character of travelling Englishwoman, suddenly seized with an unaccountable passion for wooden dishes, I questioned the Cooper as to the *Past and Present* of his town. He was the very man for me, being ready to talk the tongue small in his head about his town's-folks, men, women, and children of them. He told me amongst other interesting things, that 'Doctor Welsh's death was the sorest loss ever came to the Place'; – that myself 'went away into England and

– died there'! adding a handsome enough tribute to my memory –
'Yes! Miss Welsh! he remembered her famously, – used to think her
the *tastiest* young lady in the whole Place – but she was very – not
just to call *proud*, – very *reserved in her company.*' – In leaving this man
I felt more than ever like my own ghost; if I had really been *walking*
after my death and burial, there could not I think have been any
material difference in my sensations.

My next visit was to the front gate of Sunny Bank, where I stood
some minutes, looking up at the beautifully quiet House; not unlike
the 'outcast *Peri*' *done into prose*. How would my old godmother and
the others have looked, I wondered, had they known who was there,
so near them! I longed to go in and kiss them once more, but positively *dared* not; I felt that their demonstrations of affection would
break me down into a torrent of tears, which there was no time for;
so I contented myself with kissing – the *gate*(!) and returned to my
Inn, it being now near Dark. Surely it was the silentest Inn on the
Planet! not a living being male or female to be seen in it except when
I rung my bell, and then the Landlord or Waiter (both old men) did
my bidding promptly and silently and vanished again into space. On
my reentrance I rung for candles, and for a glass of sherry and hot
water; my feet had been wetted amongst the long grass of the churchyard, and I felt to be taking cold; so I made myself negus as an antidote, and they say I am not a *practical* woman! Then it struck me; I
would write to Mr Carlyle, – one more letter from the old place,
after so much come and gone. Accordingly I wrote till the Town
clock (the first familiar voice I had heard) struck eleven, then twelve,
and near *one* I wrote the Irish address on my letter and finally put
myself to bed – in the George Inn of Haddington, good God! – I
thought it too strange and mournful a position for ever falling
asleep in; nevertheless I *slept* in the first instance; for I was 'a-weary
a-weary', body and soul of me! But, alas! the *only noise* I was to hear
in Haddington '*transpired*' exactly at the wrong moment; before I
had slept one hour I was awoke by – an explosion of cats! The rest
of that night I spent betwixt sleeping and waking, in night-mare-
efforts to 'sort up my thoughts'. At half after five I put my clothes on,
and began the business of the day by destroying in a moment of
enthusiasm – for *silence* – the long letter 'all about feelings' which I
had written the night before. Soon after six I was *haunting* our old
house, while the present occupants still slept. I found the garden
door *locked*, and *iron stanchions*, – my Heavens! – on the porch and
cellar windows, 'significative of much'! for the rest, there was a

general need of paint and whitewash: in fact the whole premises had a bedimmed melancholy look as of having '*seen better days*'. It was difficult for me to realise to myself that the people inside were only *asleep* – and not *dead* – *dead since many years*. Ah! one breathed freer in the churchyard, with the bright morning sunshine streaming down on it than near that (so-called) habitation of the living! I went straight from the one to the other. The gate was still locked; for I was an hour before my time; so I made a dash at the wall, some seven feet high I should think, and dropt safe on the inside – a feat I should never have imagined to *try* in my actual phase, not even with a mad bull at my heels; if I had not trained myself to it at a more elastic age. Godefroi Cavaignac's '*Quoi donc je ne suis pas mort?*' crossed my mind but *I* had none of that feeling – *moi*, – was morte enough, I *knew*, whatever face I might put on it! only, what one has well learnt one never forgets.

When I had scraped the moss out of the inscription, as well as I could with the only thing in my dressing case at all suited to the purpose, namely *his own* button hook with the mother-of-pearl handle; I made a deliberate survey of the whole churchyard; and most of the names I had missed out of the *signboards* turned up for me once more on the *tombstones*. It was strange the feeling of almost *glad* recognition that came over me, in finding so many familiar figures out of my childhood and youth all gathered together in one place; But still more interesting for me than these later graves were *two* that I remembered to have weeped little innocent tears over before I had a conception what real weeping meant, – the grave of the little girl who was burnt to death, thro' drying her white muslin frock at the fire, and that of the young officer (Rutherford) who was shot in a duel. The oval tablet of white marble over the little girl's grave looked as bright and spotless as on the first day – as emblematic of the child existence it commemorated; it seemed to my somewhat excited imagination that the youthfulness and innocence there buried had impregnated the marble to keep it snow-white for ever! – When the sexton came at eight to let me in; he found me ready to be *let out*. 'How in the world had I got in?' – 'over the wall.' 'No! surely I couldn't mean *that*?' – 'Why not?' – 'Lordsake then,' cried the man in real admiration, 'there is *no end* to you!' –

He told me at parting; 'there is *one* man in this Town, Mem you might like to see – James Robertson, your Father's old servant.' Our own old Jamie! he was waiter at *The Star* good gracious! had returned to Haddington within the last year. 'Yes indeed' – I said, 'he

must be sent to me at The George an hour hence; and told only that
a Lady wanted him.'

It was still but eight o'clock, so I should have time to look at Sunny
Bank from the *back* gate, and streamed off in that direction; but
passing my dear old schoolhouse, I observed the door a little ajar,
walked in and sat down in my old seat; to the manifest astonishment
of a decent woman who was sweeping the floor. *Ach Gott*! our maps
and Geometrical Figures had given place to *Texts from Scripture* and
the foolishest *half-penny pictures*! it was become an *Infant School* Good
God! and a *Miss* Alexander was now Teacher where Edward Irving
and James Brown had taught! – Miss A. – and her Infants were not,
it seemed early risers; their schoolroom after eight o'clock was only
being swept; it was at *seven* of the morning that James Brown once
found *me* asleep there – after two hours hard study – asleep betwixt
the leaves of *the Great Atlas*, like a *keep lesson*! but 'things have been
all gone to the Devil ever since the reform bill'; as my Uncle is
always telling us. The woman interrupted her sweeping to inform
me amongst other things that it 'was a most terrible place for dust';
that 'a deal was put into *Bairns* now, which she *dooted* was *waste*
wark'; that 'it was little one got by *cleaning after them*', and 'if her
Husband *had his legs*, they might *have* the school that liked'.

Not the vestige of a Boy or even of a *girl* was to be seen about *the
Grammar* School either; *that* school, I afterwards heard from Jamie
'had gone to just perfect nonsense' – 'There was a *Master* (one
White) but no *scholars*.' 'How *is* that, I asked; '*are* there no children
here any longer?' 'Why, its not altogether the want o' children,'
said Jamie, with his queer old *smudge* of inarticulate fun; 'but the
new Master is *rather* severe, – *broke the jawbone of a wee Boy* – they tell
me; but indeed the whole place is sore gone down.' I should think
so! But I am not got to Jamie yet; another meeting came off before
that one.

Sunny Bank looked even lovelier 'in the light of a new morning'
than it had done in the evening dusk. A hedge of red roses in full
blow extended now from the House to the gate; and I thought I might
go in and gather one without evoking any – Beast. Once inside the
gate I passed easily to the idea of proceeding as far as the backdoor,
just to ask the servant how they all were, and leave compliments
without naming myself; the servants only would be a-stir so early.
Well! when I had knocked at the door with my finger 'sharp but
mannerly'; it was opened by a tidy maidservant exhibiting no more
surprise than if I had been the Baker's boy! Strange, was it not, that

anybody should be in a calm state of mind, while *I* was so full of emotions? strange that the universe should pursue its own course without reference to my presence in Haddington!! – 'Are your Ladies quite well'; I asked nevertheless. 'Miss Jess and Miss Catherine are quite well, Miss Donaldson rather *complaining*; you are aware Mem that Mr Donaldson is dead?' 'Oh dear yes!' I said, thinking she meant Alexander. 'At what hour do your Ladies get up?' 'They *are* up Mem and done breakfast. Will you walk round to the front door?' – Goodness gracious! *should* I 'walk round' or not? – My *own* nerves had got braced somewhat by the morning air; but *their* nerves – how would the sight of me thus '*promiscuously*' operate on *them*? 'You had better go round and let me tell the Ladies,' put in the servant, as if in reply to my cogitations; 'what name shall I say?' – 'None, I think, perhaps my name would startle them more than myself; tell them; *someone they will be glad to see.*' And so, flinging the responsibility on *Providence*, who is made for being fallen back upon in such dilemmas, ('Providence must have meant me to see them in raising them out of bed so betimes!'), I did 'go round', with my heart thumping, 'like, – like, – like – *anything*'.

The maidservant met me at the front-door and conducted me to the Drawingroom, where was – nobody; but on a table lay a pile of *black*-bordered note-paper which explained to me, that it was Mr Donaldson of London who was *dead*; the last Brother – dead in these very days! I wished I had not come in; but it was out of time now. – The door opened and showed me Miss Catherine changed into an *old* woman, and showed Miss Catherine *me*, changed into one of – a *certain* age! She remained at the door, motionless, speechless, and *I* couldn't rise off my chair, at least I didn't; but when I saw her eyes staring 'like watch-faces', I said, 'Oh Miss Catherine don't be frightened at me!' – and then she quite *shrieked* 'Jeannie! Jeannie! Jeannie Welsh! *my* Jeannie! *my* Jeannie!' – Oh mercy I shan't forget that scene in a hurry! I got her in my arms and kissed her into her wits again; and then we both cried a little – naturally –; both of us had had enough since we last met to cry for. I explained to her 'how I was *situated*', as Mr C. would say, and that I was meaning to visit them after – like a Christian; and she found it all 'most wisely done – done like my own self'. – Humph! – Poor Miss Catherine! it's little she knows of my own self's and perhaps the less the better! She told me about their Brother's death, which had been sudden at the last. Supposing me still in London as usual, and that in London we hear of one another's deaths; they had been saying it was strange I did not write to them and my godmother had remarked, 'it is not like her!' – just while I was standing at their gate most likely; for it was 'the evening before, about dark', they had been speaking of me.

But again the door opened and showed Miss Jess – *Ach!* – *she* had to be *told* who I was, and pretty *loudly* too; but when she *did* take in the immense fact, oh *my*! if she didn't '*show feeling enough*' (her own favourite expression of old)! – Poor Jess after all! We used to think she *showed* even more *feeling* than she *felt*, and nothing came out on the present emergence to alter our opinion of her. But enough – *the very old*, it seems to me, should be admitted, by favour, to the privilege of *the Dead*, – have '*no ill*' spoken of them, that can possibly be helped.

My 'Godmother' was keeping her bed 'with rheumatism' and grief; as I 'would *really* come back soon', it was settled to leave her quiet. They offered me breakfast, – it was still on the table: but '*horrible was the thought*' to me! It was all so solemn and doleful there that I should have heard every morsel going down my throat! besides I was engaged to breakfast with *myself* at *the George*. So, with blessings for many days, I slipt away from them like a knotless thread. My friend the Cooper, espying me from his doorway, on the road back, planted himself *firmly* in my path: 'if I would just compli*ment* him with my name, he would be *terribly* obliged; we had been *uncommon comfortable* together, and he *must* know what they called me'! I told him, and he neither died on the spot nor went mad; he looked pleased and asked how many children I had had. *None*, I told him. 'None!' (in a tone of astonishment, verging on horror.) 'None at all! then what on the Earth had I been *doing* all this time?' 'Amusing myself,' I told him. He ran after me, to beg I would give him a call on my return (I had spoken of returning) 'as he might be making something, belike, to *send south* with me, something *small* and *of a fancy sort, liker myself* than *them* I had bought'.

Breakfast stood ready for me at the Inn, and was discussed in five minutes. Then I wrote a note to Mr C., a compromise betwixt '*all about feelings*' and '*the new silent system*' – of the *Prisons*. Then I went to my bedroom to pack up. The chambermaid came to say a *gentleman* was asking for me. 'For me?' 'Yes! he asked for *the lady stopping* here' (no influx of company at the George it seemed) 'Did you see him' I asked, divining Jamie, 'are you sure it is a *gentleman?*' 'I am sure of his being *put on* like one.' I flew down to my parlour, and there was Jamie sure enough! Jamie to the Life! and I threw my arms round his neck, that did I! – He stood quite passive and quite pale with *great* tears rolling down; it was minutes before he

spoke, and then he said only, low under his breath; 'Mrs – Carlyle!'
So nice he looked, and hardly a day older, and really as like 'a
gentleman' as some Lords; he had dressed himself in his Sunday
clothes for the occasion, and they were capital good ones. 'And you
knew me, Jamie, at first sight' I asked? 'Toot! *we* knew ye *afore* we
seed ye.' – 'Then you were told it was me?' – 'No! they told us just
we was to speak to a Lady at the George, and I knew it was Mrs
Carlyle.' – 'But how *could* you tell, dear Jamie?' 'Hoots! *who else
could it be?*' Dear funniest of created Jamies! – While he was ostler at
the Black Bull, Edinburgh; 'one of them what-ye-call *Bagmen
furgottet* his patterns' at Haddington, and he (Jamie) was 'sent to
take them up; and falling in talk with *Him* of *the Star*, it came out
there was no waiter, and so in that way, said Jamie, 'we came back
to the old place.' He told me all sorts of particulars 'more profitable
to the soul of man' than anything I should have got out of Mr
Charteris in three *years*, never to say 'three weeks'. But 'a waggon
came in atween ten and eleven and he must be stepping west'. 'He
was glad to have seen me looking so (dropping his voice) – stootish!'
(I saw him, from the omnibus, after, unloading the waggon, in his
workday clothes, almost on the very spot where, for a dozen years,
he had helped me in and out of our carriage!)

And now there only remained to pay my bill and await the omnibus. I have that bill of 6/6 in my writing-case; and shall keep it all
my days; not only as an eloquent memorial of human change – like
grass from graves and all that sort of thing; but as the first Inn bill I
ever in my life contracted and paid *on my own basis*.

Another long look from the George Inn window, – and then into
the shabby little omnibus again; where the faces of a Lady next me
and a gentleman opposite me tormented my memory without result.

In the railway carriage which I selected, an old gentleman had
taken his seat, and I recognised him at once as Mr Lea – the same
who made the little obelisk which hangs in my bedroom at Chelsea.
He had grown old like a golden pippin, merely *crined* [shrunk] with
the bloom upon him. I laid my hand on his arm, turning away my
face, and said, 'Thank God here is one person I feel no difficulty
about.' 'I don't know you,' he said in his old blunt way, 'who are
you?' – 'Guess!' – 'Was it you who got over the churchyard wall
this morning? I saw a stranger-lady climb the wall and I said to
myself that's Jeannie Welsh! – no other woman would climb the
wall instead of going in at the gate – *are* you Jeannie Welsh?'

I owned the soft impeachment; then such shaking of hands! em-

bracing even! But so soon as things had calmed down a little between us; Mr Lea laid his hand on my shoulder and said as if *pursuing knowledge under difficulties*; 'Now tell me, my Dear, why *did* you
get over the wall instead of just asking for the key?'

He spoke of William Ainsley's death; I said I had never known
him, that he went to India before I could remember. 'Nonsense,'
said Mr Lea; 'not remember William Ainsley? – never knew William
Ainsley? What are you thinking of? Why; didn't he wrap you in a
shawl and run away with you to our house the *very day you were born*,
I believe?' – I said it might be very true but that the circumstance
had escaped my recollection. Mr Lea was left at Longniddry where
he came daily, he said, to bathe in the sea. What energy!

While waiting there for the train from London, I saw again my
Lady and Gentleman of the omnibus, and got their names from Mr
Lea; they were not people I had ever visited with, but I had been at
school with them both. We passed and repassed one another without
the slightest sign of recognition on their side.

George Cunningham too was pacing the Longniddry-platform,
the Boy of our school who never got into *trouble* and never helped
others out of it, – a slow bullet-headed boy who said his lessons like
an eight-day clock and never looked *young*; now, on the wrong side of
forty it might be doubted if he would ever look *old*. He came up to me
and shook hands, and asked me by name how I did, exactly as tho'
we met *on change* every day of our lives! To be sure I had seen him
once since we were at school together, had met him at Craik's some
twelve years ago. – Such as he was; we stood together till the train
came up, and 'talked of geography, politics, and *nature*'.

At Edinburgh Jeannie's sweet little face looked wildly into the
carriage for me, and next minute we were *chirping* and *twittering*
together on the platform whilst the eternal two boxes writing-case
and carpet-bag were being once more brought into one focus. –
'Look, look, cousin' said Jeannie, '*there* are people who know you!'
and looking as I was bid; who but the pair who had accompanied me
from Haddington were standing, with their heads laid together, and
the eyes starting out of them *me*-ward! The Lady the instant she saw
I noticed them sprang forward extending her hand; the husband
'emboldened by her excellent example' did the same; they were
'surprised', 'delighted', everything that could be wished; 'had not
had a conception of its being me till they saw me *smiling*' – 'Eh,
sirs!' said my Mother's old nurse to her after a separation of twenty
years, 'there's no a *featur* o' ye left, but just *the bit smile*!'

I will call for these Richardsons when I go back to Haddington; I liked their *hop-skip-and-jump* over ceremony – their oblivion in the enthusiasm of the moment that we had '*belonged to different circles*' (*Haddingtonly* speaking).

And now having brought myself to Edinburgh and under the little protecting wing of Jeannie, I bid myself adieu and 'wave my lily hand' – I was back into the Present! and it is only in connection with the Past that I can get up a sentiment for myself. The Present Mrs Carlyle is what shall I say? – *detestable* – upon *my* honour.

A KIND REMEMBRANCE FROM THE WALL-CLIMBER

110. To Mr Lea at Haddington

5 Cheyne Row, Chelsea/ 23 November 1849

My dear Mr Lea

You will presently receive, – if indeed you have not already received it, a copy of my Husbands *Cromwell*, a new edition of which is just come out. It was directed to be sent in a Bookseller's parcel to Edinburgh; whence they would forward it to you by the railway. I do not remember whether you liked *reading* in old times, and suppose you liked it ever so well twenty years ago; it does not follow that you should be still of the same mind – one's taste for reading I find, to my sorrow, is after all but a *taste*, which one may lose like one's taste for dancing or for *climbing walls*! but whether you *read* the book, or no; I am sure you will like to *have* it, as a token of kind remembrance from me, and of my Husbands participation in my grateful feelings towards you.

Dear Mr Lea! You did me a world of good with your kind looks and words – not merely good *for the time*, but to this hour I feel happier for having seen you – Indeed my visit to Haddington was altogether good for me; tho' trying for my nerves, and *very* sad! – There is a preciousness in the affection bestowed on me *for the sake of my parents* which no other affection has or ever can have for me in this world – and I needed to go back to dear old Haddington to know how much of such affection still remained for me there – God bless you all! It may be a while before you *see* me again *climbing the Churchyard* Wall, but I am often there, for all that, in my *dreams* and in my waking thoughts too –

197

Give my kind love to your wife and to Kitty Brown – dear Kitty! except that she looked paler I did not see a bit of difference in *her* – Tell our old Jamie at the Star Inn that you have heard from me, and that I send him my compliments – and tell William Dodds to be sure and call for me when he comes to London.

If you can't be troubled writing a line yourself make Kitty write when you have got the book that I may be sure of its having reached you safe.

Ever your affectionate
Jeanie Welsh Carlyle

[on first page – upside down]

Do you remember the little obelisk you made for my Mother with my Fathers hair? It hangs in my bedroom here beside my Mothers miniature.

VIII *Guardian angel*

Jane often quoted, in a half-comical, half-rueful way, a verse that ran

> O little did my Mammy think
> The day she cradled me,
> The lands I was to travel in,
> The death I was to dee.

This was 'a natural wail for a much "made of" *Only Child*!' she told the second Lady Ashburton, 'But extremely little to the practical purposes of the wife of a nervous Man of Genius.'

It was at Craigenputtoch that she discovered what 'the duty nearest hand' was going to mean for her, and how what mattered was the spirit in which she did it. Darning socks, sewing buttons, baking bread, 'putting down' barking dogs with gifts of whisky, silencing crowing cocks, wrestling with Tax Commissioners, writing the letters he was too busy to write himself, mending his boots on New Year's Day – all these services Jane performed, though not always without complaint, for her genius husband. Without her he was a babe in the woods. Her last victory over the infernal cocks was won within a few months of her death. She said that she stood between him and any new, untrained servant, imitating 'in a small humble way the Roman soldier who gathered his arms full of the enemy's spears and received them all into his own breast!' She was indeed his guardian angel, and it was 'No sinecure I can tell him!'

WATCHING A LOAF OF BREAD

111. TO MARY SMITH AT CARLISLE

5 Cheyne Row, Chelsea/ 11 January 1857

Dear Miss Smith

...So many talents are wasted, so many enthusiams turned to smoke...for want of recognising that it is not the greatness or littleness of 'the duty nearest hand', but the spirit in which one does it, that makes one's doing noble or mean!

I can't think how people who have any natural ambition, and any sense of power in them, escape going *mad* in a world like this, without the recognition of that! I know I was very near mad when I found it out for myself (as one has to find out for oneself everything that is to be of any real practical use to one). Shall I tell you how it came into my head? Perhaps it may be of comfort to you in similar moments of fatigue and disgust.

I had gone with my husband to live on a little estate of *peat bog*, that had descended to me, all the way down from John Welsh, the Covenanter, who married a daughter of John Knox. *That* didn't, I'm ashamed to say, make me feel Craigenputtoch a whit less of a peat bog, and most dreary, untoward place to live at. In fact, it was sixteen miles distant on every side from all the conveniences of life – shops, and even post office!

Further, we were very *poor* and, further and worst, being an only child, and brought up to 'great prospects', I was sublimely ignorant of every branch of useful knowledge, though a capital Latin scholar and a very fair mathematician!! It behoved me in these astonishing circumstances to learn – to sew! Husbands, I was shocked to find, wore their stockings into holes! and were always losing buttons! and *I* was expected to 'look to all that'. Also, it behoved me to learn *to cook*! No capable servant choosing to live at 'such an out of the way place', and my husband having 'bad digestion' which complicated my difficulties dreadfully. The *bread* above all, brought from Dumfries, 'soured on his stomach' (oh Heavens!); and it was plainly my duty as a Christian wife to bake at home! So I sent for Cobbett's '*Cottage Economy*' and fell to work at a loaf of bread. But knowing nothing of the process of fermentation or the heat of ovens, it came to pass that my loaf got put into the oven at the time myself ought to have put into bed, and I remained the only person not asleep, in a house in the middle of a desert! One o'clock struck, and then two and then three; and still I was sitting there in an intense solitude, my whole body aching with weariness, my heart aching with a sense of forlornness and *degradation*. 'That I who had been so petted at home, whose comfort had been studied by everybody in the house, who had never been required to *do* anything but *cultivate my mind*, should have to pass all those hours of the night watching *a loaf of bread*! which mightn't turn out bread after all!'

Such thoughts maddened me, till I laid my head on the table and sobbed aloud. It was then that somehow the idea of Benvenuto Cellini's sitting up all night watching his Perseus in the oven came into my head; and suddenly I asked myself, 'After all, in the sight of the upper powers, what is the mighty difference between a statue of Perseus and a loaf of bread, so that each be the thing one's hand hath found to do?' The man's determined will, his energy, his patience, his resource, were the really admirable things, of which the statue of Perseus was the mere chance expression. If he had been a woman living at Craigenputtoch with a dyspeptic husband, sixteen miles from a baker, *and he a bad one*, all these same qualities would have come out most fitting in a *good* loaf of bread!

I cannot express what consolation this germ of an idea spread over an uncongenial life, during five years we lived at that savage place; where my two immediate predecessors had gone *mad*, and the third had taken to *drink* . . .

Yours truly
Jane W. Carlyle

PUTTING DOWN THE DOG NEXT DOOR

112. To Thomas Carlyle at Scotsbrig

5 Cheyne Row, Chelsea/ 10 October 1845

Well! now I am subsided again – set in for a quiet evening – at leisure to write, and with plenty to write about. I know not how it is; I seem to myself to be leading a most solitary and *virtuous* and eventless life here at this *dead* season of the year; and yet when I sit down to write, I have so many things to tell always that I am puzzled where to begin! Decidedly, I was meant to have been a subaltern of the Daily Press – not 'a Penny-Lady',[1] but a Penny-a-liner – for it is not only a faculty with me, but a necessity of my nature to make a great deal out of nothing!

To begin with something I have been treasuring up for a week (for I would not hollo till we were out of the wood)! I have *put down the Dog*! 'The Dog! wasn't he put down at Christmas, with a hare?' – It seemed so, and 'we wished we might get it'! But on my return, I found him in the old place, at the back of the wall, barking 'like – like – anything'! 'Helen'! I said, with the calmness of a great despair, 'is not that the same Dog?' ''Deed is it!' said she, 'and the whole two months you have been away, its tongue has never lain! – it has driven *even me* almost distracted!' I said no more; but I had my own thoughts on the subject – *poison*! – a pistol-bullet! the Metropolitan Police! One way or other that Dog – or I – must

---

[1] Subscribers of a penny a week for good works.

terminate! Meanwhile I went on cleaning with what heart I could. – 'My Dear – will you hasten to the catastrophe!' – I *am* hastening, slowly! – *festina lente* – bless your heart 'there's nothing pushing – the rowans[1] are a' in the loft' for this night! – Well! it was the evening after John's departure. I had been too busy all day to *listen* – the candles were lit, and I had set myself down with my feet on the fender to enjoy the happiness of being *let alone*, and to – bid myself 'consider'. 'Bow-wow-wow', roared the Dog, 'and dashed the cup of fame from my brow'! 'Bow-wow-wow' again and again, till the whole Universe seemed turned into one great Dog-Kennel! I hid my face in my hands and groaned inwardly. 'Oh, Destiny accursed! what use of scrubbing and sorting! All this availeth me nothing so long as *The Dog* sitteth at the Washerman's gate!' I could have burst into tears; but I did not! 'I was a republican – before the Revolution; and I never wanted energy!' I ran for ink and paper, and wrote –

'Dear Gambardella

You once offered to shoot some cocks for me; *that* service I was enabled to dispense with; but now I accept your devotion. Come, if you value my sanity, and –.' But here 'a sudden thought struck me.' He could not take aim at the Dog without scaling the high wall, and in so doing he would certainly be seized by the Police – so I threw away that first sibylline leaf, and wrote another – to the Washerman! Once more! I offered him 'any price for that horrible dog – *to hang* it', offered 'to settle a yearly income on it if it would hold its accursed tongue'. I implored, threatened, imprecated! and ended by proposing that, in case he could not take an immediate final resolution, he should in the interim 'make the dog dead-drunk with a bottle of whiskey which I sent for the purpose'! Helen was sent off with the note and the whiskey – and I sat all concentrated, awaiting her return, as if the fate of nations had depended on my diplomacy – and so it did – to a certain extent! Would not the inspirations of 'the first man in Europe' be modified, for the next six months at least by the fact, who should come off victorious, I or the Dog? Ah it is curious to think how *first men in Europe*, and first *women* too, are acted upon by the inferior animals!

Helen came – but even before *that* had 'the raven down of Night' smoothed itself in heavenly silence! God grant this was not mere

---

[1] Saying of my indolent sister-in-law, brother Alick's wife, on one occasion. 'Rowins' are wool completely carded, ready for the wheel when it comes down from 'the loft' – T.C.

accident! Oh no! verily it was not accident! The washerman's two daughters had seized upon and read the note – and what was death to *me* had been such rare amusement to *them* that they 'fell into fits of laughter' in the first place; and in the second place, ran down and untied the dog, and solemnly pledge themselves it should 'never trouble me more'! At Christmas they had sent it into the Country for three months '*to learn to be quiet*', and then chained it in the old place. Now they would take some final measure. Next morning came a note from the Washerman himself – written on glazed note-paper, with a crow-quill, apologising, promising – he could not put it away entirely – as it was 'a great protection' to him and '*belonged to a relation*' (who shall say where *sentiment* may *not* exist!) but he 'had untied it', and would take care it gave me no further trouble, and he 'returned his grateful thanks for *what 'as been sent*'. It is a week ago, and one may now rest satisfied that *the tying up* caused the whole nuisance. The Dog is to be seen going about there all day in the yard, like any other Christian Dog, 'carrying out' *your* principle of *Silence*, not merely '*platonically*', but *practically*. Since that night, as Helen remarks, 'it has not said one word'! So 'thanks God', you still have quietude to return to! . . .

Good night. Schlaf wohl . . .

J.C.

SILENCING THE INFERNAL COCKS

113. To Mrs Russell at Thornhill

5 Cheyne Row, Chelsea/ 31 December 1853

My dear Mrs Russell

Ever since I received your note by Mrs Pringle, I have been meaning to write to you, yet always waited for 'a more *cheerful* season', and now here is New Year's day at hand, and my regular letter due, and the season is not more cheerful, and besides I am full of business, owing to the sudden movements of the last two weeks, and Mr C.'s absence, leaving me *his* affairs to look after as well as my own.

We went to the Grange, (Lord Ashburton's) in the beginning of December to stay till after Christmas. I was very glad to get into the country for a while, and have nothing to do but dress dolls for a Christmas-tree – for the last months had quite worn me out. I had had nothing but building and painting for so long, varied with Mr

C.'s outbursts against the 'infernal cocks' next door, which had made our last addition of a 'Silent Apartment' necessary. Alas! and the silent apartment had turned out the noisiest apartment in the house! and the *cocks* still crowed, and the *macaw* still shrieked! and Mr C. still stormed! At the Grange I should at least escape *all that* for the time being I thought. The first two days I felt in Paradise, and so *well*! the third day I smashed my forehead against a marble slab – raised a lump the size of a hen's egg on it, and gave a shock to my nerves that quite unfitted me for company. But I struggled on amongst *the eighteen other visitors*, better or worse, till at the end of a fortnight I was recovered, except for a slight lump *still* visible – when Mr C. came to me one morning, all of a sudden, and told me I must go up to London myself, and take charge of some business – nothing less than trying to *take* the adjoining house ourselves, on the chance of *letting* it, and get our disobliging neighbours turned out; and there being but six days till Christmas (the time for giving them notice to quit) of course despatch was required, especially as the owner of the house lived away in Devonshire. I thought it a most wildgoose enterprise I was sent on, and when Lady Ashburton and the others asked him why he sent poor me instead of going himself, and when he coolly answered, 'Oh, *I* should only spoil the thing, *she* is sure to manage it'; it provoked me the more – I was so sure I could not manage it. But he was quite right. Before the week was out I had done better than take a house we did not need, for I had got the people bound down legally 'under a penalty of £10, and of immediate notice to quit, never to keep, or allow to be kept, fowls, or macaw, or other nuisance on these premises', in consideration of £5 given to them by Mr Carlyle. I had the lease of the house, and the *notice* to quit lying at my disposition; but the threat having served the end, I had no wish to turn the people out. You may fancy what I had suffered, thro' the effects of these nuisances on Mr C, when I tell you that, on having this agreement put in my hand by their house agent, I – burst into tears! – and should have kissed the man, if he had not been so *ugly* . . .

Your affectionate
J. W. Carlyle

APPEALING TO THE TAX COMMISSIONERS

114. EXTRACTS FROM JANE'S JOURNAL

November 20 [1855] – I have been fretting inwardly all this day at the prospect of having to go and appeal before the Tax Commissioners at Kensington tomorrow morning. Still, it must be done. If Mr C. should go himself he would run his head against some post in his impatience; and besides, for me, when it is over it will be over, whereas he would not get the better of it for twelve months – if ever at all.

November 21. – *O me miseram*! not one wink of sleep the whole night through! so great the 'rale mental agony in my own inside' at the thought of that horrid appealing. It was with feeling like the ghost of a dead dog, that I rose and dressed and drank my coffee, and then started for Kensington. Mr C. said 'the voice of honour seemed to call on him to go himself'. But either it did not call loud enough, or he would not listen to that charmer. I went in a cab, to save all my breath for appealing. Set down at 30 Hornton Street, I found a dirty private-like house, only with Tax Office painted on the door. A dirty woman-servant opened the door, and told me the Commissioners would not be there for half-an-hour, but I might walk up. There were already some half-score of men assembled in the waiting-room, among whom I saw the man who cleans our clocks, and a young apothecary of Cheyne Walk. All the others, to look at them, could not have been suspected for an instant, I should have said, of making a hundred a year. Feeling in a false position, I stood by myself at a window and 'thought shame' (as children say). Men trooped in by twos and threes, till the small room was pretty well filled; at last a woman showed herself. O my! did I ever know the full value of any sort of woman – as woman – before! By this time some benches had been brought in, and I was sitting nearest the door. The woman sat down on the same bench with me, and misery acquainting one with strange bedfellows, we entered into conversation without having been introduced, and I had 'the happiness', as Allan termed it, 'of seeing a woman more miserable than myself'. Two more women arrived at intervals, one a young girl of Dundee, 'sent by my uncle that's ill'; who looked to be always recapitulating inwardly what she had been told to say to the Commissioners. The other, a widow, and such a goose, poor thing; she was bringing an appeal against no overcharge in her individual paper, but against the doubling of the Income Tax. She had paid the double tax once, she said, because she was told they would take her goods for it if she didn't – and it was so disgraceful for one in a small business to have her goods taken; besides it was very disadvantageous; but now that it was come round again she would give up. She seemed to attach an irresistible pathos to the title of *widow*, this woman. 'And me a widow, ma'm', was the winding up of her every paragraph. The men seemed as worried as the women, though they put a better face on it, even carrying on a sort of sickly laughing and bantering with one another. 'First-come lady', called the clerk, opening a small side-door, and I stept forward into a *grand peut-être*. There was an instant of darkness while the one door was shut behind and the other opened in front; and there I stood in a dim room where three men sat round a large table spread with papers. One held a pen ready over an open ledger; another was taking snuff, and had taken still worse in his time, to judge by his shaky, clayed appearance. The third, who was plainly the cock of that dungheap, was sitting for Rhadamanthus – a Rhadamanthus without the justice. 'Name,' said the horned-owl-looking individual holding the pen. 'Carlyle.' 'What?' 'Car-lyle.' Seeing he still looked dubious, I spelt it for him. 'Ha'! cried Rhadamanthus, a big, bloodless-faced, insolent-looking fellow. 'What is this? why is Mr Carlyle not come himself? Didn't he get a letter ordering him to appear? Mr Carlyle wrote some nonsense about being exempted from coming, and I desired an answer to be sent that he must come, must do as other people.' 'Then sir,' I said, 'your desire has been neglected, it would seem, my husband having received no such letter; and I was told by one of your fellow Commissioners that Mr Carlyle's personal appearance was not indispensable.' 'Huffgh! Huffgh! what does Mr Carlyle mean by saying he has no income from his writings, when he himself fixed it in the beginning at a hundred and fifty?' 'It means sir, that, in ceasing to write, one ceases to be paid for writing, and Mr Carlyle has published nothing for several years.' 'Huffgh! Huffgh! I understand nothing about that.' 'I do,' whispered the snuff-taking Commissioner at my ear. 'I can quite understand a literary man does not always make money. I would take it off, for my share, but (sinking his voice still lower) I am only one voice here, and not the most important.' 'There,' said I, handing to Rhadamanthus Chapman and Hall's account; 'that will prove Mr Carlyle's statement.' 'What am I to make of that?

Huffgh! we should have Mr Carlyle here to swear to this before we believe it.' 'If a gentleman's word of honour written at the bottom of that paper is not enough, you can put me on my oath: I am ready to swear to it.' 'You! you, indeed! No, no! we can do nothing with your oath.' 'But, sir, I understand my husband's affairs fully, better than he does himself.' 'That I can well believe; but we can make nothing of this,' flinging my document contemptuously on the table. The horned owl picked it up, glanced over it while Rhadamanthus was tossing papers about, and grumbling about 'people that wouldn't conform to rules'; then handed it back to him, saying deprecatingly: 'But, sir, this is a very plain statement.' 'Then what has Mr Carlyle to live upon? You don't mean to tell me he lives on that?' pointing to the document. 'Heaven forbid, sir! but I am not here to explain what Mr Carlyle has to live on, only to declare his income from literature during the last three years.' 'True! true!' mumbled the not-most-important voice at my elbow. 'Mr Carlyle, I believe, has landed income.' 'Of which,' said I haughtily, for my spirit was up, 'I have fortunately no account to render in this kingdom and to this board.' 'Take off fifty pounds, say a hundred – take off a hundred pounds,' said Rhadamanthus to the horned owl. 'If we write Mr Carlyle down a hundred and fifty he has no reason to complain, I think. There, you may go. Mr Carlyle has no reason to complain.' Second-come woman was already introduced, and I was motioned to the door; but I could not depart without saying that 'at all events there was no use in complaining, since they had the power to enforce their decision'. On stepping out, my first thought was, what a mercy Carlyle didn't come himself! For the rest, though it might have gone better, I was thankful that it had not gone worse. When one has been threatened with a great injustice, one accepts a smaller as a favour.

Went back to spend the evening with Geraldine when Mr C. set forth for Bath House. Her ladyship in town for two days . . .

WRITING FAMILY LETTERS FOR HIM

115. To Mrs Austin at The Gill, Annan

5 Cheyne Row, Chelsea/ 25 December 1857

My dear Mary

I understood that your brother would write himself to-day, to announce the safe arrival of your box, the contents of which were exhibited to him in succession last night. When it came to the goose, carried in on my arms like a strange new kind of baby (with that belly-band about it!), he burst into such a laugh! 'That fellow I think has got his quietus' (he said).

But now he has just come down, and is off for his ride, and when I asked 'had he written to Mary?' he exclaimed wildly that he had 'fifteen hours of the most awful work of correcting proofs ahead of him, that I who had nothing to do should have written to Mary'! With all the pleasure in life! had I known in time, instead of within just half an hour of post-time – from which is to be subtracted ten minutes for putting on my things and running to the post-office! But better a line than no letter at all till tomorrow – you thinking the while that those blessed birds may be coming to harm from being too long on the road!

No, my dear! one 'Chucka' is boiling at this moment for the master's dinner (I dine on anything at two o'clock; not being up to waiting for Mr C.'s six or seven o'clock dinners). But I had one of the eggs to my breakfast, and it was the very best and biggest I ever ate in my life! There were only two broken, and not wasted even these; I lifted up the yolks, which lay quite round and whole, in a spoon (for puddings).

I wish I had begun in time, for I had plenty of things to say; but I must keep for this time to mere acknowledgment of your present – another day I may tell you the rest.

Yours ever affectionately,

Jane Carlyle

IGNORING NOISE WHEN CARLYLE IS AWAY

116. To Thomas Carlyle at Chelsea

Wellington Crescent, Ramsgate/ 6 August 1861

Very charming doesn't that look, with the sea in front as far as eye can reach?[1] And *that* seen (the East Cliff), you needn't wish to ever see more of Ramsgate! It is made up of narrow, steep, confused streets like the worst parts of Brighton. The shops look nasty, the people nasty, the smells are nasty! (spoiled shrimps complicated with cess-pool!) Only the *East Cliff* is clean, and *genteel*, and airy, and *would be* perfect as sea-quarters, if it weren't for the noise! which is so extraordinary as to be almost laughable!

Along that still-looking road or street between the Houses and the Gardens, are passing and re-passing, from early morning to late night, criers of Prawns, Shrimps, Lollipops, things one never wanted, and will never want, of the most miscellaneous sort, and if that were all! But a Brass Band plays all thro our Breakfast, and repeats the performance *often* during the day, and the Brass Band is succeeded by a Band of Ethiopians, and that again by a Band of female fiddlers! and interspersed with these are individual Barrel-organs, individual Scotch Bagpipes, individual French Horns! – Oh Lord, it is 'most expensive'![2] – And the night noises were not to be estimated by the first night! – These are so many and frequent as to form a sort of *mass of* noise – perhaps *easier to* get some sleep thro than an individual nuisance of cock or dog. There are *hundreds* of cocks! and they get waked up at, say, *one* in the morning! by some outburst of drunken song or of cat-wailing! and never go to sleep again (these cocks) but for *minutes*! and there are three steeple clocks that strike *in succession,* and there are doors and gates that slam, and dogs that bark *occasionally,* and a *saw mill,* and a *Mews,* and – and – in short, everything you could wish *not* to hear! and I hear it all and am getting *to sleep in hearing it*!! the bed is so soft and clean, and the room so airy; and then I think under every shock, so triumphantly, 'Crow away' – 'roar away' – 'bark away; you can't disturb Mr C. at Cheyne Row – that can't you!' – and the thought is so soothing, I go off asleep – *till next thing*! I might try Geraldine's

---

[1] A reference to the picture of the harbour on the Ramsgate notepaper.
[2] An expression of the housemaid, Helen. She used it 'promiscuously'.

room;[1] but *she* has now got an adjoining Baby! Yesterday we drove to Broadstairs – a quieter place, but we saw no *lodgings* that were likely to be quiet, except *one* villa at *six guineas a week* – already occupied! I sleep about – in intervals of the Bands – on sofas – during the day – and am less *sick* than when I left home, and we get good enough food *very* well cooked – and I don't repent coming on the whole – Tho' *I hate* living in lodgings – in strange places . . .

PAMPERING A 'SPOILED BABY'

117. To Mrs Russell at Holm Hill

5 Cheyne Row, Chelsea/ 30 August 1861

Darling!

I want to hear about you; and that is lucky for *you*, if you be at all wanting to hear about *me*! For I'll be hanged if mere unassisted sense of duty – and that sort of thing, could *nerve me* to sit down and write a letter in these days – when it takes pretty well *all* the sense and strength I have left, to keep myself soul and body together, doing the thing forced into my hands to do, and answering when I am spoken to! A nice woman I am! But I know you have been in such *depths* yourself occasionally, and will have sympathy with me, instead of being contemptuous or angry, as your strong-minded, able-bodied women would be – and accordingly strong-minded, able-bodied women are my aversion, and I run out of the road of one as I would from a mad cow! The fact is, had there been nobody in the world to consider except myself, I ought to have 'carried out' that project I had set my heart on of streaming off by myself to Holm Hill – and taking a life-bath, as it were, in my quasi-native air, in the scene of old affections, not *all* past and gone, but some still there as alive and warm, thank God, as ever! and only the dearer for being mixed up with those that *are* dead and gone.

Thursday [1 September 1861]

. . . Ah, my Dear, your kindness goes to my heart, and makes me like to cry, because I *cannot* do as you bid me! My servants are pretty well got into the routine of the house now, and if Mr C. were

---

[1] Geraldine Jewsbury accompanied Jane to Ramsgate.

like other men, he might be left to their care for two or three weeks without fear of consequences! But he is much more like a spoiled Baby than like *other men*! I *tried* him alone for a few days, when I was afraid of falling seriously ill unless I had change of air. Three weeks ago I went with Geraldine Jewsbury to Ramsgate, one of the most accessible sea-side places, where I was within call, as it were, if anything went wrong at home; but the letter that came from him every morning was like the letter of a *Babe in the Wood*! who would be found buried with dead leaves by the Robins if I didn't look to it! So, even if Ramsgate hadn't been the horridest, noisiest place, where I knew nobody, and had nothing to do except swallow sea air (the best of sea air indeed), I couldn't have got stayed there long enough to make it worth the bother of going. I *had thought* in going there, that if he got on well enough by himself for the few days, I might take two or three weeks later and realise my heart's wish after all. But I found him so out of sorts on my return that I gave it up – with inward protest and appeal to posterity!

Again a glimmer of hope arose. Lady Sandwich had taken a villa on the edge of Windsor Forest, for a month, and invited us to go with her there. Mr C. is very fond of that old lady, partly for her own sake, and partly for the late Lady Ashburton's (her daughter). He can take his horse with him there, and his books, and if he miss his sleep one night he can come straight home the next. So, on the whole, after much pressing, he consented to go. And the idea came to me, if *he* were all right *there*, mightn't I slip away meanwhile to *you*. Before however it had been communicated, he said to me one day: 'What a poor shivering nervous wretch I am grown! I declare if *you* weren't to be there to take care of me, and keep all disturbance off me, nothing would induce me to go to that place of Lady Sandwich's! tho' I dare say it is very necessary for me to go somewhere.' Humph! very flattering! but very inconvenient! And one can't console oneself at my age for a present disappointment, with looking forward to next year – one is no longer so sure of one's next year!

One thing I *can* do, and you can do - we can write oftener. It is a deal nicer to speak face to face from heart to heart. But we might make our correspondence a better thing than it is, if we prevented the need of beginning our letters so often with an apology for silence.

Thanks for all your news. Every little detail about Thornhill people and things is interesting to me - And, oh many many thanks for your kind messages to us all – God bless you, Dear, and love to the Doctor.

Affectionately
Jane W. Carlyle

MENDING HIS BOOTS
ON NEW YEAR'S DAY

118. TO DR RUSSELL AT HOLM HILL

5 Cheyne Row, Chelsea/ 6 January 1863

My dear Dr Russell,

. . . You wonder, perhaps, what a woman like me has to take up her time with. Here, for example, is one full day's work, not to say two. On the New Year's morning itself, Mr C. 'got up off his wrong side', a by no means uncommon way of getting up for him in these overworked times! And he suddenly discovered that his salvation, here and hereafter, depended on having, 'immediately, without a moment's delay', a beggarly pair of old cloth boots, that the street-sweeper would hardly have thanked him for, 'lined with flannel, and new bound, and repaired generally'! and 'one of my women' – that is, my one woman and a half – was to be set upon the job! Alas! a regular shoemaker would have taken a whole day to it, and wouldn't have undertaken such a piece of work besides! and Mr C. scouted the idea of employing a shoemaker, as subversive of his authority as master of the house. So, neither my one woman, nor my half one, having any more capability of repairing 'generally' these boots than of repairing the Great Eastern, there was no help for me but to sit down on the New Year's morning, with a great ugly beast of a man's boot in my lap, and scheme, and stitch, and worry over it till night; and next morning begin on the other! There, you see, were my two days eaten up very completely, and unexpectedly; and so it goes on, 'always a something' (as my dear mother used to say).

The accounts from Paris[1] continue more favourable. But they sound hollow to me somehow.

Love to Mary.

Your ever affectionate
Jane Carlyle

[1] Concerning Lord Ashburton, who was mortally ill.

A LAST VICTORY

119. To Mrs Russell at Holm Hill

5 Cheyne Row, Chelsea/ 25 December 1865

Dearest Mary

... But the grand worry of all – that which perfected my sleeplessness, was an importation of nine hens, and a magnificent *Cock* (!!!), into the adjoining garden! For years back there has reigned over all these Gardens a heavenly quiet! thanks to my heroic exertions in exterminating nuisances of every description! But I no longer felt the hope or the energy in me requisite for such achievements! Figure then my horror, my despair, on being waked one dark morning with the crowing of a Cock, that seemed to issue from under my bed! I leapt up, and rushed to my dressing-room window; but it was still all darkness. I lay with my heart in my mouth, listening *to* the Cock, crowing hoarsely from time to time, and listening *for* Mr C.'s foot stamping frantically, as of old, on the floor above! – But strangely enough, he gave no sign of having heard his Enemy – his whole attentions, having been, ever since his visit to Mrs Aitken, morbidly devoted to – *Railway Whistles*! So soon as it was daylight I looked out again, and *there* was a sight to see! – a ragged, *Irish*-looking hen-house, run up over night; and sauntering to and fro, nine goodly hens, and a *stunning* Cock! I didn't know whether Mr C. remained really deaf as well as blind to these new neighbours, or whether he was only magnanimously resolved to observe silence about them; but it is a fact, that for a whole week he said no word to enlighten me – while I expected and expected the crisis which would surely come! and shuddered at every Cock-Crow, and counted the number of times he crowed in a night! at two! at three! at four! at five! at six! at seven! Oh, terribly at seven! For a whole week I bore my hideous secret in my breast! and slept none to speak of! At the week's end I fell into one of my old sick headaches. I used always to find a sick headache had a fine effect in clearing the wits. So, even this time, I rose from a day's agony with a scheme of operation in my head, and a sense of ability to 'carry it out'. It would be too long to go into details – enough to say my negotiations with 'Next door' ended in an agreement that the Cock should be shut up in the cellar inside the owner's own house, from three in the afternoon till ten in the morning! and, in return, I give the small boy of the house a lesson every morning in his *Reading made Easy*!! the small boy being 'too excitable' for being sent to school! It is a house full of *mysteries* – *No. 6*! I have thoughts of writing a novel about it. Meanwhile, Mr C. declares me to be his '*Guardian Angel*'! No sinecure I can tell him! . . .

Your ever affectionate

Jane Carlyle

IX *Lady Ashburton*

Lady Harriet Baring, eldest daughter of the sixth Earl of Sandwich, had married into one of the great commercial dynasties of her times. 'The Barings', she once said, 'are everywhere. They get everything. The only check upon them is, that they are all members of the Church of England; otherwise, there is no saying what they would do.' Lady Harriet had some scornful things to say about her husband's family; but she could be equally scornful about aristocratic pedigrees, including her own. Satire, high-spirited mockery of pretensions of all kind, was her element. 'In my childhood', she told her friends, 'I was constantly punished for any impertinence, and you see the results. I think I have made up for it since.' Bingham Baring, her husband, was one of those men who are inevitably condemned to look less clever than their wives. It was said that Lady Harriet's brilliance as a hostess may even have retarded his political fortunes instead of advancing them, so blinding was her sunshine. He succeeded the first Lord Ashburton in 1848 and gave her new theatres for her talents by adding the Grange, in central Hampshire, and Bath House, in Piccadilly, to the two houses he already owned – Bay House, at Alverstoke on the Hampshire coast, and Addiscombe Farm, in the Croydon suburbs of London. Not every guest was comfortable at these performances. 'I do not mind being knocked down,' said one, 'but I can't stand being danced upon afterwards.' But Lady Harriet's genius was not ill-natured; it was her gaiety, an intellectual gaiety compared with the frivolities of the empty-headed rich, that impressed her contemporaries.

Lady Harriet was the cleverest, wealthiest, most regal woman Jane had ever met. She was surrounded by a pride of literary lions (not to mention an adoring zoo of noblemen and statesmen) and she was intent on displaying her dear prophet Carlyle as the noblest lion of them all. What could be more intriguing or cosseting for Jane than to enter the golden gates of this aristocratic paradise after the austerities of Cheyne Row? Did not Carlyle prefer Jane to all other women? Were not habits much stronger in him than passions? Was not his indifference to all women as women a sufficient protection against this woman? Why not make the most of her friendship and hospitality?

But gnawing away at this cheerful optimism was the conscience of Scottish puritanism (the Ashburtons toil not neither do they spin!), the wariness of the rival performer (who wanted the centre of the stage more than Jane?), the sense of inferiority imposed by the normal on the neurotic (Lady Harriet could be sick but she was never depressed!), and, worst of all, fears for Carlyle. Temptations of the flesh were out of the question. But was his spirit seducible?

Lady Harriet summons Carlyle to a work of charity and piety; she is ill, she explains, and not allowed out; will he come and talk to her? Lady Harriet receives Carlyle one evening a week and at her farm on Sundays; her little notes are 'a pleasing titillation to Mr. Carlyle's philosophic spirit'. Lady Harriet meets *Mrs* Carlyle for the first time at tea and chides Mr Carlyle, 'I meditate paying my respects to Mrs Carlyle . . . she is a reality whom you have hitherto quite suppressed.' Lady Harriet, like the Queen, must have her court about her; Mr Carlyle is invited to the Grange for at least a week while Mrs Carlyle dusts his books, papers his dressing room and lays a carpet. Lady Harriet takes Mrs Carlyle to the opera – and Mr Carlyle is there, too, God help us! Nobody knows what he can do until he tries, or rather till a Lady Harriet tries! Lady Harriet is not the haughty creature she is made out to be, perhaps only a little brusque out of high spirits. Lady Harriet is immensely large; she might had been one of the ugliest women you ever met, if her intelligence and cordiality had not made her almost beautiful. Lady Harriet is the most masterly coquette of modern times – look at what she does to Mazzini and John Stuart Mill, not to mention Carlyle! Lady Harriet is a very lovable, spoilt child of fortune whom a little judicious whipping (Jane had not yet heard about the repressed childhood) might have turned into a first-class woman.

Thus this delicate observer, every sense aquiver, sketches her rival in the early years of an intimacy which was to flourish or fester for more than a decade, with annual visits to the Grange at Christmas, Bay House in January, Addiscombe in the spring; with Lady Harriet usually very considerate but always in command; with Carlyle seeing nothing to be 'fashed' about; and with Jane herself, when she was not 'making wits' or 'churned up to froth', shedding tears on her sofa, or in her journal, or on the bosom of a friend.

Anyone as cosmopolitan, as grand, as triumphant, as free from despair as Lady Ashburton could be no intimate of Jane's. Eventually, she gave up trying to love her. How could she love anyone who did not believe in *feelings*, who shared her mind but not her heart, who notoriously preferred men to women, and who seemed to have bewitched Carlyle? She could turn to Lord Ashburton for comfort; he was a good man who did not mind his place in the shade. She could love Lady Ashburton's mother, the old Countess of Sandwich, who was both clever and warmhearted. But what was she to do with the Lady herself? The closer they seemed, to the outside world, the less they had in common; on the rare occasions when they were left alone together in a huge mansion like the Grange, with its troops of guests and servants, these two great wits had nothing to say to each other.

The Ashburton relationship was a trial which Jane bore, like many others, with a divided spirit. It meant everything to Carlyle, and she had made it her life's work to put him first. It could also be a wonderful stimulation for her in her buoyant moods. But to the wounded, proud Jane, who was made to feel that her husband had outgrown her, it was like the death of the soul. Someone said of her at these times that she looked 'like a mourner by an unclosed grave'.

Was it reasonable to feel humiliated? Froude thought that Carlyle should have shown more understanding. It was not good enough for 'the philosopher in chains' to act like a puzzled innocent when his wife upbraided him. He was having a love affair of a kind. It was a literary intimacy like his own courtship of Jane – was he not offering to teach Harriet German, lending her books, urging her to write, talking about his own writings? It was an escape from a sick wife, a flight into romance, a flirtation with the great world of statesmen and prime ministers. Froude was fascinated by what he found in Jane's private journal of 1855–6 and by the discovery that Carlyle was not prepared to see all of it published. He turned to Geraldine for an explanation of the mood that lay behind the mournful entries and convinced himself, as she had done, that there were faults on both sides. He quoted Carlyle as often saying to him, after Jane's death, 'Oh, if I could but see her for five minutes to assure her that I had really cared for her throughout all that! But she never knew it, she never knew it!'

The anti-Froudians would have none of this. It was a simple case of irrational conduct on Jane's part – her mind had been deranged by a nervous breakdown which made her prey to morbid jealousies. A modern reader might feel that she was right to resent the embarrassments of the relationship but wrong not to extract herself from it; that this was one more phase in her life when she should have asserted her independence. Carlyle would not have liked it, but what of that?

It is pleasant to recall that the ordeals of Jane's relationship with the first Lady Ashburton were succeeded by her love affair with the second. Eighteen months after the death of his first wife, Lord Ashburton married, on 17 November 1858, a warmhearted Mackenzie, with whom Jane soon swore one of her everlasting friendships. Louisa, Lady Ashburton, was young and beautiful and responsive. Visits to the Grange continued, with the most ardent outpourings of affection from the liberated, if frail, Jane to the young mother and her baby. The letter printed at the end of 'Self-portrait' (see p. 81 above) was one of dozens which passed between them in a friendship which was now shared equally by Carlyle and Jane.

'ONE *NEW FEMALE*'

120. To Jeannie Welsh at Liverpool

5 Cheyne Row, Chelsea/ 28 May 1843

Private

My darling,

. . . Yes, there is one . . . *new female* in whom he takes a vast of pleasure, Lady Harriet Baring –

I have always omitted to tell you how marvellously that liaison has gone on. Geraldine seemed horribly *jealous* about it – nay almost '*scandalized*' – while she was here – for my part I am singularly inaccessible to jealousy, and am pleased rather that he has found *one* agreeable house to which he likes to go and goes regularly – one evening in the week at least – and then *he* visits them at their 'farm' on Sundays and there are flights of charming little notes always coming to create a pleasing titillation of the philosophic spirit! – Mrs Buller in her graceful quizzical way insisted I should 'see a little into the thing with my own eyes', and promised to give me notice the first time she knew beforehand of the Intellectual Circe's coming to her house – And accordingly Mr Buller came last Monday to ask me to meet her that evening at tea at seven o'clock.

. . . I liked her on the whole – she is immensely *large* – might easily have been one of the *ugliest* women living – but *is* almost beautiful – simply thro' the intelligence and cordiality of her expression – I saw nothing of the impertinence and hauteur which people impute to her – only a certain *brusquerie* of manner which seemed to me to proceed from exuberant spirits and absence of all affectation. She is unquestionably very clever – just the *wittiest* woman I have seen – but with many aristocratic prejudices – which I wonder *Carlyle* should have got over so completely as he seems to have done – in a word I take her to be a very lovable spoilt Child of Fortune – that a little *whipping*, judiciously administered would have made into a first rate woman – we staid till eleven – and as there were no other strangers, I had ample opportunity of estimating the amount of her seductions.

What *she* thought of *me* I should rather like to know – she took prodigious looks at me from time to time. In the *last* note to Carlyle inviting him to Addiscombe for next Sunday she says – 'I meditate paying my respects to Mrs Carlyle – so soon as I am again making visits – she is a *reality* whom you have hitherto *quite suppressed*'. . .

Your own J.C.

SLEEPLESS NIGHTS AT ADDISCOMBE

121. To Jeannie Welsh at Liverpool

5 Cheyne Row, Chelsea/ 9 July 1845

Dearest Babbie,

. . . I have been in a sad way for a long while, and was not saying anything about it to any one – indeed I was ashamed to talk of illness which had taken the form chiefly of frightful depression of spirits – . . . But every body's fortitude has limits, and so my determination never to tell Carlyle or any one what I had been swallowing down and was still swallowing down in the shape of suffering did not hinder me the other day from giving way to a dreadful fit of crying and telling him all about it – He was not a little horrified at my revelations and immediately declared that I must get away into the country as fast as possible – But where – To Dumfriesshire with him or before him? – impossible – he may call it 'weak' 'unworthy of a rational creature' – I cannot help it – I cannot go there yet – it is just *weakness* and irrationality that I complain of – if I were *strong* – *rational* there would be no need for my flying out of London at all.

To Haddington – to the Miss Donaldsons? – that also were painful enough – but I felt as if after the first horror of it I should rather like being there – many places were spoken of – but in every one a lion was in the way – Haddington remained the most possible looking – when I had to dry my eyes and go off with the Lady Harriet to Addiscombe for four mortal days! Fancy it! – in such a state of mind – having to get up fine clothes and fine 'wits'! having to proceed with my *first season* of *fashionable life* while I was feeling it the dreadfulest problem to *live* at all! In the whole *three* nights I lay in bed at Addiscombe I slept just *one hour and forty minutes* by my watch! the first night an hour and half – the second none at all – and the third ten minutes! Oh dear dear what do the glories of upholstery help one when there is no sleep to be had – how gladly would I have exchanged my Throne-like bed – with cambric sheets bordered with lace (!) to have had the deep sleep of a Peasant on the top of a dung cart! The house was full of fine people among whom there was only one (Lord Ashburton) who did not feel it his duty to make 'incessant wits'. These said '*wits*', in my sleepless state of nerves, grew to look like a shower of fire sparks falling falling for ever about my ears till I had not a grain of common sense remaining – one night that I walked in the dark for an hour with Lord Ashburton I felt myself human again – able to talk – and it was a mournful little satisfaction for me that *he* at least might recognise me for something a few degrees above an *Idiot* – At Addiscombe I received your letter – Carlyle brought it with him when he came to spend his Sunday (as usual) (he has established a small permanent wardrobe there!) . . .

Kind regards wherever they are due.

J.C.

AN INTERVIEW WITH LADY HARRIET AT BATH HOUSE

122. To Thomas Carlyle at Scotsbrig

28 September 1845

. . . Last night I received a note from Lady Harriet stating that she was in town for only a few days – not able to go out – but would send the Brougham for me today at two, if 'perchance' I could come and see her. Of course, today at two, I was all in readiness. 'guy ticht aboot the head; I *think* I had on *my new bonnet*.' I was rather surprised to be set down at a great unknown House – and conducted thro' large Halls and staircases by unknown servants – if it had not been for the indubitability of *the Brougham* I should have begun to fancy myself kidnapped, or in a Fairy Tale! *Eventually*, in a large dressing room at the top of the house, I found the Lady on a sofa – a gentleman was just coming out – *Irish* I should fancy from the fact of his leaving – his *hat* behind him! on search being made for it by a servant some five minutes after, it was found – with difficulty – under the chair *I* had sat down upon! – The Lady was *ill* only in a feminine sense – 'My dear, I am not *up to* going out just at present' – that sort of thing – she 'would be able to return to the Grange on Tuesday' – spoke of being to dine at Lansdowne house on Monday – She was very gracious[1] and agreeable – repeated pressingly the invitation to Alverstoke . . . The German books had reached her safely – if you wrote about them, that letter had not yet reached her – the one you wrote on your arrival, she bade me say, was duly received and she would have answered it before now, 'if she had not been moving about more than she had anticipated'. When she got back to the Grange she expected to rest for a while and would then write. It was to Richard Milnes I owed the pleasure of seeing her – he had been there the same evening he called on me, and mentioned having just seen me in an unprecedented state of confusion.

I recommended her to read *Cecil* (which I like immensely) and she recommended me to read Blanco White's Memoirs about which she was all agog. She asked what I had heard said about it – and I told her Darwin's criticism – that 'it greatly took away from one's sympathy with a man's religious scruples to find that they were merely symptoms of a diseased liver' – To which she replied very justly that 'until the dominion of the liver was precisely ascertained, it were safer to speak respectfully of it'! The Brougham was waiting to take me back again, and she was *on a sofa* – so for both reasons I was careful not to make my visit too long: although she *did* ask me *in a sort of way* to stay and dine with them at five o'clock. On the whole our interview went off, quite successfully – and I daresay in spite of Mrs Buller's predictions we shall get on very well together – altho I can see that the Lady has a genius for *ruling* – whilst I have a genius for – not being ruled!

[1] In a letter two days later, to her confidante Jeannie Welsh, Jane wrote: 'More than *gracious*! *Incomprehensible* upon *my* honour! she insisted that I had promised to "give her *my whole winter* at Alverstoke"! – and yet I have an unconquerable persuasion that she does not and never can like me.'

AT BAY HOUSE, ALVERSTOKE

123. To Jeannie Welsh at Liverpool

17 November 1845

. . . Lady Harriet insists we are to stay here 'all the winter' – to stay 'till parliament meets in February' – but I fancy Carlyle's need to be ugly and stupid and disagreeable without restraint (never to speak of my own) will send us back to London in a month or so.

I feel as if I should get on here in an even, middlingly pleasant sort of a way. I am not in the horribly excitable state I was in when I went to Addiscombe – I take things now very calmly – almost coolly – Lady Harriet seems a woman of *good sense* and perfect good breeding – and with a person of that sort one need not, unless one be a fool oneself have any *collisions* – at the same time she seems to me so *systematic* and *superior* to her *natural feelings* that however long and pleasantly I may live beside her I am sure I shall never feel *warm affection* for her nor inspire her with warm affection – her intercourse will remain *an honour for me* never be a heartfelt delight – as it might be if she were as loving as she is charming – and Bay House will consequently not suit one as well as Seaforth House . . .

WORN OUT WITH 'STRENUOUS IDLENESS'

124. To Mrs Russell at Thornhill

5 Cheyne Row, Chelsea/ 30 December 1845

Dearest Mrs Russell

We are just returned from our Hampshire visit – and I can answer for one of us being so worn out with '*strenuous idleness*' as I do not remember ever to have been before! Six weeks have I been doing absolutely nothing but playing at battledore-and-shuttlecock – chess – talking nonsense – and getting rid of a certain fraction of this mortal life as *cleverly* and uselessly as possible – nothing could exceed the sumptuosity and elegance of the whole thing – nor its *uselessness*! – Oh dear me! I wonder why so many people wish for high position and great wealth when it is such an 'open secret' what all *that* amounts to in these days – merely to emancipating people from all those practical difficulties which might teach them the *fact* of things and sympathy with their fellow creatures. This Lady Harriet Baring whom we have just been staying with is the very cleverest woman – out of sight – that I ever saw in my life (and I have seen all our 'distinguished Authoresses'). Moreover she is full of energy and sincerity – and has I am quite sure an excellent heart – yet so perverted has she been by the training and life-long humouring incident to her high position that I question if in her *whole life* she have done as much for her fellow creatures as *my* mother in *one year* – or whether she will ever break thro the cobwebs she is entangled in so as to be anything other than the *most amusing* and most *graceful* woman of her time. The sight of such a woman should make one very content with one's own trials even when they feel to be rather hard! . . .

Yours,

J. Carlyle

INSOLUBLE PSYCHOLOGICAL PUZZLE

125. To Jeannie Welsh at Liverpool

5 Cheyne Row, Chelsea/ 10 March 1846

Here goes Dearest Babbie! just to *try* whether the Devil or I shall be strongest today, in the matter of writing to you – how often *he* has had the upper hand of late, to the utter suppression of the many things I have wished to say to you, I am ashamed to think! for if one cannot make head against the Devil in a world where one meets him at every turn, one may as well take a little arsenic at once and spare oneself the sin and sorrow of being nothing but a Spooney in God's universe. For ten days I was nearly out of my wits with want of sleep – and I say this not *figuratively* nor even *exaggeratively* but in simple truth. Four nights in one week I never *once* closed my eyes, and *henbane* even in large quantities of no more use to me than cold water – The consequence was such a state of nervous excitation as nobody ever saw in me before – Carlyle declares me to have been 'quite mad' for half an hour – and I can well believe him – I have for a long while back been dreadfully haunted with the apprehension of going *mad* some day – and I am only too thankful to have got off with 'half an hour' of it thus far. For the last week I have been sleeping – and in the reactionary state – that is to say *dead stupid*. Oh! the blessedness of *stupidity* at times! I feel as if I would not make 'a wit' just now for fifty guineas.

On the 20th I am going with Lady Harriet to Addiscombe for a month and that will be good for me I suppose – Carlyle is so hard at work that he will not miss me – besides if he takes a notion of seeing me at any time he can be there by railway in half an hour. We two *women* go alone. Mr Baring and Charles Buller of course – will be there on the Saturdays and Sundays – And we are to come up to town once a week *for two hours*, her Ladyship to take a Drawing lesson(!) I to bless my family with a sight of me and regulate the week's accounts. If all proceeds according to Programme it will be a pleasant month but I cannot fancy Lady Harriet anywhere leading *a life of privacy*; however, she may propose it to herself. She needs the excitement of company, imagining all the while that she is bored with it – and so many people are ready to follow her into Siberia – if she chose to take her flight even there! She is 'a bit of fascination' (as the Countrymen said of '*Tagglioni*)[1] a very *large bit*. I profess never to this hour to have arrived at a complete understanding of her – but *that* I fancy is just a part of her fascination – the insoluble psychological puzzle which she is and bids fair to remain for me! . . .

Ever your affectionate

Jane Carlyle

'THE ONLY WOMAN OF *GENIUS*'

126. To Jeannie Welsh at Liverpool

1846

. . . Lady Harriet is returned and seems disposed to keep up our country intimacy – she sends her carriage for me often in the evenings and sends me back – treats me in all respects with a *consideration* for which I cannot but be grateful to her. She never *says* to anyone that she likes them – she goes upon *the silent system* as to all the thoughts of her *heart* – it is only the thoughts of her *head* which she gives one the benefit of – and so she has never *said* what one could call a *kind* word to *me* – but she proves by all her behaviour that she is rather fond of me – the mere fact of her having *kissed* me at parting and meeting

---

[1] Two London mechanics paused at a print-shop window where I was. 'Ha!' said one to the other in a jaunty knowing tone. '*Tag-li-oni*! Bit of fascination there' – T.C.

again proves more affection for me than twenty reams of protestations from a Geraldine would do – for her Ladyship is *sincere* to death – and would think much less of boxing the ears of a person indifferent to her than of kissing her! for my part I *love* her now as much as I *admired* her in the beginning – She is the only woman of *genius* I have found amongst all our pretenders to it - I only wish I had got to know her twenty years ago when I was better capable of enjoying the advantages of such an acquaintance – the 'getting-on-in-Society' part of it looks to me often enough a practical irony at this time of day rather than a good fortune to thank my stars for.

You would be amused to see the increase of charm I have for the smaller gentry since Lady Harriet took me up! — I could not help answering a *kind* note I had from Lady Monteagle the other day after a *twelve-months' silence* - in a tone of very *frank sarcasm* . . .

AN ANGUISHED BIRTHDAY

127. To Thomas Carlyle at Chelsea

Seaforth/ 14 July 1846

Oh! my dear Husband

Fortune has played me such a cruel trick this day! - but it is all right now! and I do not even feel any resentment against fortune for the suffocating misery of the last two hours. I know always, when I seem to you most exacting, that whatever happens to me is nothing like so bad as I deserve – But you shall hear all how it was – . . .

– *None* for *me* the postmistress averred! - not a line from you on my birthday . . . I did not burst out crying – did not faint – did not *do* anything absurd, so far as I know – but I walked back again without speaking a word, and with such a tumult of wretchedness in my heart as you who know me can conceive – And then I shut myself in my own room to fancy everything that was most tormenting – Were you finally so out of patience with me that you had resolved to write to me no more at all? – had you gone to Addiscombe and found no leisure *there* to remember my existence? Were you taken ill so ill that you *could* not write? That last idea made me mad to get off to the railway, and back to London – Oh mercy what a two hours I had of it! – And just when I was at my wits end, I heard Julia crying out thro the house – 'Mrs Carlyle Mrs Carlyle! Are you there? here is a letter for you!'

And so there was after all! – the postmistress had overlooked it – and given it to Robert when he went afterwards not knowing that we had been. I wonder what *love-letter* was ever received with such thankfulness! – Oh my dear I am not fit for living in the World with this organisation – I am as much broken to pieces by that little accident as if I had come thro an attack of Cholera or Typhus fever – I cannot even steady my hand to *write* decently. But I felt an irresistible need of thanking you by return of post – Yes I have kissed the dear little card case – and now I will lie down a while, and try to get some sleep – at least to quieten myself – will try to believe – oh why can I not believe it once for all – that with all my faults and follies I *am* 'dearer to you than any earthly creature' – I will be better for Geraldine here; she is very quiet and nice *become* – and as affectionate for me as ever.

Your own

J.C.

LIFE AT THE GRANGE

128. To Jeannie Welsh at Auchtertool

The Grange, Hampshire/ 30 October 1846

Dearest Babbie,

I have no prospect of being able to write you a deliberate letter even at this late date. Tho, for the moment, I have not a room merely but a suite of rooms all to myself, where no one may come to molest me – still my soul is in a state of hurry-scurry which makes *deliberate* writing quite impossible. The very look of this bedroom with its immense dimensions, its vaulted and carved ceiling its princely magnificence of every sort makes me ill at ease – I feel to have got out of my latitude – as much as if I were hanging on to the horns of the moon! and then the recollection of all the idle restless people under the same roof with me – whose idleness and restlessness is so contagious! In fact *this* is 'a country house' with a vengeance! and I do not find that my Destiny has done amiss in casting *my* lot amongst '*the poorer orders*'. We are here professedly on a visit to the Ashburtons *virtually*, at least so far as C. is concerned, on a visit to Lady Harriet – and besides Lady Harriet and Mr Baring, there are some dozen visitors besides – The Marchioness of Bath, Lord Ashburton's

eldest daughter with two tiny Ladyships and their French governess –
Old Rogers – an Honble Mr Byng – a beautiful Miss Dalton – a rich
Mr Portal etc., etc. In all *my* life I never drew my breath in such a
racket! Some of the People go tomorrow and then others will come.
It is the ruling Principle of the Host and Hostess to keep the house
always full – *We* shall remain till the end of next week and by that
time I shall have had enough of it I fancy. The Ashburtons one and
all of them are excellent people – very *homely* – and very kind – they
make me as much at home as it is possible for a *fish* to be in the *air* –
Lady H. also continues *kind* to me after her fashion – But, as you can
easily conceive, I feel myself in *a false position* – and find it very
difficult to guide myself in it – I have always however the consolation
of feeling quite sure that nobody knows nor can divine my difficulties – except C. – who since I make no noise about them is bound to
recognise them with respectful toleration. 'One fire' they say, 'drives
out another'! or (another version of it) 'one devil drives out another'
– and *that* at least is something to be thankful for! My natural shyness
and over-modesty, of which I have a great deal (tho' neither you nor
anyone else perhaps ever found it out) – has entirely given place to
more powerful feelings – so that I have no more care than a cat about
things that would have fussed me once on a time – I used to be
apprehensive that my toilette might look defective, that my manner
might look *gauche* – that my speech might sound flat – amongst
sumptuous, self-possessed, brilliant people – Now I am so entirely
absorbed in thoughts far away from all outward *appearances* that if I
had been brought up at court all the days of my life I could not feel
more perfectly regardless on these points.

But it were more amusing for you to hear something of the Place
and People than of *my* feelings toward them – The Place is like, not
one, but a conglomeration of Greek Temples set down in a magnificent wooded Park some five miles in length – The inside is magnificent to death – the ceilings all painted in fresco – some dozen public
rooms on the ground floor all hung with magnificent paintings – and
fitted up like rooms in an Arabian night's entertainment – but the
finest part of it is the entrance hall and staircases – which present a
view of columns, frescos and carved wood and Turkey carpet – that
one might guess at a quarter of a mile long! In the Hall which indeed
resembles a church Lord A. reads prayers every morning to a numerous congregation consisting of men and women-servants ranged on
opposite sides and his own wife and daughters kneeling beside him –
The *effect* as seen from the *gallery above* is very pretty!! but I did not

meddle with it personally further than looking over the balustrade – and I saw old Rogers this morning doing the same. They are very *good* in the religious sense of the word – the whole family of them – except of course Lady Harriet – who *goes* on nothing of that sort – but they are not bigotted and let one hold one's own opinions. They have had their own trials poor people – a favourite daughter the beauty and genius of the family – when grown to womanhood was burnt to death in Italy some years ago – and the Marquis of Bath *drank* himself to death – this poor Lady now here has spent night after night in holding the basin to him and hiding it away with her own hands that the servants might not see the Brute he made of himself – She has still such a suffering patient look! And this morning she was maintaining against me the Beauty and holiness of *Marriage* even in these days!!! Every mortal woman I fancy is born to be made miserable thro one cause or other, and with this moral reflection I will conclude.

Ever your affectionate,

J.C.

BACK FROM THE GRANGE

129. To Helen Welsh at Liverpool

5 Cheyne Row, Chelsea/ 7 November 1846

Dearest Helen

I am just returned from the Grange – *that* is *one* good job over – and I may calculate now on being let alone till after Christmas – so I write to urge with all solemnity that you should *immediately* fling some clothes into a trunk and come off to me. The programme is that after Christmas we shall go for a month to Bay House where we were the last year. *So* the Lady Harriet wills *at present* – and her Ladyship's will is become the law of this house! – even her *whims* are as imperative as the ten commandments! – In March she will be at Addiscombe – only twelve miles from here – and if she wish us to amuse her ennui there also of course; it will be so arranged – then in April what Darwin calls 'the 5 Cheyne-Row-spring-fever' begins – frantic speculations about where to go – etc. etc. So that it seems to me on the whole, there is no time so good as the present. We have six clear weeks till Christmas – if you start immediately you may have a tolerable view of London in that time – So let me have a letter by return of post to say what day you will be here – the journey is the simplest thing in nature – nothing in the shape of *escort* need be waited for. You have only to bid a Policeman at the station get you a cab – (Meeting people is *impossible* in Euston Square) and you will be fetched safe here without a word spoken – I am too much occupied with the prospect of seeing you to enter into any detail of my visit – it was *grand* to Death! – people with eighty thousand a year can *afford* to do things in style. I will tell you things that will amuse you when we meet . . .

Ever your affectionate

J. Carlyle

'LOVER OF ALL MIRTHFUL THINGS'

130. TO JEANNIE WELSH AT LIVERPOOL

5 Cheyne Row, Chelsea/ 5 February 1849

Dearest Babbie

. . . The Ashburtons have been in town for a week, returned today to the Grange for another week and then back to London for *the Season*. Lady A. came to see me on her arrival with an *armful of shawl* which she laid into *my* arms, saying 'there, dear Mrs Carlyle – there is my *late* new year to you – at new years day we had so much to think of else!' and she kissed me. It was well and graciously *done* – still *valuable* presents for which I can make no return, distress me always from that quarter – there are people from whom I can take things without any *spoiling* sense of obligation, but then I feel that I can repay them with love – now Lady A. can do perfectly well *without* love of mine – love from *me* beyond a certain point would bore her rather than otherwise. She looked quite herself again – all her wild grief over C. Buller crushed down out of sight into the bottom of her heart, or perhaps *out of it* altogether – She spoke of him with *supreme* composure – and was in a racket of company all the time of her stay – Poor Mr C. will never succeed in making her 'more *earnest*', dear, gay hearted, high spirited woman that she is! God bless her for her seeming determination *not* to be '*earnest*' for *his* pleasure, or anyone else's but to be just what God has made her, the enemy of *cant* and lover of all mirthful things – It is a great faculty that of being able to throw off grief – I would not somehow care to have it, and yet I see well enough how much better people, who have it, both enjoy their life and contribute to the enjoyment of 'others' ...

Ever your affectionate
Jane C.

A GRILLING ABOUT CARLYLE'S INFATUATION

131. To Jeannie Welsh at Auchtertool

5 Cheyne Row, Chelsea/ Holy Thursday 1849

Dearest Babbie

... I have had no more headaches since that dreadful one I told Helen about – now that the weather is warmer I can stand a pitcher of cold water on the back of my neck every morning and that always agrees with me. I have been to several parties – a dinner at Dickens's last Saturday where I never went before. 'A great fact!' Forster might have called it. Such getting up of the steam is unbecoming to a literary man who *ought* to have his basis elsewhere than on what the old Annandale woman called 'Ornament and grander'. The dinner was served up in the new fashion – not placed on the table at all – but handed round – only the dessert on the table and quantities of *artificial* flowers – but such an overloaded dessert! pyramids of figs raisins oranges – ach! At the Ashburton dinner served on those principles there were just *four cowslips* in china pots – four silver shells containing sweets, and a silver filigree temple in the middle! but here the very candles rose each out of an artificial rose! Good God! Mrs Gaskell the Authoress of *Mary Barton* was there – I had already seen her at my own house, a natural unassuming woman whom they have been doing their best to spoil by making a lioness of her. Before dinner, old Rogers, who ought to have been buried long ago, so old and ill-natured he is grown, said to me pointing to a chair beside him, 'sit down my Dear – I want to ask you; is your husband as much infatuated as ever with Lady Ashburton? – 'Oh of course' I said *laughing*, 'why shouldn't he?' – 'Now – do *you* like her – tell me honestly is she kind to *you* – as kind as she is to your husband?' 'Why you know it is impossible for *me* to know *how* kind she is to my husband; but I *can* say she is extremely kind to *me* and I should be stupid and ungrateful if I did *not* like her.' 'Humph! (disappointedly) Well! it is very good of you to like her when she takes away all your husband's company from you – he is always there isn't he?' 'Oh

229

good gracious no! (still laughing *admirably*) he writes and reads a great deal in his own study.' 'But he spends all his evenings with her I am told?' 'No – not all – for example you see he is *here* this evening.' 'Yes,' he said in a tone of vexation, 'I *see* he is here *this* evening – and *hear* him too – for he has done nothing but talk across the room since he came in.' Very devilish old man! but he got no satisfaction to his devilishness out of *me* –

> 'On Earth the living
> Have much to bear!'[1] . . .

Your affectionate
Jane Carlyle

THE BATH HOUSE BALL

132. To Helen Welsh at Liverpool

5 Cheyne Row, Chelsea/ 4 July 1850

Dearest Helen

. . . The Bath House Ball threw me into a perfect fever for one week – as I had got no dress for it; not understanding that I was to go – but Mr C. was 'quite determined for once in his life to see an aristocratic Ball and if I chose to be so peevish and ungracious as to stay away there was no help for me' - I pleaded the want of a dress - he 'would pay for any dress I chose to get'; and then I fell back on the horror of *stripping* myself, of 'being bare' - at my age after being muffled up so many years! and that if I didn't I should be like no one else – to which he told me angrily – 'true propriety consisted in conforming to other peoples fashions!!! and that Eve he supposed had as much sense of decency as I had and *she* wore no clothes at all!!!' So I got a white silk dress – which first was made high and long sleeved – and then on the very day of the ball was sent back to be cut down to the due pitch of indecency! – I could have gone into *fits* of crying when I began to put it on – but I looked so astonishingly well in it *by candle light*, and when I got into the fine rooms amongst the universally *bare* people I felt so much in *keeping*, that I forgot my neck and arms almost immediately. I was glad *after* that I went – not for any pleasure I had at the time being past dancing, and knowing but few people – but it is an additional idea for life, to have seen such a party – all the Duchesses one ever heard tell of blazing in diamonds, all the young beauties of the season, all the distinguished statesmen,

---

[1] From Thomas Carlyle's translation of Tieck's *Phantasma*.

etc. etc. were to be seen among the six or seven hundred people present – and the rooms all hung with artificial roses looked like an Arabian Nights entertainment. What pleased me best was the good look I got *into the eyes* of the old Duke of Wellington – one has no notion, seeing him on the streets what a dear kind face he has – Lady Ashburton receiving all these people with her grand-Lady airs was also a sight worth seeing. On Saturday I went to Addiscombe with a party of *boys* and *girls* and returned on Monday night. Mr C. and Thackeray came to dinner on Sunday but had to return at night, every room being taken up. I can't imagine why Lady A. always asks *me* to help her with these flirting young ladies and gentlemen. I feel more disposed to wring their necks than take part in their riotous nonsense.

Now; all is changed in *that* quarter by the death of Peel – Lady A. was deeply attached to him – she is off into the country again to escape parties; came here on her way, all in tears, and asked Mr C. to come by himself *this* week – as one asks the Clergyman when one is in affliction! – indeed this death has produced a greater dismay than any public event of my time. Not only among his own set but crowds of working people pressed round his house all the time of his illness demanding news which a Constable, lifted above their heads tried to make heard in vain – and written bulletins were finally hoisted up to be read by the crowd from hour to hour. Mr C. is mourning over him as I never saw him mourn before – went today to look at the house where he lies dead! – But no impression lasts long in London Society – in a few weeks they will all be visiting and 'making wits' again as if nothing had happened.

I have seen little of Geraldine; she comes pretty often but has always engagements to hurry her away – She has sworn friendship with Fanny Lewald the German Authoress who is also lionizing in London at present – and gives me much of her semi-articulate company – I also met Jane Eyre (Miss Bronte) one night at Thackeray's a less figure than Geraldine and extremely unimpressive *to look at* . . .

Ever your affectionate J.C.

GIFTS AND SLIGHTS

133. To Jeannie Welsh at Liverpool

5 Cheyne Row, Chelsea/ 15 October 1851

Dearest Babbie

... Mr C has been sleeping like a top and eating vigorously since his return from Paris – the Ashburtons were only two days behind him – a fact which threw some light on his return sooner than was expected – They (the Ashburtons) are now in town. She brought me a woollen scarf of *her own knitting* during their stay in Switzerland and a cornelian bracelet and – a similar scarf only smaller for Mr C. – in fact I believe the dear woman would never have done all that knitting for *me* unless as a handsome preparation for doing the comforter for Mr C. She is really 'what shall I say? – *strange* upon *my* honour' – On her first arrival in London she staid only two hours and drove down here with these things – I was gone out so she left them – with Mr C. whom she saw – and then wrote me a note of invitation to the Grange – which I answered negatively – 'being so wearied of visiting for the present' – but begged she would let me see her on her coming to town this week – I would go up to her at any hour morning or evening – After knitting me a scarf one might have supposed she would have *cared* to see me for ten minutes in six months and after having Mr C. away in Paris she might have felt it *decent* to constrain herself to receive his wife whether she liked it or no. But not at all! When Mr C. who of course was there so soon as she arrived and before I knew she was to arrive that day, asked 'if she would be disengaged at any time so that I might see her' *she made no answer* – he said, and on the following morning comes a note which I will enclose.

Because she must go to the Exhibition with Lady Sandwich one day she could not have me come to see her any of the three days she was to be in town! and the very day this note came – and after reading it Mr C. walked off and sat an hour with her and is off now again thro' a pouring rain to sit till dinner time – And he 'could not see what the devil business I had to find anything strange in that or to suppose that any slight was put on *me*' – on the contrary she 'had spoken of the *impossibility* of receiving me *in the most goodnatured manner*'!!

I suppose I ought to feel by this time quite resigned to such annoyances – or rather I ought to feel and to have always felt quite superior to them – but I am angry and sorrowful all the same. It is not of course any caprice *she* can show to me that annoys me – I have long given up the generous attempt at loving her – But it is to see *him* always starting up to defend every thing she does and says and no matter whether it be capricious behaviour towards his *wife* – so long as she flatters himself with delicate attentions –

This did not get finished in time for the post – thro' the Sterling girls coming to call – and while they were here your letter came – thanks for it dear Babbie – it is very kind of you to write at such length besides so often – when you must have your hands and head and heart all so busily employed – With your letter came a note from Lady A. to Mr C. which turned out to be an invitation to *him* for this evening at 9 and after that another note came begging he would come at 8 – and he is now off there again – I will not write any more tonight being in rather a bitter mood and the best in such moments is if possible to consume one's own smoke – since one cannot help *smoking*. God bless you all.

Your affectionate

J. Carlyle

134 EXTRACTS FROM JANE'S JOURNAL (1855–6)

Only part of this journal has been preserved. The texts of all but the last three of the following extracts have been taken from Froude's *Letters and Memorials of Jane Welsh Carlyle*.

October 21, 1855. – I remember Charles Buller saying of the Duchess de Praslin's murder, 'What could a poor fellow do with a wife who kept a journal but murder her?' There was a certain truth hidden in this light remark. Your journal all about feelings aggravates whatever is factitious and morbid in you; that I have made experience of. And now the only sort of journal I would keep should have to do with what Mr. Carlyle calls 'the fact of things'. It is very bleak and barren, this fact of things, as I now see it – very; and what good is to result from writing of it in a paper book is more than I can tell. But I have taken a notion to, and perhaps I shall blacken more paper this time, when I begin quite promiscuously without any moral end in view; but just as the Scotch professor drank whisky, because I like it, and because it's cheap.

October 22. – I was cut short in my introduction last night by Mr. C.'s return from Bath House. That eternal Bath House. I wonder how many thousand miles Mr. C. has walked between there and here, putting it all together; setting up always another milestone and another betwixt himself and me. Oh, good gracious! when I first noticed that heavy yellow house without knowing, or caring to know, who it belonged to, how far I was from dreaming that through years and years I should carry every stone's weight of it on my heart. About feelings already! Well, I will not proceed, tho' the thoughts I had in my bed about all that were tragical enough to fill a page of thrilling interest for myself, and tho', as George Sand has shrewdly remarked, '*rien ne soulage comme la rhétorique*'.

October 23. – A stormy day within doors, so I walked out early, and walked, walked, walked. If peace and quietness be not in one's own power, one can always give oneself at least bodily fatigue – no such bad succedaneum after all. Life gets to look for me like a sort of kaleidoscope – a few things of different colours – black predominating, which fate shakes into new and ever new combinations, but always the same things over again. To-day has been so like a day I still remember out of ten years ago; the same still dreamy October weather, the same tumult of mind contrasting with the outer stillness; the same causes for that tumult. Then, as now, I had walked, walked, walked with no aim but to tire myself.

October 25. – . . . My heart is very sore to-night, but I have promised myself not to make this journal a 'miserere', so I will take a dose of morphia and do the impossible to sleep.

November 1. – At last a fair morning to rise to, thanks God! Mazzini never says 'thank God' by any chance, but always 'thanks God'; and I find it sound more grateful. Fine weather outside in fact, but indoors blowing a devil of a gale. Off into space, then, to get the green mould that has been gathering upon me of late days brushed off by human contact.

November 5. – Alone this evening. Lady A. in town again; and Mr. C. of course at Bath House.

Extracts from Jane's journal

When I think of what I is
And what I used to was,
I gin to think I've sold myself
For very little cas.

November 6. – Mended Mr. C.'s dressing-gown. Much movement under the free sky is needful for me to keep my heart from throbbing up into my head and maddening it. They must be comfortable people who have leisure to think about going to Heaven! My most constant and pressing anxiety is to keep out of Bedlam! that's all . . . Ach! If there were no feelings 'what steady sailing craft we should be', as the nautical gentleman of some novel says.

November 7. – Dear, dear! What a sick day this has been with me. Oh, my mother! nobody sees when I am suffering now; and I have learnt to suffer 'all to myself'. From 'only childless' to that, is a far and rough road to travel.

Oh, little did my mother think
The day she cradled me,
The lands I was to travel in,
The death I was to dee.

December 11. – Oh dear! I wish this Grange business were well over. It occupies me (the mere preparation for it) to the exclusion of all quiet thought and placid occupation. To have to care for my dress at this time of day more than I ever did when young and pretty and happy (God bless me, to think that I was once all that!) on penalty of being regarded as a blot on the Grange gold and azure, is really too bad. *Ach Gott!* if we had been left in the sphere of life we belong to, how much better it would have been for us in many ways!

March 24, 1856. – We are now at the 24th of March, 1856, and from this point of time, my journal, let us renew our daily intercourse without looking back. Looking back was not intended by nature, evidently, from the fact that our eyes are in our faces and not in our hind heads. Look straight before you, then, Jane Carlyle, and, if possible, not over the heads of things either, away into the distant vague. Look, above all, at the duty nearest hand, and what's more, do it. Ah, the spirit is willing, but the flesh is weak, and four weeks of illness have made mine weak as water. No galloping over London as in seven-leagued boots for me at present. To-day I walked with effort one little mile, and thought it a great feat; but if the strength has gone out of me, so also has the unrest. I can sit and lie even very patiently doing nothing. To be sure, I am always going on with the story in my head, as poor Paulet expressed it; but even that has taken a dreamy contemplative character, and excites no emotions 'to speak of'. In fact, sleep has come to look to me the highest virtue and the greatest happiness; that is, good sleep, untroubled, beautiful, like a child's. Ah me!

March 26. – To-day, it has blown knives and files; a cold, rasping, savage day; excruciating for sick nerves. Dear Geraldine, as if she would contend with the very elements on my behalf, brought me a bunch of violets and a bouquet of the loveliest most fragrant flowers. Talking with her all I have done or could do . . .

March 30. – Plattnauer told me how the 'grande passion' between — and — had gone to the dogs utterly – the general recipients of '*grandes passions*'.

> Oh, waly, waly, love is bonnie
> A little while when it is new;
> But when it's auld
> It waxeth cauld,
> And melts away like morning dew.

Beautiful verse, sweet and sad, like barley sugar dissolved in tears. About the morning dew, however! I should rather say, 'Goes out like candle snuff' would be a truer simile; only that would not suit the rhyme.

April 11. – To-day I called on 'my lady' come to town for the season. She was perfectly civil, for a wonder.

April 21. – I feel weaklier every day, and 'my soul is also sore vexed'. Oh 'how long?' I put myself in an omnibus, being unable to walk, and was carried to Islington and back again. What a good shilling's-worth of exercise! The Angel at Islington! It was *there* I was set down on my first arrival in London; and Mr. C with Edward Irving was waiting to receive me –

'The past is past; and gone is gone!'

May 29. – . . . Old Mrs. Dermont said to me the other day when I encountered her after 2 years – 'Yes mam my daughter is dead! – only Child, House and everything gone from me! and I assure you *I stand up in the world as if it was'nt the world at all any more'* . . .

Mr. Barlow says nine tenths of the misery of human life proceeds according to *his* observation from *The Institution of Marriage.* He should say from the demoralisation – the desecration of the Institution of Marriage, and then I should cordially agree with him . . .

June 27. – Went with Geraldine to Hampstead; preferring to be broiled on a heath to being broiled in Cheyne Row. dined at *The Spaniard* and came home to tea – dead weary, and a good many shillings out of pocket.

135   GERALDINE'S COMMENTS
ON JANE'S JOURNAL

Froude felt that various passages in Jane's journal required explanation, and he therefore sent it to Geraldine Jewsbury, who returned it with a letter. Froude published extracts from this letter, which follow.

The reading has been like the calling up ghosts . . . It was a very bad time with her just then. No one but herself or one constantly with her knows what she suffered physically as well as morally.

She was miserable: more abidingly and intensely miserable than words can utter. The misery was a reality, no matter whether her imagination made it or not . . . Mr. C. once said to me of her that she had the deepest and tenderest feelings, but narrow. Any other wife would have laughed at Mr. C.'s bewitchment with Lady A.; but to her there was a complicated aggravation which made it very hard to endure. Lady A. was admired for sayings and doings for which she was snubbed. She saw through Lady A.'s little ways and *grande-dame* manners, and knew what they were worth. She contrasted them with the daily, hourly endeavours she was making that *his* life should be as free from hindrances as possible. He put her aside for his work, but lingered in the 'Primrose path of dalliance' for the sake of a great Lady, who liked to have a philosopher in chains.

Lady A. was excessively capricious towards her, and made her feel they cared more about *him* than about *her*.

She was never allowed to visit anywhere but at the Grange; and the mortifications and vexations she felt, though they were often and often self-made, were none the less intolerable to her. At first she was charmed with Lady A., but soon found she had no real hold on her, nor ever could or would have. The sufferings were real, intense, and at times too grievous to be borne. C. did not understand all this, and only felt her to be unreasonable.

The lines on which her character was laid down were very grand, but the result was blurred and distorted and confused.

In marrying she undertook what she felt to be a grand and noble life task: a task which, as set forth by himself, touched all that was noble and heroic, and inspired her imagination from its difficulty. She believed in him, and her faith was unique. No one else did. Well, but she was to be the companion, friend, helpmate – her own gifts were to be cultivated and recognised by him. She was bright and beautiful, with a certain star-like radiance and grace. She had devoted to him her life, which so many other men had desired to share. She had gone off into the desert with him. She had taken up poverty, obscurity, hardship even, cheerfully, willingly, and with an enthusiasm of self-sacrifice, on asking to be allowed to minister to him. The offering was accepted, but, like the precious things flung by Benvenuto into the furnace when his statue was molten, they were all consumed in the flames; and he was so intent and occupied by what he was bringing forth that he could take no heed of her individual treasures. They were all swallowed up in the great whole. In her case it was the living creature in the midst of the fire which felt and suffered. He gave her no human help nor tenderness.

Bear in mind that her inmost life was solitary – no tenderness, no caresses, no loving words; nothing out of which one's heart can make the wine of life. A glacier on a mountain would have been as human a companionship. He suffered too; but he put it all into his work. She had only the desolation and barrenness of having all her love and her life laid waste. Six years she lived at Craigenputtock, and she held out. She had undertaken a task, and she knew that, whether recognised or not, she *did* help him. Her strong persistent will kept her up to the task of pain. Then they came back to the world, and the strain told on her. She did not falter from her purpose of helping and shielding him, but she became warped.

– GERALDINE E. JEWSBURY.

A SHREWING FOR CARLYLE

136. To Thomas Carlyle at Kinloch Luichart, Dingwall

Scotsbrig/ 18 September 1856

Well, I am safe here, tho' not without a struggle for it . . .

Your letter this morning is a *degree* more *legible* than the first one! – but dear me! what galloping and spluttering over the paper; as if you were writing in a house on fire! and bent on making *a little* look *as much as possible*! I have measured the distance between your lines in the letter just come, and it is precisely *one inch*! In the first letter it must have been an inch and half! – I call that a foolish waste of writing-paper! – If you have an excellent bedroom, could you not retire into it for, say one hour, in the course of a whole week, and write composedly and leisurely – *Why* write in the midst of four people?

For the rest, in spite of all objections 'for the occasion got up'; I dare say you are pretty comfortable. Why not? When *you* go to any house, one knows it is because you *choose* to go, and when you stay it is because you *choose* to stay – *You* dont, as weakly amiable people do, *sacrifice* yourself for the pleasure of 'others' – So pray do not think it necessary to be *wishing yourself at home* and 'all that sort of thing,' on paper. 'I don't believe thee!' If I were inclined *to*; I should only have to call to mind the beautiful letters you wrote to me during your former visit to the Ashburtons in the Highlands, and which you afterwards *disavowed* and *trampled into the fire*!!

. . . Lady Ashburton is very kind to offer to take me back pray make her my thanks for the offer – But tho' a very little *Herring* I have a born liking to '*hang by* my own head'. 'And when it is a question simply of paying my own way or having it paid for me – I prefer 'lashing down' my four or five sovereigns *on the table all at once*! – If there were any *companionship* in the matter it would be different – and if *you* go back with the Ashburtons it would be different – as then I should be going merely as part of your luggage – without self responsibility – Settle it as you like; it will be all one to me – meeting you at Scotsbrig, or in Edinburgh, or going home by myself from Thornhill.

This is the 19th of September, the day of my Father's death . . .

Yours faithfully,

Jane W. C.

THE MIGHTY FALLEN

137. To Mrs Russell at Holm Hill

5 Cheyne Row, Chelsea/ March 1857

My dearest Mary,

... We had a letter from Lord Ashburton yesterday. He is very ill content with Lady A.'s progress – but the Doctors say, he writes, she is going on very favourably. They are meaning to come to Paris in the middle of next month and to remain there till the middle of May. Poor woman! this sick life must be a sorer trial to her than to any of us. She has been so used to have everything bend to her will. Her life looked to me always like a *Triumph*! A person so admired, and so prosperous is apt to slight those sympathies and affections which make one's consolation in times of sickness, or of sorrow. And so she will hardly admit anyone to see her now – and those she chooses to see are almost solely *clever men*!!

Oh my Dear Mary, in mourning over that dear good father, who loved you to his last breath, and to whom you were ever loving and dutiful; how much happier are you, than that grand Lady Ashburton fallen into sickness, and with a Mother *living* whom she *would rather not see*! A clever warmhearted woman is the old Countess of Sandwich, and her heart is broken with the accounts of her only daughter's illness – but – that Mother and daughter have lived like so many other Mothers and daughters in Fashionable life – always fenced around with ceremonies – and durst no more enter one another's sick room, without leave asked and obtained, or take any kind freedom with one another, than a pair of entire strangers! ...

I will write soon again

Your affectionate

Jane Carlyle

138   CARLYLE ON THE DEATH OF LADY ASHBURTON

Monday, May 4, 1847 – At Paris, on her way home from Nice, Lady Ashburton (born Lady Harriet Montague) suddenly died: suddenly to the doctors and those who believed them; in which number, fondly hoping against hope, was I. A sad and greatly interesting event to me and to many! The most queen-like woman I had ever known or seen. The honour of her constant regard had for ten years back been among my proudest and most valued possessions – lost now; gone – for ever gone! This was our first visit to Addiscombe after. I rode much about with Lord A. in intimate talk, and well recollect this visit of perhaps a week or ten days, and of the weeks that preceded and followed. How well I still remember the evening Richard Milnes brought down the news; the moonlit streets, and dirge-like tone of everything, as I walked up to Lady Sandwich's door and asked for the weak, devoted, aged mother. In no society, English or other, had I seen the equal or the second of this great lady that was gone; by nature and by culture *facile princeps* she, I think, of all great ladies I have ever seen.

My Jane's miserable illness now over, a visit to Haddington was steadily in view all summer.

JANE ON THE SAME SUBJECT

139. To Mrs Russell at Holm Hill

5 Cheyne Row, Chelsea/ May 1857

Dearest Mary

I have been long in answering your dear letter. If you saw Lady Ashburton's death in the newspapers you would partly guess why; that I was shocked, and dispirited, and feeling *silence* best. *But* you could *not* guess the *outward* disturbance consequent on this event! The letters and calls of inquiry and condolence that have been eating up my days for the last two weeks! distressingly and irritatingly – For it does not require any particular acuteness to detect: in this fussy display of feeling more impertinent curiosity than genuine sympathy. *Some* Ladies (of her circle) who never were here before, have come out of *good* motives, taking to us as *her* friends, out of regard for her memory – But the greater number of these *condolers* have come to ask particulars of her death (which we were likely to know) and to see how we, especially *Mr Carlyle*, were taking her loss!

At no moment since the time she was first declared in danger could her death have come with more shock. Lord Ashburton had just been here for a week, making preparations for her immediate return to England, and he represented her as 'progressing most favourably'. Sir James Clark who had been to Paris to see her said the same. Lord

A was to have gone back to Paris on the Sunday, but on Saturday he got a letter from *her*, telling him to go to St Leonards and take a house there: 'that she might be at the seaside, *if she liked*, during September'! He went and took the house, and so did not get to Paris till the Monday, when she had been *dead* two hours! I never heard of so easy a death! She was dressing about four o'clock, felt faint and called for Dr Rous (her private Dr) he told her, in answer to her question: 'what is this?' 'you are going to faint, it is nothing; you mustn't mind these faintnesses.' He put his arm round her to support her, she clasped her hands over his other arm, leant her forehead on his shoulder, gave a sigh, and was dead!

Last Tuesday Mr C. went to the Grange to be present at her funeral. It was conducted with a sort of royal state, and all the *Men*, who used to compose a sort of *Court* for her, were there; *in tears*! I never heard of a gloomier funeral . . .

Affectionately yours
Jane W. Carlyle

X *Illness*

Sir James Crichton-Browne, the Scottish surgeon whom Alexander Carlyle enlisted in his campaign against 'Froudulencies', easily persuaded himself that Jane was a poor risk as far as health was concerned long before she met Carlyle. In his Introduction to the *New Letters and Memorials of Jane Welsh Carlyle* he pointed out that her father had died of typhus fever at forty-three; that almost all her Welsh relatives had died out before she did – there was not a single descendant to inherit from her the ancestral farm at Craigenputtoch; that Jane's mother had passed on to Jane her own intensely nervous temperament; that Jane was a seven-month baby; and that her hot-house upbringing, as an over-stimulated, over-educated, only child, had prematurely weakened her. 'As the inevitable consequence of all this,' said Sir James, 'she grew up a highly neurotic woman.'

After describing the sick headaches which had got a firm hold before her marriage, the annual colds and influenzas, the sleeplessness, and the 'pretty frequent' use of morphia with its tendencies to induce delusions of persecution, Sir James delivers his verdict: 'She was in short the very woman in whom the physician would expect a nervous breakdown at a critical epoch of life.' He places this breakdown in the year 1846, when she was forty-five, and says that it lasted until 1857, by which time it was 'all but completely dispelled'. He classifies it as 'a mild, but protracted attack of mental disturbance, which would be technically called on its psychical side climacteric melancholia, and on its physical side neurasthenia'.

In his view this breakdown was the key to Jane's frame of mind during the 'Ashburton years', morbid despondency and unfounded jealousies being its typical characteristics. After it was over, he says, Jane never experienced delusions again, but her bodily health and nervous system were seriously impaired. He ended his analysis by describing the violent neuralgia which deprived her of the use of her left hand and arm in 1863 and which returned to plague her right hand and arm in 1865. The pain, he says, could be excruciating; it brought thoughts of suicide and a desperate turning to religion; but there was no longer any jealousy of her husband.

How far Jane's medical history was predetermined in this fashion is obviously a matter of opinion. No one doubts that she was delicate, sensitive, excitable, highly strung; a prey to melancholy imaginings. But there was a buoyant Jane as well as a drooping Jane; not curled up but fighting back; tough and indomitable. She told the Thackeray children never to underrate the powers of the human will, that she had faced insanity in her life and fought it back. Carlyle once wrote, 'Jane is not at all strong, sleeps very ill . . . but she is very tough, and a bit of good stuff too. I often wonder how she holds out, and braves many things, with so thin a skin.'

Jane knew her own psychic needs – for calm as well as excitement, for rest as well as activity, for frequent changes of scene, and for cheerful, loving attention.

Illness

Would another world than Craigenputtoch, Cheyne Row and Thomas Carlyle have taxed her strength and spirits less? Carlyle gave her a life-time of love in his own way. But his hypochondria aggravated hers; his demands – for peace, quiet, protection, and every other condition deemed necessary to his work – were a terrible ordeal for overwrought nerves; and his self-absorption often condemned her to loneliness. He discovered after her death that he had never known how much more she needed from him than he was able to give.

Could the doctors have done more for her? Probably not. She and Carlyle took what the doctors of their day had to offer, with a mixture of scepticism and dependence. They were grateful for the devotion of her doctors – Doctor Barnes in Chelsea, Doctor Quain, Doctor Blakiston at St Leonards, and above all, Doctor Russell. Jane wrote at the end of her life that Doctor Russell was the best doctor she had ever had; nerves were real things for him, like muscles, not something in the imagination; if she had had someone like him at the beginning of her illness, it might not have taken such a fearful hold. But medical science could do little for her. Carlyle, at the depth of her depression in 1864, found the doctors as puzzled as he was.

Could Jane have done more for herself? Carlyle preached fresh air and exercise. 'Do you walk daily? Every day?' He once wrote, 'There is no drug or doctoring in the whole pharmacopœia that is worth a pin without this.' His brother, who preached cheerfulness to Thomas as a cure for his troubles, preached hard work for Jane's! She was ironical about Carlyle's favourite prescription – 'Mr Carlyle walked and rode and bathed himself into a bilious crisis', was one of her comments – and she was furious about John's. One wish she confessed to Mrs Russell at the end of her life, as she thought of the prodigious procession of sedatives and stimulants that had wound its way through her anatomy – that young ladies might be given a course of instruction by wise women about their bowels!

Readers with a clinical taste can try to find chapters in Jane's medical history. In the love letters of the long courtship it is not she but Thomas who is constantly complaining about ill health. The 'incessant torture' which his dyspepsia has inflicted on him is not a subject for humour. Did she develop her headaches out of self-defence? Of course not; but she makes a good story out of her bouts of illness whenever she can and is usually matter of fact when she cannot. One of the earliest surviving references to a disabling headache is in December 1823, when she was twenty-two. The pattern soon becomes clear. It can last up to three days; the pain can make her almost insensible; she is left shattered and listless until a few nights of good sleep, or a new excitement, restore her spirits. She connects her headaches with worries – about herself, her mother, Carlyle; but noise can also produce headaches. After the headache is gone, her wits feel sharper than they were before. Sick headaches were to be part of Jane's life for many years, but not for ever; they seem to have disappeared in her early fifties, and she was caught by surprise when one returned in December 1865, within a few months of her death.

The Craigenputtoch years are a controversial chapter. Froude believed that Jane's health never recovered from the strains of this period – the drudgery, roughness, loneliness of the moorland farm, and the limits to companionship with Carlyle. Alexander Carlyle protested that her health, though never good, was better at Craigenputtoch than it had ever been! Perhaps the real development of these years is the discovery by both Jane and Carlyle that poor health is going to be part of her existence. Winters get worse, bringing 'headaches, heartaches and all kinds of aches'. Looking back in 1833 Jane writes, 'To say the truth, my whole life has been a sort of *puddling* as to health.' And brother John is already saying at this date what so infuriated her when he repeated it in her later depressions, 'Could I give you some agreeable occupation to fill your whole mind, it would do more for you than all the medicine in existence.'

The first decade in London, which we have called 'The creative years', brought all sorts of stimulations for the mind. If Carlyle, when editing her letters after death, pauses over a letter of 1839 to record sadly that winter colds and 'fierce torturing nervous headaches' will accompany her for the rest of her days, nonetheless, she makes fun of her afflictions, rouses herself for 'earthquakes' and 'outings' and writes hosts of spirited letters. The next decade has all the sombre hues which we connect with 'the Ashburton episode'. But was there really a breakdown in 1846, followed by years of protracted mental disturbance, of the kind Sir James postulated? Carlyle's editorial notes, which he attached to her letters after her death, provide no support for this view. He says she was in poor health in the summer and autumn of 1846; but it was no poorer than it had often been before, and he was soon telling how she rose victorious again. It was only the camp-followers of Sir James who repeated his view. What Jane's letters seem to reveal, either directly or indirectly, is not a major breakdown but simply a grievous sense of estrangement over Carlyle's intimacy with Lady Ashburton. This was the inference which Froude drew from them, and it was Froude's judgment that Carlyle, however unwittingly, had put himself in the wrong that seems to have provoked Sir James into developing the theory of Jane's breakdown, in order to vindicate Carlyle. It is also very interesting to notice that the year which Sir James selects, without explanation, as marking the end of Jane's delusions is the year in which Lady Ashburton, their target, passed away!

All in all, it seems much more reasonable to assume that the Ashburton relationship was just an added strain on a constitution already weakened by strain. Jane was getting no younger; living with Carlyle no easier. Was it necessary to aassume a middle-aged breakdown, and an over-indulgence in drugs, to explain the anguish of these years? Lady Bliss, one of Jane's most perceptive interpreters, was nearer the mark when she referred to the tensions of the summer of 1846 as 'a small climax in their mutual misery'.

And of course all was not black. Froude described the impression which the Carlyles made on him when he met them for the first time in 1849. James Spedding took him on a June evening after dinner into the little court at Cheyne Row where Carlyle was puffing his disgust over a poor book he was reading.

We went afterwards into the dining-room, where Mrs. Carlyle gave us tea. Her features were not regular, but I thought I had never seen a more interesting-looking woman. Her hair was raven black, her eyes dark, soft, sad, with dangerous light in them. Carlyle's talk was rich, full, and scornful; hers delicately mocking. She was fond of Spedding, and kept up a quick, sparkling conversation with him, telling stories at her husband's expense, at which he laughed himself as heartily as we did.

Her letters of the 1850s were often written by a prisoner indoors, or by a convalescent just risen from her bed, but it was only in the 1860s that the full extent of her sickness became evident to Carlyle. The misery begun by the neuralgia of 1863, and aggravated by the street accident in October of that year, developed into torments the like of which she had never before suffered. It was not the positive pain that reduced her; she said she could stand as much of that as anyone; but the black terrors of nervous misery. Before these, her stoicism dissolved in fears of insanity and cravings for death; Doctor Blakiston at St Leonards, kind but unimaginative, talked about her 'hysterical mania'. If there was any single experience in her medical history which deserved to be called a breakdown, it was this. When she finally struggled out of it under the care of Doctor and Mrs Russell at Thornhill in Scotland, and returned to Chelsea in early October 1864, she described herself as 'a *Living Miracle*'. It was like a resurrection from the dead.

Her last eighteen months were to be troubled enough, with her right arm disabled in the summer of 1865 as her left arm had been before – how moving those left-handed letters! – and with only limited strength for the remaining calls that Carlyle would make on her. But anything was better, she wrote to her closest friends, than 'the miserable nervous illness which kept me so ruined for more than a year'.

The thought that anyone would ever make a selection of her letters to illustrate her ill-health – a sick-room anthology! – would have horrified Jane. She knew how boring ill-health could be; made light of her own in company; confided only in intimates; and never talked freely to her male doctors (there were no female ones) before pain had burnt out her delicacy.

In the following selection we have drawn on the playful and the caustic; on letters to a bosom friend like Mary Russell; on the vivid, poignant description of her accident and breakdown in 1863–4, which Carlyle wrote as he looked back in anguish after her death; and on her heart-rending letters from St Leonards and Holm Hill. The depths of her torments were at St Leonards in the spring of 1864, where she went to be near Doctor Blakiston in the hope that a change from Chelsea might do something for her. The special carriage that took her from Cheyne Row to the station felt like a hearse. From St Leonards she turned in despair to Scotland. Carlyle's doctor-brother John took her first to the family farm at The Gill, Annandale, where their sister Mary Austin lived, and then to Doctor and Mary Russell at Holm Hill, Thornhill, where her ordeal finally ended.

TRYING A 'CHANGE'

140. TO MRS RUSSELL AT THORNHILL

5 Cheyne Row, Chelsea/12 July 1845

My dearest Mrs Russell

. . . For us here; we go on in much the old fashion – my Husband always *writing* – I always *ailing*, which is perhaps the most laborious business of the two, tho' yielding less result – I was confined four months to the house during winter and spring, taking care of a cough – but it went when the warm weather came – Since then however I have never felt to have got back even my usual limited amount of strength and spirits – so I am going to try what people call a 'change' – My Husband is going to Scotsbrig so soon as his weary book [on Cromwell] is completed which he expects will be in the course of next month – and he has been very urgent on me to go to Scotland also, and even without waiting his time which will be rather late in the season. But I do not fancy the object of my going from home would be attained by encountering so much painful emotion as a visit to a country made so desolate for me would excite. I have tried to bring my mind to it – but it will not do – So I am going to Liverpool some ten days hence – and then to Seaforth a place in the neighbourhood belonging to a favourite friend of mine [Mrs Paulet] – where I enjoy the inestimable advantage of being *let alone* – My uncle and Jeannie start for Helensborough again on the first of August and would have had me go *there* with *them* – but on one hand there was the sea voyage which occasions me such horrible suffering that only the hope of seeing my Mother at the end of it ever could make me undertake it – or if I went by land I must have passed thro' Dumfriesshire – staid some days at Scotsbrig – and the notion of all that was too sad – If there were any positive duty to be accomplished by going to Scotland, I hope I would not be so weak as to let the pain of it withold me. But going there merely to recover my *strength* and *spirits*! – No no it would be labour worse than lost . . .

Ever affectionately

Yours

Jane Carlyle

MORALIZING ON DEATH

141. To Thomas Carlyle at Chelsea

Seaforth House, Liverpool/15 July 1846

My dear Husband

. . . Jeannie writes me from Auchtertool that the old Minister is suddenly dead – . . . Poor mortals 'after all'! What a mighty pother we make about our bits of lives, and Death, so surely on the way to cut us out of *all that* at least – whatever may come after! Yes nobody out of Bedlam even *educated* in *Edinburgh* can contrive to doubt of *Death*. One may go a far way in Scepticism – may get to disbelieve in God and Devil, in *Virtue and in Vice*, in Love, in one's own Soul, never to speak of *Time and Space* – *Progress of the Species* – *Rights of Women*, – Greatest *Happiness of the greatest Number* – *isms* world without end everything in short that the human mind ever believed in, or 'believed that it believed' in – only *not* in *Death*! The most outrageous Sceptic – even I after two nights without sleep – cannot go ahead against *that* fact – a rather cheering one on the whole – that let one's earthly difficulties be what they may, Death will make them all smooth sooner or later, and either one shall have a trial at existing again under new conditions, or sleep soundly thro all eternity. That last used to be a horrible thought for me – but is not so any longer. I am weary, weary to such a point of moral exhaustion that *any* anchorage were welcome even the stillest coldest where the wicked should cease from troubling and the weary be at rest, understanding both by the *wicked* and the weary – *myself* – But if I had been meaning to moralize I should have taken larger notepaper – Adieu, then.

Ever yours
Jane W. C.

REASSURING CARLYLE

142. TO THOMAS CARLYLE AT SCOTSBRIG

5 Cheyne Row, Chelsea/ 22 September 1847

. . . You are to know then that ever since I wrote the last letter to you I have had no *history* 'to speak of' – having been confined pretty constantly to bed – When I wrote the last letter I was already ill – in fact I had never felt *well* from the first day of my return – but at that writing I perceived I was in for some sort of regular illness. I thought at first it was going to be a violent cold – but it has not turned to a cold – I suppose a Dr would call it some sort of bilious or nervous fever – Whatever it has been I have suffered horribly from irritation nausea and languor – but now I am in the way of getting well again. I am out of bed today and able to write to you as you see. John has been very kind to me since he knew of my illness which was not till Sunday afternoon. He has come to see me *twice* a day – and one time staid *four hours* in my bedroom, reading to me &c. I prohibited him from telling you of it – as I did not want you to be kept anxious – but now I am so much better that there is not the slightest occasion for anxiety – and as to your being *there* and not *here*, I assure [you] it has been the greatest possible *Comfort* to me that it so happened– I can be twice as patient and composed I find when there is nobody put about by my being laid up – Had you been here I should have struggled on longer without taking to bed and been in the desperatest haste to get out of it – All the Nursing possible has been given me by Anne and Mrs Piper – and the perfect quiet of the house could not have been had on other terms – nor could Anne have had time to attend to me as I required if we had not had the house all to ourselves.

So do not be *vexed* and do not be uneasy – I have no ailment now but weakness and so soon as I can get into the air *that* will wear off.

And now I must stop for this time.

Ever yours,
J.W.C.

[Postscript]   23 September

You must have another little letter today, Dear; in case you take a notion to *fret*. I continue to mend rapidly, had a good deal of sleep last night – without henbane – and today I astonished Anne by telling her I was '*very* hungry' . . .

One of the People who has been kindest to me during my illness is Mr Chambers's 'Old John' – He has actually reduced all the *pianos* to utter silence. Hearing Anne say that the noise of his Ladies was enough to drive *her* mistress mad, he said '*I* will put a stop to *that*' and went immediately himself into the Drawing-room, and told the Ladies then at the piano 'he wondered they were not ashamed of themselves making such a noise and Mrs. Carlyle at death's door on the other side the wall' – And there has not been a note struck since – five days ago . . .

J. C.

'I HAVE BEEN "PACKED"'

143. To Thomas Carlyle at Galway, Ireland

Benrydden/ 20 July 1849

Oh my Dear! I have been '*packed*'. The Dr proposed to 'pack' me, for courtesy, and I for curiosity accepted – so at six in the morning, just when I had fallen into sound sleep; I was roused by a bath-woman coming to my bedside, in a huge white flannel gown, and bidding me turn out. I got onto the floor in a very bewildered state, and she proceeded to double back one half of my bed clothes and feather-bed; spread a pair of blankets on the mattress; then a sheet wrung out of cold water; then bid me strip and lie down. I lay down and she swathed me with the wet sheet like a mummy, then swathed me with the blankets, my arms pinioned down, exactly in fact like a mummy then rolled back the feather bed and original bedclothes on the top of me, leaving out the head – and so left me – for an hour – to *go mad* at my leisure! – I had no sooner fairly realized my situation – of being bound hand and foot under a heap of things, than I felt quite frantic, cursed my foolish curiosity, and made horrid efforts to release myself – thought of *rolling* to the bell and ringing it with my *teeth*, but could not shake off the feather bed! – did ultimately get one of my hands *turned round* – and was thankful for even *that* change of posture. Dr Nicol says the bath-woman should have *stayed* with me during the first 'pack' and put a wet cloth on my head – that it was the blood being sent to my head that 'caused all this wildness', Whatever it was; I would not undergo the thing again for a hundred guineas. When the bath-woman came back at seven I ordered her to take me out instantly – 'But the Dr?' The Dr I told her had no business with *me*, I was not a patient – 'Oh! then you have only been *packed* for *foon*, have you?' – 'Yes – and very bad fun!' so she filled a slipper-bath to 'put me to rights again' – and I plunged into *that* so soon as I was set loose, and she plashed pitcher after pitcher- ful of water on my head – and this shall be the last of my water- curing, for the present. I feel quite shattered still, with an incipient headache, and am wishing that Forster would come, and take us back to Rawdon . . .

Your affectionate
Jane W. C.

SURVIVING NINETEEN WINTERS IN ENGLAND

144. To Mrs Russell at Holm Hill

5 Cheyne Row, Chelsea/ Spring 1857

My dearest Mary
    . . . If only you could get back your sleep, Darling! – It is dreadful when Sorrow[1] cannot have the relief which Nature has appointed it in sleep, in forgetfulness – but must be endured by night as well as by day! and every sad image that presents itself is thrown out in such

---

[1] Mrs Russell's father had recently died.

gigantic relief on the darkness; and made so haggard by bodily weariness! There is nothing I feel so much sympathy with as sleeplessness! for there is nothing I have suffered so much from, myself. – (However kindly disposed one may be; it needs always that one should *understand* another's *trouble* before one can rightly sympathise with it) – My comfort about *you* is, that your Husband, besides being a kind Husband, is a skilful Doctor – and whatever *can* be done to overcome your wakefulness will assuredly be done. Do you know he has helped *me* to get better sleep, by what he said when I was at Thornhill, about the injuriousness of Morphia and such things; which both Dr Carlyle and Dr Rouse had recommended and urged on me *without restriction*! Except *one* dose of Morphia which Dr C. forced me to take at the beginning of this last cold, and which did me manifest hurt, I have taken *none of these things* whatever – and tho I had spent many nights almost wholly without sleep the sleep I *did* get was more like real human sleep, and of late weeks I have even had from five to six hours a-night of it. I have also abstained from something else Dr Russell did *not* prohibit, nay rather *by example* inculcated; I take no *tea* – only what they call in Scotland '*content*' – not even *that* quite; for I take milk and water without sugar. For the rest: I am decidedly recovering now; and even while your mind must needs be full of your own sad loss – I know you are unselfish enough, and love me enough, to be interested in what I write of myself, and glad that it is so favourable. I have been out four times in a carriage – and I feel stronger body and mind. The cough is not gone yet, but there is no pain connected with it now; and it will need warmer weather to break *the habit* of coughing. I was beginning to think with Dr Russell, that I had taken a too serious responsibility on myself in Doctoring myself thro this last illness: but now I am glad; for any of these slapdash medical *Eminences* who had seen me a few weeks ago; not knowing how many of the same sort of seizures I had weathered, would for certain have ordered me to Madeira, or the south of Italy; to the complete upsetting of one's domestic convenience and the progress of *Frederick the Great*!

It is seventeen years now since a Dr Morrah who attended me here, in such another illness, told me 'I *should never live thro' another winter in England*'!! He was a man of high reputation, whom I shouldn't have disliked having again; but he died soon after – Well; I resolved when the next winter came to *stay*, and take my chance! – and I have *lived 19 winters in England*! and ten of them [I] have walked about in the coldest frosts; at the rate of six or ten miles a day! To be sure the Pitcher goes often to the well and gets broken at last. *This* time again, however, the poor little brittle Pitcher will come back from the well, whole, I think, or – with only a *little crack* in it – And cracked things often hold out as long as whole things; one takes so much better care of them! . . .

God bless J.W.C.

TURNING OVER A NEW LEAF

145. To Thomas Carlyle at Chelsea

Sunny Bank, Haddington/ 23 July 1857

The pens you made me, Dear, are all ground down on this lime-paper, and I am obliged to write now with the *backs* – which has a perverse effect on my ideas, and my ideas are rather awry to begin with. I feel *provoked* that having 'made an effort', like this, to get well; I do not succeed in doing it *effectually* and *at once*. '*Very* absurd!' – I ought to be thankful for ever so little amendment: above all, even if no cure should be worked on me by all this fresh air, and sweet milk, and riding in carriages, and having my own entire humour out; I ought to be thankful for the *present* escape from that horrid *sickness* which nobody that has not felt it can know the horror of.

Tho my nights are no better than they were at Chelsea, indeed worse latterly; still it is only oppression and weariness I feel during the day – not that horrid feeling as if Death were grasping at my heart – But 'Oh *My!*' – What a shame! when you are left alone there with plenty smoke of your own to consume, to be puffing out mine on you from this distance! It is certainly a questionable privilege one's best friend enjoys; that of having all one's darkness rayed out on him! – If I were writing to – who shall I say? – Mr Barlow, now – I should fill my paper with '*wits*' and elegant quotations, and diverting anecdotes; should write a letter that would procure me laudation sky-high, on my 'charming unflagging spirits'!! and my 'extraordinary freshness of mind and feelings'! but to *you* I cannot for my life be anything but a bore! . . .

Affectionately yours,
Jane Welsh Carlyle

Turning over a new leaf

146. To Thomas Carlyle at Chelsea

Sunny Bank, Haddington/ 26 July 1857

Thanks for your note, meant to be very *soothing* I can see; but it rather soothes me *the wrong way of the hair* somehow! makes me feel I had been making a Baby of myself and a fractious Baby – Well never mind, As Miss Madeline Smith[1] said to old Dr Simpson, who attended her during a short illness in prison, and begged to use 'the privilege of an old man, and speak to her seriously at parting', 'My dear Doctor! it is *so* good of you! But I wont let you trouble yourself to give *me* advice; for I assure you I have quite made up my mind *to turn over a new leaf*'!!! That is a fact! Simpson told it to Terrot who told *me*.

And so, *I* have made up my mind to turn over a new leaf; and no more give words to the impatient or desponding thoughts that rise in my mind about myself: It is not a *natural* vice of mine, that sort of egoistical babblement; but has been fostered in me by the patience and sympathy shown me in my late long illness. I can very easily leave it off – as I did *smoking* – when I see it to be getting a bad habit . . .

EIGHT INFLUENZAS ANNUALLY

147. To Mrs Russell at Thornhill

2 October 1857

. . . I could not for shame write to you last week – for I couldn't in writing have withheld the fact that I had – got a shocking bad *cold*! – (again!) – Really I found myself making apologies, and explaining *the cause* to every body who came in – as if it had been a punishable offence against society I was committing. Harriet Martineau used to say of me, with that show of *accuracy* never accurate, which distinguishes her, 'Jane Carlyle has *eight* Influenzas *annually*; I wonder how she survives it!' Now it is getting to be *one* Influenza lasting all the year round – However I must not lose heart; tho it *was* disappointing to fall ill just when I had been taking all that trouble to *strengthen* myself, and with tolerable success apparently. But really

[1] The Glasgow murderess, under sentence of death.

253

I should have needed the thick skin of a horse, instead of being 'born without skin' as the Germans call those born, (as I was), in *the seventh month*; to resist the masked batteries of cold air, Mr C. brought to bear on me during the east wind ten days ago! He has a mania about 'fresh air', this Man – and is never happy unless all the doors and windows are open . . .

REPROACHING CARLYLE

148. To Thomas Carlyle at The Gill

25 June 1858

. . . Don't let your enjoyment of 'the Country' be disturbed by thoughts of *me* still 'in Town'. I won't stay here longer than I find it good for me. But what *I* feel to need *at present* is, above all things human and divine, *rest from 'mental worry'*! and no where is there such fair outlook of *that* for me as just at home, under the present conditions. 'The *Cares of Bread*' have been too heavy for me lately – and the influx of 'cousins' most wearing! and to see *you* constantly discontented, and as much so with *me* apparently as with all other things, when I have neither the strength and spirits to bear up against your discontent, nor the obtuseness to be indifferent to it – that has done me more harm than you have the least notion of. You have not the least notion what a killing thought it is to have put into one's heart, gnawing there day and night, that one *ought* to be *dead*, since one *can* no longer make the same exertions as formerly! – that one was taken only 'for better' – not by any means 'for worse'; and in fact, that the only feasible and dignified thing that remains for one to do is to just *die*, and be done with it!

Better, if possible, to recover some health of body and mind, you say – Well yes! *if possible*! In that view I go with Neuberg this evening to view a field of hay! . . .

OPENING CARLYLE'S EYES

149. To Mrs Russell at Thornhill

5 Cheyne Row, Chelsea/ 27 June 1858

Dearest Mary

. . . First, my Dear, the *heat* has really been nearer killing me than the cold – London heat! – nobody knows what *that* is till having tried it! so breathless and sickening, and oppressive as no other heat I ever experienced! Then the quantities of visitors rushing about me at this season, complicated by an influx of *cousins*, to be entertained on special terms, have taken out in talk my dregs of strength and spirit!

Then Mr Carlyle, in the collapse from the strain of his book, and the biliousness developed by the heat, has been so wild to 'get away' and so incapable of determining where to go and when to go! that living beside him has been like living the life of a weathercock, in a high wind, blowing from all points at once! *sensibility* superadded! So long at least as he involved *me* in his 'dissolving views'! The imaginary houses, in different parts of the Kingdom, in which I have had to look round me on bare walls, and apply my fancy to *furnishing*; *with the strength I have*(!) – (about equal to my canary's, which, every now and then, drops off the perch on its back and has to be lifted up!) – would have driven me crazy I think, if one day I hadn't got desperate and burst out *crying*!! Until a woman *cries*, men never think she can be suffering! Bless their blockheadism! However when I *cried*, and declared I was not strong enough for all that any more; Mr C. opened his eyes to the fact so far, as to decide that for the present he would go to his Sister's (the Gill) and let me choose my own course after. And to the Gill he went last Wednesday night, and since then I have been *resting* – and already feel better for the rest, even *without* 'change of air' –

What my own course will be, I haven't a notion! The main point in my system of *rest* is, to postpone not only all doing, but all making up my mind to do! to reduce myself as much as possible to a state of vacant, placid idiocy! *That* is the state, I am sure, a judicious Doctor would recommend for the moment! When the time comes for *wishing* for change and action – it will be time to decide where to go – Meanwhile I shall see what being *well let alone* will do for my health! All the cousins are gone now, the visitors going – no household cares! ('*cares of bread*' as Mazzini calls them!) For, with no Husband to *study*, housekeeping is mere play, and my young maid is a jewel of a creature! It seems to me the best chance I have had for picking up a little strength this good while . . .

> Your affectionate
> Jane W. Carlyle

STAYING AWAY FROM CARLYLE

150. To Mrs Russell at Holm Hill

5 Cheyne Row, Chelsea/ 17 August 1860

Dearest Mary

I haven't leisure to commence this letter with reproaches, for the reproaches would be very long! and my time for writing is very short! In an hour hence a carriage will come to take me to a sick old *Lady* – I myself being quite as sick, and nearly as old! – and there are directions to be given to diverse workmen before I start. For Mr Carlyle is absent – and I have taken the opportunity of turning a carpenter, and a painter, and a paperhanger into his private apartment!

Yes: after repeatedly assuring you that Mr C. would not go North this summer, but restrict his travels to some sea side place near hand, I am almost ashamed to tell you that he *has* gone 'north' after all! and further north than he ever was in all his life before! Being on a visit to Sir George Sinclair at Thurso Castle – the northernmost point of Scotland! A trial of Brighton had been made, and had ended abruptly and ignominiously, in flight back to Chelsea; to get out of the sound of certain *cocks*! Of all places in the world Brighton was the last one could have expected to be infested with *poultry*! But one week of Brighton had only increased Mr C.'s desire for *sea*; and indeed he had got into such a sleepless, excited condition, thro' prolonged over-work, that there could be no doubt about the need of what they call '*a complete change*' for him. So he looked about for a sea residence, where he might be safe from *cocks* and cockneys, and decided for Thurso Castle – which could moreover be reached by *sailing*, which he prefers infinitely to railwaying – and whence there had come a pressing invitation for us both – to spend a couple of months. Accordingly he streamed off there a fortnight ago – I remaining behind, for several reasons; first that *sailing* is as much as my life is worth! and seven hundred miles of railway would have been just about as fatal! Second, if I was going to undertake a *long* journey, I might take it in directions that would better repay the trouble and expense than Thurso Castle, presided over by an unknown Lady Camilla; my only friend there Sir George himself more good than interesting! And third; the long worry and anxiety I had had with Mr C.'s nervousness had reduced myself to the brink of a nervous fever, and my Dr was peremptory as to the unfitness of my either going with Mr C., or rejoining him at Thurso. Indeed I was not to leave home at all, in the state I was in – but to take three *composing draughts* a-day! and go to bed for two hours every forenoon! A fortnight of this, and perfect quiet in the house has calmed me down amazingly – only I feel as *tired* as if I were just returned from 'the thirty years' war'. – And *now* Mr Barnes does not object to my going away, provided I don't go to Mr C.!!! and don't over exert myself. Mr C. who is already immensely improved by his residence at Thurso Castle, is all for every body 'going into the Country', and has made up his mind that, like it or not, *I* must go 'instantly' to – the Gill! (Mary Austin's!), which as it suits *his* milk-loving and solitude-loving habits he imagines would equally suit *me*! – And I myself, would like very well to turn my two or three remaining weeks of liberty to some more agreeable use than superintending the house-cleaning here! But decidedly mooning about, all by myself, at *the Gill*, lapping milk which doesn't agree with me, and being *stared at* by the Gill children as their 'Aunt!' is not the happy 'change' for which I would go far! much as I like Mary Austin, and like to speak with her – *for a few hours*! . . .

Your affectionate
Jane W. Carlyle

'THIS DEVILRY IN MY ARM'

151. To Mrs Russell at Holm Hill

5 Cheyne Row, Chelsea/ 16 September 1863

How absurd of you, my dearest Mary, to make so many apologies about a trifling request like that! Why, if you had asked for twenty autographs, Mr C. could have written them in twenty minutes, and would have written them for *you* with pleasure. Certainly, my Dear, as I have often said before, *faith* is not your strong point!

Well, we have done our '*outing*' (as the people here call going into the country); and it is all the 'outing!' we are likely to do till next summer (if we live to see next summer), unless Lord Ashburton should be well enough, and myself well enough, to make another expedition to the Grange during the winter.

I had some idea of going to Folkestone, where Miss Davenport

Bromley has a house at present, and pressed me to come and take some tepid sea water baths. but my experience of the wretchedness of being from home, with this devilry in my arm, has decided me to remain stationary, for the present. In spite of the fine air and beauty of the Grange, and Lady Ashburton's[1] superhuman kindness, I had no enjoyment of anything, all the three weeks we staid; being in constant pain, day and night, and not able to comb my own hair, or do anything in which a *left* arm is needed as well as a right one! I think I told you I had had pain more or less in my left arm for two months before I left London. It was trifling in the beginning; indeed nothing to speak of, when I did not move it *backwards* or *upwards*. I did not think it worth sending for Mr Barnes about at first, and latterly, he was away at the seaside for some weeks, having been ill himself. There was nobody else I like to consult. Besides, I always flatter myself that anything that ails me more than usual is sure to be removed by change of scene; so I *bore* on, in hope that so soon as I got to the Grange the arm would come all right. It did quite the reverse however, for it became worse and worse, and I was driven at last to consult Dr Quain, when he came down to see Lord A. He told me, before I had spoken a dozen words, that it wasn't rheumatism I had got but neuralgia (if any good Christian would explain to me the difference between these two things I should feel edified and grateful!) It had been produced he said by extreme weakness; and that I must be stronger before any impression could be made on it. Could I take quinine? I didn't know – I would try – so he sent me quinine pills from London to be taken twice a day if they gave me no headache, which they don't do, and an embrocation of opium, aconite, camphor, and chloroform (I tell you all this that you may ask *your* Dr if he thinks it right, or can suggest anything else) moreover; I was to take castor oil every two or three days. I have been following these directions for a fortnight, and there is certainly an improvement in my general health. I feel less cowardly and less fanciful, and feel less disgust at human food; but tho' the embrocation relieves the pain while I am applying it and for a few minutes after, it is as stiff and painful as ever when left to itself . . .

Yours ever affectionately,
Jane Carlyle

[1] This is the *second* Lady Ashburton.

LOOKING BACK IN ANGUISH:
CARLYLE'S NOTES

These notes, written by Carlyle in the months following his wife's death, were
published in Froude, *Letters and Memorials*, III, 174–81, 192–5.

Of all these dreary sufferings and miseries, which had been steadily
increasing for years past, I perceive now, with pain and remorse, I
had never had the least of a clear notion; such her invincible spirit
in bearing them, such her constant effort to hide them from me
altogether. My own poor existence, as she also well knew, was laden
to the utmost pitch of strength, and sunk in perpetual muddy darkness, by a task too heavy for me – task which seemed impossible, and
as if it would end me instead of I it. I saw no company, had no
companion but my horse (fourteen miles a day, winter time, mainly
in the dark), rode in all, as I have sometimes counted, above 30,000
miles for health's sake, while writing that unutterable book.[1] The
one bright point in my day was from half an hour to twenty minutes'
talking with her, after my return from those thrice dismal rides,
while I sat smoking (on the hearthrug, with my back to the jamb,
puffing firewards – a rare invention!) and sipping a spoonful of
brandy in water, preparatory to the hour of sleep I had before
dinner. She, too, the dear and noble soul, seemed to feel that this
was the eye of her day, the flower of all her daily endeavour in the
world. I found her oftenest stretched on the sofa (close at my right
hand, I between her and the fire), her drawing-room and self all
in the gracefullest and most perfect order, and waiting with such a
welcome; ah, me! ah, me! She was weak, weak, far weaker than I
understood; but to me was bright always as stars and diamonds; nay,
I should say a kind of cheery sunshine in those otherwise Egyptian
days. She had always something cheerful to tell me of (especially if
she had been out, or had had visitors); generally something quite
pretty to report (in her sprightly, quiet, and ever-genial way). At
lowest, nothing of unpleasant was ever heard from her; all that was
gloomy she was silent upon, and had strictly hidden away. Once, I
remember, years before this, while she suffered under one of her bad
influenzas (little known to me how bad), I came in for three succes-
ive evenings, full of the 'Battle of Molwitz' (which I had at last got
to understand, much to my inward triumph), and talked to her all
my half-hour about nothing else. She answered little ('speaking

[1] *History of Frederick the Great* (1858–65).

not good for me', perhaps); but gave no sign of want of interest – nay, perhaps did not quite want it, and yet confessed to me, several years afterwards, her principal thought was, 'Alas, I shall never see this come to print; I am hastening towards death instead!' These were, indeed, dark days for us both, and still darker unknown to us were at hand. One evening, probably the 1st or 2nd of October, 1863 . . . on my return from riding, I learned rather with satisfaction for her sake that she had ventured on a drive to the General Post Office to see her cousin, Mrs Godby, 'matron' of that establishment; and would take tea there. After sleep and dinner, I was still without her; 'Well, well, I thought, what a nice little story will she have to tell me soon!' and lay quietly down on the sofa, and comfortably waited – still comfortably, though the time (an hour or more) was longer than I had expected. At length came the welcome sound of her wheels; I started up – she rather lingered in appearing, – I rang, got no clear answer, rushed down, and, oh, what a sight awaited me! She was still in the cab, Larkin speaking to her (Larkin lived next door, and for him she had sent, carefully saving me!) Oh, Heavens! and, alas! both Larkin and I were needed. She had had a frightful street-accident in St Martin's, and was now lamed and in agony! This was the account I got by degrees.

Mrs Godby sent a maid-servant out with her to catch an omnibus; maid was stupid, unhelpful, and there happened to be some excavation on the street which did not permit the omnibus to come close. Just as my poor little darling was stepping from the kerbstone to run over (maid merely looking on), a furious cab rushed through the interval; she had to stop spasmodically, then still more spasmodically try to keep from falling flat on the other side, and ruining her poor neuralgic arm. In vain, this latter effort; she did fall, lame arm useless for help, and in the desperate effort she had torn the sinews of the thigh-bone, and was powerless to move or stand, and in pain unspeakable. Larkin and I lifted her into a chair, carried her with all our steadiness (for every shake was misery) up to her bed, where, in a few minutes, the good Barnes, luckily found at home, made appearance with what help there was. Three weeks later, this letter gives account in her own words.[1]

The torment of those first three days was naturally horrible; but it was right bravely borne, and directly there-upon all things looked up, she herself, bright centre of them, throwing light into all things.

[1] To Mrs Russell, 16 September 1863 (151, p. 257 above).

Looking back in anguish

It was wonderful to see how in a few days she seemed to be almost happy, contented with immunity from pain, and proud to have made (as she soon did) her little bedroom into a boudoir, all in her own likeness. She sent for the carpenter, directed him in everything, had cords and appliances put up for grasping with and getting good of her hand, the one useful limb now left. It was wonderful what she had made of that room, by carpenter and housemaid, in a few hours – all done in her own image, as I said. On a little table at her right hand, among books and other useful furniture, she gaily pointed out to me a dainty little bottle of champagne, from which, by some leaden article screwed through the cork, and needing only a touch, she could take a spoonful or teaspoonful at any time, without injuring the rest: 'Is not that pretty? Excellent champagne (Miss Bromley's kind gift), and does me good, I can tell you.' I remember this scene well, and that, in the love of gentle and assiduous friends, and their kind little interviews and ministrations, added to the hope she had, her sick room had comparatively an almost happy air, so elegant and beautiful it all was, and her own behaviour in it always was. Not many evenings after[1] I was sitting solitary over my dreary Prussian books, as usual, in the drawing-room, perhaps about 10 P.M., room perhaps (without my knowledge) made trimmer than usual, when suddenly, without warning given, the double door from her bedroom went wide open, and my little darling, all radiant in graceful evening dress, followed by a maid with new lights, came gliding in to me, gently stooping, leaning on a fine Malacca cane, saying *silently* but so eloquently, 'Here am I come back to you, dear!' It was among the bright moments of my life – the picture of it still vivid with me, and will always be. Till now I had not seen her in the drawing-room, had only heard of those tentative pilgrimings thither with her maid for support. But now I considered the victory as good as won, and everything fallen into its old course again or a better. Blind that we were! This was but a gleam of sunlight, and ended swiftly in a far blacker storm of miseries than ever before.

. . . [After a visit of old friends on 23 November] she silently at once withdrew to her bed, saying nothing to me of the state she was in, which I found next morning to have been alarmingly miserable, the prophecy of one of the worst of nights, wholly without sleep and full of strange and horrible pain. And the nights and days that followed continued steadily to *worsen* day after day, and month after month, no end visible . . .

---

[1] I.e. about the end of October or beginning of November 1863.

Barnes, for some time, said the disease was 'influenza, merely accidental cold, kindling up all the old injuries and maladies', and promised speedy amendment; but week after week gave dismally contrary evidence. 'Neuralgia!' the doctors then all said, by which they mean they know not in the least what; in this case, such a deluge of intolerable pain, indescribable, unaidable pain, as I had never seen or dreamt of, and which drowned six or eight months of my poor darling's life as in the blackness of very death; her recovery at last, and the manner of it, an unexpected miracle to me. There seemed to be pain in every muscle, misery in every nerve, no sleep by night or day, no rest from struggle and desperate suffering. Nobody ever known to me could more nobly and silently endure pain; but here for the first time I saw her vanquished, driven hopeless, as it were looking into a wild chaotic universe of boundless woe – on the horizon, only death or worse. Oh, I have seen such expressions in those dear and beautiful eyes as exceeded all tragedy! (one night in particular, when she rushed desperately out to me, without speech; got laid and wrapped by me on the sofa, and gazed silently on all the old familiar objects and me). Her pain she would seldom speak of, but, when she did, it was in terms as if there were no language for it; 'any honest pain, mere pain, if it were of cutting my flesh with knives, or sawing my bones, I could hail that as a luxury in comparison!'

And the doctors, so far as I could privately judge, effected approximately to double the disease. We had many doctors, skilful men of their sort, and some of them (Dr Quain, especially, who absolutely would accept no pay, and was unwearied in attendance and invention) were surely among the friendliest possible; but each of them – most of all each new one – was sure to effect only harm, tried some new form of his opiums and narcotic poisons without effect; on the whole I computed, 'Had there been no doctors, it had been only about half as miserable.' Honest Barnes admitted in the end, 'We have been able to do nothing.' . . . December was hardly out till there began to be speech among the doctors of sea-side and change of air: the one hope they continued more and more to say; and we also thinking of St Leonards and our Dr Blakiston and bountiful resources there, waited only for spring weather, and the possibility of flight thither. How, in all this tearing whirlpool of miseries, anxieties, and sorrows, I contrived to go on with my work is still an astonishment to me. For one thing, I did not believe in these doctors, nor that she (if let alone of them) had not yet strength left. Secondly, I always counted 'Frederick' itself to be the prime source of all her sorrows as well as my own; that to end it was the condition of new life to us both, of which there was a strange dull hope in me. Not above thrice can I recollect when, on stepping out in the morning, the thought struck me, cold and sharp, 'She will die, and leave thee here!' and always before next day I had got it cast out of me again. And, indeed, in all points except one I was as if stupefied more or less, and flying on like those migrative swallows of Professor Owen, after my strength was done and coma or dream had supervened, till the Mediterranean Sea was crossed! . . .

Early in March, weather mild though dim and wettish, this sad transit [to St Leonards] was accomplished by railway; I escorting, and visiting at every stage; Maggie Welsh and our poor patient in what they called a 'sick carriage', which indeed took her up at this door, and after delays and haggles at St Leonards, put her down at Dr Blakiston's; but was found otherwise inferior to the common arrangement for a sick person (two window-seats, with board and cushion put between), though about five or six times dearer, and was never employed again. She was carried downstairs here in the bed of this dreary vehicle (which I saw well would remind her, as it did of a hearse, with its window for letting in the coffin); she herself, weak but clear, directed the men. So pathetic a face as then glided past me at this lower door I never saw nor shall see! . . .

In those seven or eight months of martyrdom (October 1863–May 1864) there is naturally no record of the poor dear martyr's own discoverable; nothing but these small, most mournful notes written with the left hand, as if from the core of a broken heart, and worthy to survive as a voice *de profundis*.

TORMENTS AT ST LEONARDS

153. To Thomas Carlyle at Chelsea

St Leonards-on-Sea/ 8 April 1864

Oh my own Darling! God have pity on us! – Ever since the day after you left – whatever flattering accounts may have been sent to you – the *truth* is, I have been wretched – perfectly wretched day and night with that horrible malady: – Dr B. *knows nothing* about it more than the other Drs – So God help me – for on earth is no help –

Lady A. writes that Lord A. left you two thousand pounds – not

in his will – to save the Duty – but to be given you as soon as possible
– 'The wished for come too late!' *Money* can do nothing for us now' –
Your loving and sore suffering
Jane W. Carlyle

Today I am a *little* less tortured – only *a little* – but a letter having
been promised I write.

154. To Thomas Carlyle at Chelsea

St Leonards-on-Sea/ 19 April 1864

It is no 'morbid despondency'; it is *positive* physical torment day
and night – a burning, throbbing maddening sensation in the most
nervous part of me ever and ever. How be in good spirits or have any
hope but to die! When I spoke of going home it was to *die* there; here
were the place for *living* – if one could!

It was not *my* wish to leave here. It was the Blakistons' *own*
suggestion and wish that we should get a little house of our own. I
have rather wondered at the short time their benevolence has held
out – but it is natural as not even the honour of a *cure* is to be gained
for all their pains!

Oh have pity on me – I am worse than ever I was in that terrible
malady.

I am yours as ever
Jane Carlyle

155. To Thomas Carlyle at Chelsea

St Leonards-on-Sea/ 25 April 1864

Oh, my Husband! I am suffering torments! each day I suffer
more horribly.

Oh I would like you beside me! – I am terribly *alone* – But I don't
want to interrupt your work. I will wait till we are in our own hired
house and – then, if am no better you must come for *a day*.

Your own wretched J.W.C.

156. To the Misses Welsh at Edinburgh

St Leonards-on-Sea/ End of April 1864

My own dear Aunts,

I take you to my heart and kiss you fondly one after another. God knows if we shall ever meet again! and *His* will be done! – My Dr has hopes of my recovery, but I myself am not hopeful; My sufferings are terrible.

The malady is in my womb – you may fancy! – It is the consequence of that unlucky fall – no *disease* there, the Drs say, but some nervous derangement – Oh what I have suffered, my Aunts! What I may still have to suffer! Pray for me that I may be enabled to endure!

Don't write to myself; reading letters excites me too much. And Maggie tells me all I should hear. I commit you to the Lord's keeping – whether I live or die. Ah my Aunts, I shall die; that is my belief.

Jane Carlyle

EXTRACTS FROM HOLM HILL, SCOTLAND, 23 JULY – 28 SEPTEMBER 1864

157. To Thomas Carlyle at Chelsea

23 July

I have arrived safe . . . *They* met me at the station, and are kind, as indeed many are – John offered to accompany me here, but I declined. I have not had so much pleasure in him as to prolong our intercourse a moment beyond what I could help – He has been very hard and cruel – and *mean* inconceivably! but *that* is *his own* affair! Fancy him telling me in my agony yesterday that 'if I had ever *done* anything in my life, this would not have been! that no *poor* woman with *work* to mind had ever had such an ailment as this of mine since the world began'!!![1] . . . Oh my dear I think how near my mother I am! – how still I should be laid beside *her*! – But I *wish* to live – for *you* if only – I could live out of torment– . . .

[1] Carlyle annotated this, saying that Jane never could forget this unkindness.

158. To Thomas Carlyle at Chelsea

2 August

I am cared for here as I have never been since I lost my mother's nursing – and everything is good for me – the *quiet* airy bedroom – the new milk – the beautiful drives – and when all this fails to bring me human sleep or *endurable* nervousness, can you wonder that I am in the lowest spirits about myself. So long as I had a noisy bedroom or food miscooked – etc. etc. I had something to attribute my sleeplessness to – *Now* I can only lay it to my diseased nerves – and at my age such illness does not right itself . . .

159. To Thomas Carlyle at Chelsea

5 August

. . . Except for this wakefulness, I am better than when I left Marina – and it is unaccountable that I should be so well, in spite of getting less sleep than I ever heard of anyone, *out of a medical Book*, getting, and living with! I was weighed yesterday and found a gain of five *pounds* since Dr Blackiston weighed me in April. If sleep would come; I think I should *recover*! – the first time I have had this hope seriously – but – if it won't come – I *must* break down sooner or later – being no Dutchman nor Jeffrey[1] – and I fear horribly for – not my life – but my reason – It is almost sinfully ungrateful, when God has borne me thro such prolonged agonies, with my senses intact, to have so little confidence in the future – but courage and hope have been *ground* out of me – *submission* – acknowledgment that my sufferings have been no greater than I deserved is just the most I am up to . . .

160. To Thomas Carlyle at Chelsea

22 August

I have no wholly sleepless nights to report now. I don't sleep *well*, by any means; but to sleep *at all* is such an improvement. I continue

---

[1] In Cabanis, case of a Dutch gentleman who lived twenty years without sleep! which I often remembered for my own sake and hers. Jeffrey is Lord Jeffrey: sad trait of insomnia reported by himself – T.C.

to gain flesh. Andrew (the 'man') declares that in the last ten days I have gained four pounds! But that must be nonsense . . .

161. To Thomas Carlyle at Chelsea

30 August

. . . I got *no* sleep *at all* last night. Had no chance at sleep, for the neuralgic pains piercing me from shoulder to breast, like a sword.

162. To Thomas Carlyle at Chelsea

1 September

I am profoundly disheartened just now! Every way I turn it looks dark, dark to me. I had dared to *hope* – to look forward to some years of health no worse at least than I had before and that revival of Hope makes my present hopelessness doubly bitter for me . . . I cannot write cheerfully – I am not cheerful . . .

163. To Thomas Carlyle at Chelsea

6 September

Oh, that it was as easy to put tormenting thoughts out of one's own head as it is for others to bid one do that! I wish to heaven you were delivered from these paperhangers. I did not think it would have been so long in the wind. I, the unlucky cause, am quite as sorry for the botheration to *you* as Jane expresses herself; tho I have more appreciation of the terrible half-insane sensitiveness which drove me on to bothering you. Oh if God would only lift my trouble off me so far that I *could* bear it in all silence! and not add to the own troubles of others! . . .

164. To Thomas Carlyle at Chelsea

7 September

I cannot write a letter today. I have passed a terrible night – sleeplessness and restlessness, and *the old pain* (worse than it has ever been since I came here) and in addition to all that, an inward blackness of darkness! Am I going to have another winter like the last? I cannot live thro another such time – my reason at least cannot live thro' it . . . Oh, God bless you and help me! . . .

165. To Thomas Carlyle at Chelsea

9 September

I am very stupid and *low*. God can raise me up again – but will He? Oh I am weary, weary! . . .

166. To Thomas Carlyle at Chelsea

13 September

My Dear! When I have been giving directions about the House *there* – a feeling like a great black wave will roll over my breast; and I shall say to myself, whatever pains be taken to gratify me, shall I ever more have a day of ease, of painlessness, or a night of sweet rest, in that House, or in any House, but the dark narrow one where I shall arrive at last? . . .

167. To Thomas Carlyle at Chelsea

16 September

Oh if there were any sleep to be got in it wherever it stands![1] But it looks to my excited imagination, that Bed I was born in, a sort of instrument of red hot torture; after all those nights that I lay meditating on self-destruction as my only escape from insanity! Oh, the terriblest part of my suffering has not been what was *seen*! has not been what *could* be put into human language! . . .

168. To Thomas Carlyle at Chelsea

26 September

. . . John is coming to-day to settle about the journey. When I spoke so bravely about going alone I was much better than I am at present. I am up to nothing of the *sort* now, and must be thankful for

[1] Jane is alluding to a change in the position of her red bed at Chelsea.

his escort, the best that offers! He says Saturday is the best day. But I don't incline to arriving on a Sunday morning; so I shall vote for Friday night. But you will hear from me again and again before then . . .

169. To Thomas Carlyle at Chelsea

28 September

Again a night *absolutely* sleepless, except for a little dozing between six and seven. There were no shooting pains to keep me awake last night; altho I felt terribly chill, in spite of a heap of blankets that kept me in a sweat; but it was a *cold* sweat. I am very wretched today. Dr Russell handed me the other night a medical Book he was reading, open at the chapter on 'neuralgia' that I might read, for my practical information, a list of 'counter-irritants'.

I read a sentence or two more than was meant, ending with 'this Lady was bent on self-destruction'. You may think it a strange comfort; but it was a sort of comfort to me to find, that my dreadful wretchedness was a not uncommon feature of my disease, and not merely an expression of individual cowardice.

Another strange comfort I take to myself under the present pressure of horrible nights. If I had continued up till now, to feel as much better as I did in the first weeks of my stay here; I should have dreaded the return to London as a sort of suicide. *Now* I again want a change – even *that* change! There lies a *possibility*, at least, of benefit in it; which I could not have admitted to myself had all gone on here as in the beginning . . .

XI *Living miracle*

On 1 October 1864, Doctor John Carlyle brought Jane home from Scotland, tremulous but spared. The stay with the Russells at Holm Hill had released her from her worst torments. Thomas Woolner, the sculptor, wrote to Tennyson on 3 November that he was 'charmed to see how well she was looking: she is too weak to do much more than stand upright; but her spirits are good, and her state may almost be called a resurrection of the dead'. When he came to annotate the letters of this period, Carlyle wrote,

My poor martyred darling continued to prosper here beyond my hopes – far beyond her own; and in spite of utter weakness (which I never rightly saw) and of many fits of trouble, her life to the very end continued beautiful and hopeful to both of us – to me more beautiful than I had ever seen it in her best days. Strange and precious to look back upon, those last eighteen months, as of a second youth (almost a second childhood with the wisdom and graces of old age), which by Heaven's great mercy were conceded her and me. In essentials never had she been so beautiful to me; never in my time been so happy.[1]

She rode daily through the London parks in the carriage Carlyle had bought her, gave little tea-parties, scribbled her notes, emerged from the 'valley of the shadow of Frederick' when Carlyle sent his final chapter to the press in January 1865; had a month in the spring with the second Lady Ashburton in Devonshire, a summer visit to Scotland, and a few weeks of sea air with Miss Bromley at Folkestone. 'Cheerful weakness' would best describe her health for much of this time. It was in the summer that neuralgia attacked her right arm, but there was no return of the nervous disease and all was tenderness between her and Carlyle. She even resumed her career – never quite abandoned at the worst of times – of guardian angel; battling with the cocks and hens in Number 6 and dealing firmly with the goings-on downstairs.

In November 1865 Carlyle was elected Rector of the University of Edinburgh, an office of dignity in the gift of the students. His defeated rival was Disraeli, his predecessor, Gladstone. This tribute from his old University, and from a Scotland which had done less for its prophet than most other countries, was a touching experience for both him and Jane. But it revived all his horrors of platform performances. As the installation drew nearer, Jane writes half-seriously, half-comically, about both his terrors and hers.

She decided she would not risk the strains of the journey to Scotland and kissed him goodbye – twice, he remembers – on Thursday, 29 March. This was the last time he saw her. He and his companion, Professor Tyndall, broke their journey for two nights at Fryston Hall in Yorkshire, the home of their old friend Lord Houghton, and then went on to Thomas Erskine's house in Edinburgh. The

[1] Froude, *Letters and Memorials*, III, 215.

Rectorial Address was given to an enthusiastic audience in the Music Rooms on George Street on 2 April. Professor Tyndall's telegram – 'a perfect triumph' reached Cheyne Row the next day. While congratulations poured in at Chelsea, Carlyle enjoyed the festivities in Edinburgh, all gloom forgotten, and then went on to see his brother and sister at Scotsbrig. Jane sent him all the news from London for a fortnight while he rested there, recovering from a sprained ankle. She wrote her last letter, in high spirits, on Saturday morning 21 April, and drove off in her brougham. By nightfall in Dumfries, with the letter still on its way, a telegram brought the news of her death.

The story of that afternoon in London was pieced together by Geraldine Jewsbury, who talked to Jane's coachman, Silvester, and to her housekeeper, Mrs Warren, and who herself went with Froude to St George's Hospital to bring back Jane's body to Cheyne Row. It had long been promised that Jane would be buried with her father at Haddington, in that grave in the ruined choir of the old abbey, open to the sky, from which the moss had just been removed when she visited it in 1849. Today a restored roof protects the grave. Inside this beautiful church, the visitor filled with memories of Jane's radiant youth – the schoolhouse, the parapet of the bridge, the churchyard wall, the suitors, the two young men who stayed at the George Hotel – can read on her tombstone what she came to represent for one of those young men – 'the true and ever-loving helpmate of her husband'; and who 'unweariedly forwarded him, as none else could, in all of worthy that he did or attempted'.

It was a noble career. But was it enough?

A BLESSING ON THE RUSSELLS

170. TO MRS RUSSELL AT HOLM HILL

5 Cheyne Row, Chelsea/ 3 October 1864

Oh, my Darling! my Darling! God for ever bless you! you and dear Dr Russell, for your goodness to me, your patience with me, and all the good you have done me! I am better aware *now* how much I have *gained* than I was *before* this journey – how much stronger I am, both in body and mind, than I was on my journey *to* Scotland. I felt no fatigue on the journey down, but I made up for it in nervous excitement! On the journey *up*, all my nervousness was over when I had parted with *you two*. Even when arrived at my own door (which I had always looked forward to as a most terrible moment, remembering the hearse-like fashion in which I was carried away from it) I could possess my soul in quiet, and meet the excited people who rushed out to me, as gladly as if I had been returned from any ordinary pleasure-excursion!

Living miracle

Very *excited* people they were! Dr C. had stupidly told his brother he might look for us about ten, and as we did not arrive till half after eleven, Mr C. had settled it in his own mind, that I had been taken ill somewhere *on* the road, and was momentarily expecting a Telegram to say I was dead. So he rushed out in his dressing gown, and kissed me, and *wept* over me as I was in the act of getting down out of the cab! (much to the edification of the neighbours at their windows, I have no doubt) and then the maids appeared behind him, looking *timidly*, with flushed faces, and tears in *their* eyes! and the little one (the cook) threw *her* arms round my neck, and fell to kissing me in the open street; and the big one (the Housemaid) I had to kiss, that she might not be made *jealous* the first thing!

They were all astonished at the improvement in my appearance. Mr C. has said again and again, that he would not have believed anyone who had sworn it to him, that I should return so changed for the better. Breakfast was presented to me, but tho' I had still Holmhill things to eat, I had not my Holmhill appetite to eat them with. All Saturday there was nothing I cared to swallow but Champagne (Lady Ashburton had sent me two dozen, first-rate, in the winter). So I took the Blakiston blue pill that first night instead of the next as Dr Russell had advised. And oh such a heavenly sleep I had! awoke only twice the whole night! It is worth while passing a whole night on the railway to get such blessed sleep the night after! Last night again *I slept* – not so well as the first night, of course; but wonderfully well for *me*. And this morning my breakfast was not contemptible. But it is a great hardship to have lost my warm milk in the morning. I thought by paying an exorbitant price, it might have been obtained: – but No! the stuff offered me yesterday at eight oclock, was impossible to swallow – And my poor 'Bowels', perfectly bewildered by all the sudden changes put on them, don't seem to have any clear idea left, when to 'act' or when to let it alone! so I am driven back into the valley of the shadow of *pills*!

I had a two-hours drive yesterday in Battersea Park and Clapham Common. When one hasn't the Beauties of Nature, one must content oneself with the Beauties of Art.

Today my drive must be townward – so many things wanted at the shops! There is hardly a dish or kitchen utensil left unbroken – all broken by 'I-*can't-imagine-who-did-it* –' Still it might have been worse – there seems to have no *serious* mischief been done . . .

Oh my Darling if I might continue just as well as I am *now*! But that is not to be hoped! Anyway, I shall always feel as if I owed my life chiefly to your Husband and you, who procured me such *rest* as I could have had nowhere else in the world.

Your own
Jane W. C.

THE JOY OF OLD FRIENDS

171. TO MRS RUSSELL AT HOLM HILL

5 Cheyne Row, Chelsea/ 10 October 1864

Dearest

Nature prompts me to begin the week with writing to you. Tho' I have such a pressure of *work* ahead as I can't see day-light thro' – with no *help* in putting to rights: for my large beautiful Housemaid is like a Cow in a flower-garden, amongst the '*curiosities and niceties*' of a civilised House! – Oh thank God for the precious layer of impassivity which that stone-weight of flesh has put over my nerves! I am not like the same woman who trembled from head to foot and panted like a duck in a thunder-storm at St Leonards, whenever a human face showed itself from without, or anything worried from within! Indeed, my nerves are stronger than they have been for years! Just for instance yesterday, *what* I went thro' without having '*the irritation*' increased, or my sleep worsened! As soon as I was in the Drawingroom George Cooke came – the same who wrote to tell you of my accident – Now this George Cooke is a man betwixt thirty and forty – tall, strong, silent, sincere – has been a sailor, a soldier, a New Zealand settler, 'a Man about Town', and a Stock Broker!!! The last man on earth one would have expected to make one '*a scene*'. But lo! What happened! I stood up to welcome him, and he took me in his arms, and kissed me two or three times, and then he sank into a chair and – burst into tears! and sobbed and cried for a minute or two, like any schoolboy! Mercifully I was not infected by his agitation; but it was I who spoke *calmly* and brought him out of it! He accompanied me in my drive after, and when I had come home and was going to have my dinner, a carriage drove up. Being nothing like so polite and self-sacrificing as *you*, I told Helen, to say I was tired, and dining, and would see no one – She returned with a card 'Please Mam the Gentleman says, if you will look at his name, he thinks you will see *him*' – The name on the card was Lord Houghton a very old friend whom you may have heard me speak of as Richard Milnes. – 'Oh yes! *He* might come up' – Nobody could have predicted *sentiment* out of Lord Houghton! – but good gracious! it was the same thing over again – He clasped me in his arms! and kissed me, and dropt on a chair, – not *crying* – but quite pale, and gasping, without being able to say a word! –

... After these two enthusiastic meetings, I was sure I should get no sleep – But I slept much as usual during the last week. Not at all as I slept the first night but better than my fashion of sleep during the last weeks with you. My bed room is extremely quiet; my comfort well attended to by – myself! I miss little Mary for more things than the 'clipping o' the taes!' Bless her!

I was at Elise's, to get the velvet bonnet she made me last year stript of its finery! White lace and red roses don't become a woman wha haes been looking both death and insanity in the face for a year! – I told her (Elise) that I had seen two of her bonnets on a Mrs Henry in Scotland – 'Oh yes, *she* has every article she wears from here' – 'you made her Court dress – didn't you – that was noticed in the Morning Post'? 'Yes – yes I dressed the whole *three*. Mrs Henry's dress cost three hundred pounds! but she doesn't mind cost.'

Dear love to *the* Doctor.

Your affectionate

J. Carlyle

RETURNING FROM LADY ASHBURTON'S

172. To Mrs Warren at 5 Cheyne Row

Seaton, Devonshire/ 29 March 1865

Dear Mrs Warren,

We have made out our visit, you see, with greater deliberation than I predicted, in leaving! Not that Mr Carlyle has not talked of *being off 'this very day'*, every morning after a restless night! And he has had too many of these; since his habits have been turned all heels over head, and there has been no punctual Mrs Warren at hand to *measure* out his dinners! – So I have been in constant uncertainty all the time; and no woman living hates uncertainty more than I do! It would spoil my pleasure in Heaven itself!

Tho' I am in no haste to go, then; and never wearying of either the *sea* or Lady Ashburton; still it is a sort of a melancholy satisfaction to know, that our departure is finally *fixed* for Saturday next: –

when I hope to find you well, and glad to see us! And to find the kitchen smartened up, and the cistern cured of leaking!

I don't know yet what hour we shall arrive; it will probably be in time for a late dinner. Mr C. likes mutton-broth after a journey, and *I like – nothing*!! so I can dine with *Him* that day. and you must get in things for Sunday; but I need not be telling *you* what to do; for, thank God, you have *sense*; which is not so common a qualification as one might think! Oh dear me! there hasn't been a day here that I have not wished I could have brought one half of you with me and left the other half to take care of the House! The times and times I have been put into a rage is quite disgraceful!

Please tell the Postman of our coming; in time to prevent his sending off the letters that may come on Saturday.

> Good by!
> Yours kindly
> Jane W. Carlyle

I don't forget that I only left money up to Wednesday. But what you need after til Saturday had best be put down in the Bills as I have no means of sending money from here except in a letter which wouldnt be safe.

AND NOW THE RIGHT ARM!

173. TO MRS RUSSELL AT HOLM HILL

4 May 1865

. . . How absurd! in telling you on the other sheet how I was bodily, I quite forgot to mention my most serious ailment for the last six weeks. My right arm has gone the way that my left went two years ago, gives me considerable pain, so that I cannot lie upon it, or make any effort (such as ringing a bell, opening a window &c, &c) with it and if anyone shakes my hand heartily, I – shriek! Geraldine Jewsbury is always asking, '*Have* you written to Dr Russell yet about your arm?' But what could anyone do before for the other arm? All that was tried was useless, except quinine and quinine destroys my sleep. I must just hope it will mend of itself as the other did . . .

174. TO THOMAS CARLYLE AT THE GILL, DUMFRIES

27 May 1865

. . . My quinine and castor oil has quite failed of doing the good to my *right* arm which they formerly did to my *left*. The pain gets more severe and more continuous from day to day. Last night it kept me almost entirely awake. I often wonder that I am able to keep on foot during the day, and take my three hours drives and talk to the people who come to relieve my loneliness, with that arm always in pain, as if a dog were gnawing and tearing at it! But *anything* rather than the old nervous misery which was not to be called pain at all! *positive natural pain* I can bear as well as most people. But I wish Dr Blakiston would come! Perhaps he can deal with a *reality* like this tho he could 'do nothing against *hysterical mania*'! I got the thing he mentioned, *veratrine* lineament, yesterday from Quiller, and Geraldine rubbed it in for an hour last night. But as I said, last night was the worst! . . .

WITH MISS BROMLEY AT FOLKESTONE

175. TO THOMAS CARLYLE AT LINLATHEN, DUNDEE

4 Langhorne Gardens, Folkestone/ 15 August 1865

Here I am Dear! Safe and Slept!

I arrived last evening about seven. Miss Bromley had gone for a walk with the girl staying with her and they has *lost* their way! So I had ample time to unpack all the things into my drawers, before I was called upon to dress for dinner.

It is a nice House – for Sea-lodging – but I am afraid *you* would find the same fault to it as to the West Cliff Hotel, viz: 'an eternal ripple-tippling of venetian blinds'! Also there is a terrible super abundance of – earwigs! They are found in your *hair-brush*! in *the Book* you are reading! in fact, I defy you to say where they will *not* be found!

But the '*Flight of Skylarks*'[1] is always charming to live beside; and the air of the West Cliff is understood to be all one could wish! And

---

[1] This was how the Carlyles referred to Miss Bromley.

'*Change*' (Dr Blakiston wrote to me the other day) 'is for illness like mine the one available medicine'! So, I suppose it is all right! – Certainly my sleeping facilities were nothing like so great here last night, as they were at home; nevertheless, in spite of 'ripple-tippling', and too much light, and the sense of novelty, I patched together Sleep enough to be called a goodish night.

It is blowing hard to-day with a dull grey sky, and skiffs of rain; so I see no prospect of 'Varrying the Schene!' as there are no carriages but open ones.

Oh my Dear! I could tell you something that would make you die of laughing, if I hadn't to dilute it in ink! And I was solemnly charged to '*not* tell Mr Carlyle'! Lady William told me, that Mr and Mrs Grote, having lived to the respective ages of 72 and 74, in the expression of the most outrageously George-Sandish opinions, had tried the thing in practice and found it 'no go'! 'Yes, my Dear Lady! Mr Grote, sad to say, has committed – an *infidelity*!! And poor Mrs Grote, so far from agreeing that a grand passion is omnipotent, and showing the generosity of Jacques, has fallen ill about it and had to go off to the Continent for her health!' I did hear from George Cooke that Lady Trelawny had taken Mrs Grote to Paris and then returned immediately. 'Mrs Grote for all her strong-mindedness not being equal to crossing the sea *alone* and Mr Grote couldnt accompany her.' . . . Yours ever

J.W.C.

176. To Mrs Russell at Holm Hill

4 Langhorne Gardens, Folkestone/ 23 August 1865

I am again going to make an attempt, at putting on paper the letter that has been in my head for you, Dear, ever since I came to this place. I had even begun to *write* it two or three days ago, when at the first words my conscience gave me a smart box on the ear, reminding me that I hadn't written one word to Mrs Ewart since I left her – after all her kindness to me! whereas to you I had written once and again – So my pen formed, quite unexpectedly for *myself*, the words 'dear Mrs Ewart', instead of 'dearest Mary'. To be sure there have been leisure hours enough since! Life here is made up of 'leisure hours'; But just the less one does, I long ago observed, the less one can find time to do! I get up at nine, and it takes me a whole mortal hour to dress: – without assistance. At ten we sit down to breakfast, and talk over it till about eleven. Then I have to write my letter to Mr Carlyle. Then I make a feeble attempt at *walking*, on the cliff by the shore – which never fails to weary me dreadfully; so that I can do nothing after, till the *first* dinner (called Luncheon), which comes off at 2 o'clock. Then, between three and four we go out for a drive, in an open barouche, with a pair of swift horses and explore the country for three or four hours. On coming home we have a cup of tea, then rest, and dress for the *second* dinner at eight (nominally, but in reality half-past eight!) At eleven we go to bed, very sleepy generally with so much open air! There is not a soul to speak to from without! But Miss Bromley and I never bore one another. When we find nothing of mutual interest to talk about, we have the gift, both of us, of being able to sit silent together without the least embarrassment! She is adorably kind to me, that 'fine Lady'! and in such an unconscious way! always looking and talking, as if it were *me* that was kind to *her*, and *she* the one benefited by our intimacy! And then she has something in her face, and movements, and ways that always reminds me of my Mother – at *her* age.

I am sorry that Mr Carlyle after all his objections to *my* returning to London in August should have taken it in his head to return to London in August himself! I find it so pleasant here, and am sleeping so wonderfully, that I feel no disposition to go back to Chelsea already; Miss Bromley having taken her house for five weeks, and being heartily desirous I should stay and keep her company. But a demon of impatience seems to have taken possession of Mr C., and he has been rushing thro' his promised visits as if the Furies were chasing him! Everything right seemingly wherever he went! the people all kindness for him; the bedrooms quiet and airy; Horses and carriages at his command; and behold! it was impossible to persuade him to stay longer than *three days* with Mr Erskine of Linlathen! – ditto with Stirling of Keir! and just three hours (*for Luncheon*) at Newbattle with the Lothians, and by this time he is back at Scotsbrig (if all have gone right) to stay '*one* day or at most two' preparatory for starting for Chelsea!

It is really so unreasonable, this sudden haste, after so many months of dawdling, that I do *not* feel it my duty to rush home 'promiscuously' to receive him. I promised to stay here a fortnight *at* the least, and the fortnight does not complete itself till Monday next - so I have written to him that I will be home on Monday - not sooner - and begging him to break the journey, and amuse himself for a couple of days at Alderley Park – and then he would find me at home to receive him, since he won't do as Miss Bromley and I wish, and come here – for a little sea-bathing to finish off with!

It really *is* miraculous how soundly I have slept here! tho' I take two glasses of champagne – besides Manzanilla – every day at the late dinner! It couldn't have been sound that champagne of poor kind Mrs Ewart's or it wouldn't have so disagreed with me – *Here* it always does me good! And the pain is entirely gone out of my arm! I can't *move* it any better yet – but *that* is small matter in comparison! I can do many things with my hand – write (as you see) knit, I have knitted myself a pair of garters – I can play on the piano a little, and do a few stitches with a very coarse needle.

Kindest love to the Doctor.

Your ever affectionate
Jane Carlyle

CARLYLE'S APPROACHING ORDEAL

177. To Grace Welsh at Craigenvilla, Morningside, Edinburgh

5 Cheyne Row, Chelsea/ 23 January 1866

My dear Grace

. . . Perhaps I am even more stupid than sad: and no shame to me, with a *cold in my head*, dating from before Xmas! It is the only illness I have had to complain of this winter; and is no illness 'to speak of'; but, none the less, it makes me very sodden and abject; and instead of having *thoughts* in my head, it (my head) feels to be filled with *Wool*! *Fuzzy* is the word for how I feel all thro'! But I continue to take my three hours drive daily, all the same. Since I returned from Folkestone in September, I have only missed *two days*! the days of the snowstorm a fortnight ago; when it was so dangerous for horses to travel that the very omnibuses struck work. And besides the forenoon drive, I *occasionally*, with this wool in my head, go out to dinner!!! With a hot bottle at my feet, and wrapt in fur, I take no hurt, and the talk stirs me up. Dr Quain told me I 'couldn't take a better remedy, if only I drank plenty of champagne', – a condition which I for one, never find any difficulty in complying with!

My chief Intimates have been away all this winter, which has made my life less pleasant. Lady Ashburton on the Continent, and Miss Davenport Bromley waiting in the country till the new-paint smell should have gone out of her house. But there are always nice people to take the place of those absent. It made me laugh, Dear, that Edinburgh notion that because Mr C. had been made Rector of the University, an office purely honorary; we should immediately proceed to tear ourselves up by the roots, and transplant ourselves *there*! After *thirty years of London*, and with such society as we have in London, to bundle ourselves off to Edinburgh to live out the poor remnant of our lives, in a new and perfectly uncongenial sphere; with no consolations that I know of but your three selves – and dear old Betty –! Ach! 'A *Wishing Carpet*' on which I could sit down, and be transported to Craigenvilla, for an hours talk with you all – two or three times a week, and – *back again*! – would be a most welcome fairy gift to me! – But no 'villa at Morningside' tempts me – except *your* villa! And for Edinburgh people! – those I knew are mostly dead and gone – and the new ones would astonish me much if they afforded any shadow of compensation for the people I should leave here! No! my Dear, we shall certainly not go 'to live in Edinburgh', I only wish Mr C. hadn't to go to deliver a speech in it; for it will tear him to tatters

Love to you all.

Affectionately
J.W.C.

HOME AS THE BEST PLACE FOR 'LIVING MIRACLES'

178. To Henry Inglis at Edinburgh

5 Cheyne Row, Chelsea/ March 1866

Dear 'Henry Inglis'!

That is the name I knew you by, and have remembered you by, for the third part of a Century: *that*, and no other!

Mr Masson asked me some days ago; 'Wasnt Mr Inglis a friend of mine?' – 'Mr Inglis?' I repeated after reflection, and in the truthfulest ignorance, '*No*! I don't know any Mr Inglis!'

'Are you *sure*?' said Masson; '*your Husband* knows him very well! He staid at his house when he was in Edinburgh last summer.' – 'Oh! *Henry* Inglis you mean! I exclaimed enthusiastically. Oh yes! *of course* I know *Henry* Inglis! Why; He baptised my Horse! – broke a cigar over his nose, and named him *Harry* – after *himself.*'

Mr Masson looked as grave as tho' I had suggested that *his* next own Baby should be baptised after that fashion! 'A *rather* strange one,' he remarked!

Well! but about *coming*. – Indeed I should like to be beside you, long enough to make your acquaintance again! And I am glad – very – of your invitation even tho' it lead to nothing beyond!

The nearer we get to the end of March, the more I shudder at a journey of eight hundred miles (there and back) and *a Speech* for object! I am not so strong as when galloping 'Harry' over the Moors! In fact I am *now*, what is pleasantly called 'a *Living Miracle*'! – That is a woman who ought in the course of Nature to have been dead and buried; but has come alive again; for *some* purpose; – *what?* one does not *see!* – But surely it could not have been for the *purpose* of killing myself after all, by outrageous fatigues and agitations, wilfully encountered – to hear my own Husband *speak*!!

I did not answer your letter by return of post; because there was still enough of indecision in my mind, to make me pause before committing myself to let Mr C. go alone, but the frost and snow of the last day or two have chilled my spirit of enterprise into one lump of ice! And now I have no hesitation about staying at home; as the suitablest place for Living Miracles!

So, you see; *I* am done with! And if you are the Henry Inglis I cared for; you will not forget to come and see me next time you are in London!

For Mr C.; I don't think *he* has taken a single detail of his visit to Edinburgh into his head yet; any more than a single *head* of his '*Address*'. – When I ask him anything, he merely says 'for God's sake my Dear, leave all that dreadful business lying over till the time comes'!

Lord Lothian is not *worse* only not *better* – after all the attempts at curing him by electricity! If *they* get home in time, Mr C. will stay there, having promised from the very first. If not, he has invitations to David Masson's, to David Laing's, not, I think, *absolutely* refused; but the man he will go to, I will confide to you privately, will not be the man he likes best, but the man who lies furthest away from – '*Railway Whistles*'!

Most likely he will write himself and tell you all about it, when he *has* a plan –

Ever yours affectionately
Jane Carlyle

179. HENRY INGLIS' REPLY TO JANE CARLYLE

16 Queen Street, Edinburgh/ 5 March 1866

My dear Mrs Carlyle

In my latest Will and Testament, I shall leave your letter to the British Museum; whence, in ages to come, it will be reproduced by some hungry literary scavenger. There is no doubt that you are 'a living Miracle'. – What, or who else, could have produced such a resurrection of the past; which now however, that it is narrated, comes before me as if it had occurred yesterday. But you must have astonished Mr Masson, with whom I have met only twice; under circumstances quite foreign to any such theological liberties as you ascribed to me in the Craigenputtoch era.

I am very sorry that you are not coming here; but cannot blame you for declining to face such a frosty pilgrimage. I still hope that Carlyle may prefer his old quarters at Torsonce; whence the railway whistle is far distant, and very occasional; but be this as it may, of this rest assured, that your letter was a great joy to me; and that whether we should meet again in this hemisphere or not, I shall ever remain,

Most truly and affectionately

yours,

Henry Inglis

Many thanks for the photographs.

180. TO LORD HOUGHTON AT FRYSTON

5 Cheyne Row, Chelsea/ March 1866

My dear, kind Lord Houghton

I have been out in far worse winds than yesterday's since I came to depend on my drives for *sleep*! And I am not afraid of the *journey* to Fryston, nor of *bodily* fatigue, generally. For you see I am what is pleasantly called '*A Living Miracle*'! meaning – a woman who, according to Nature, should have been dead and buried away two years ago and is here still, going about in society alive and well! (To be sure both the aliveness and the wellness '*may be strongly doubted*' as they say in Edinburgh!)

What I *am* afraid of, and what has determined me against accompanying Mr C. on this 'accursed adventure' (I don't mean the

Fryston part of it!) is the agitation that was getting hold on me about *his* agitation! I had visions of his breaking down in his '*Address*'! of his lying ill with stress and *dinners*! of his going to wreck and ruin in every possible way! And *I* unable to do anything, *now*, for his furtherance, but just to take the terrible *pain in my back* which assails me under all violent emotion. In intervals of good sense I perceived that my only chance of escaping an illness was to cut myself loose from him, till 'the accursed affair' was over. 'What the Eye sees not, the Heart grieves not!' When he is gone, out of my sight, I shall calm down! But if I should *prolong* the nervousness of these days, going with him and the others to Fryston; I should get no good of Fryston and risk a spell of illness – I want to go to Fryston (it would be the first time remember) in a state of mind that would not interfere with my enjoyment of it.

Mr C. says he 'cannot give me any advice – will not take the responsibility of my going; but if I don't think it wise to go with him now; I may say that I will come in the summer weather *if you like* and bring *him* along with me'! Will you let me come later? And will you believe how much I should like it in my normal state? and how much I – like *you*? Lady Houghton too has written to me so kindly

Affectionately
yours
Jane Carlyle

181. To Ann Welsh at Edinburgh

5 Cheyne Row, Chelsea/ 27 March 1866

My dear Aunts

It is long since I have written; and I have not leisure for a satisfactory letter even now. But I want you to have these two admissions in good time, in case you desire to hear poor Mr C.'s *Address*, and don't know how to manage it. If you dont care about it or cant for any other reason use the admissions, or either of them; please return them to me forthwith. For the Thing comes off this day week and there is a great demand for them.

Mr C. was too modest when asked by the University people *how many* admissions he wished reserved for himself and required only *twenty* for men, and *six* for women – or, as I suppose they would say in Edinburgh – '*Ladies*'! Four have been given away to *Ladies* who have shown him great kindness at one time or other, and the two left he sends to you in preference to some dozen other *Ladies* who have applied for them directly or indirectly – so you see the propriety of my request to have one or both returned if you are prevented from using them yourselves.

I am afraid and he himself is certain; his address will be a sad break-down to Human expectation! He has had no practice in Public Speaking – hating it with all his heart! And then he *does speak* – does not merely read or repeat from memory a composition elaborately prepared – in fact, as in the case of his predecessors *printed before* it was 'delivered'!!

I wish him well thro' it, for I am very fearful the worry and flurry of the thing will make him *ill*. After speculating all winter about going myself; my heart failed me as the time drew near, and I realised more clearly the nervousness and pain in my Back that so much fuss was sure to bring on. I did not dread the bodily fatigue but the mental. We were to have broken the journey into two by stopping a few days at Lord Houghtons in Yorkshire, and after giving up Edinburgh, I thought for a while I would still go as far as the Houghtons, and wait there till Mr C. returned. But *that* part of the business I also decided against, only two days since! preferring to reserve Yorkshire till summer, and till I was in a more tranquil frame of mind.

Mr C. is going to stay while in Edinburgh at Thomas Erskine's, our dear old friend – not however because of liking him better than anyone else there, but because of his being most out of the way of – *railway whistles*!! It was worth while however to have talked of accompanying Mr C. to have given so much enthusiastic hospitality an opportunity for displaying itself!

One of the letters of invitation I had quite pleasantly surprised me by its warmth and eagerness; being from a quarter where I hardly believed myself remembered – David Aitken and Eliza Stodart! – They had both grown into sticks I was thinking! But I have no time to gossip – . . .

Affectionately yours,
J. W. Carlyle

TERRORS OF THE IMAGINATION

182. To Thomas Carlyle at T. Erskine's,
Edinburgh

5 Cheyne Row, Chelsea/ 2 April 1866

Dearest

By the time you get this, you will be out of your trouble, better or worse, – but *out of it*, please God! And if ever you let youself be led or driven into such a horrid thing again, I will never forgive you! never!

What I have been suffering, vicariously, of late days, is not to be told! If you had been to be *hanged*, I don't see that I could have taken it more to heart. This morning, after about two hours of off-and-on sleep, I awoke – long before daylight – to sleep no more! While drinking a glass of wine and eating a biscuit at five in the morning, it came into my mind, what is *He* doing, I wonder, at this moment? and then instead of picturing you sitting smoking, up the stranger chimney, or anything else that was likely to *be*; I found myself always dropping off into details of a regular *execution*! – Now they will be telling him it is time! now they will be pinioning his arms! and saying last words! Oh mercy! was I dreaming or waking? was I mad or sane? – Upon my word I hardly know *now*! – Only that I have been having next to no sleep all the week – and that at the best of times I have a too 'fertile imagination', like 'oor David'![1]

When the thing is *over* I shall be content – however it have gone, as to making a good 'appearance' or a bad one! That you have made your 'address' and are *alive* – *that* is what I long to hear, and please God *shall* hear in a few hours! My 'Imagination' has gone the length of representing you getting up to speak before an awful crowd of people; and what with fuss and 'bad air' and confusion, dropping down dead! –

Why on Earth did you ever get into this galley?

J. W. C.

[1] A lying boy at Haddington, whom his mother excused in that way – T.C.

A PERFECT TRIUMPH

183. To Thomas Carlyle at Edinburgh

5 Cheyne Row, Chelsea/ 3 April, 1866

I made so sure of a letter this morning – from some of you! and 'nothing but a double letter *for* Miss Welsh!'[1] Perhaps I should, that is, *ought* – to have contented myself with Tyndall's adorable Telegram, which reached me at Cheyne Row five minutes after six last evening, considering the sensation it made! –

Mrs Warren and Maggie were helping to dress me for Forster's Birth day when the Telegraph Boy gave his double knock. 'There it is!' I said. 'I am afraid, cousin, it is only the Postman' said Maggie. Jessie rushed up with the Telegram. I tore it open and read, '*From John Tyndall* (Oh God bless John Tyndall in this world and the next!) *to Mrs Carlyle, A perfect triumph*' – I read it to myself and then read it aloud to the gaping chorus. And chorus all began to dance and clap their hands – '*Eh, Mrs Carlyle*! Eh, Hear to *that*' cried Jessie. '*I* told you Mam! cried Mrs Warren; *I* told you how it would be!' 'Im so glad, Cousin! you'll be all right now Cousin!' twittered Maggie, executing a sort of leap-frog round me. And they went on clapping their hands, till there arose among them a sudden cry for – Brandy! 'Get her some Brandy!' '*Do* Mam swallow this spoonful of Brandy! – just a spoonful'! For you see the sudden solution of the nervous tension with which I had been holding in my anxieties for days nay weeks past, threw me into as pretty a little fit of hysterics as you ever saw.

I went to Forster's nevertheless, with my Telegram in my hand, and 'John Tyndall' in the core of my heart! And it was pleasant to see with what hearty good will all there, Dickens, Wilkie Collins, as well as Fuz, received the news. And we drank your health with great glee! Maggie came in the evening and Fuz in his joy over you, sent out a glass of Brandy to Silvester!! Poor Silvester by the by showed as much glad *emotion* as anybody on my telling him you had got well thro' it!

Did you remember Craik's paper? I am going to take Maggie to the Railway for Liverpool. I suppose I shall now calm down and get sleep again – by degrees. I am *smashed* for the present.   J. W. C.

[1] Maggie Welsh, her Liverpool cousin, who was staying with her.

A perfect triumph

5 Cheyne Row, Chelsea/ 4 April 1866

Well! I do think you might have sent me a *Scotsman* this morning; or ordered one to be sent! I was up and dressed at 7, and it seemed such an interminable time till a quarter after nine, when the Postman came, bringing only a note about – Cheltenham, from Geraldine!

The letter I had from Tyndall yesterday might have satisfied any ordinary man – or woman; you would have said. But I don't pretend to be an ordinary man – or woman; I am perfectly *extra*ordinary; especially in the power I possess of fretting and worrying myself into one fever after another, without any cause to speak of!

What do you suppose I am worrying about now, because of the Scotsman having *not* come? That there may be in it something about your having *fallen ill – which you wished me not to see*! *This* I am capable of fancying at moments; tho' last evening I saw a man who had seen you 'smoking very quietly at Masson's', and had heard your speech, and, what was more to the purpose, (his semi-articulateness taken into account) – brought me what he said was as good an account of it as any *he* could give – already in *The Pallmall Gazette*, written by a hearty admirer of long standing, evidently. It was so kind of Macmillan to come to me – *before he had slept*. He had gone in the morning straight from the Railway to his shop and work. He seemed still under the *Emotion* of the Thing – Tears starting to his black eyes every time he mentioned any *moving* part!!

Now just look at that! If here isn't – at half after eleven, when nobody looks for the Edinburgh post – your letter – *two* newspapers, and letters from my Aunt Anne, Thomas Erskine, David Aitken besides.

I have only as yet read *your* letter. The rest will keep *now* – I had a nice letter from Henry Davidson yesterday – as good as a Newspaper *Critic*. What pleases me most in this business – I mean the business of your *success*, is the hearty *personal affection towards you* that comes out on all hands. These men at Forsters, with their cheering, our own people; even old Silvester turning as white as a sheet, and his lips quivering when he tried to express his gladness over the telegraph, *all that* is positively delightful, and makes the success 'a good joy' to me. No appearance of envy or grudging in anybody;

but one general, loving, heartfelt throwing up of caps with young and old, male and female! If we could only *sleep* Dear, and what you call *digest*; wouldn't it be nice? . . .

Affectionately yours,

Jane W. Carlyle

185 PROFESSOR TYNDALL'S DESCRIPTION OF THE RECTORIAL INSTALLATION

. . . Carlyle was lodged in the house of his gentle and devoted friend, Erskine of Linlathen. He was placed as far from the noises of the street, in other words as near the roof, as possible. I saw him occasionally in his skyey dormitory, where, though his sleep did not reach the perfection once attained at Freystone, it was never wholly bad. There was considerable excitement in Edinburgh at the time – copious talking and hospitable feasting. The evening before the eventful day I dined at Kinellan with my well-beloved friends, Sir James and Lady Coxe, whose permanent guest I was at the time. Sir David and Lady Brewster were there, and Russell of the *Scotsman*. The good Sir David looked forward with fear and trembling to what he was persuaded must prove a *fiasco*. 'Why,' he said to me, 'Carlyle has not written a word of his Address; and no Rector of this University ever appeared before his audience without this needful preparation.' In regard to the writing I did not share Sir David's fear, being well aware of Carlyle's marvellous powers of utterance when he had fair play. *There*, however, was the rub. Would he have fair play? Would he come to his task fresh and strong, or with the pliancy of his brain destroyed by sleeplessness? This surely is the tragic side of insomnia, and of the dyspepsia which frequently generates it. 'It takes all heart out of me, so that I cannot speak to my people as I ought.' Such were the words of a worthy Welsh clergyman whom I met in 1854 among his native hills, and whose unrest at night was similar to that of Carlyle. Time would soon deliver its verdict.

The eventful day came, and we assembled in the anteroom of the hall in which the address was to be delivered – Carlyle in his rector's robe, Huxley, Ramsay, Erskine, and myself in more sober gowns. We were all four to be doctored. The great man of the occasion had declined the honour, pleading humorously that in heaven there might be some confusion between him and his brother John, if they both bore the title of doctor. I went up to Carlyle, and earnestly scanning his face, asked: 'How do you feel?' He returned my gaze, curved his lip, shook his head, and answered not a word. 'Now,' I said, 'you have to practise what you have been preaching all your life, and prove yourself a hero.' He again shook his head, but said nothing. A procession was formed, and we moved, amid the plaudits of the students, towards the platform. Carlyle took his place in the rector's chair, and the ceremony of conferring degrees began. Looking at the sea of faces below me – young, eager, expectant, waiting to be lifted up by the words of the prophet they had chosen – I forgot all about the degrees. Suddenly I found an elbow among my ribs – 'Tyndall, they are calling for you.' I promptly stood at ''tention' and underwent the process of baptism. The degrees conferred, a fine tall young fellow rose and proclaimed with ringing voice from the platform the honour that had been conferred on 'the foremost of living Scotchmen'. The cheers were loud and long.

Carlyle stood up, threw off his robe, like an ancient David declining the unproved armour of Saul, and in his carefully-brushed brown morning-coat came forward to the table. With nervous fingers he grasped the leaf, and stooping over it looked earnestly down upon the audience. 'They tell me,' he said, 'that I ought to have written this address, and out of deference to the counsel I tried to do so, once, twice, thrice. But what I wrote was only fit for the fire, and to the fire it was compendiously committed. You must therefore listen to and accept what I say to you as coming straight from the heart.' He began, and the world already knows what he said. I attended more to the aspect of the audience than to the speech of the orator, which contained nothing new to me. I could, however, mark its influence on the palpitating crowd below. They were stirred as if by subterranean fire. For an hour and a half he held them spellbound, and when he ended the emotion previously pent up burst forth in a roar of acclamation. With a joyful heart and clear conscience I could redeem my promise to Mrs Carlyle. From the nearest telegraph-office I sent her a despatch of three words: 'A perfect triumph', and returned toward the hall. Noticing a commotion in the street, I came up with the crowd. It was no street brawl; it was not the settlement of a quarrel, but a consensus of acclamation, cheers and 'bravos', and a general shying of caps into the air! Looking ahead I saw two venerable old men walking slowly arm-in-arm in advance of the crowd. They were Carlyle and Erskine. The rector's audience had turned out to do honour to their hero. Nothing in the whole ceremony affected Carlyle so deeply as this display of fervour in the open air.

EXTRACTS FROM JANE'S LAST LETTERS

186. To Thomas Carlyle at Scotsbrig

10 April 1866

Alas I missed Tyndall's call! and was '*vaixed*'! He left word with Jessie that you were 'looking well; and everybody worshipping you'! and I thought to myself; A pity if he have taken the habit of being *worshipped,* for he may find some difficulty in keeping it up, *here*! – . . .

187. To Thomas Carlyle at Scotsbrig

12 April 1866

. . . I sent you better than a letter yesterday – a charming *Punch* – which I hope you received in due course; but Geraldine undertook the posting of it, and as Ann said of her long ago, '*Miss* can write Books but I'm sure it's the only thing she's fit for'! Well! there only wanted, to complete your celebrity, that you should be in the chief place of Punch! and there you are, cape and wideawake, making a really creditable appearance. I must repeat what I said before, that the best part of this '*success*' is the general feeling of *personal goodwill* that pervades all they say and write about you. Even *Punch* cuddles you and purrs over you as if you were his favourite son! From *Punch* to Terry the greengrocer, is a good step; but let me tell you, he (Terry) asked Mrs Warren: *was* Mr Carlyle the person they wrote of as *Lord Rector,* and Mrs Warren having answered in her stage voice, 'the *very* same'! Terry shouted out ('quite *shouted* it, Mam!') 'I never was so glad of anything! – by George! - I *am* glad!' – Both Mrs Warren and Jessie rushed out and bought *Punches* to send to their families; and in the fervour of their mutual enthusiasm they have actually ceased hostilities – for *the present*. It seems to me that on every new compliment paid you, these women run and *fry something*; such savoury smells reach me upstairs! . . .

188. To Thomas Carlyle at Scotsbrig

13 April 1866

Oh, what a pity, Dear, and what a stupidity, I must say! After coming safely thro so many fatigues and dangers to go and sprain your ankle off your own feet! And such treatment the sprain will get! Out you *will* go with it, morning and night, along the roughest roads, and keep up the swelling heaven knows how long! The only comfort is that, 'Providence is kind to women, fools, and drunk people', and in the matter of taking care of yourself, *you* come under the category of '*fools*', if ever any wise man did – . . .

189. To Thomas Carlyle at Scotsbrig

17 April 1866

. . . I called at the Royal Institution yesterday to ask if Tyndall had returned. He was there; and I sat some time with him in his room, hearing the minutest details of your doings and sufferings on the journey. It is *the* event of Tyndall's life! – Crossing the hall I noticed, for the first time, that officials were hurrying about, and asked the one nearest me, 'is there to be *Lecturing* here to-day?' The man gave me *such* a look, as if I were 'de*e*ranged,' and people going up the stairs turned and looked at me as if I was de*e*ranged; Neuberg – whose complexion has become that of a lobster (boiled) – ran down to me and asked '*wouldn't* I hear the Lecture?' – And by simply going *out* when everyone else was going *in* I made myself an object of general interest. As I looked back from the carriage window I saw all heads in the Hall and on the stairs turned toward me! . . .

190. To Thomas Carlyle at The Hill, Dumfries

5 Cheyne Row, Chelsea/ 21 April 1866

Dearest –

It seems 'just a consuming of Time' to write today, when you are coming the day after tomorrow. But – 'if there were nothing else in it' – (*your* phrase) such a piece of liberality, as letting one have letters on Sunday if called for, should be honoured, at least by availing oneself of it! All *long* stories however may be postponed till next week.

Living miracle

Indeed, I have neither long stories not short ones to tell this morning. Tomorrow, after the Tea-party, I may have more to say, provided I survive it! Tho' how I am to entertain, on 'my own *base*' eleven people, in a hot night '*without refreshments*' (to speak of) is more than I '*see my way*' thro'! Even as to *cups*! – there *is* only *ten* cups of company-china, and *eleven* are coming; myself making 12! 'After all, said Jessie; you had *once eight* at tea; *three* mair won't kill us'! I'm not so sure of *that*! – Let us hope the motive will sanctify the end; being 'the welfare of others'! – an unselfish desire to make two *Bai ings* happy'! Principal Tulloch and Froude who have a great liking for one another! The Spottiswoodes were added in the same philanthropic spirit. We met in a shop, and they begged permission to come again; so I thought it would be clever to get them over (handsomely, with Froude and Mrs Oliphant) before *you* came. They couldn't '*ask for more*', for a long time! Miss Wynne offered herself, by accident, for that same night.

The Marchioness was here yesterday *twice*; called at four when I hadn't returned, and called again at five. She brought with her yesterday a charming old Miss Talbot, with a palsied head, but the most loveable Babyish old face! She seemed to take to me as I did to her; and Lady Lothian staid behind a minute, to ask if I would go with *her* someday, to see this Miss Talbot who had a Houseful of the finest Pictures.

You should have sent *the address* to Lord Lothian or Lady. I see several names on the list less worthy of such attention.

Chapman is furious at Hotten – no wonder! When he went round to the Booksellers, he found that everywhere Hotten had got the start of him. Smith and Elder had bought *five hundred* copies from Hotten! And poor Frederick did not receive his copies from Edinburgh till he had 'telegraphed' six-and-thirty hours after I had received *mine*!

I saw in an old furniture-shop window at Richmond a copy of the Frederick picture that was lent you – not bad; coarsely painted; but the likeness well preserved. Would you like to have it? I will, if so, make you a present of it – being to be had 'very equal'. I 'descended from' the carriage, and asked: 'What was *that*?' (meaning what price was it). The Broker told me impressively: '*That*, Mam, is *Peter the Great*.' 'Indeed! and what is the price?' - 'Seven and sixpence.' I offered *five shillings* on the spot, but he would only come down to six shillings. I will go back for it if you like, and can find a place for it on my wall.

Yours ever, J. W. C.

A DESCRIPTION OF JANE'S DEATH

191. GERALDINE JEWSBURY TO THOMAS CARLYLE AT CHELSEA

43 Markham Square, Chelsea/ 26 May 1866

Dear Mr Carlyle,

I think it better to write than to speak on the miserable subject about which you told me to inquire of Mr Silvester [Carlyle's coachman]. I saw him to-day. He said that it would be about twenty minutes after three o'clock or thereabouts when they left Mr Forster's house; that he then drove through the Queen's Gate, close by Kensington Gardens, that there, at the uppermost gate, she got out, and walked along the side of the Gardens very slowly, about two hundred paces, with the little dog running, until she came to the Serpentine Bridge, at the southern end of which she got into the carriage again, and he drove on till they came to a quiet place on the Tyburnia side, near Victoria Gate, and then she put out the little dog to run along. When they came opposite to Albion Street, Stanhope Place (lowest thoroughfare of Park towards Marble Arch), a brougham coming along upset the dog, which lay on its back screaming for a while, and then she pulled the check-string; and he turned round and pulled up at the side of the footpath, and there the dog was (he had got up out of the road and gone there). Almost before the carriage stopped she was out of it. The lady whose brougham had caused the accident got out also, and several other ladies who were walking had stopped round the dog. The lady spoke to her; but he could not hear what she said, and the other ladies spoke. She then lifted the dog into the carriage, and got in herself. He asked if the little dog was hurt; but he thinks she did not hear him, as carriages were passing. He heard the dog squeak as if she had been feeling it (nothing but a toe was hurt); this was the last sound or sigh he ever heard from her place of fate. He went on towards Hyde Park Corner, turned there and drove past the Duke of Wellington's Achilles figure, up the drive to the Serpentine and past it, and came round by the road where the dog was hurt, past the Duke of Wellington's house and past the gate opposite St George's. Getting no sign (noticing only the two hands laid on the lap, palm uppermost the right hand, reverse way the left, and all motionless), he turned into the Serpentine drive again; but after a few yards, feeling a little surprised, he looked back, and seeing her in the same posture, became alarmed, made for the streetward entrance into the Park a few yards westward of gatekeeper's lodge, and asked a lady to look in; and she said what we know, and she addressed a gentleman who confirmed her fears. It was then fully a quarter past four; going on to twenty minutes (but nearer the quarter); of this he is quite certain. She was leaning back in one corner of the carriage, rugs spread over her knees; her eyes were closed, and her upper lip slightly, slightly opened. Those who saw her at the hospital and when in the carriage speak of the beautiful expression upon her face.

On that miserable night, when we were preparing to receive her, Mrs Warren [the housekeeper] came to me and said, that one time, when she was very ill, she said to her, that when the last had come, she was to go upstairs into the closet of the spare room and there she would find two wax candles wrapt in paper, and that those were to be lighted and burned. She said that after she came to live in London she wanted to give a party; her mother wished everything to be very nice, and went out and bought candles and confectionery, and set out a table, and lighted the room quite splendidly, and called her to come and see it when all was prepared. She was angry; she said people would say she was extravagant, and would ruin her husband. She took away two of the candles and some of the cakes. Her mother was hurt and began to weep. She was pained at once at what she had done; she tried to comfort her, and was dreadfully sorry. She took the candles and wrapped them up, and put them where they could be easily found. We found them and lighted them, and did as she desired.

G.E.J.

192. CARLYLE TO LOUISA, LADY ASHBURTON

28 April 1866

Dear Kind Lady,

I cannot write even to you: silence (in the utmost seclusion I can get) can alone express to myself or others the state I am in since Saturday 21st. Sudden, like a bolt from the skies all shining bright, the stroke fell; and has shattered my whole existence into immeasurable ruin. Since that Saturday (10 p.m. at Dumfries, *perhaps* about $3\frac{1}{2}$ p.m. *in Hyde Park*), the nine days that have passed are like no other I ever had since I was born. My heart feels as if broken; overwhelmed, in mean wreck of things secular and prosaic, and in deluges of sacred sorrow, to which, except slowly from time and reflexion, there is no alleviation possible.

Thursday last, she was committed to her Father's Grave, in the Abbey Kirk at Haddington, and now sleeps there, – as was the covenant between us, 40 years ago or nearly so. Her death was swift (as had always been her prayer); swift, I am led to think, almost as lightning from the skies; and she passed away as in a blaze of splendour, *Victory* (late, but bright and complete to her) crowning her whole noble life and end. For her life from the time we met was and continued all mine; and she had fought and toiled for *me*, valiantly at all moments up to that last, – how loyally, lovingly, and bravely, and thro' what sore paths and difficulties, is now known only to God and one living mortal. Sixteen hours after the fatal telegram at Dumfries, there came to me a letter written on the Saturday morning (perhaps two hours before her death), in the cheeriest spirits any had yet been (and they were all cheerful, prosperous, even joyful, after 'April 3'), and I think, the *longest* of all, – in bright hope that we should meet 'the day after tomorrow'. Indeed for a fortnight before, all testimony is, that she looked brighter, gayer, and felt *better*, than for years past. That is the last value I shall ever get of my poor bits of 'successes', which for her sake, were and now are really precious to me, but had otherwise the character mainly of mere confusions, and can henceforth have no value to me.

Maggie Welsh is here, unravelling the dismal chaos to me (for I did not even know a *key* in the house); my Brother too has attended me throughout; and I am gradually recovering my sleep; – day after day, since Friday morning last, endeavouring slowly to settle the wreck of my existence into some incipiency of order; and to see round me [incomplete]

Carlyle's Inscription on Jane's Tomb in Haddington Church

HERE LIKEWISE NOW RESTS

JANE WELSH CARLYLE,

SPOUSE OF THOMAS CARLYLE, CHELSEA, LONDON.

SHE WAS BORN AT HADDINGTON, 14th JULY 1801: ONLY CHILD OF THE ABOVE JOHN WELSH, AND OF GRACE WELSH, CAPLEGILL, DUMFRIESSHIRE, HIS WIFE. IN HER BRIGHT EXISTENCE SHE HAD MORE SORROWS THAN ARE COMMON; BUT ALSO A SOFT INVINCIBILITY, A CLEARNESS OF DISCERN-MENT, AND A NOBLE LOYALTY OF HEART, WHICH ARE RARE. FOR FORTY YEARS SHE WAS THE TRUE AND EVER-LOVING HELPMATE OF HER HUSBAND; AND, BY ACT AND WORD, UNWEARIEDLY FORWARDED HIM, AS NONE ELSE COULD, IN ALL OF WORTHY THAT HE DID OR ATTEMPTED. SHE DIED AT LONDON, 21st APRIL 1866; SUDDENLY SNATCHED AWAY FROM HIM, AND THE LIGHT OF HIS LIFE AS IF GONE OUT.

Further reading

PUBLISHED COLLECTIONS OF JANE'S LETTERS

The Duke–Edinburgh edition of the correspondence of Thomas and Jane Carlyle will supersede all previous publications so far as the text of Jane's letters is concerned. Begun in 1952, the first four volumes were published in 1970 (*The Collected Letters of Thomas and Jane Welsh Carlyle, 1812–28.* General Editor, Charles Richard Sanders; Associate Editor, K. J. Fielding. Duke University Press) and the next three are expected in 1977. This will carry the story up to 1834, when the Carlyles left Craigenputtoch for 5 Cheyne Row. Readers with access to this superlative edition may choose to ignore the letters published by J. A. Froude in *Thomas Carlyle, A History of the First Forty Years of His Life 1795–1835* (2 vols. 1882), David G. Ritchie's *Early Letters of Jane Welsh Carlyle* (1889) and Alexander Carlyle's *The Love Letters of Thomas Carlyle and Jane Welsh* (2 vols. 1909).

For the thirty-two years in Cheyne Row, the following collections are still essential: J. A. Froude, *Letters and Memorials of Jane Welsh Carlyle* (3 vols. 1883); Alexander Carlyle, *New Letters and Memorials of Jane Welsh Carlyle* (2 vols. 1903); Leonard Huxley, *Jane Welsh Carlyle: Letters to Her Family, 1839–1863* (John Murray, 1924); and Townsend Scudder, *Letters of Jane Welsh Carlyle to Joseph Neuberg, 1848–1862* (Oxford University Press, 1931).

Lawrence and Elisabeth Hanson, whose *Necessary Evil: The Life of Jane Welsh Carlyle* was published by Constable in 1952, began by planning an edition of Jane's letters. Their comprehensive biography contains extensive extracts from her letters, many of which had not been published before.

Jane Welsh Carlyle: A New Selection of Her Letters, arranged by Trudy Bliss (Victor Gollancz, 1949) is the best popular selection. Lady Bliss's design was to let Jane speak for herself, helped by a slender, sensitive thread of narrative.

Further reading

MANUSCRIPT COLLECTIONS OF JANE'S LETTERS

The editors of the Duke–Edinburgh edition reported in 1970 that they had located over 3,000 letters by Jane, of which about 800 were unpublished; and that roughly 1,380 of these letters were in The National Library of Scotland at Edinburgh. They listed about thirty other libraries and private collections in English-speaking countries which held either Thomas's or Jane's letters. There are more of Thomas's than of Jane's in these collections, but the University of Edinburgh, the New York Public Library, and the Ashburton collection at Castle Ashby are among those with substantial numbers of her letters.

REMINISCENCES OF CONTEMPORARIES

Unique among these are Carlyle's *Reminiscences*, which included his Memoir of Jane. Published by Froude in 1881 and republished by Norton in 1887, it has been reissued in 1972 by Ian Campbell in J. M. Dent's Everyman's University Library.

Fascinating impressions of the Carlyles were recorded by many contemporaries, either in their lifetimes or in retrospect. Lovers of Jane will be interested in:

William Allingham's Diary, ed. Geoffrey Grigson (Centaur Press, 1967)

Mrs. Brookfield and her Circle, by Charles and Frances Brookfield (1905)

Autobiography, by Moncure Daniel Conway (1904)

Emma Darwin, A Century of Family Letters, 1792–1896, ed. Henrietta Litchfield, 2 vols. (1915)

Conversations and Correspondence with Carlyle, by Sir C. Gavan Duffy (1892)

Literary Recollections and Sketches, by Francis Espinasse (1893)

Life of Charles Dickens, by John Forster (1872–74)

Memories of Old Friends, by Caroline Fox (1882)

'Carlyle and Mrs Carlyle: A Ten Year's Reminiscence', *British Quarterly Review*, by Henry Larkin (July 1881)

Autobiography, by Harriet Martineau (1877)

Memories of London in the Forties, by David Masson (1908)

'Mrs. Carlyle', *Contemporary Review*, by Mrs Oliphant (May 1883)

'Thomas Carlyle', *Macmillan's Magazine*, by Mrs Oliphant (April 1881)

Chapters from Some Unwritten Memoirs, by Anne Thackeray Ritchie (1895)

Further reading

Thomas Woolner, R.A., Sculptor and Poet, His Life in Letters, by Amy Woolner (1917)

New Fragments, by John Tyndall (1896)

'Personal Recollections of Carlyle', *Fortnightly Review*, vol. 277, by John Tyndall (1890)

'Some Reminiscences of Jane Welsh Carlyle', *Temple Bar Magazine* (October 1883). Unsigned, but thought to have been written by Mrs Brookfield

BIOGRAPHIES

J. A. Froude's four-volume biography of Thomas Carlyle, and the biography of Jane Carlyle by Lawrence and Elisabeth Hanson have already been cited.

An admirable short biography of Thomas Carlyle, reflecting the latest scholarship, is by Ian Campbell, lecturer in English literature at Edinburgh University and a member of the Duke–Edinburgh editorial team: *Thomas Carlyle* (Hamish Hamilton, 1974; Scribner's, 1975).

ESSAYS AND STUDIES

The incomparable essays by Virginia Woolf ('Geraldine and Jane', *Times Literary Supplement* (22 February, 1929), reprinted in her *Second Common Reader*) and Iris Origo ('The Carlyles and the Ashburtons: A Victorian Friendship', *Cornhill Magazine* (Autumn 1950), no. 984, pp. 441–83) have been cited.

J. M. Sloan's *The Carlyle Country* (1904), R. Blunt's *The Carlyles' Chelsea Home* (1895), Thea Holme's *The Carlyles at Home* (Oxford University Press, 1965) are good territorial guides.

The guidebook to the Chelsea house, *Carlyle's House*, published by the National Trust in 1976, is based on the original guidebook of 1896, written by Carlyle's nephew, Alexander, and is excellent.

Two selections from the letters of Jane's most faithful correspondents are 'musts' on any short reading list – *Thomas Carlyle: Letters to His Wife*, edited by Trudy Bliss (Harvard University Press, 1953), and *Selections from the Letters of Geraldine Endsor Jewsbury to Jane Welsh Carlyle*, edited by Mrs Alexander Ireland (1892).

Victorian Prose, A Guide to Research, edited by D. J. DeLaura (Modern Language Association of America, 1973) contains an exhaustive bibliographical essay entitled 'The Carlyles', by G. B. Tennyson.

Further reading

And, finally, there are two excellent collections of essays which have been published within the past year: *Carlyle Past and Present. A Collection of New Essays*, edited by K. J. Fielding and Rodger L. Tarr (Vision Press, 1976); and *Carlyle and His Contemporaries: Essays in Honor of Charles Richard Sanders* (Duke University Press, 1976).

Index

Index

Index

Darwin, Erasmus: brother of Charles, 70, 83, 109, 115, 118, 119, 141, 220, 227
Davidson, Henry, 287
Dermont, Mrs, 237
Dickens, Charles, 20, 22, 60, 83, 109, 181, 229, 286
Disraeli, Benjamin, 270
Dodds, William, 99, 198
Donaldson, Miss: Jane's godmother, of Sunny Bank, Haddington, 95, 193, 194, 219
Donaldson, Miss Catherine: of Sunny Bank, 193
Donaldson, Miss Jess: of Sunny Bank, 95, 190, 193, 194
Donaldson, Mr: of London, 193
Drem, Scotland, 187
Duke University, 21
Dunbar, Scotland, 186
Dürer, Albert, 164

Ecclefechan, 3, 16
Edinburgh University, 11, 21, 270
Elise, Madame: Jane's dressmaker, 274
Elizabeth: Elizabeth Sprague, a maid, 1849-50, 128, 138
Elizabeth: a maid in 1862, 148, 150, 152
Ellen: a maid in 1837, 128, 165
Elliot, Frederick, 103
Ellis, Sarah Stickney: author of *The Women of England*, 18
Emerson, Ralph Waldo, 5, 15, 109
Emma: a maid in 1850, 128
Erskine, Thomas (1788-1870): of Linlathen, author, advocate and theologian, 123, 270, 278, 284, 287, 288
Ewart, Mrs, 277, 279
Eyre, Edward John: Governor of Jamaica, disgraced for his harsh treatment of rebellious Blacks, 103

Fanny: a maid in 1852, 128, 130, 140
Farrar, Miss, 160
Fergusson, 179
Fielding, Kenneth J., 21
'Flo': a housemaid in 1863, 150, 151, 152
Folkestone, 257-8, 270, 276-7, 279
Forster, John: editor of the *Examiner*, 1847-56, author of *The Life of Charles Dickens*, 20, 60, 93, 100, 229, 286, 287, 293
Forster, William Edward: statesman (Education Act of 1870 and Ballot Act of 1872), Chief Secretary for Ireland 1880, 184, 185, 186, 250
Frederick the Great, 109, 123, 127, 162, 251, 262, 270

Frome, 180
Froude, James Anthony (1818-94): historian, biographer of Thomas Carlyle, 1, 9, 11, 12, 13, 14, 15, 16, 17, 20, 109, 216, 233, 237, 244, 245, 270, 271, 292
Fryston Hall, Yorkshire: home of Lord Houghton, 270, 282, 283
Fuz, 286

Gambardella, Spiridione: Italian portrait painter working in England, 202
Gaskell, Elizabeth, 229
George Inn, Haddington, 186-92, 271
Gill, The, Annandale: home of T.C.'s sister, Mary Austin, 101, 106, 162, 246, 255, 257
Gladstone, W. E., 270
Glen, William, 78
Glover, Miss: mistress of Duke of Marlborough, 167
Godby, Mrs: J.W.C.'s cousin, 260
Grace (Macdonald): a maid at Craigenputtoch, 113, 127
Graham, Mr and Mrs, 165
Grange, The: Ashburton estate at Alresford, 8, 102, 130, 158, 159, 203, 204, 215, 216, 217, 220, 225-8, 232, 235, 238, 242, 257, 258
Great Britain, 162
Grote, George: M.P. for London 1832-41, 277
Grote, Mrs George: Harriet Lewin, popularly known as 'Queen of the Radicals', 277

Haddington: J.W.C.'s girlhood home in, East Lothian, Scotland: 2, 3, 4, 6, 11, 16, 20, 22, 26, 49, 51, 101, 112, 114, 142, 161, 184-98, 219, 271, 295
Hahn-Hahn, Countess, 118
Hall's, Miss: school J.W.C. attended in Edinburgh, 70
Hall, Mrs, 62
Hanning, Mrs Robert: *see* Carlyle, Janet
Hayward, Abraham: barrister, editor and writer, 103
Helen: Helen Mitchell, 'Kirkcaldy Helen', a maid in 1837-46, 1848-9, 67, 70, 108, 115, 116, 117, 120, 127, 128, 130, 132, 133, 135, 136, 137, 138, 141, 171, 175, 183, 201, 202, 203
Helen: a maid in 1864, 155, 156, 272, 273
Henry, Mrs, 274
Hiddlestone, Jessie: *see* Jessie (Hiddlestone)
Hiddlestone, Margaret: *see* Margaret (Hiddlestone)
Hill, Lady Alice, 143, 144

Index

Index

Index